Water and Wetland Plants
of the Prairie Provinces

by Heinjo Lahring

Canadian Plains Research Center, 2003

UNIVERSITY OF
REGINA

Canadian Plains Research Center
University of Regina
Regina, Saskatchewan S4S 0A2
Canada
Tel: (306) 585-4758
Fax: (306) 585-4699
e-mail: canadian.plains@uregina.ca
http://www.cprc.uregina.ca

National Library of Canada Cataloguing in Publication Data
Lahring, Heinjo, 1957–

Water and wetland plants of the Prairie Provinces/Heinjo Lahring

(Canadian plains studies, ISSN 0397-6290 ; 44)
Includes bibliographical references and index.
ISBN 0-88977-162-6

1. Aquatic plants–Prairie Provinces–Indentification. 2. Wetland plants–Prairie Provinces–Identification. 3. Wetland ecology–Prairie Provinces. I. University of Regina. Canadian Plains Research Center. II. Title. III. Series.
QH106.2.P6L34 2003   581.7'6'09712   C2003-911222-5

Cover design: Donna Achtzehner, Canadian Plains Research Center

Printed and bound in Canada by Houghton Boston, Saskatoon, Saskatchewan
Printed on acid-free paper

This book is dedicated to three young explorers:

Grant, Kiana, and Wade

Love,
Dad

Table of Contents

Preface

As a young boy growing up in Alberta's foothills, I would always look forward to taking my fishing rod and venturing down to the Little Red Deer River with its many backwaters and beaver ponds. It was a time for exploration and adventure.

Moments from casting my lure, I would be retrieving my first catch of weeds for the day. After perhaps half an hour I'd have cleaned off my share of hooks from the first pond and would soon set off for the next. Before long I had a pretty good idea of the aquatic plant life associated with each fishing hole. In later years I took up fly-fishing, and learned how to sample the shoreline vegetation as well. Apparently I was not alone since I noticed other fishermen practicing similar methods of plant sampling. Little did I know at the time that my hard-earned technique of 'cast and sample' was to lead me into a lifetime of aquatic plant study.

Eventually I built a 12"x12" water window which, when placed on the water's surface, eliminated the surface ripples and reflection. I could then view the underwater world from the comfort of my canoe. I would get into my canoe at one end of the lake and slowly drift by current or wind until I had reached the opposite shore. This was a huge improvement over pulling little plant fragments off of sharp hooks. The world it revealed was remarkable. I saw huge beds of single plant species with their varying shades of green. Some plants grew as short velvety mounds, others were long and stringy, waving in the undulating currents. Fish darted in and out of this underwater forest. Large pike would be waiting in ambush within the shadows of pond lilies. Plant communities were alive with bubbles of oxygen rising to the surface. An overwhelming number of invertebrates were busily going about their business within this underwater garden.

Each pond was different from the next. Some water conditions were very turbid while others were crystal clear. Plants in fast-moving streams were firmly anchored. Warm, calm waters had different species from the streams and several plant types were free-floating. Each pond, bog, seepage and puddle had its own flora. By mid-summer many of the submerged plants could be seen pushing their flowers above the water's surface.

This book was born out of a love for water plants and the places in which they grow. It is meant for those who don't mind getting their rubber boots filled with water or putting up with muggy summer heat, mud, mosquitoes, and biting flies. Northern wetlands have much to offer to those who are patient and observant. The rewards are many and often very unexpected.

I hope that the plants presented in this guide will be of interest not only to those familiar with our wetland flora, but especially to those young explorers who may one day discover an unknown plant at the end of their hook.

Good luck on your journey through the fascinating world of water plants!
Heinjo M. R. Lahring

Acknowledgements

This book would not have been possible without the generous support and contributions of many people. Above all, I would like to thank my wife, Jan, for her support, encouragement, suggestions and understanding from the project's conception through to its completion.

I would like to give special thanks to the following individuals for their patience and willingness in sharing their expertise and knowledge while reviewing the manuscript: Dr. C. Barre Hellquist (Massachusetts College of Liberal Arts, MA); Mr. John Hudson (Biologist, SK); Dr. Vernon Harms (Prof. Emeritus, University of Saskatchewan, SK); Dr. Bruce Ford (University of Manitoba, MB); Dr. Mary Vetter (Luther College, University of Regina, SK).

Special thanks go to Denis Johnson and the staff of Red Deer Press for originally asking me to take on the project and for allowing me the freedom to proceed at my own pace over the past few years, although the project eventually moved on under the direction of another publisher.

I would like to thank Brian Mlazgar and Donna Achtzehner of the Canadian Plains Research Center (University of Regina) for taking on the daunting task of transforming the manuscript into a field guide, and thanks to Diane Perrick for preparing the maps in the introduction.

Thank you to the following individuals for their efforts and valuable contributions to the project: Eric Watton for preparing the glossary, Kristen Murray for searching for maps, Angela Sutherland for her organizational skills, Alison and Edna Bakken for being my e-mail connection, Lory Sanders and Wendy Daly for their assistance in the Olds College Herbarium, the Olds College Library staff, Bonnie Smith for the use of the University of Calgary Herbarium, Joan Willams for access to specialized botanical references, David and Jennifer Wells for their computer assistance, Terry Roszko for joining me on field trips, and Ray Huene for trusting me with his camera equipment in knee-deep mud and pouring rain.

I would like to recognize the following people for their generosity in sharing information and referring me to other sources: John Morgan of Prairie Seeds Inc. (Manitoba); Dean Nernberg of the Canadian Wildlife Service (Saskatchewan); Leslie Hall of the Saskatchewan Wetland Corporation; Kathleen Wilkinson (biologist, British Columbia); Bret Calverly of Ducks Unlimited (Alberta); Paul Gregory of Interlake Conservation Seeds (Manitoba); Gord Pearse of Newfield Seed (Saskatchewan); Frank Switzer (plant photographer and author, Saskatchewan); Donna Lawrence of Alberta Agriculture; Andy Hamerston of the Native Plant Society (Saskatchewan); Joseph Tomocik of the Denver Botanic Gardens; Linda Oestry of the Missouri Botanical Gardens; the Devonian Botanical Gardens Herbarium (Alberta); Dave, Bill and Pat Kester of Kester's Wild Game Food Nurseries (Wisconsin); John, Theresa, Jim and Sue Lemberger of Wildlife Nurseries (Wisconsin); Henry and Isolde Lahring for their encouragement, support and fax machine; and finally, the staff of Bearberry Creek Water Gardens (Sundre, Alberta).

Photos and illustrations were provided by the author unless otherwise noted. Thank you to the following individuals for their generous slide contributions: Alison Bakken (Bearberry Creek Water Gardens, Alberta), Christa Edwards (Ducks Unlimited, Alberta), Dr. C.B. Hellquist (Massachusetts College of Liberal Arts), Myrna Pearman (Ellis Bird Farm, Alberta), Pat Porter (Alberta Agriculture, Alberta), Dr. J. Romo (University of Saskatchewan, Saskatchewan), Colin Stone (Alberta Agriculture, Alberta), Glen Suggett (Manitoba Natural Resources, Wildlife Branch, Manitoba), Joan Williams (Botanist, Calgary, Alberta).

HEINJO LAHRING

Watercress

x

Introduction

Thinking is more
Interesting than
Knowing, but less
Interesting than
Looking.

Goethe (Schiller, 1994)

This field guide has been created as a reference for those who are curious about the many mysteries of our natural world, and for those who would like to know more about a plant than just its name.

Water is essential to life. As such, all of us are affected by wetlands in one way or another. The ability of these areas to filter and purify water is incredible and the quantity, diversity and uniqueness of wildlife that a wetland supports is truly remarkable. Continued loss of these biologically diverse ecosystems will be detrimental to our long-term well-being.

Interestingly, although humans are destroying valuable habitat through development, they also construct new drainage channels, ponds and even lakes. With the use of modern heavy equipment this can affect rather large areas. Often these disturbed and barren areas are isolated and require replanting. It is one of the many goals of this book to compile a collection of reference species that could be used for this purpose. The appropriate plant material would depend on the type of habitat created, water depths, water quality, nutrient load, and other factors.

Humans have long employed water plants in daily life. The descriptions in this book include anecdotes pertaining to history, survival, edibility, and ecology.

Water plants in general are recognized to be a tremendous resource for basic survival needs. Most marginal and emergent aquatics produce palatable roots and tubers, and have been used by indigenous populations for centuries. At the same time, one must be especially cautious when collecting for human consumption. A few select species—in particular Water-hemlock and Poison Hemlock of the *Apiaceae*—are extremely toxic, making proper identification of collected plants crucial.

Since open water in the form of springs and seepages is often accessible during the winter, it is possible to gather water plants for food year-round. Emergent species such as reeds and cattails can produce abundant stands of vegetation that protrude well above the snow. Thus shelter and fire-starter material can be readily at hand when other material is scarce.

As development continues in the Prairie provinces, native wetlands will become increasingly rare. Their value for wildlife, water conservation, and as a native seed bank is immeasurable. As well, many of the species listed in this guide are very important economically, being used in projects involving revegetation, water filtration, reclamation, water gardening, recreation and wildlife enhancement. Thus, those involved in aquatic landscaping will find this water plant manual particularly useful.

The search for new species continues. With only a sprinkling of amateur and professional botanists in the field collecting and identifying wetland plants, the odds of finding something 'yet-to-be-named' are quite good. A short collecting season and the thousands of square kilometres of wetland habitat combine to offer a considerable challenge to those who study wetland flora. While we can enjoy the plants through photography, observation and collection, it is important to sample and not over-collect. The appropriate location for pressed specimens is the herbarium, where many more people can see them and learn to understand our rich wetland flora.

HEINJO LAHRING

Water plant communities are dynamic and change with the rise and fall of water levels.

BIOGEOGRAPHY

Wetland plant distribution patterns in the Prairie provinces have been determined by geological and climatic forces which have shaped the landscape we see today.

Topography

During past ice ages, glaciers have scoured, left deposits on, and contoured much of our northern landscape. As the atmosphere warmed, the glaciers retreated. Since then, climatic change has resulted in a steady decline in water replenishment to our aquifers. Unless major climatic trends once again swing in favor of increased precipitation, we may be in for a continuing pattern of drying-out. Ponds and lakes which were once filled with water and teeming with fish and waterfowl have, over time, succumbed to community succession and now contain only dryland species. Water plant presence or absence is a way of monitoring this change.

The Prairie provinces have an elevation gain from sea level in the northeast to over 3000 m in the extreme west. The major landforms include the Cordilleran Region (mountains, highlands, and foothills), the Interior Plains (relatively flat topography with small hills, river valleys, and potholes), and the Canadian Shield (exposed rock formations). Water is held in or moves through these varying landforms, and their geologic structure is a very important factor in the quality of water in our wetlands, strongly influencing pH levels and presence of dissolved minerals. Generally we find that sedimentary deposits such as limestone, sandstone, shale, and conglomerate are common south of a line drawn from approximately the center of the Alberta–Northwest Territories border in the north to the center of the Manitoba–United States border in the south. This area is dominated by **basic** (alkaline) waters, rich in calcium carbonates and bicarbonates. Northeast of this line we find waters to be more or less neutral to **acidic** because of the exposed Precambrian (Canadian) Shield, acidifying rocks such as granite, granite gneiss, and quartz-diorite. Plant life tends to follow this pattern, with acid-loving plants in one area and plants preferring basic conditions in the other.

Map 1. Major landforms and watersheds of the Prairie provinces (adapted from Natural Resources Canada online Atlas of Canada).

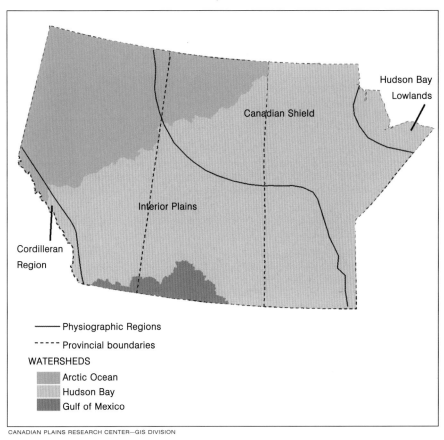

CANADIAN PLAINS RESEARCH CENTER—GIS DIVISION

Watersheds

The prairie provinces include portions of three great watersheds: the **Arctic**, the **Hudson Bay**, and the **Gulf of Mexico** (see Map 1). Plant material found in one location, depending on latitude and underlying parent material, is often found in other sites within the same watershed.

Bird migratory flyways contribute greatly to the dispersal of water plant material from one watershed to the next. Birds will feed in one location and carry plant fragments or seeds in their feathers or droppings to the next site. Although ponds may be quite isolated, in effect they are linked by this seasonal movement.

As we move into the northern sections of the prairie provinces we find discontinuous permafrost. Continuous permafrost occurs inland along the Hudson Bay coast. This results in poor drainage, with water collecting and flowing over the surface.

Map 2. Climatic regions west of Hudson Bay (adapted from Canadian Oxford Atlas of the World).

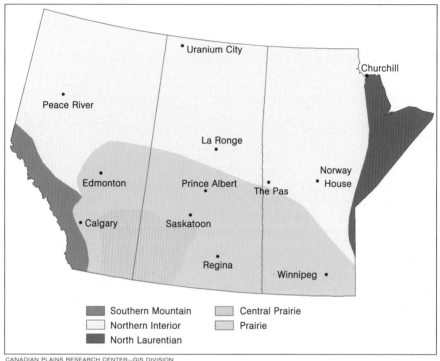

Climate

The maintenance of our wetlands is in part determined by climate. The prevailing winds in the Prairie provinces are from the northwest at these latitudes, with much of the Pacific moisture being blocked by the Rocky Mountains to the west. This inland climate is generally quite dry with moisture levels increasing as one moves towards eastern Manitoba. As well, the snowfall increases from 800–1600 mm per year in western Alberta to 1600–2800 mm in northeastern Manitoba. Five major climatic regions occur west of Hudson Bay (see Map 2):

NORTHERN INTERIOR: boreal forest with long, cold winters and mean annual precipitation of under 200 mm (decreasing from south to north)

SOUTHERN MOUNTAIN: warm mountain, valley and plateau country with highly variable conditions due to the influence of Pacific moisture, Chinook winds and elevation gradients (mean annual precipitation of 400–1000+ mm)

CENTRAL PRAIRIE: hot summers and cold winters with a semi-arid climate (mean annual precipitation of 250–400 mm, of which 30% comes as rainfall)

PRAIRIE: temperature extremes with warm summers and long, cold winters (mean annual precipitation 400–600 mm)

NORTH LAURENTIAN: cool summers and long winters; land is covered with snow for more than half of the year (mean annual precipitation of 600–1000 mm)

Map 3. Ecozones of the Prairie provinces (adapted from www.ccea.org/ecozones/terr).

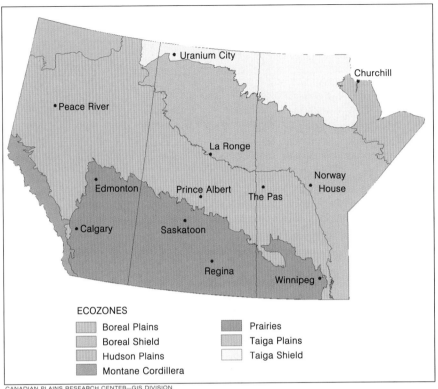

CANADIAN PLAINS RESEARCH CENTER—GIS DIVISION

Ecozones

The prairie provinces occupy one fifth of Canada's total area. Although we tend to think of them as primarily **prairie,** in actual fact, prairie occupies only one-sixth of the total area of the three provinces (almost 2,000,000 square kilometres or 757,985 square miles). The Prairie provinces are comprised of seven ecozones: Montane Cordillera, Taiga Plains, Boreal Plains, Prairie, Boreal Shield, Taiga Shield, and Hudson Plains (see Map 3). Some of the major plant cover types within each ecozone include:

MONTANE CORDILLERA: herb and shrub alpine communities; lodgepole pine, white spruce, Engelmann spruce, alpine fir, Douglas fir, ponderosa pine, and trembling aspen forests; forage grass and bunchgrass/sedges grasslands.

TAIGA PLAINS: black spruce, white spruce, jack pine, tamarack, paper birch, trembling aspen, and balsam poplar forests with shrubs, lichens, and mosses.

BOREAL PLAINS: white spruce, black spruce, jack pine, paper birch, trembling aspen and balsam poplar forests.

PRAIRIES: shortgrass and moist mixed grasslands with aspen, chokecherry, saskatoon, Manitoba maple groves; aspen parkland along northern edge.

BOREAL SHIELD: white spruce, black spruce, tamarack, balsam pir, jack pine, paper birch, trembling aspen, and balsam poplar closed forests.

TAIGA SHIELD: open black spruce and jack pine forests with mosses and lichens; tamarack, sedges, dwarf birch, Labrador tea, small bog cranberry and spaghnum bogs.

GLEN SUGGETT

HUDSON PLAINS: arctic tundra; open black spruce and tamarack forests; dwarf birch and willow shrublands; dense sedges, mosses, and lichens.

Cape Churchill, Manitoba
(Hudson Plains Ecozone).

Particularly unique to the Prairie provinces are the Cypress Hills. They are located along the southern Alberta–Saskatchewan border, at an altitude of from 870 m to 1350 m. The higher parts of this area of low hills surrounded by prairie were not glaciated during the last ice age, and it has retained its own unique forest flora.

The Peace River District has a warmer and drier climate than surrounding areas and is classified as parkland and prairie. Because of its agricultural potential, considerable clearing and draining of land is occurring in this region.

Alkali Sloughs and Sand Hills

Some prairie water bodies are quite saline, including many of the lakes and sloughs in southern Alberta and Saskatchewan. In these areas groundwater passes through ancient marine deposits picking up salts which are later drawn up to the surface by evaporation. Groundwater movement, especially with seasonal flooding, will also concentrate salts in depressions and hollows. The alkali precipitates left behind form a white crust on the ground's surface. Only certain wetland species can survive under these saline conditions, with shorelines and mud flats often dominated by seaside arrowgrass, red samphire, and species indigenous to each site. These plants are also known to occur along sea coasts with similar salty conditions.

Several areas are very well drained due to natural sand accumulations. Even so, wetlands and lakes occur here in depressions and are important staging and nesting areas for waterfowl. They include the Middle, Great and Little Sandhills of southeastern Alberta and southwestern Saskatchewan and the Athabasca Sand Dunes near Lake Athabasca in the north.

Water levels in prairie wetlands typically fluctuate with the seasons. Melt waters recharge prairie potholes in spring. Low summer rainfall causes them to shrink, some drying up completely. These changes affect plant communities and wildlife use. Awned sedge and reed grasses usually dominate these sites.

A large number of northern wetland plants are circumpolar in distribution, making this guide suitable for use in other parts of Canada, the United States and even Eurasia.

Map 4. Hardiness zones—Prairie provinces (adapted from www.nrcan-rncan.gc.ca).

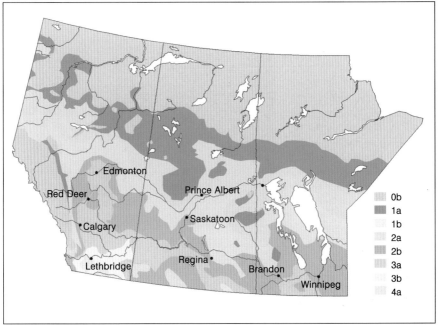

▦	0b
▦	1a
▦	1b
▦	2a
▦	2b
▦	3a
▦	3b
▦	4a

CANADIAN PLAINS RESEARCH CENTER—GIS DIVISION

PLANT HARDINESS ZONES

Geographic regions can be divided into **Plant Hardiness Zones**. These are based on average climatic conditions in each area and represent where plants will most likely survive. In Canada we go from the harshest value of 0 to the mildest value of 8. These can be further divided into sub-zones (e.g., 2a or 2b).

To produce the latest Hardiness Zone map, Natural Resources Canada's Forest Service updated Agriculture Canada's 1967 Hardiness Map using new climatic data collected since the first issue. Variables taken into account include minimum winter temperature, length of frost-free period, summer rainfall, maximum temperature, snow cover, January rainfall and wind speed.

In the Prairie provinces we generally have a range from Zone 0b (northeastern Manitoba) to Zone 4a (southwestern Alberta). For this guide we have rated each plant variety according to the harshest Hardiness Zone in which the plant can be found growing according to herbarium collection records. Although at times a plant will occur in a very cold area, it may not necessarily flower and may be dependent on vegetative reproduction or reintroduction (e.g., by waterfowl) from another zone in order to survive. Plants may also live within mild microhabitats in a colder zone. The actual change from one zone to the next is, in reality, a gradient and not a definite line. Nevertheless, the Hardiness Zone classification system can serve as a valuable guide to those interested in growing wetland plants.

WETLAND CLASSIFICATION

When we speak of **wetlands** we are referring to areas where the water table is at or above the level of the soil for the entire year.

The term **riparian** is used to refer to the transitional zone between open water and dry upland areas. It includes the margins of ponds, lakes, streams, and rivers. A wetland might be described as being grassy riparian or shrubby riparian or some other combination depending on which plants dominate the shoreline.

HEINJO LAHRING

Riparian.

HEINJO LAHRING

Above: Wet meadow (with boardwalk).

Below: Alkali slough.

HEINJO LAHRING

Wet meadows of lush grasses will often support wetland plants. These regions are flooded by spring runoff or heavy rainfalls but eventually dry out during the hot summer months. They are prone to dry and wet cycles which limits the plant life to those species which are able to tolerate these changing conditions. Ditches often fall into this category.

Sloughs are wet depressions or shallow ponds usually associated with open prairie-like areas.

Wetlands are classified into five major groups. These are **bogs**, **fens**, **marshes**, **swamps**, and **shallow open water**. **Muskegs** are a complex of several types of these wetlands and are common in Canada's poorly drained north.

Sphagnum moss.

HEINJO LAHRING

Bogs

Bogs are very low in plant nutrients. They are often isolated from external sources of water and, thus, nutrients. Calcium and magnesium levels are extremely low. Rainfall, deposition of particulate matter from the atmosphere, and animal droppings are often the only significant nutrient sources. Bogs are dominated by *Sphagnum* moss which often form characteristic hummocks or mounds. Deep organic deposits (often greater than 40 cm) build up over the years as a result of the accumulation of poorly decomposed vegetation. Conditions are very acidic (pH less than 4.6). Bogs can be classified as treed or open.

ALISON BAKKEN

Above: Graminoid fen.
Below: Marshes provide valuable habitat for waterfowl.

HEINJO LAHRING

Fens

Fens have high nutrient and pH (5.5–7.0) levels in contrast to bogs. The fen terrain is often sloped, allowing water to slowly move through the area bringing with it nutrients from the surrounding topography. The calcium and magnesium levels are high. Fens are dominated by sedges, grasses, and brown mosses. Floating mats sometimes form over the open water. Fens are classified as either graminoid fens (dominated by grasses and sedges), shrub fens, or treed fens.

Marshes

Marshes are known for their emergent vegetation of rushes, sedges, and grasses. Periods of sustained flooding are common, with slow moving water often running through them. Oxygen levels are relatively high. Plant and animal productivity is usually high in marshes and peat accumulation is minimal. The water is neutral to slightly alkaline. Zonation of vegetation takes

9

Exploring native wetlands.

HEINJO LAHRING

place according to water depth, wave action and salinity. Marshes can be further divided into freshwater marshes and saline or brackish wetlands.

Swamps

Swamps are tree dominated and nutrient rich with dissolved oxygen and mineral levels relatively high. The pH is neutral to moderately acidic. Water may be flowing or standing. The root zone is commonly waterlogged. The water table often fluctuates with the season. Peat-forming mosses are absent, so peat accumulation is low. Much of the organic deposition is due to herbaceous and woody plant decay. Swamps are classified as either coniferous or deciduous.

Shallow Water

A shallow water wetland has a depth of less than 2 m and less than 25% of its surface is occupied by scattered emergent vegetation. Plants tend to be floating or submerged. The underlying substrates may be mineral or organic. The shallow water zone is actually a continuation of a riparian zone, bog, fen, swamp or marsh into open water.

Deep Water

When the water exceeds 2 m in depth, we consider this the deep water zone. Plant life in this zone must be able to withstand being totally submerged. Open water areas are classed as being oligotrophic (nutrient poor), mesotrophic (of moderate nutrient levels), eutrophic (nutrient rich), or dystrophic (acid water bodies which are nutrient poor and have high levels of tannic and organic acids). Ponds may be defined as those waterbodies where light reaches the bottom, whereas in lakes, very little if any light reaches the bottom.

HEINJO LAHRING

Above: Shallow stream.

Below: Deep mountain lake.

HEINJO LAHRING

WETLAND PLANT CATEGORIES

Botanists classify plants according to floral structure and other related anatomical features. This is extremely handy when it comes to applying names to plants, and tells us a considerable amount about a plant's relative evolutionary placement.

Water gardeners have devised their own system. It has little to do with taxonomy but much to do with ecology. In a wetland ecosystem, as we move from dry land to open water, we go through several life zones. Each zone has a characteristic depth of water. This in turn is associated with parameters such as the amount of light which travels through a given depth of water, the amount of oxygen available in bottom sediments, and the effects of wave action to name a few.

Every species of water plant has its own adaptations in order to survive under these limiting environmental conditions. Some are anchored with strong root systems so they won't be carried away by waves; others are free-floating, dangling their roots into the water in a hydroponic fashion and allowing currents to transport them to uncolonized areas.

Understanding this relationship between a plant's adaptations and its environment allows us to group plants with similar features together. This is a very practical tool since, by knowing its group, we can easily place a given plant in the appropriate environment.

Presently we recognize four major water plant groups:

WETLAND PLANTS occur where the water table is at or above the level of the soil for the entire year.

Wetland

MARGINAL PLANTS inhabit the shoreline of open water. This is a shoreline zone where water levels may fluctuate with the season (i.e., flooding during spring followed by drought in late summer). It is actually more accurate to further divide this transitional zone into **marginal** (including those plants adjacent to dryland conditions but with roots in saturated soil, e.g., sedges) and **emergent** (including those plants that are actually emerging or growing out of and above the water, e.g., cattails).

Emergent

FLOATING-LEAVED PLANTS are those that have floating leaves. These can be **rooted** (e.g., waterlilies) or **free-floating** (e.g., duckweed).

Floating-leaved

SUBMERGED PLANTS have all or most of the plant foliage under water. During times of low water levels, or late in the season when the plant reaches the water's surface, floating and/or aerial leaves may form which look quite different from the submerged leaves (e.g., many of the pondweeds). Most, but not all, submerged plants will also have an emergent life stage, allowing flowering to occur above the water's surface.

Submerged

11

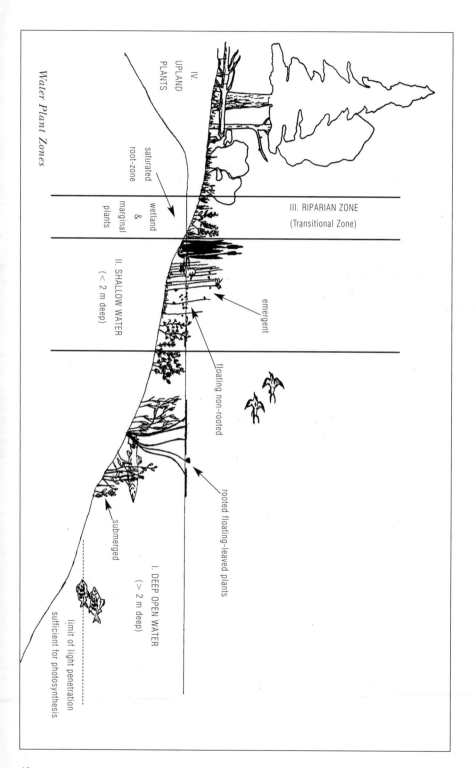

Water Plant Zones

IV. UPLAND PLANTS

saturated root-zone

wetland & marginal plants

III. RIPARIAN ZONE (Transitional Zone)

II. SHALLOW WATER (< 2 m deep)

emergent

floating non-rooted

rooted floating-leaved plants

submerged

I. DEEP OPEN WATER (> 2 m deep)

limit of light penetration sufficient for photosynthesis

12

Although placement into these groups may at times seem somewhat arbitrary, especially since some aquatics will survive on dry land (including waterlilies) if pushed through a drought, it gives us guidance for locating and handling water plants. Each category plays a role in a wetland ecosystem. In pond management it is important to include plants from each category in order to establish a healthy pond.

WETLAND ECOLOGY

The water plants presented in this book represent a sampling of the continuum of vegetation found from the 'dryland' to the 'deep-water' zones. What all of these plants share is the ability to survive under very wet conditions.

Water Levels

Those plants growing in the driest parts of wetlands live where water levels are not always stable. Many prairie sloughs dry out as the summer progresses. The water slowly evaporates or works its way into the ground, salt concentrations rise, and salt pans form. Few plants can survive under such extreme conditions. These alkali mud flats often have dense stands of one or two well-adapted species (e.g., *Chenopodium rubrum* or *Salicornia europaea*). Some plants have adjusted to these conditions by growing and reproducing on an annual cycle. Flowering occurs while water levels are adequate, and the dry season is passed in seed form.

In areas where the water level is more dependable, marginal and emergent species predominate. Here, perennial plants are generally abundant and space is often densely colonized. It is not a coincidence that many of the rushes, reeds, and grasses look very similar. Space may be limiting. Foliage is commonly upright with narrow blades. The saturated mud is anaerobic, so roots tend to be shallow and creeping and filled with air-storage tissue. The inconspicuous flowers are held high and are predominantly wind-pollinated. These parameters, plus the influence of the local climate, nutrient availability, light levels, and herbivory, combine to determine which plants can survive in this zone.

This beaver pond in the foothills is an example of a naturally created wetland.

The Highly Productive Emergent and Shallow Water Zones

Amphibians, birds, and mammals find an abundance of food and shelter in shallow water areas. The emergent plants growing here protect the area from wind and wave action. Light can generally reach the bottom resulting in high photosynthetic activity throughout the water column. This produces a highly complex array of microbial and invertebrate life. In turn they support larger wetland creatures.

As the water depth increases, we move into a region of true aquatics. Many are rooted and some, such as the duckweeds, are free-floating. With increased water volume, water temperatures are buffered from large fluctuations during the growing season. The underwater foliage provides homes for many creatures including snails, beetles, hydras, rotifers, protozoans, water mites, and fresh water sponges. The undersurface of leaves is often covered with egg masses and larvae, all potential prey for damselflies, dragonflies, mayflies and frogs.

GLEN SUGGETT

Emergent shallow water zone: American avocet in Manitoba marsh.

Living Underwater

Submerged plants live in a world quite different from terrestrial plants and have developed features that permit them to survive in an aqueous environment. For instance, water loss is not a problem so underwater foliage lacks the waterproof cuticle often found on land plants. Stomata are normally not present except on the upper surface of floating leaves. The epidermis (outer cell layer) allows for the absorption of water and nutrients and exchange of gases. Since nutrients can be taken in over the entire plant surface, roots play only a minor role in nutrient uptake and serve primarily as a form of anchorage. Total immersion can be a problem in water plants. To avoid 'drowning,' leaves and stems may be covered with a layer of slime and mucilage. This is especially true of young plants (Thompson et al. 1985).

Although plants have evolved ways of acquiring oxygen from the water, the amount that is held in solution regulates plant growth. High altitude water bodies hold less oxygen due to lower atmospheric pressure. The diffusion of oxygen in water is very slow. In water bodies with large amounts of plant life the deoxygenation of the water can be rapid (especially at night when photosynthesis is not occurring to replace it) and the oxygen demand is greater. Water plants adapt to this low oxygen by developing air canals. Many aquatics store oxygen in intercellular spaces known as aerenchyma. Often these are linked to form a continuous passage to all parts of the plant.

14

Cattails, Water-hemlock, and water lilies all have these very porous aerenchyma tissues used for oxygen storage. At night, when photosynthesis activity stops but respiration continues, these reserves are slowly utilized to keep the plant metabolically active.

Carbon is a critical element for life. In water, carbon is available for photosynthesis in the form of carbon dioxide and bicarbonates. Carbon dioxide is 200 times more soluble in water than oxygen. How much of each is present determines the amount of plant production which can occur.

In terrestrial plants, strong sunlight can damage chloroplasts (those organelles in which photosynthesis takes place). Chloroplasts in terrestrial plants are deep within the leaf tissues. The chloroplasts of submerged plants, however, growing under diffused light conditions tend to be distributed in the outer layer of cells of stems and leaves.

The depth in the water to which light can penetrate and the quality of light present at that level determine how far down plants are able to grow. Water that is clear allows blue-green wavelengths to penetrate more deeply. In medium clear water the yellow wavelengths penetrate more deeply. Brown water only allows the red and orange parts of the spectrum to reach the depths. The depth to which 1% of the surface value of light energy penetrates is usually the lowest depth at which plants can photosynthesize (Mitchell 1974).

Submerged plants tend to be buoyant due to gas-filled tissues and are partially supported by the water itself. The firm, rigid structure of land plants is not necessary. When submerged species, such as water-crowfoots and milfoils, are removed from the water, they collapse. Surface and underwater leaves are often dramatically different. For example, mare's-tail has whorls of thin, flaccid and brownish underwater leaves but the above-water foliage is thick, stiff and deep green. Thus, water plants at one stage of their annual growth cycle will sometimes appear entirely different from a later stage, adding to the challenge of water plant identification.

Wetlands and Water Quality

Productive wetlands improve water quality. A wetland acts as a giant sponge. Rainfall and runoff are collected and filtered by the vegetation and microbial life. Water slowly works its way through the wetland. Sediments are deposited and nutrients that are held in solution are utilized by plant and animal life. The purified water leaves the wetland and continues on its way either on the surface, in the ground water or into the atmosphere through evaporation.

The local climate is affected by the presence of a wetland. Soil moisture and air humidity is controlled through evaporation and plant transpiration, helping to maintain a healthy environment. Through photosynthesis, aquatic plants contribute significantly to the amount of oxygen in the water. High oxygen levels favor the aerobic breakdown of compounds. A rise and fall in oxygen levels occurs over a 24-hour period. During the day, photosynthesis takes place and oxygen is released into the water. During the night, photosynthesis stops but respiration continues, lowering the amount of oxygen in solution.

The absence of plants results in oxygen-poor waters and less efficient anaerobic decomposition predominates. The result is stagnant conditions with the end products of ammonia, methane and hydrogen sulfide being released by biological activity. This gives some areas their distinctive swampy odor. On the other hand, an over-abundance of plants (a high plant volume to water volume ratio) will result in oxygen depletion on warm summer nights (resulting in high fish mortality). Respiration levels are high at a time when the water (warmed from the day) will not hold very much oxygen in solution.

Wetland systems are dynamic and change over time. Sediment accumulation and excessive plant growth can eventually fill in a wetland. The flora slowly changes with the drying out of the landscape, and terrestrial conditions take over as wetland becomes dryland. This process, known as succession, can take place in 10 to 20 years or over thousands of years depending on the drainage basin and the amount of water input replenishing the wetland.

HEINJO LAHRING

Beaver lodge.

Nature renews wetlands in many ways. Past glaciations have played a major role in wetland creation. Beavers build dams that flood large tracts of land. Landslides or fallen trees can block a drainage channel.

Humans create wetlands through road building and land development. Drainage channels become modified and water fills ditches and low-lying areas. Wetland reclamation projects focus on large excavations in order to improve habitat for waterfowl.

Invasive Plants

Several species of water plants have become problems in our native wetlands.

Purple Loosestrife (*Lythrum salicaria*) is an example of an introduced plant from Europe that now covers large areas of the northeastern United States and southeastern Canada. A beautiful plant with showy purple spikes, *Lythrum salicaria* has nonetheless become a problem because of a combination of factors. The plant is a prolific seed producer and is difficult to eradicate, spreading with each successive season. It is not favored by wildlife.

HEINJO LAHRING

Lythrum salicaria *growing in native wetland.*

Many non-native plants, especially those introduced through water gardening, barely survive in our cold northern climate and must be given special conditions in order to survive. These are easily displaced by native plants. However, caution is advised in disposal of water plants. *Do not plant non-natives in native wetlands!* A great number of native species can be considered invasive in that they will easily outcompete other more favored wetland plants when conditions are suitable. Not all non-native species are invasive, and not all invasive species are non-native.

Aquatic Plant Control

The maintenance of irrigation canals and the use of lakes and ponds for recreation may at times necessitate the removal of aquatic plants.

Eurasian Water-milfoil (*Myriophyllum spicatum*), a problem in the Okanagan Valley of British Columbia as well as drainages in the eastern United States, is a highly productive aquatic plant which, once established, chokes out native plants and fills in shallow waters. Small fragments attached to a boat propeller or a bird's plumage are all it takes to move it from one water body to the next. Eliminating this plant once it is established is extremely difficult to achieve.

When conditions are favorable, native aquatics can also grow in profusion and overwhelm a pond. This is actually a normal phase of succession. Unfortunately this usually indicates the end of a productive wetland, as the pond soon fills in and water plants become replaced by land plants. Plant control methods include the following:

1. Underwater mats can be placed to cover the bottom sediments, discouraging plant life from growing. This is quite successful in beach areas. The mats must be removed and replaced since sediment fallout from the water eventually allows plants to grow on top of the mats.

2. Chemical control is useful in some locations. Herbicides, many with a copper base, are added to the water and kill the vegetation. This can be quite effective but is not always appropriate. The sudden death and decay of plants resulting from herbicide use often causes a serious oxygen deficiency that can result in fish-kill. Repeated seasonal use is usually necessary to maintain some form of control from year to year. In some forms, copper accumulates (toxic).

3. Although labour intensive, mechanical removal of water plants is quite effective. Rakes, chains, scythes, and cutter-bars are used to crop the plants during the growing season. Maintenance staff at golf courses, botanical gardens, and swimming areas employ this safe method to keep waterways weed-free. The resulting piles of vegetation can be used to produce compost, mulch or fertilizer.

4. Many aquatic macrophytes can be harvested for useful purposes. Duckweed (*Lemna* spp.) and Canada waterweed (*Elodea canadensis*) have been used to feed livestock. Reeds have been used for centuries throughout the world for thatching roofs.

5. Biological control is employed in some areas. This is especially effective in isolated trout and golf course ponds. Herbivorous fish, such as the Triploid White Amur or Grass Carp (a native fish of China and Siberia), graze on the plants, helping to keep excessive plant growth in check. However, many of these species require warm water to do well and are not suited to the cold northern waters found in many parts of the prairie provinces. Government regulations may restrict the use of this method.

GLEN SUGGETT

Delta Marsh, Manitoba.

PLANT CLASSIFICATION AND NOMENCLATURE

This field guide is intended to highlight the water and wetland plants of the Prairie provinces that are of common occurrence and/or of special interest.

For ease of reference the grass-like monocots have been grouped together in one section (i.e., grasses, sedges and rushes). Similarly, the woody dicots have been listed together under the heading "Shrubs." Apart from these modifications, the families have been arranged in an order similar to that found in the two most popular floras used in the region, *Flora of Alberta* (Moss, 1983) and Budd's *Flora of the Canadian Prairie Provinces* (Looman and Best, 1979). Although some changes have occurred since these were published, they are still very popular. This guide has been designed to act as a supplement to these floras. For a more recent and detailed taxonomic treatment, see *Aquatic and Wetland Plants of Northeastern North America* (Crow and Hellquist, 2000) and *The Flora of North America* (Flora of North America Committee, 1997). Taxonomic nomenclature essentially follows that outlined by these last two updated floras. When there were alternate valid plant names, it was necessary to make informed decisions as to taxonomic nomenclature. I will take full responsibility for any errors and omissions that may have occurred in the process.

It is surprising how many common names have become attached to plants over the years. Finding one that is recognized by all is not always possible. Fortunately, standardized lists of many of the common names exist and have been helpful in selecting proper common names used in this guide (Brako et al. 1995).

Although identification keys can be overly technical for the lay reader, a key to the families is included, beginning on page 20, along with keys to *Potamogeton, Eriophorum, Myriophyllum,* and *Scirpus* in order to assist in identifying the species in these frequently encountered but difficult to identify genera.

When identifying water plants, remember that:

1. growth stages and environmental conditions (especially submerged versus aerial) can result in variations in plant form. For example, compare long ribbons of *Sagittaria* (submerged leaves) at right, with the emergent leaves of *Sagittaria latifolia* below.

HEINJO LAHRING

HEINJO LAHRING

2. non-vascular plants may resemble vascular plants. For example, *Chara sp.* (below, left), an alga, and *Ricciocarpus natans* (below, right) a floating aquatic liverwort, can easily be misidentified as vascular plants.

HEINJO LAHRING

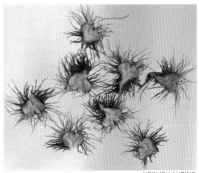

HEINJO LAHRING

KEY TO FAMILIES

(adapted from Moss, 1983)

DIVISION PTERIDOPHYTA (Ferns and Fern Allies)

DIVISION SPERMATOPHYTA (Seed Plants)

CLASS MONOCOTYLEDONEAE (MONOCOTS)

- leaves parallel-veined
- vascular bundles of stem irregularily arranged
- cambium absent
- flower parts in 3s or 6s (never in 5s)
- embryo with 1 cotyledon
- mostly herbaceous

CLASS DICOTYLEDONEAE (DICOTS)

- leaves usually net-veined
- vascular bundles of stem commonly in a single ring
- cambium present
- flower parts usually in 5s or 4s
- embryo with 2 cotyledons
- herbaceous or woody

1. perianth parts in 1 series or entirely absent
    2. flower imperfect, the staminate (and generally the pistillate too) in catkins; trees or shrubs
        3. plants monoecious ....**BETULACEAE** (Birch Family) 146
        3. plants dioecious (sometimes monoecious in Myricaceae)
            4. ovules many; fruit a many-seeded capsule; seeds hairy
            .... **SALICACEAE** (Willow Family) 136
            4. ovules 1 or 2; fruit a gland-dotted nutlet with 2 corky bracts; seeds not hairy
            ....**MYRICACEAE** (Bayberry Family) 144
    2. flowers perfect (or if imperfect, the plants herbaceous); flowers not in catkins
        5. plants woody
            6. stamens 4 or 8; leaves with silvery or rusty brown scales
            ....**ELAEAGNACEAE** (Oleaster Family) 152
            6.stamens 5 (sometimes 4); leaves otherwise ..**CAPRIFOLIACEAE** (Honysuckle Family) 168
        5. plants herbaceous
            7. plants aquatic; flowers small and sessile in leaf axils or in spikes held above water
                8. small tufted plants; leaves opposite ...**CALLITRICHACEAE** (Water-starwort Family) 220
                8. plants growing as long strands; leaves whorled
                    9. leaves entire; flowers in leaf axils ....**HIPPURIDACEAE** (Mare's-tail Family) 236
                    9. leaves finely dissected; flowers in leaf axils or on spikes
                        10. leaves pinnately branched; flowers on spikes; stamens 8
                        ....**HALORAGACEAE** (Water-milfoil Family) 232
                        10. leaves dichotomously branched; flowers in leaf axils; stamens 12–16
                        ....**CERATOPHYLLACEAE** (Hornwort Family) 192
            7. plants terrestrial/wetland; flowers otherwise
                11. ovary inferior or partly so, or closely enclosed by the calyx and appearing inferior
                    12. ovary or its locules with many ovules ....**SAXIFRAGACEAE** (Saxifrage Family) 208
                    12. ovary or its locules with only 1 or 2 ovules
                        13. inflorescence a dense head, subtended by an involucre of separate
                        bracts ....**ASTERACEAE** (Composite Family) 286
                        13. inflorescence otherwise
                            14. leaves whorled ....**RUBIACEAE** (Madder Family) 280
                            14. leaves alternate or basal
                                15. flowers in terminal or axillary cymules (sometimes forming a cluster);
                                leaves simple and entire.............**SANTALACEAE** (Sandalwood Family) 173
                                15. flowers in umbels; leaves compound (occasionally simple), usually
                                much divided ....**APIACEAE** (Carrot Family) 238

11. ovary superior

16. ovary or its locules with many ovules, or gynoecium consisting of many one-seeded ovaries

17. leaves simple or compound (often ternate); flowers mostly regular, corolla not 2-lipped ....**RANUNCULACEAE** (Crowfoot Family)　　194

17. leaves simple or pinnately divided but not ternate; flowers irregular, corolla 2-lipped ....**SCROPHULARIACEAE** (Figwort Family)　　266

16. ovary or its locules with only 1 or 2 ovules

18. leaves opposite (sometimes alternate); stinging hairs present ....**URTICACEAE** (Nettle Family)　　170

18. leaves alternate; stinging hairs absent

19. flowers imperfect

20. flowers borne in axillary staminate or pistillate clusters; ovary 1-loculed, 1-seeded ....**URTICACEAE** (Nettle Family)　　170

20. flowers borne 1–3 in leaf axils; ovary 2-loculed (4-lobed), 4-seeded ....**CALLITRICHACEAE** (Water-starwort Family)　　220

19. flowers perfect, in terminal racemes or clustered along stem

21. ovary 2-loculed (rarely 1 loculed); fruit a pod-like capsule ....**BRASSICACEAE** (Mustard Family)　　199

21. ovary 1 or 3-loculed; fruit otherwise

22. ovary 1-loculed; stipules (ocreae) sheathing the stem at nodes; stamens 5 or 6 (3–9) ....**POLYGONACEAE** (Buckwheat Family)　　174

22. ovary 1 or 3-loculed; stipules not sheathing; stamens 1–5

23. leaves opposite, at least below (often united at base); stems usually swollen at nodes................................**CARYOPHYLLACEAE** (Pink Family)　　184

23. leaves alternate; nodal swelling of stems absent; sepals 5 or less; petals absent; stamens 1–5........**CHENOPODIACEAE** (Goosefoot Family) 150, 178

1. perianth in two series

24. corolla of separate petals

25. stamens more than twice as many as the petals

26. plants aquatic with leaves floating, peltate and entire ....**NYMPHAEACEAE** (Waterlily Family)　　186

26. plants terrestrial or aquatic but leaves not as above

27. leaves basal, margins fused to form a winged, obconical pitcher; stigma umbrella shaped, 3–4 cm wide..............**SARRACENIACEAE** (Pitcher-plant Family)　　204

27. plants otherwise

28. ovary inferior, leaves alternate...................................**ROSACEAE** (Rose Family)　　212

28. ovary superior

29. ovary 2 or more, separate from one another or united only at base

30. stamens inserted on the receptacle, at the base of the ovaries; stipules absent ....**RANUNCULACEAE** (Crowfoot Family)　　194

30. stamens inserted on a disc or hypanthium; stipules usually present...**ROSACEAE** (Rose Family)　　212

29. ovary solitary

31. leaves punctate with translucent or black dots ....**CLUSIACEAE** (St. John's-wort Family)　　224

31. leaves not punctate

23

61. stamens 5

    64. plants woody ....**ERICACEAE** (Heath Family)   154

    64. plants herbaceous

        65. leaves trifoliate; corolla-lobes fimbriate.......**MENYANTHACEAE** (Bogbean Family)   254

        65. leaves not trifoliate; corolla-lobes not fimbriate

            66. corolla-tube with 5 lobes often bearing 5 appendages in the throat; fruit of 4 nutlets (each 1-seeded); whole plant usually coarsely hairy ....**BORAGINACEAE** (Borage Family)   257

            66. corolla-tube appendages absent; fruit a capsule with many seeds

                67. ovary 1-loculed; leaves opposite, entire; fruit a 2-valved capsule ....**GENTIANACEAE** (Gentian Family)   252

                67. ovary 2-loculed or more; leaves alternate or opposite; fruit a 2 or 3-valved capsule

                    68. corolla tube 5-lobed but not 2-lipped; ovary 3-loculed; stigma 3-cleft; fruit a 3-valved capsule.........................**POLEMONIACEAE** (Phlox Family)   256

                    68. corolla-tube 2-lipped (upper 2-lobed, lower 3-lobed); ovary 2-loculed; fruit a 2-valved capsule...............**SCROPHULARIACEAE** (Figwort Family)   266

57. ovary inferior

    69. flowers (often present as ray and disc flowers) in heads subtended by an involucre of bracts ....**ASTERACEAE** (Composite Family)   286

    69. flowers otherwise

        70. plants woody....................................**CAPRIFOLIACEAE** (Honeysuckle Family)   168

        70. plants herbaceous

            71. leaves alternate; flowers blue or purplish; ovary 3-(5)-loculed; irregular corolla of 5 joined petals, 5-stamens (filaments and anthers wholly united to form a tube around stigma) ....**CAMPANULACEAE** (Bluebell Family)   283

            71. leaves opposite or whorled; flowers white, pinkish, lilac or yellow; 3,4, or 5 stamens (filaments not united to form a tube around the stigma)

                72. flowers white or yellow

                    73. leaves opposite or whorled, simple and entire; corolla of 3–4 lobes ....**RUBIACEAE** (Madder Family)   280

                    73. leaves opposite and in basal rosette; cauline leaves pinnately divided; corolla 5-lobed ....**VALERIANACEAE** (Valerian Family)   282

                72. flowers pinkish or lilac

                    74. plants erect; corolla 3–4-lobed.............................**RUBIACEAE** (Madder Family)   280

                    74. plants trailing; corolla 5-lobed and 2-lipped ....**CAPRIFOLIACEAE** (Honeysuckle Family)   168

—PTERIDOPHYTA—
FERN ALLIES

- herbaceous vascular plants reproducing by spores
- plants lacking true flowers
- spores develop into a small prothallus (gametophyte). The prothallus produces gametes which, when united, form a zygote. The zygote develops into an embryo growing into a plant. Part of this plant then forms sporangia which release spores to continue the cycle. The sporophyte phase is separate from the gametophyte phase for part of the lifecycle.

Equisetum hyemale (pp. 32–33)
Common Scouring-rush

HEINJO LAHRING

Equisetum fluviatile (pp. 30–31)
Swamp Horsetail

HEINJO LAHRING

Isoetes echinospora Dur.

ISOETACEAE (Quillwort Family)

Northern Quillwort

Syn.: *I. muricata* Dur., *I. braunii* Dur., *I. echinospora* Dur. var. *braunii* (Dur.) Engelm.
Other Common Names: Quillwort Fern, Braun's Quillwort

Isoetes means 'green throughout the year.' *Echinospora* refers to the megaspores which are armed with prickles or spines.

Submerged
Perennial
Native
Rare
Hardiness Zone: 0

DESCRIPTION

This onion-like, evergreen plant has hollow, tubular leaves which form a basal rosette from forked, fibrous roots. **Leaves** are linear, 5–15 cm long by 1–1.5 mm wide, spoon-shaped and clasping at base. Each leaf contains 4 large, longitudinal air cavities.
Sporangia (4–7 mm long) are inconspicuous and on the adaxial (inner) face of the leaf-base.
Spore clusters are covered by a velum (thin membrane). Two spore types exist. The first are megaspores (female) which are white, 0.3–0.5 mm wide and resemble salt with tiny spines covering them. The second type are microspores (male). These are fawn coloured and 23–50 micrometers in length.

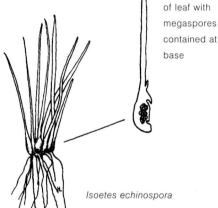

cross-section of leaf with megaspores contained at base

Isoetes echinospora

HABITAT AND DISTRIBUTION

Northern Quillwort is usually found growing submerged on sand or rocky lakeshores across the prairies. Occasionally it grows as an emergent just above the water-line. In wet meadows, it resembles a clump of bunchgrass. Noncalcareous, oligotrophic waters are preferred.

Distribution is circumpolar. Range extends from southern Mackenzie region (Lake Athabasca) in Alberta, across northern Saskatchewan and Manitoba.

SPECIAL FEATURES

This often overlooked plant sometimes covers large areas. It is valued as a food for diving ducks, muskrats and deer. It is an indicator species for soft-water or acid habitats where it may form dense stands over lake bottoms.

RELATED SPECIES

Isoetes bolanderi Engelm., **Bolander's Quillwort**, is slightly shorter (5–10 cm long) and softer-leaved than *I. echinospora*. Its microspores are more spiny than *I. echinospora*. Habitat is restricted to mountain ponds and lakes of southwestern Alberta. *Isoetes echinospora* hybridizes with *I. lacustris* (=*I. x hickeyi* A. A. Eaton).

Isoetes lacustris L., **Lake Quillwort**, is similar to *I. echinospora* but has larger megaspores which are ridged (rarely smooth) but not spiny. Lake Quillwort is found across the Prairie provinces.

Equisetum fluviatile L.   **EQUISETACEAE (Horsetail Family)**

Swamp Horsetail

Syn.: *Equisetum limosum* L.

Other Common Names: Water Horsetail, River Horsetail, Joint Grass, Scrub Grass

Equisetum is a compound word derived from *equus* (horse) and *seta* (bristle). The species epithet, *fluviatile*, pertains to 'rivers,' which is where it is often found growing.

**Emergent
Perennial
Native
Common
Hardiness Zone: 0**

DESCRIPTION

The green, segmented, hollow stems are circular in cross-section, often over 1 m tall, and gradually taper to a point. They are quite soft to the touch and collapse easily when squeezed. Stems are fluted and somewhat rough due to silica (SiO_2) deposits along the ridges and in epidermal cell walls. **Leaves** are reduced to small, whorled scales at the stem and branch nodes (joints). These are fused together to form a tightly appressed, dark brown sheath with a 15–20 toothed, narrow, white margin (may be black throughout). Side branches, when present, are quite fine. Aerial stems persist for 1 year or less. Reproduction is vegetative, by rooting along the stem and underground stolons, or sexually, by spore production. Whorls of 5–10

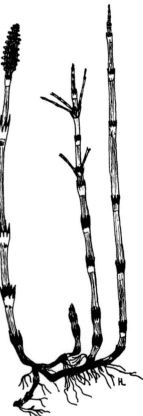

sporangia are borne in terminal cones called strobili.

Spherical **spores** are released at maturity, each provided with 4 elastic hygroscopic elaters. Spores germinate in damp locations to produce a prothallus (gametophyte).

HABITAT AND DISTRIBUTION

Water Horsetail is tolerant of a wide range of habitats including shallow water in bogs, fens, ditches, swamps, streams, lakes and wet meadows. This is a widely distributed horsetail found across the Prairie provinces.

Equisetum fluviatile L.

Equisetum fluviatile

HEINJO LAHRING

SPECIAL FEATURES

Equisetum fluviatile is an important food for muskrats. Some birds such as grouse, geese and swans will utilize the upper parts of the stems for grit. Black bears are known to feed on the rhizomes and stems. Moose occasionally feed heavily on the stems. One report claims horsetails to be responsible for the deaths of horses, cattle and sheep.

Native peoples have utilized the shoots as a food source. The stiff outer part of mature stems containing the silica deposits were peeled and discarded. The sweet, pulpy inner material was eaten raw. Young shoots are also considered edible. Europeans have used the starchy rhizomes of *E. fluviatile* as food. When young, they are tender and juicy and the taste is usually fairly mild. Older plants may be edible but tend to be somewhat unpalatable. Raw horsetails, in quantity and improperly prepared, could be fatal to humans, so caution is advised.

RELATED SPECIES

Equisetum fluviatile is easily confused with *E. hyemale* L., **Common Scouring-rush**. *Equisetum fluviatile* tends to be a lighter green colour, often has some side branching, stems are usually thinner and die back each fall. *Equisetum hyemale* has sharp cone tips (*E. fluviatile* does not) and usually grows in drier habitats.

Equisetum palustre L., **Marsh Horsetail**, is shorter (20–60 cm tall) than *E. fluviatile*, tends to be more heavily branched and has fewer than 11 teeth per sheath with prominent white margins and dark centers.

HEINJO LAHRING

Equisetum fluviatile

(Also see photo of *Equisetum fluviatile* on page 28.)

HEINJO LAHRING

31

Equisetum hyemale L.   EQUISETACEAE (Horsetail Family)
Common Scouring-rush

Syn.: *Equisetum prealtum* Raf., *E. robustum* A. Br.
Other Common Names: Dutch-rush, Gun-bright

Equisetum is a compound word derived from *equus* (horse) and *seta* (bristle).
The species epithet, *hyemale*, pertains to winter or wintery.

Emergent
Perennial
Native
Common
Hardiness Zone: 0

DESCRIPTION

Deep green, unbranched stems stand erect to 1 m tall. The aerial stems persist for more than one year. Stems are jointed with a hollow central cavity. **Leaves** are reduced to a toothed sheath at most of the joints. Each sheath may have 14 or more teeth. In southern, central, and western regions the plants tend to be taller and have more persistent teeth. The stomata are sunken in single lines down the stem. Siliceous cross-bands, or tubercles, are present on stem ridges, giving a very rough feel when touched.

Vegetative reproduction occurs by rooting along creeping black rootstocks. **Sporangia** are borne in terminal cones on stems.

Spores are released at maturity (late summer) and, under moist conditions, will grow into a prothallus (gametophyte).

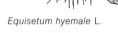
Equisetum hyemale L.

HABITAT AND DISTRIBUTION

Scouring rush grows on riverbanks, along roadsides, lakeshores and in moist woodland habitats. It has a preference for sandy soils and is a reliable sign of a very high water table. Distribution is circumpolar and can be found throughout the Prairie provinces.

SPECIAL FEATURES

This is a living relic of prehistoric times. Giant tree-forms of the now extinct *Calamites*, probably related to our *Equisetum* of today, existed in the Carboniferous era and contributed in forming the coal of today.

Scouring-rush refers to its use as an abrasive in cleaning and sanding. This is due to the high silicon content of the stems

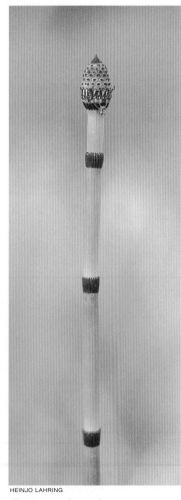
HEINJO LAHRING

Equisetum hyemale

HEINJO LAHRING

HEINJO LAHRING

HEINJO LAHRING

Equisetum laevigatum

HEINJO LAHRING

(5–10% of dry weight). In the past, dried stems were used in brightening gun-stocks, cleaning pots and pans, and polishing wood finishes by European cabinet makers. A bundle of horsetails for cleaning was as commonly used by early pioneers and Native peoples as it is by today's campers.

Dyes can be obtained from the green stalks. Stems in an alum solution give a yellow colour, with copper sulfate a green colour, and ferrous sulfate a greenish gray colour. The dyes were used to colour wool, cotton and linen.

As a food source young shoots from the green sterile stems can be used as one would asparagus, or they can be boiled and fried. Mature plants should be avoided and have even proved lethal to livestock in quantity (especially horses due to the plant's thiaminase content). Never harvest from heavily fertilized ditches or meadows since high levels of nitrates may render them toxic. *Equisetum* is one of a number of plants which will collect selenium (when present in soil) to a major degree.

Medicinally, a decoction applied externally has been reported to stop the bleeding of wounds. It has been used to treat urinary infections in the past but excessive amounts can result in irritation of the intestinal mucosa.

RELATED SPECIES

Worldwide, many varieties of *E. hyemale* have been identified.

Equisetum laevigatum A. Br., **Smooth Scouring-rush**, and *E. variegatum* Schleich., **Variegated Horsetail**, are also closely related evergreen-types of horsetails, but are not nearly as rough stemmed, rigidly erect and resistant to being crushed as *E. hyemale*.

Marsilea vestita Hook. & Grev.
Hairy Water-clover

MARSILEACEAE (Water-clover Family)

Syn.: *Marsilea mucronata* A. Br., *M. fournieri* C. Christensen, *M. uncinata* A. Br., *M. tenuifolia ex.* A. Br. Hooker & Greville, *M. vestita* ssp. *tenuifolia* (Engelmann *ex* A. Br.) D. M. Johnson
Other Common Names: Hairy Pepperwort

Marsilea is named for the Italian naturalist Luigi Fernando Conte Masigli, 1658–1730. The species epithet, *vestita*, means clothed or covered.

Emergent
Perennial
Native
Rare
Hardiness Zone: 3

DESCRIPTION

Marsilea is an aquatic fern. The appearance reminds one of *Oxalis* (Shamrock). It forms dense colonies of 4-foliate, palmately compound **leaves**. The leaflets are from 0.5 to 1.5 cm in length. Two or three leaves (rarely solitary) grow from a slender rhizome or shortened rootstock. The quadrifoliate blade arises from a slender petiole. The petiole can get quite long when submersed or very short when growing on shore (forming turf). Leaves may be aerial or floating in the water.

Marsilea vestita Hook. & Grev.

sporocarp

A nut-like **sporocarp**, borne laterally on the petiole, releases **spores** when the plant matures. A second spore-producing structure, a stalked **sporangiophore**, can be found growing on short peduncles near the leaf base. The sporangiophores start out green when young and change to brown with long hairs upon maturity. *Marsilea* also reproduces rapidly by proliferation from horizontal rootstocks.

HABITAT AND DISTRIBUTION

Hairy Water-clover can be found in ponds, lakes, wet depressions, ditches, river flood plains and even on dry ground where water once was earlier in the season. *Marsilea vestita* is known to colonize dried-up sloughs in tilled fields.

Plants occur in the southern parts of Alberta and Saskatchewan.

SPECIAL FEATURES

Sporangiophores are noted to be used by waterfowl for food.

RELATED SPECIES

Marsilea vestita is the only species native to the Prairie provinces.

Marsilea vestita

BARRE HELLQUIST

—SPERMATOPHYTA—
MONOCOTS
(EXCLUDING GRASSES, SEDGES, RUSHES)

- herbaceous vascular plants reproducing by seeds
- embryo with 1 cotyledon (seed leaf)
- flower parts in 3s or multiples of 3 (never 5s)
- stems, when present, lacking central pith; vascular bundles arranged irregularily in stem
- leaves parallel-veined

Tofieldia glutinosa (pp. 74–75)
Sticky False Asphodel

JOAN WILLIAMS

Typha latifolia L.
Common Cattail

TYPHACEAE (Cattail Family)

Typha is from an old Greek name, *Typhe*. *Latifolia* refers to the broad leaves. The Ojibway call this plant *pukawayaushkawi*, meaning "the common reed that splits."

Emergent
Perennial
Native
Common
Hardiness Zone: 0
Flowering Season: late summer

DESCRIPTION

Thick, creeping rhizomes give rise to tall (over 1 m), alternate, flat sword-like leaves. The **leaves** are sheathing at the bottom, green, spongy and have a strong network of fibers. The underground (or at times floating just below the water's surface) rhizomes produce numerous side shoots and will propagate rapidly given space and adequate nutrients. Flower stems act as the core of the plant with leaves enveloping them. The **flowers** are borne in a long (10–20 cm), thick spadix held above the foliage. Each spike is composed of multitudes of tiny male flowers towards the top, and female mixed with sterile flowers below. The female section of the spike starts out green, narrow and hard, and becomes thick (2.5 cm), soft and brown with age. The **male flowers** are composed of 1–7 (usually 3) stamens plus numerous hairs. The **female flowers** are essentially a one-celled ovary, a short style with stigma, and numerous long hairs on the stipe. The dense mass of these gives the spike its soft, furry character. The hairs help carry the **achenes** away in the wind when mature.

*Typha
latifolia* L.

HABITAT AND DISTRIBUTION

Typha is found throughout the region in marshes, ditches, ponds and lakes. It tends to be less common in swamps. Established colonies release a substance which is toxic to their own seedlings thereby preventing germination of seedlings in established stands. Cattails prefer areas where the water persists until at least mid-summer. Common throughout the Prairie provinces.

Typha latifolia

HEINJO LAHRING

SPECIAL FEATURES

Cattail stands form the backbone to many wetland ecosystems. They are used for nest building by birds such as Marsh Wrens, Red-winged Blackbirds, Swamp Sparrows, American Bitterns, Pied-billed Grebes, American Coots and Soras. Canada Geese feed on their rhizomes and, occasionally, young spikes. Cattail rhizomes also serve as one of the main foods for muskrat and beaver. Countless invertebrates (eg., cattail moth) rely on them for food and shelter in order to complete their life cycles.

From a year-round survival point of view, cattails are not only the easiest to recognize but also one of the most abundant and palatable of wild foods available in the Canadian wilds. The inner core at the base of the leaves can be eaten raw. The roots, when pounded into a meal or 'flour,' have a pleasant taste, and are rich in starch (up to 55% carbohydrates) and proteins. The resulting powder is similar to cornstarch. In early summer the young spikes can be boiled and eaten like corn on the cob. When the pollen (which is high in protein and a rich source of vitamin A) is ripe it can be shaken off and added to wheat flour. Later when the spike matures, the seeds can be obtained by burning the heads and then winnowing or sifting in order to obtain the seeds for cooking.

The long leaves are excellent for weaving mats and baskets, or shelter construction. The long fibers make it an excellent choice for emergency cordage. Cattail-fluff from the mature spikes makes excellent insulation for blankets and clothing, as well as tinder for starting fires.

RELATED SPECIES

In the southeastern region of the Prairie provinces native populations of *T. angustifolia* L., **Narrow-leaved** or **Pencil Cattail**, may be found. It differs from *T. latifolia* in having narrower, ribbon-like leaves. *Typha angustifolia* flower spikes are much thinner, with a space between the staminate (above)and pistillate flowers (below). *Typha angustifolia* is being used quite frequently in water gardening and is establishing itself in farm ponds and wetlands where it has been introduced. *Typha x glauca*, the hybrid formed from *T. angustifolia x T. latifolia*, is at times more common than either of the parents in some parts of Manitoba.

Typha angustifolia L.

Typha angustifolia

HEINJO LAHRING

Sparganium eurycarpum Engelm.

SPARGANIACEAE (Bur-reed Family)

Giant Bur-reed

Other Common Names: Broad-fruited Bur-reed

The genus name is from the Greek *sparganion*, a derivative of *sparganon* (swaddling-band) and refers to the ribbon-like leaves. *Eurycarpum* can be broken down as *'eu'*, meaning well, good or thoroughly completed, and *'carpum'* relating to the fruit.

Emergent
Perennial
Native
Common
Hardiness Zone: 0
Flowering Season: mid- to late summer

DESCRIPTION

Plants grow from fibrous roots and creeping rhizomes to over 1 m in height with stout and robust stems. The green **leaves** are alternate, narrow (0.5–1.5 cm wide), and stiff. They are characteristically without prominent longitudinal veins and have cross and longitudinal veinlets forming a pattern of rectangular spaces. The leaves are trough-shaped or keeled on the back, particularly towards the spongy base. In off-shore locations, submerged leaves (up to 80 cm long) develop before the main stem.

Flower heads (3–20) are formed along an erect, zigzag-patterned stem. Male flower heads develop above and female (1–4) below. Each head contains numerous very small, greenish, unisexual **flowers**. The perianth of staminate flowers consists of very small scales. Pistillate flowers have 2 stigmas, and 3–6 sepals.

Large, bristly, 1–2 cm wide, 'burs' form later in the season and are composed of nut-like **achenes** each with a 2-pronged, persistant style.

Sparganium eurycarpum Engelm.

(See additional photo of *Sparganium eurycarpum* on page 57.)

SPARGANIUM ACHENES	
Sparganium eurycarpum	*Sparganium angustifolium*
2 stigmas	• beak of achene often quite curved • anthers < .8mm long • *Sparganium fluctuans* is similar but anthers are ≥.8mm long

Sparganium eurycarpum

HEINJO LAHRING

HABITAT AND DISTRIBUTION

Giant Bur-reed can be found growing in quiet marshes, rivers, sloughs, roadside ditches and ponds. Preferred water depth is usually less than 1 m and where the water persists until at least late June. It tends to be more common in the shady wetlands of the parkland than elsewhere.

Range extends across each of the Prairie provinces.

Sparganium angustifolium Michx.
(1–several staminate heads)

SPECIAL FEATURES

The large, bur-like fruits are a favourite of wildlife. Waterfowl which eat them include Mallards, Coots, Black Ducks, Common Snipe and Rails. The stems and leaves are a preferred food and deer. Muskrats devour the entire plant.

This is another prized survival plant for people, providing edibles year round. The tubers and bulb-like base can be dried and pounded into flour in the same way as cattails. They can also be cooked, boiled or roasted.

Sparganium was one of the plants used by the founder of medicine, Dioscorides (50 years BC). It was claimed that the root and seeds drunk in wine would help cure snake bites.

Insects, and especially flies, assist in pollination.

RELATED SPECIES

Sparganium eurycarpum is the only bur-reed in the region with only 2 stigmas (all others have only 1).

Sparganium angustifolium Michx., **Narrow-leaved Bur-reed**, is similar to *S. fluctuans* but has erect stems as well as floating leaves. The perianth segments are attached near the top of stipe. [syn. *S. emersum* var. *angustifolium* (Michx.) Taylor & MacBryde, *S. multipedunculatum* Rydb.]

HEINJO LAHRING

Sparganium emersum Rehmann, **Stemless Bur-reed**, has erect stems (75 cm) with 2–10 mm wide leaves which extend beyond the flower spike. There are 4–9 male flower heads above and 1–4 female heads (1.5–2.5 cm dia.) below. The beak of the achene is half the length of the achene body. [syn. *S. chlorocarpum* Rydb.]

Sparganium fluctuans (Morong) Robins., **Floating Bur-reed**, is found in shallow water. It has slender stems (up to 150 cm long) with floating, ribbon-like leaves. The inflorescence is usually branched with each branch containing a few male and female heads. The perianth segments are attached near the bottom of the stipe. This is a rare species confined to the north, preferring the soft water of the Precambrian formation.

Sparganium natans var. *minimum* Hartm., **Slender Bur-reed**, is a relatively small plant with floating (and sometimes erect) leaves, 1–4 female heads and 1 male head. [syn. *S. minimum* (Hartm.) Fries]

Sparganium natans var. *minimum*

Najas flexilis (Willd.) Rostk. & Schmidt

NAJADACEAE (Naiad Family)

Slender Naiad

Other Common Names: Northern Water-nymph

Najas means water-nymph and *flexilis* refers to its flexible and bending underwater stems.

Submerged
Annual
Native
Common
Hardiness Zone: 0
Flowering Season: mid-summer

DESCRIPTION

This is an aquatic plant with slender, densely branching underwater stems arising from fibrous roots. Stems are forked, becoming quite long (over 1 m) with widely spaced leaves in deep water, or short and compact with closely spaced leaves in shallow water. The opposite, toothed **leaves** (0.2–0.6 mm wide) are broad at the base and taper towards a sharp recurving tip. Margins are inrolled.

The tiny **flowers** can be found in the leaf axils and are often hidden by broad, sheathing leaf bases. Solitary male and female flowers can be found on the same plant. The male flower consists of a single stamen enclosed in a papery sheath. The female flower is a single pistil (style over 1 mm long) without any sheath. This plant fragments very easily, with broken-off sections dispersing easily throughout the waterbody.

The Naiad's **fruit** consists of a shiny, pale brown achene (2.5–3.7 mm long) which is released into the water upon ripening. Obscure, fine, hexagonal reticulation is evident on surface.

HABITAT AND DISTRIBUTION

Slender Naiad makes its home in lakes, ponds, rivers and streams. It can be found in scattered patterns mixed with other aquatic plants, such as *Ranunculus* and *Potamogeton*, or it can form extensive patches. This plant is intolerant of pollution. It is not often seen since it is mainly a bottom dweller. This northern aquatic plant is widely distributed across the Prairie provinces.

Najas flexilis (Willd.) Rostk. & Schmidt

SPECIAL FEATURES

The Slender Naiad is a very important plant for water aeration. It provides food and shelter for fish and invertebrates. The small seeds are eaten by small aquatic organisms. Waterfowl such as Black Ducks, Buffleheads, Pintails, Ring-necked Ducks, Scaups, Teals, geese and Coots feed on the plants and seeds.

Najas flexilis

HEINJO LAHRING

40

HEINJO LAHRING

Najas flexilis, above and left.
Left, note flower in leaf axil.

HEINJO LAHRING

Najas guadalupensis (Spreng.) Magnus

RELATED SPECIES

Najas guadalupensis (Spreng.) Magnus, **Guadalupe Naiad**, has been reported from the Prairies. Its flat leaves have non-curled tips which are acute to rounded at the apex. The style is at most 0.5 mm long and the anthers 4-locular. The seed is dull with rather squarish reticulation. It is known from warmer areas including southern Ontario and Quebec. Its range extends into Minnesota and Wisconsin, Colorado, Oregon to Idaho, south to Baja California, and Texas to Florida.

Key to *Potamogeton*

(adapted from Crow and Hellquist, 2000)

1. Leaves stiff, conspicuously 2-ranked, with basal lobe at junction with stipule..............*P. robbinsii*
   ROBBIN'S PONDWEED

1. Leaves lax, not conspicuously 2-ranked, basal lobes lacking
   2. Submersed leaves linear, thread-like to ribbon-like, 0.1–10 mm wide
      3. Floating leaves present (at least on some plants), 2.5–6 cm wide, usually cordate at base (floating leaves in strong currents not cordate at base), 1.5–12 cm long, 7–37-veined, petiole pale at junction with blade; submersed (phyllodial) leaves 0.8–2 mm wide; fruit usually 3.5–5 mm long, keels obscure ....*P. natans*
         FLOATING-LEAF PONDWEED
      3. Floating leaves absent
         4. Nodal glands at leaf base absent
            5. Leaves 15–35-veined, more than 2 mm wide; stem conspicuously flattened; fruit 3–3.5 mm wide ....*P. zosteriformis*
               FLAT-STEMMED PONDWEED
            5. Leaves 3–5-veined, usually less than 2 mm wide, stem round in cross-section; fruit less than 3 mm wide...*P. foliosus*
               LEAFY PONDWEED
         4. Nodal glands at leaf base present
            6. Stipules fibrous, often whitish
               7. Leaf apex rounded or apiculate; leaves 5–7 (9)-veined; winter buds with inner leaves at right angle to outer leaves ....*P. friesii*
                  FRIES PONDWEED
               7. Leaf apex usually bristle-tipped, acute or rarely obtuse to apiculate; leaves 3–13-veined; winter buds flattened, with inner and outer leaves in same plane ....*P. strictifolius*
                  STIFF-LEAVED PONDWEED
            6. Stipules not fibrous, usually delicate, greenish, brown, or white
               8. Leaves 1–3.5 mm wide, often reddish brown, apex rounded or slightly apiculate; fruit with dorsal keel or ridge ....*P. obtusifolius*
                  BLUNT-LEAF PONDWEED
               8. Leaves 0.2–2.5 mm wide, usually green, apex obtuse, apiculate, or acute; ruit with a rounded dorsal surface
                  9. Leaves with up to 2 rows of lacunae along each side of midrib, apex acute, rarely apiculate; stipules mostly connate (surrounding stem); peduncles usually terminal, 1–6.2 cm long, 1–3 per plant; inflorescence usually of 2–4 distinct, interrupted whorls ....*P. pusillus* ssp. *pusillus*
                     SLENDER PONDWEED
                  9. Leaves with up to 5 rows of lacunae along each side of midrib, apex obtuse to acute; stipules mostly convolute (wrapped around stem, but split); peduncles axillary or terminal, 0.5–4.6 (6.6) cm long, more than 3 per plant; inflorescence crowded ....*P. pusillus* ssp. *tenuissimus*
                     POINTED-LEAF SLENDER PONDWEED

Key (continued)

2. Submersed leaves broadly linear-oblong to lanceolate to elliptic to subcircular, 10–75 mm wide (in *P. gramineus* stranded terrestrial forms sometimes lack submersed leaves)

   10. Leaf margins conspicuously toothed; stem flattened; fruit beak 2–3 mm long; winter buds commonly present and extremely hard ....*P. crispus*
                                   CURLY-LEAVED PONDWEED

   10. Leaf margins entire; stem round in cross-section; fruit beak 1 mm long or less; winter buds rarely present, soft

      11. Submersed leaves sessile (but not clasping) or petioled; floating leaves absent or present

         12. Submersed leaves 27–37-veined, distinctly arced. ....*P. amplifolius*
                                 LARGE-LEAVED PONDWEED

         12. Submersed leaves with fewer than 27 veins, not arced

            13. Submersed leaves with petiole 1–13 cm long; stipules 3–9 cm long, disintegrating early; fruit 3.5–4.3 mm long ....*P. nodosus*
                                 LONGLEAF PONDWEED

            13. Submersed leaves sessile; fruit 1.7–3.5 mm long

               14. Submersed leaves 7-veined (often up to 6 additional obscure veins), with a reticulate portion along midvein; leaf apex obtuse or acute; leaves with reddish colour on drying; stipules blunt; fruit plump, tawny olive, stalked ....*P. alpinus*
                                   RED PONDWEED

               14. Submersed leaves (3) 5–9 (11)-veined (all conspicuous), lacking an obvious reticulate portion along midvein; leaf apex acute or awl-shaped; leaves without reddish colour on drying; stipules acute; fruit laterally flattened, reddish brown, not stalked ....*P. gramineus*
                                   VARIABLE PONDWEED

      11. Submersed leaves clasping stem; floating leaves absent

         15. Rhizomes spotted with rusty red; leaves linear-lanceolate to ovate-oblong, (5) 10–20 (25) cm long, apex boat-shaped (curved upward) and splitting when pressed; stipules usually persistent and conspicuous ....*P. praelongus*
                                  WHITESTEM PONDWEED

         15. Rhizomes unspotted; leaves roundish-ovate or circulate to lanceolate, 1–10 cm long, apex flat; stipules deciduous or disintegrating into fibers

            16. Leaves ovate-lanceolate to narrowly lanceolate, 3–10 cm long, with 7–33 strong veins; stipules coarse deciduous to persistant white fibers, even on lower portion of stem...*P. richardsonii*
                                 RICHARDSON'S PONDWEED

            16. Leaves circular to ovate, becoming lanceolate in soft water, 1–6 cm long, 0.5–2 cm wide, with 7–17 weak veins; stipules disintegrating and deciduous, absent on lower portions of stem...*P. perfoliatus*
                                 CLASPING-LEAVED PONDWEED

MONOCOTS

Potamogeton natans L.   POTAMOGETONACEAE (Pondweed Family)

Floating-leaf Pondweed

Other Common Names: Floating Pondweed, Broad-leaved Pondweed

Potamos is Greek for river, and *geton* is derived from *geiton* which is Greek for neighbour. *Natans* means to be swimming, floating on or under the surface of water.

Submerged
Perennial
Native
Common
Hardiness Zone: 1
Flowering Season: mid- to late summer

DESCRIPTION

This is one of the few Potamogetons commonly found in the Prairie provinces which have obvious floating leaves. These **leaves** are elliptic to oval, 4–9 cm long by 2–6 cm wide, many-veined, leathery with a waxy texture on the upper surface, bronzy green, and connected by a petiole longer than the blade. Submerged leaves (often lacking) are bladeless, without a petiole, 10–40 cm long by 1–2 mm wide, and 3–5-veined.

Potamogeton natans reproduces freely from creeping underground rhizomes, and broken-off sections of stem. The **flowers** can be found later in the season at the water surface or held just above. They are arranged in whorls along a 2–5 cm long spike at the tip of the stem. The flowers are quite small with both male and female parts present. Each flower has 4 sepal-like bracts at its base, 4 stamens and 4 separate ovaries.

The drupe-like **fruit** is 3–5 mm long with a small nutlet on the inside. When immature, the nutlet is encased in a more or less spongy pericarp. The two layers become difficult to distinguish upon maturity. The ripe fruit is released into the water where it moves with water currents, establishing itself where conditions are favourable.

Potamogeton natans L.

HABITAT AND DISTRIBUTION

Potamogeton natans is one of the easiest pondweeds to identify from shore or boat due to its floating leaves. It has a preference for organic lake or pond bottoms. Water depth can vary from 0.5 to 2 m or more. It occurs throughout all three of the Prairie provinces.

SPECIAL FEATURES

Floating-leaved pondweed provides habitat for invertebrates and thus is an important provider of food for fish. Waterfowl and other animals eat the seeds and young roots and

Potamogetan natans

HEINJO LAHRING

44

shoots which are rich in starch. It is a rapid grower, utilizing nutrients and providing oxygen to the aquatic environment. The plants add substantial amounts of organic matter to the pond or lake bottom each fall when they die back.

RELATED SPECIES

Potamogeton alpinus Balb., **Red Pondweed**, has floating leaves (when present) which are more tapered at the base than *P. natans*. The submersed leaves are sessile, 7-veined (at times with up to 6 obvious veins), and have a net-like pattern along the midvein. The leaves dry a reddish colour. Stipules are blunt. It's found in alkaline waters.

HEINJO LAHRING

Potamogeton gramineus L., **Variable Pondweed**, has branching stems. Its surface leaves are greenish and smaller (2–6 cm long) than *P. natans*. Submersed leaves are sessile, 3–17-veined and more than 5 mm wide. Stipules are acute. Leaves lack the net-like pattern along the midvein and reddish colour upon drying which are characteristic of *P. alpinus*. *Potamogeton natans* is confined to the boreal forest, while *P. gramineus* extends into southern prairie regions in acid to alkaline waters. *Potamogeton natans* forms hybrids with *P. gramineus* L. (=*P. x sparganifolius* Laest. ex Fries).

Potamogeton alpinus Balb.

Potamogeton gramineus L.

Above and below:
Potamogetan gramineus

HEINJO LAHRING

Potamogeton nodosus Poir., **Longleaf Pondweed**, has floating leaves which are somewhat more tapered at the base than *P. natans*. Submersed leaves have 3–13 cm long petioles. Stipules are 3–9 cm long and disintegrate early. It occurs in still to swiftly moving alkaline waters. [*P. americanus* C. & S.]

HEINJO LAHRING

Potamogeton nodosus Poir.

Potamogeton nodosus

Potamogeton pusillus L.
Slender Pondweed

POTAMOGETONACEAE (Pondweed Family)

Potamos is Greek for river, and *geton* is derived from *geiton* which is Greek for neighbour. *Pusillus* is Latin for very small.

DESCRIPTION

Stems are thin and freely branching. Narrow (0.2–2.5 mm) 1–3-nerved **leaves** are 1–8 cm long with a nodal gland where the blade meets the stem. Delicate stipules surround the stem and are soon deciduous.

Short **flower** spikes are held on 0.5–6 cm long peducles and have 1–5 whorls of flowers. Each tiny flower consists of 4 sepal-like bracts, 4 stamens, and 4 separate ovaries.

The rounded drupe-like **fruit** (2–2.5 mm long) has a very low dorsal keel and contains a small nutlet on the inside.

Potamogeton pusillus

> Submerged
> Perennial
> Native
> Common
> Hardiness Zone: 0
> Flowering Season: mid-summer

Potamogeton pusillus L.

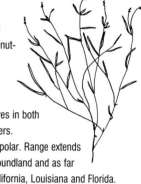

HABITAT AND DISTRIBUTION

Slender Pondweed lives in both acid and alkaline waters. Distribution is circumpolar. Range extends from Alaska to Newfoundland and as far south as northern California, Louisiana and Florida.

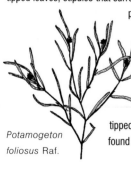

HEINJO LAHRING

SPECIAL FEATURES

Potamogeton pusillus is one of several slender-leaved submerged pondweeds offering generous amounts of surface area for sheltering and feeding aquatic invertebrates. It is a very effective oxygenator within the water column but its fast growth rate can, at times, choke shallow waters by mid-summer.

RELATED SPECIES

Two subspecies are recognized to occur in the area. *Potamogeton pusillus* ssp. *pusillus* L. (preferring alkaline waters) has acutely tipped leaves, stipules that surround the stem, and mostly terminal peduncles (1–3 per plant). *Potamogetum pusillus* ssp. *tenuissimus* (Mert. & Koch) Haynes & Hellquist (preferring acid waters) has obtuse to acutely tipped leaves, stipules that surround stem (split), and terminal and axillary peduncles (3 or more per plant).

Other pondweeds **lacking surface leaves** and in which the **submersed leaves are narrow (but not threadlike)** include: *Potamogeton foliosus* Raf., **Leafy Pondweed**, has submersed leaves usually less than 2 mm wide, 3–5-veined and acute-tipped. Nodal glands at the base of leaf are absent. It is found in alkaline water.

Potamogeton foliosus Raf.

HEINJO LAHRING

Potamogeton foliosus

Potamogeton friesii Rupr.

Potamogeton friesii Rupr., **Fries Pondweed**, has submersed leaves 0.1–3.2 mm wide, 5–9-veined and rounded or apiculate at tip. Stipules are fibrous and often whitish. Winter buds within the inner leaves are at right angles to outer leaves. Nodal gland at leaf base is present.

Potamogeton obtusifolius Mert. & Koch, **Blunt-leaf Pondweed**, has submersed leaves (often brownish) 1–3.5 mm wide, 3–5-veined and rounded or slightly apiculate at tip. Nodal gland at base of leaf is present. It is found in moderately alkaline waters.

Potamogeton robbinsii Oakes, **Robbin's Pondweed**, has submersed leaves which are rigid and 2-ranked (alternating in one plane) up the stem. The base of the leaves have lobes. This species rarely forms fruit. It occurs in still and slow moving water (at times deep).

Potamogeton robbinsii Oakes

Potamogeton obtusifolis Mert. & Koch

Potamogeton zosteriformis Fern.

Potamogeton strictifolius Ar. Benn., **Stiff-leaved Pondweed**, is similar to *P. friesii* but differs in having a bristle-tipped leaf apex, 3–13-veined leaves, flattened winter buds (inner and outer leaves are in the same plane). It grows in alkaline water.

Potamogeton zosteriformis Fern., **Flat-stemmed** or **Eel-grass Pondweed**, has submersed leaves 2–3.2 mm wide (15–35-veined). Stems are conspicuously flattened. It occurs in alkaline waters.

P. friesii   *P. strictifolius*

BARRE HELLQUIST

Potamogeton friesii

Potamogeton obtusifolius
BARRE HELLQUIST

HEINJO LAHRING

Potamogeton zosteriformis

Potamogeton richardsonii (Benn.) Rydb.   POTAMOGETONACEAE (Pondweed Family)
Richardson's Pondweed

Syn.: *P. perfoliatus* L. var. *richardsonii* Benn.
Other Common Names: Clasping-leaved Pondweed

Potamogeton is of Greek origin with *Potamos* meaning 'river,' and *geton* (from *geiton*) 'neighbour.'

> Submerged
> Perennial
> Native
> Common
> Hardiness Zone: 0
> Flowering Season: mid-summer

DESCRIPTION

This is one of the most beautiful of underwater plants. Rounded, branching stems rise upward from creeping rhizomes (rusty red spotting absent). Clasping onto the stem are alternate, undulating (wavy edged), somewhat translucent, green **leaves** (usually less than 10 cm long and 2 cm wide) with 3–7 strong (and several finer) parallel veins. Stipules are deciduous but tend to persist as white fibers (even on lower portion). Young leaves are especially bright, glossy green.

Dense whorls of **flowers** are formed at the stem tip in the form of a narrow spike (1.5–3 cm long). Each tiny flower consists of 4 sepal-like bracts, 4 stamens, and 4 separate ovaries. The mature **fruit** (about 3 mm long) is a drupe containing a small nutlet on the inside. The fruit has a short beak (less than 1.5 mm long).

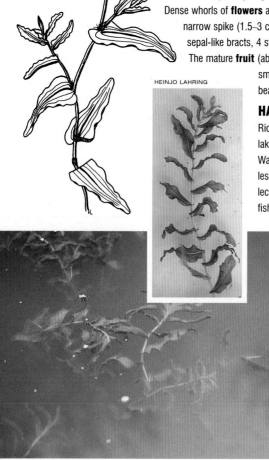

Potamogeton richardsonii (Benn.) Rydb.

HEINJO LAHRING

HABITAT AND DISTRIBUTION

Richardson's Pondweed makes its home in lakes, ponds, streams, and occasionally rivers. Water depth is quite variable but tends to be less than 4 m deep. This is a frequently collected water plant and often found clinging to fishing lures, boat propellers and paddles. In very alkaline water it will accumulate a white calcium carbonate precipitate known as marl on its foliage.

Range is transcontinental with a wide prairie, boreal, and parkland distribution pattern.

SPECIAL FEATURES

The large surface area of the leaves makes especially suitable habitat for many aquatic organisms. Richardson's Pondweed is

Left and inset:
Potamogeton richardsonii

BARRE HELLQUIST

48

an important waterfowl food. The attractive, glossy, undulating, green leaves make excellent show pieces in aquariums and home ponds. Unfortunately, as with many submerged pondweeds, the plants grow and develop according to the water chemistry they are growing in, and moving plants to water of a different quality often sets them back until they have had a chance to grow new leaves better suited to their new environment.

surface leaves

Potamogeton amplifolius Tuckerm.

RELATED SPECIES

Other Potamogetons with **broad underwater leaves** include:

Potamogeton amplifolius Tuckerm., **Large-leaved Pondweed**, develops petioled surface leaves. Distinctly arced submersed leaves are sessile (non-clasping), broad and undulating with 27–37 veins. Plants are found in acid to alkaline waters (often quite deep).

Potamogeton crispus L., **Curly-leaved Pondweed**, lacks surface leaves. Submersed leaves are minutely toothed along the margin (versus *P. richardsonii*'s smooth leaf margins), 3–8 cm long, 3–5-nerved and undulating. The fruit has a relatively long (2–3 mm) beak. This is an introduced pondweed from Eurasia which spreads mainly vegetatively in the region. It is found in alkaline and, at times, eutrophic waters.

Potamogeton crispus L.

toothed leaf margin

BARRE HELLQUIST

Potamogeton amplifolius

Potamogeton perfoliatus L., **Clasping-leaved Pondweed**, is very similar to *P. richardsonii* but differs in having shorter (1–6 cm) more circular to ovate leaves (becoming lanceolate in soft water). Its stipules are deciduous and disintegrate (absent on lower portions of stem).

Potamogeton praelongus Wulf., **Whitestem Pondweed**, lacks surface leaves. Submersed leaves are linear lanceolate to ovate-oblong, 5–25 cm long, with a boat-shaped apex. White stipules (2–8 cm long) are conspicuously long. There is rusty red spotting on the rhizomes. It is found in moderately alkaline, deep water.

Potamogeton praelongus L.

HEINJO LAHRING

Stuckenia pectinata (top)
P. richardsonii (middle)
P. praelongus (bottom)

Stuckenia pectinata (L.) Borner   **POTAMOGETONACEAE (Pondweed Family)**
Sago Pondweed

Syn.: *Coleogeton pectinatus* (L.) Les Haynes, *Potamogeton interruptus* Kit., *P. pectinatus* L.

Other Common Names: Fennel-leaved Pondweed, Bushy Pondweed

Pectinata means 'in the form of a comb' (i.e., with narrow, close-set divisions), and describes the plant's narrow leaves.

> Submerged
> Perennial
> Native
> Common
> Hardiness Zone: 0
> Flowering Season: mid-summer

DESCRIPTION

Plants are normally submerged, with no floating leaves. Long (30–100 cm or more), rounded (1 mm thick) stems arise from slender, tuber-forming rhizomes. The stems freely branch and sometimes produce large, overwintering buds in the leaf axils. The long (3–10 cm), narrow (1–2 mm wide) and sharply pointed **leaves** are alternate and have light-coloured bands on either side of the midvein. Each leaf has an inconspicuous 1–3 cm sheathing stipule at its base.

A 1–4 cm flower spike emerges from the water in mid-summer. It consists of many loose whorls of tiny **flowers** each having 4 sepal-like bracts, 4 stamens and 4 separate ovaries.

The mature drupe-like **fruit** contains a small nutlet on the inside. Fruit is distinctly beaked.

HABITAT AND DISTRIBUTION

Sago Pondweed inhabits highly alkaline or brackish water less than 4 m deep. It can be found in lakes, ponds and rivers and rapidly colonizes new areas. Dense underwater stands can slow water movement causing organic matter to settle out, further stimulating aquatic plant growth. Distribution is circumpolar. In Saskatchewan *Stuckenia pectinata* occurs throughout the prairie region, invading hard or subsaline waters.

SPECIAL FEATURES

Sago Pondweed is fast growing and provides excellent underwater habitat for aquatic invertebrates. The plants, achenes, and

*Stuckenia
pectinata* (L.)
Borner

overwinter-
ing tubers

BARRE HELLQUIST

Stuckenia pectinata

HEINJO LAHRING

tubers are all important foods for wildlife. It is known to provide up to half of the dietary needs of waterfowl and marsh birds including Coots, Black Ducks, Mallards, Teals, Wood Ducks, Canada Geese, Scaups, Redheads, Common Snipe and Rails. The large and abundant tubers are rich in starch.

The edible tubers are considered a survival food but are said to be somewhat lacking in taste and texture. Sago Pondweed is known for its prolific ability to produce tubers.

To control unchecked growth of Sago Pondweed, a draw-down can be done, thereby freezing out the tubers during the winter months.

RELATED SPECIES

The *Stuckenia* genus can be distinguished from *Potamogeton* by the presence of a **stipular sheath which is adnate (fused to stem) for two thirds or more of the stipule length** (it is, at most, to halfway in *Potamogeton*), channeled, opaque, septate leaves and a floating inflorescence (if at water surface).

Two other species of *Stuckenia* with their characteristic thread-like to narrowly ribbon-like leaves are also found in the region:

Stuckenia filiformis (Pers.) Borner, **Thread-leaved Pondweed**, has submerged leaves 0.2–2 mm wide with notched rounded or obtuse tips. The free-section of the stipular sheath forms a ligule up to 20 mm long and is slightly inflated (at mid-section of stems to less than twice the diameter of stem). Fruit is only slightly beaked or beakless. Found in cold, usually calcareous, flowing water. [*Potamogeton filiformis* Pers.]

Stuckenia vaginata (Turcz.) Holub, **Large-sheath Pondweed** or **Giant Poodweed**, has submerged leaves 1 to 2 mm wide with notched rounded or obtuse tips. The free-section of the stipular sheath forms a ligule up to 1 mm long which is distinctly inflated (at mid-section of stem to twice the diameter of stem). Fruit is only slightly beaked or beakless. Found in calcareous to brackish waters. [*Potamogeton vaginatus* Turcz.]

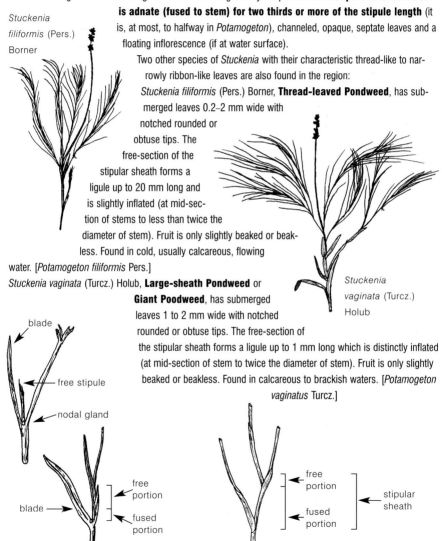

Stuckenia filiformis (Pers.) Borner

Stuckenia vaginata (Turcz.) Holub

blade

free stipule

nodal gland

blade

free portion

fused portion

Potamogeton

free portion

fused portion

stipular sheath

Stuckenia

Ruppia cirrhosa (Petango) Grande

RUPPIACEAE (Ditch-Grass Family)

Widgeon-grass

Syn.: *Ruppia occidentalis* S. Wats., *R. maritima* var. *occidentalis* (Wats.) Graebn., *R. lacustris* Macoun

Other Common Names: Ditch-grass

This plant is dedicated to Heinrich Bernhard Ruppius, a German botanist, 1689–1719. The species epithet, *maritima*, means growing by the sea and is indicative of the plant's preference for a saline habitat.

> Submerged
> Annual (rarely Perennial)
> Native
> Rare
> Hardiness Zone: 2
> Flowering Season: summer–fall

Ruppia cirrhosa (Petango) Grande

Description

This entirely submerged, grass-like plant grows upward (30–100 cm) from prostrate runners. The stems are very slender and forking with mostly basal leaves which sometimes alternate on the stem. Leaf clusters often appear to be spreading out like a fan. The **leaves** are broader at the base (forming a sheath around the stem), 5–20 cm in length, with scarious margins and a finely pointed tip. Leaf sheaths are to 7 cm long. Stipules are fused at the leaf base.

The small **flowers** (usually 2) are formed on a spadix which lengthens to become a long (to 50 cm), often spiralling, peduncle. Each peduncle (or scape) is sheathed by the leaf-base. The flowers are simple and consist of 2 sessile stamens, 4 sessile pistils (4 ovaries), and no perianth. *Ruppia*'s **fruit** is a small olivaceous (dotted with red) drupe which is ovoid in shape and about 3–4 mm long. The drupes are held up on stalks and tend to form umbel-like clusters (helpful in field identification).

HABITAT AND DISTRIBUTION

Widgeon-grass is not as common as other submerged aquatics due to its preference for very saline waters. Where conditions are acceptable, it can be found in ponds and lakes with a muddy sand-type of bottom. It has been reported to occur in brackish waters with *Zannichellia* sp., *Zostera marina*, and *Najas* sp.

Ruppia cirrhosa distribution includes the southern parts of the Prairie provinces (in general, south of the 53rd parallel). The range extends south to Nebraska and western Minnesota.

SPECIAL FEATURES

The small fruits of Widgeon-grass are much used by waterfowl. This is one of the few plants which tolerates saline growing conditions whether it be a seaside location or salt-rich prairie pond. Its preference for such conditions and its attraction as a food source for waterfowl make it especially valuable as a wildlife enhancement plant for these areas.

Ruppia maritima (closely related species of coastal areas).

RELATED SPECIES

Many of the submerged-leaved *Potamogeton* species resemble *Ruppia*. *Potamogeton* has a perianth consisting of four greenish, sepal-like bracts attached to the base of 4 stamens, whereas *Ruppia* has 2 stamens and no perianth. *Ruppia cirrhosa* is the only species known to occur in the area.

Zannichellia palustris L.   ZANNICHELLIACEAE (Horned Pondweed Family)

Horned Pondweed

Horned Pondweed is named in honor of the Venetian botanist Gian Girolamo Zannichelli, 1662–1729. *Palustris* refers to the swampy or marshy habitat in which this plant lives.

Submerged
Perennial
Native
Common
Hardiness Zone: 1
Flowering Season: early summer

DESCRIPTION

Slender, fragile, branching stems rise upward from a thin rhizome. **Leaves** are relatively sparse in number, and opposite (sometimes whorled). The narrow leaf shape (0.5 mm wide, without serrations on the margins, and narrowed symmetrically from the base to a fine point) makes them look almost thread-like.

The **flowers** (2–5) can be found in the leaf axil and are enveloped in a delicate, transparent sheath. They occur as two kinds, both in the same axil. The male flower consists of a single anther. The female flower has 1–8 separate carpels each with a short style and stigma.

Two to 4 **achenes** (2–4 mm long) are borne in a transparent spathe. They resemble an elongated, flattened nutlet with a toothed, longitudinal ridge, and a short (1 mm) point on the end. Fruit is formed from July through August.

Zannichellia palustris L.

HABITAT AND DISTRIBUTION

This aquatic herb can be found in ponds, lakes, ditches and streams across the Prairie provinces. Horned Pondweed prefers hard water and saline conditions. It known to grow in association with *Zostera marina* and *Najas* spp.

Distribution is circumpolar. It is more common in the southern half of the Prairie provinces. Its range extends southward into California, and northward up to Alaska.

SPECIAL FEATURES

Both the plants and fruits are used by many species of birds for food.

RELATED SPECIES

Horned Pondweed may be mistaken for Slender Naiad (*Najas flexilis*). If one looks closely at the leaf margins of each it can be seen that *Z. palustris* has smooth leaf margins and *N. flexilis* has minute spines or sharp serrations on the margins. Also, *Z. palustris* has 2 or more ovaries, whereas *N. flexilis* has only one solitary ovary.

Zannichellia palustris

BARRE HELLQUIST

Triglochin maritima L.
Seaside Arrow-grass

JUNCAGINACEAE (Arrow-grass Family)

Other Common Names: Greater Arrow-grass, Sourgrass, Goosegrass
Triglochin comes from the Greek terms *'treis,'* three, and *'glochis,'* point (referring to the shape of the fruit). *Maritima* is indicative of its ability to grow by the sea.

> Emergent
> Perennial
> Native
> Common
> Hardiness Zone: 0
> Flowering Season: late spring through early summer

DESCRIPTION

Long (20–80 cm), light to medium green grass-like leaves and stems stand erect from creeping rhizomes. The 4–10 **leaves** (up to 30 cm long by 1–6 mm wide) are attached basally. Each has a broad, membranous sheath that bears a pair of ligule-like lobes part way up the leaf margins. New leaves are often encased in the leaf sheaths from the previous year.

The inflorescence is a long (10–40 cm), slender spike extending above the foliage. This spike is comprised of many small-stalked **flowers**. Individual flowers have 3 petals and 3 sepals (appearing quite similar; tepals) in two floral rings. Attached to the base of each tepal is a large, stalkless anther. The pistil is composed of 6 carpels (to 5 mm long at maturity).

A winged, oval **schizocarp** (5 mm by 2.5 mm) develops late in the season and splits into 3–6 follicle-like segments. The dried, opened fruit remains on the spike well after the seeds have been released.

HABITAT AND DISTRIBUTION

Seaside Arrow-grass is very prevalent on both the east and west coasts and can be found inland in shallow alkaline marshes, wetlands with basic soils, roadside ditches, and fens. It may also occur, but somewhat less commonly, along streams and gravelly lakeshores. *Triglochin maritima* is circumpolar in distribution and is widespread across the prairie, parkland and boreal forest regions.

SPECIAL FEATURES

Seeds are known to be eaten by waterfowl such as Mallards and Black Ducks. The plants (including *T. palustris*) have been reported to be very poisonous to livestock, such as sheep and

HEINJO LAHRING

Triglochin maritima

Triglochin maritima L.

cattle, when pastures have become overgrazed and animals have had little choice but to eat large quantities of the plant.

In the past, Native peoples collected and parched the seed. They were then ground into flour or made into a coffee substitute. The seeds (and plants) contain hydrocyanic acid and the parching process renders them non-toxic.

RELATED SPECIES

Of the four species of *Triglochin* known to occur in North America, two are found in the prairie provinces.

Triglochin palustris L., **Slender Arrow-grass**, is best distinguished from *T. maritima* by close examination of the flowers on the spike. *Triglochin palustris* has 3 carpels and 3 short stigmas, whereas *T. maritima* normally has 6 carpels and 6 spreading stigmas. *Triglochin maritima* has ovoid to oblong fruit (with a wingless axis) versus narrow and linear (with a winged axis) for *T. palustris*. *Triglochin palustris* has linear carpels which are pointed at the base. The carpels separate from the axis at the proximal end, giving 3 sharp prickles.

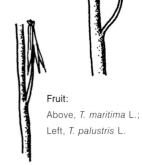

Fruit:
Above, *T. maritima* L.;
Left, *T. palustris* L.

Scheuchzeria palustris L., **Scheuchzeria**, resembles *Triglochin* to a degree and although it prefers peaty bogs it may also be found in fens. *Scheuchzeria palustris* has about 5 widely divergent flowers which develop into ovoid follicles (5–8 mm long) containing 1–2 black seeds (4–5 mm long). Each of its leaves, which go all the way up the stem, has a pore at the tip.

HEINJO LAHRING

Triglochin maritima

HEINJO LAHRING

55

Lilaea scilloides (Poir.) Haum.
Flowering Quillwort

LILAEACEAE (Flowering Quillwort Family)

Syn.: *L. subulata* Humb. & Bonpl.

Lilaea is named in honor of A. R. Delile, 1778–1850, a French authority on the flora of North Africa and Asia Minor. *Scilloides* suggests 'like *Scilla* or squill.'

> Emergent
> Annual
> Native
> Rare
> Hardiness Zone: 3
> Flowering Season: early summer

DESCRIPTION

Clusters of soft, narrow **leaves** (8–35 cm long) grow in tufts from a short stem and fibrous roots. The leaves are circular in cross-section with sheathing bases.

Lilaea scilloides (Poiret) Haum.

The small **flowers** are found in two locations. The first is in a short (to 1 cm) spike which is held up on a thin scape. The uppermost flowers in the spike are male, female are below and perfect flowers sometimes occur between the male and female ones. There are no petals or sepals. Male flowers consist of a single, sessile stamen while female flowers have one carpel. The second location is within the sheaths at the base of the leaves. These flowers are only pistillate, with one carpel and a very long (to 10 cm) filiform style topped with a capitate stigma.

The mature **fruit** of the spike is a small, 2-winged, ridged achene. Basal flowers produce a larger ribbed achene without the wings.

HABITAT AND DISTRIBUTION

Flowering Quillwort is most commonly known on the Pacific coast but has been found in saline sloughs in the southeastern parts of Alberta as well as the Cypress Hills area. It prefers brackish water in alkaline wetlands, slough margins, and mud flats. In southwestern Saskatchewan it is known to grow in cultivated slough bottoms which were either impossible to sow in spring from too much meltwater, or the crop had been flooded-out from heavy rains in early summer.

Lilaea scilloides occurs throughout the southern parts of the Prairie provinces. In Saskatchewan, there are scattered records reaching to just north of St. Albert. Its range is quite widespread elsewhere including British Columbia, California, Montana, Nevada, and even into South America.

SPECIAL FEATURES

This unusual and rare plant is an indicator of saline conditions. Flowering Quillwort is heat-loving and generally is restricted to the warmer parts of the Prairie provinces.

RELATED SPECIES

It is easy to confuse this plant with other rush-like aquatic plants. However, upon closer examination one finds quillwort to be quite unique in its two forms of flower arrangements (i.e., spike and basal), its simple 1-stamen and/or 1-pistil flowers, and its tufted 'quill-like' basal leaves.

Sparganium eurycarpum (pp. 38–39)
Giant Bur-reed
HEINJO LAHRING

MONOCOTS

Alisma triviale Pursh
Broad-leaved Water-plantain

ALISMATACEAE (Water-Plantain Family)

Syn.: *A. brevipes* Greene, *A. plantago-aquatica* var. *americanum* Schultes & Schultes

Other Common Names: Common Water-plantain, Large-flowered Water-plantain, Western Water-plantain, Mud Plantain, Mad-dog Weed, Devil-spoons, Great Thrumwort

Emergent
Perennial
Native
Common
Hardiness Zone: 0
Flowering Season: summer

Alisma is the Greek name of a water plant (derivation uncertain). The species epithet, *triviale*, means ordinary. The colloquial names 'Mad' and 'Devil' indicate a poisonous attribute which some say it has when uncooked.

DESCRIPTION

Leaves and flower stalk grow from a fleshy, corm-like base with fibrous roots. Plant height varies from 30 to 100 cm tall. The emergent long-petioled **leaves** (up to 18 cm long and attached basally) are oval-elliptic with parallel veins and smooth margins.

HEINJO LAHRING

Alisma triviale

Alisma triviale Pursh

Flowers are held above foliage in large, open, compound panicles. Each flower (up to 8 mm wide) is held out on 1–4 cm stalks and consists of 3 green sepals, 3 white to pink petals, 6–9 stamens, and a ring of pistils on a flat receptacle. **Fruits** are three-sided achenes (2–2.5 cm long) with a keel along one side and flat on the other sides.

HABITAT AND DISTRIBUTION

Broad-leaved Water-plantain is a frequently found plant of marshes, sloughs, ponds, lakes, ditches, and streams. It tends to be restricted to the muddy margins of

Alisma triviale

HEINJO LAHRING

HEINJO LAHRING

these waterbodies and is a pioneering species rapidly colonizing suitable sites. It often establishes itself in wet areas where the water does not persist beyond July. This plant is widely distributed over much of the prairie and parkland region.

SPECIAL FEATURES

Moose sometimes eat the leaves. Although not a primary food source, the achenes are occasionally eaten by waterfowl.

In more southern areas, where this plant also grows, the Cherokee poulticed the roots onto bruises, swellings, sores, and other wounds.

Early herbalists used it as a diuretic. One report claims "...bruised leaves are rubefacient and may even blister the skin" and another states, "...injurious to cattle. They could be poisonous to you." So, caution is advised when handling the leaves.

Alisma is well known for its edible starchy, swollen bulb-like base of the leaf stalk. If this part is left uncooked, but washed and dried (to remove acridity), they have a slightly bitter raw potato taste. The submerged root is also edible. It is best to cook aquatics if possible to avoid the risk of a parasitic infection.

RELATED SPECIES

Alisma gramineum Lej., **Narrow-leaved Water-plantain**, is also prevalent in the region. It has narrow, linear aerial leaves (4–8 cm long) and, occasionally, long ribbon-like submerged leaves (0.5–1 cm wide). Its flower panicles are less conspicuous, often being shorter than the leaves, with its branches being recurved. The petals are pinker than those of *A. triviale*. In Saskatchewan, *Alisma gramineum* is strictly southwestern (Brown Soil Zone). [syn. *A. geyeri* Torr.]

HEINJO LAHRING

Alisma gramineum

Alisma gramineum Lej.

① submerged
  - ribbon-like

② erect, aerial
  - lanceolate to narrowly elliptic

Sagittaria cuneata Sheld.
Arum-leaved Arrowhead

ALISMATACEAE (Water-plantain Family)

Syn.: *S. arifolia* Nutt.
Other Common Names: Wedge-leaf Arrowhead

Sagittaria means 'arrow-shaped' and refers to the floating and aerial leaves. The species name, *cuneata*, is another way of saying 'wedge-shaped' (or inversely triangular with rounded angles) and is again descriptive of the foliage.

> Emergent
> Perennial
> Native
> Common
> Hardiness Zone: 0
> Flowering Season: summer

DESCRIPTION

This tuber-forming aquatic plant initially produces submerged linear leaves. These are followed by floating leaves. The submerged **leaves** are long, thin, and ribbon-like. In deep water, floating leaves develop which are long-petioled (90 cm+) with arrow-shaped blades. In shallow water, the blades often become stiff and erect (10 cm x 4 cm wide).

The showy white **flowers** (2–3 cm wide) are grouped in whorls of 3 and are held above the water in an open spike. Each flower consists of 3 small green sepals and 3 larger white petals. Most are unisexual with male flowers (10–18 stamens, anther filaments glabrous and slender) above and female flowers (numerous carpels) below. A bract (over 1 cm long) is located at the base of each flower stalk.

Achenes are produced in dense, spherical heads. Each achene (1.8–2.6 mm long) is tipped with an erect (upright) beak.

HABITAT AND DISTRIBUTION

Arum-leaved Arrowhead grows in quiet, shallow water of lakes, streams and sloughs, as well as semi-open areas of marshes and roadside ditches.

It can dominate entire waterfront areas with its aerial foliage and flowers or be very inconspicuous with only floating leaves in amongst rushes, reeds and pond lilies.

Its range extends across the Prairies, making its home in the Far North as well as the extreme south.

Sagittaria cuneata Shield.

SPECIAL FEATURES

The Swedish have a saying, "A cherished child has many names." It seems that wherever arrowhead plants have been found, humans have discovered their many uses.

Sagittaria cuneata
(in bloom)

HEINJO LAHRING

Both *S. cuneata* and *S. latifolia* are important wildlife and human survival foods. The nutritious tubers are eaten by muskrats and ducks. The surface leaves and underwater foliage offer excellent habitat for pike and other fishes.

Arrowhead is one of the most valuable native foods available in the wild. Starting in mid-summer, Indians used their toes to dislodge the tubers from the mud which would float to the surface and were collected. They were peeled and eaten raw (best with a little salt), boiled like potatoes, or roasted (as were the roots) in hot coals in the campfire. Boiled tubers can be sliced, dried, and stored for later use. During their stay on the Columbia River, the Lewis and Clark expedition used *S. latifolia* extensively in their diet.

RELATED SPECIES

Sagittaria brevirostra Mackenzie & Bush, **Midwestern Arrowhead**, is rare in the district but has been reported from southeastern Saskatchewan. Submersed leaves are absent. Ascending emersed leaves (5–20 cm) are sagittate with basal lobes more or less equal to the remainder of blade. Flowers have 10–24 stamens. Achenes (2–4 mm long) have an erect beak. Found in sloughs and along wet shores.

Sagittaria latifolia Willd., **Broad-leaved Arrowhead**, **Wapato** or **Duck-potato**, has highly variable, sagittate emersed leaves. Basal-lobes of leaf are

HEINJO LAHRING

Sagittaria latifolia

HEINJO LAHRING

usually equal to, or slightly shorter than, the upper blade. Achenes (2.3–3.5 mm) have a horizontal beak. Staminate flowers have a stamen count of 25–40. *Sagittaria latifolia* is more common in the eastern part of the Prairie provinces and is quite rare in the west.

Sagittaria latifolia Willd.

Sagittaria rigida Pursh, **Bur** or **Sessile-fruited Arrowhead**, is rare in the region but has been reported from southern Saskatchewan and southern Manitoba. Submersed leaves are flattened and ribbon-like (30–70 cm long). Emersed leaves are slender lanceolate to broadly ovate without (or rarely with) lobes at the base. Flowers have 10–24 stamens. Female fruiting heads are sessile. It occurs in calcareous water of ponds, swamps and rivers (occasionally deep). [*S. heterophylla* Pursh, *S. heterophylla* var. *rigida* (Pursh) Engelm.]

HEINJO LAHRING

Sagittaria rigida

Elodea canadensis Michx.   HYDROCHARITACEAE (Waterweed/Frog's Bit Family)

Canada Waterweed

Syn.: *Anacharis canadensis* (Michx.) Planch., *Elodea ioensis* Wylie, *E. planchonii* Casp.

Other Common Names: Canada Pondweed, Anacharis

Elodea means 'of marshes,' referring to its wetland habitat, and *canadensis* is indicative of its Canadian distribution.

Submerged
Perennial
Native
Rare
Hardiness Zone: 1
Flowering Season: summer

DESCRIPTION

This rooted, submerged aquatic plant grows long, bright green (when young), branched, leafy strands upwards from the pond or lake bottom. Stems are round in cross section with many whorls of 3 (2–4) leaves along its length. The whorled spacing becomes tighter toward the stem tips. Stems often form long fibrous roots at the leaf nodes. **Leaves** are narrow (up to 2 mm) and 1.0–1.5 cm long with very small serrations along their margin and taper to an abrupt, blunt point. Male plants have lance-shaped leaves. Female plants have more linear-shaped leaves. Overwintering buds (short, dense branches) form in late summer.

Reproduction is mainly by fragmentation (becoming free-floating) and rooting along the stem. The **flowers**, very small and found in the upper leaf axils, are of two types. Female flowers are raised to the surface by a 3–20 cm long thread-like stalk. Each floating flower has 3 sepals, 3 white or pink petals, and 1 pistil with 3 stigmas (often 2-cleft).The long-stalked, floating male flowers have sepals which are longer than in female flowers and have 3–9 stamens. Once released, the buoyant pollen drifts to the floating female flowers.

Elodea canadensis Michx.

Fruits are oval, beaked capsules about 6 mm long. Each contains about 6 narrow, cylindrical seeds.

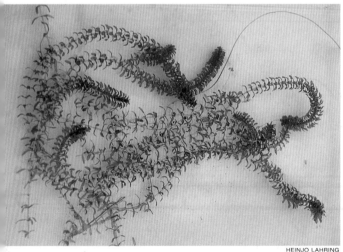

Elodea canadensis

HEINJO LAHRING

HABITAT AND DISTRIBUTION

Elodea is one of the few aquatic vascular plants which grow at depths greater than 10 m. It occurs in ponds, lakes, marshes and in slow moving streams and rivers, preferring quiet water. It frequents waterbodies of low nutrient availability and deep cold bays. In alkaline waters the foliage can become coated with lime. Canada Waterweed is not common, but can be found in Saskatchewan (to 53 degrees N) and Manitoba (north to Reindeer Lake at about 58 degrees N). Although not recorded for Alberta, it likely exists. Distribution extends southward to California, Colorado, Oklahoma, Iowa, Alabama, and North Carolina.

SPECIAL FEATURES

Elodea is one of the fastest growing submerged aquatic plants. Because of this, and the large amount of leaf surface area along its strands, it is an excellent oxygenating plant. Aquarium and pond owners find it to be of considerable help in keeping water clear and feeding fish its palatable foliage. Aquatic invertebrates, and fish fry find *Elodea* to be particularly inviting as a place of refuge and a food source. In shallow water the plant dies back to the mud bottom but in deeper water, where ice doesn't get too thick, it will remain green and continue growing the following year. The aesthetic qualities and wide habitat tolerance of this plant make it highly suitable for use in aquariums, even when light levels indoors are quite low.

RELATED SPECIES

Elodea bifoliata St. John, **Long-sheathed Pondweed**, is the only other species known to occur in the prairie provinces. It has larger (20–26 mm long), openly spaced leaves arranged on the stem mostly in twos (opposite each other). It can be found in shallow waters of sloughs, ponds, lakes and quiet running water from southern Alberta (northern edge of Milk River and Lethbridge) to southwestern Saskatchewan (Swift Current). The range extends southward to include North Dakota to Montana, Wyoming, Utah, Colorado and New Mexico [syn. *E. longivaginata* St. John].

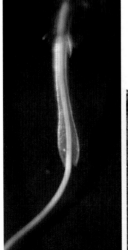

Left: *Elodea canadensis.*
Sheath at base of peduncle.

HEINJO LAHRING

Right: *Elodea* pond
in flower.

HEINJO LAHRING

Acorus americanus (Raf.) Raf.

ACORACEAE (Sweet Flag Family)

Sweet Flag

Other Common Names: Calamus, Muskrat Root, Powemenarctic, Myrtle Flag, Pine Root, Pepper-root, Beewort, Sweet Rush, Sweet Sedge, Sweet Cinnamon

Emergent
Perennial
Native
Common
Hardiness Zone: 1
Flowering Season: summer

Acorus is derived from the Greek name of a plant with an aromatic root or *akoros*. *Americanus* refers to its American distribution.

DESCRIPTION

Arising from a thick, creeping, sweetly aromatic rhizome are several erect (40–80 cm tall by 1–2 cm wide), 2-ranked sword-like **leaf** blades. Midvein of leaf is usually off-center.

The **flowering** stalk resembles a leaf with a yellowish brown spadix (3–8 cm long by 1 cm wide) to the side and towards the top. The leaf extending beyond the spadix is actually a green spathe. The many small and closely arranged flowers on the spadix are composed of 6 rudimentary sepals, a 2–3-loculed ovary (superior), a solitary pistil and 6 stamens.

The hard, dry **fruit** is berry-like with a gelatinous interior.

HABITAT AND DISTRIBUTION

Sweet Flag can be found growing to a depth of about 30 cm amongst *Typha* (which it superficially resembles) along the margins of lakes, lagoons, and marshes, and in calm areas along streams and rivers. It is tolerant of a wide range of water and soil conditions including soft, acidic locations as well as brackish mud flats. The thick rhizomes are much used by muskrats for food. Sweet Flag can be found across the Prairie provinces, particularly in the southern boreal forest zone. It extends beyond the region as far south as Louisiana.

SPECIAL FEATURES

European Sweet Flag (*Acorus calamus* L.) has a long history in Europe. It was used in making candy by cutting the rootstalk, boiling until tender, and reboiling to produce a thick syrup. Candied ginger was added for additional flavour. The roots were also sliced and candied.

The tender part of the young roots can be eaten raw. It makes a pleasant addition to a salad and, when chewed, as a breath freshener. It is also used for

Acorus americanus (Raf.) Raf.

making beer, alcoholic drinks such as gin, and an aromatic vinegar.

The perfume industry makes use of its aromatic properties. Commercial plantings can produce a ton of root per acre. Interestingly it is also an ingredient of insecticides.

Although used as a medicinal stimulant, it can be toxic in large doses. It contains an essential volatile oil (rich in *asarone*, a somewhat toxic substance with antibiotic properties), minerals, tannins, starch, a glucoside (*acorine*) and an alkaloid (*calamine*). It has been found that European Sweet Flag differs from North American Sweet Flag in the biochemical make-up and, thus, herbal applications.

Native tribes used it for colds, stomach disorders, toothache, a poultice for burns, and as a diaphretic in fevers. The Ojibwa used it to attract fish by soaking gill nets in the tea.

RELATED SPECIES

It looks quite similar to Water Irises and Cattails but has a characteristic aroma and the flowers are unmistakably different.

HEINJO LAHRING

A. americanus flower

Calla palustris L.
Water Arum

ARACEAE (Arum Family)

Other Common Names: Water Calla, Water Dragon, Wild Calla, Calla Lily

Calla, a name of unknown meaning, was used by Pliny. *Palustris* refers to its swampy or marshy habitat.

Calla palustris L.

Emergent
Perennial
Native
Common
Hardiness Zone: 0
Flowering Season: spring

DESCRIPTION

The long-stalked (10–20 cm), glossy, green **leaves** (5–15 cm long) are distinctly heart-shaped and parallel-veined with a prominent central midrib. They are arranged alternately, growing in succession along a creeping rhizome. The thick, often branching, rhizome roots along nodes and tends to travel and anchor the plant along its length. The minute, yellowish **flowers**, which lack sepals and petals, are arranged on a thick, spike-like spadix (1.5–3 cm long) and are partially enclosed within a showy white spathe. Flowers may be male towards spadix summit, but generally are perfect. Ovary contains 1 locule. The spathe (10 cm long) is an enlarged and conspicuous inflorescence bract which rots away as the fruit develops.

Numerous bright red or orange berry-like **fruits** develop into a densely packed spike. These later drop off and float to a new location. Each fruit contains a few seeds.

HABITAT AND DISTRIBUTION

Water Arum is a plant at home in wet, boggy areas. It thrives in cool, often shaded, wetlands, marshes and pond edges. It prefers stable, shallow water levels. *Calla* is native to all three Prairie provinces and tends to occur most abundantly in the boreal forest zone. Water Arum is a circumpolar plant and its range in North America extends from Alaska to Newfoundland and southward throughout the Great Lakes region.

HEINJO LAHRING

Calla palustris

SPECIAL FEATURES

The long rhizome is sometimes floating or close to the surface but is sparingly eaten by muskrats and beaver. Long rootlets tend to dangle in the water without rooting. These are quite efficient at purifing the water.

The dried berries and seeds were ground by Native peoples and made into a nutritious and palatable flour. However, some sources claim the berries to be toxic due to a high saponin content which can cause nervous, digestive and cardiac disorders. The plant itself contains calcium oxalate crystals (a poison) which causes intense burning, irritation, and swelling of the mouth, tongue and lips if eaten fresh. Heat (i.e., boiling) destroys this toxin.

In Scandinavia (where it is also native) the roots were boiled in water, dried, ground, and left for a few days. This process was repeated in order to remove the acrid properties. The resulting meal was then mixed with other kinds of flours (including fir cambium) and baked.

Native peoples used this plant medicinally to treat colds, fevers, swellings, snake bites, and sore eyes.

RELATED SPECIES

Calla is a monotypic genus. Its unique growth habit and white spathe make it easily identifiable.

Iris versicolor (p. 77)
Blue Flag or **Fleur-de-lis**

Lemna turionifera Landolt   LEMNACEAE (Duckweed Family)
Common Duckweed

The genus name, *Lemna*, was the name of a water plant mentioned by
Theophrastus. The species epithet, *turionifera*, means turion-bearing and
refers to the overwintering frond.

Free-floating
Perennial
Native
Common
Hardiness Zone: 0
Flowering Season: summer

DESCRIPTION

The small (1–8 mm across), olive to brown **fronds** (thalli) are reddish
beneath, flattened and ovate in shape. Each free-floating thallus has 1–3
faint nerves, several papules along the midline on the upper side, and a
single root (shorter than 15 cm) hanging down into the water. Thalli are
solitary or bud off to form large floating colonies.

Although the primary method of multiplication is by budding of new fronds from the base of the parent thalli,
flowers are sometimes produced. When they occur, they grow out from the base of the thalli margin. Male
flowers have one (sometimes 2) stamens. Female flowers consist of a single flask-shaped ovary with 1 or
more ovules.

Fruit is a 1–7-seeded utricle (0.8–1 mm, thin-walled and inflated). Seeds have 8–15 distinct ribs.

HABITAT AND DISTRIBUTION

Common Duckweed floats in still water of ponds, stagnant rivers, pools and ditches. It forms large mats in
nutrient rich waters.

Being of small size and easily carried from pond to pond by waterfowl, it is not surprising that this plant is
more or less circumpolar in distribution and found across the North American continent.

SPECIAL FEATURES

Lemna turionifera is a useful indicator of hardwater habitats. As the name implies it is eaten by ducks (e.g.,
Coots, Black Ducks, Mallards, Wood Ducks, Buffleheads and Rails) in great numbers. Invertebrates inhabit
the floating mats as well, which may explain why ducks consume it in large quantities when available.
Floating mats sometimes become so dense as to block light and outcompete submerged aquatic plant life.

As fall approaches, day length decreases, frosts kill off the floating plants, and duckweed forms small overwintering buds (turions) which sink to the bottom sediments for winter. When day length, light levels, and
temperatures increase the following spring, photosynthesis and
metabolism increase, and the oxygen content in the fronds rises,

HEINJO LAHRING

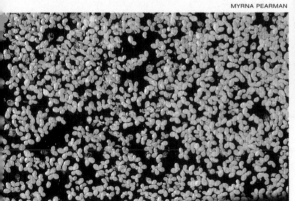
MYRNA PEARMAN

Above: *Lemna turionifera*
Single root per frond.

Left: *Lemna turionifera*

resulting in the fronds floating to the surface once again. Duckweeds are some of the fastest-replicating macrophytes in the world, doubling approximately every 48 hours.

RELATED SPECIES

Lemna minor L., **Common** or **Lesser Duckweed**, is rare in the region but has been reported from Saskatchewan. It has green (above and below same colour), ovate fronds (1–4 mm across; papules along midline are either missing or obscure) with a single root to 15 cm. Turions are not formed (likely limiting its northern distribution). Fruit is 0.5–0.6 mm across. Seeds have 30–60 indistinct ribs.

Lemna minor L.

Lemna trisulca L., **Ivy-leaved Duckweed**, is very common in the Prairie provinces. It is a subsurface floater (6–10 mm long) with 3 narrow thalli connected by long stalks. It forms small to large clustered colonies and is slower to replicate than Common Duckweed.

Spirodela polyrhiza (L.) Schleiden, **Larger Duckweed**, is much less common than either of the above two and prefers the parkland and boreal forest zones. Its thallus (3–8 mm) is slightly larger than Common Duckweed, round in shape, visibly several-nerved, maroon on undersurface and has several roots hanging down into the water beneath it. It tends to be solitary or in small, floating colonies.

Lemna trisulca L.

Spirodela polyrhiza (L.) Schleiden

(length: width)
1.3–2:1
← pointed apex

Wolffia borealis (Engelm.) Landolt

Wolffia borealis (Engelm.) Landolt, **Northern Water-meal**, has fronds which are boat-shaped (point of apex curved upwards, 0.7–1.5 mm long) and 1.3–2 times as long as wide. Pigment cells exist in the vegetative tissue. Roots are absent and it rarely flowers. It is reported from warm, eutrophic waters in central Alberta.

(length: width)
1–1.3:1

Wolffia columbiana Karst.

Wolffia columbiana Karst., **Columbia Water-meal**, is similar to *W. globosa* but differs in being slightly wider (0.4–1.2 mm wide) in proportion to length (1–1.3 times as long as wide). It is found in central Alberta, central Saskatchewan and southern Manitoba.

(length: width)
1.3–2:1

Wolffia globosa (Roxb.) Hartog & Plas, **Globose Water-meal**, has fronds which are spherical to ovoid (0.4–0.8 mm long by 0.3–0.5 mm wide; 1.3–2 times as long as wide) sometimes slightly pointed at apex. Pigment cells are absent in vegetative tissue (upper surface tansparently green). Roots are absent. It exists in warm, eutrophic waters and is likely to be found in central Alberta, central Saskatchewan and southern Manitoba.

Wolffia globosa (Roxb.) Hartog & Plas

Right: *Lemna trisulca*
Far right: *Lemna trisulca* close-up

MYRNA PEARMAN

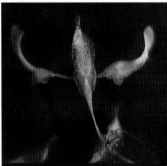

HEINJO LAHRING

Allium geyeri S. Wats
LILIACEAE (Lily Family)

Geyer's Wild Onion

Syn.: *A. rubrum* Osterh., *A. rydbergii* Macbr.

Allium is the ancient Latin name for Garlic. This wild onion is named after C. A. Geyer (1809–1853).

Wetland
Perennial
Native
Rare
Hardiness Zone: 3
Flowering Season: summer

DESCRIPTION

The flat **leaves** (20–40 cm tall by 1–5 mm wide) are not hollow as in many onions. When bruised they have a strong onion aroma. Leaves arise from a slender bulb covered with several thin layers having a netted appearance.

Flower stalk (scape) is often taller than the leaves and more or less circular in cross-section. Flowers are borne in an umbel at the top of the scape. The umbel has 1–3 small bracts at its base. Flower parts (6–8 mm long) are pink (rarely white) and in 2 whorls of 3. The 6 stamens are usually shorter than the perianth. One stigma is present. The ovary is superior with 3 locules. Flowers are mostly sterile and tend to be replaced by bulbils.

Fruit (although rarely produced) is a small, roundish, 3-loculed capsule containing 3–6 black seeds.

HABITAT AND DISTRIBUTION

Geyer's Wild Onion, and Wild Chives (see below), are the only two onions in the Prairie provinces which make their home in wet areas. They occur in wet meadows and along stream banks.

Geyer's Onion's range is restricted to Alberta's southwestern corner but extends into British Columbia and south to Arizona, New Mexico, and Texas.

SPECIAL FEATURES

This wetland onion is considered quite rare and should be left alone and protected where it grows.

Onions have served to compliment food dishes throughout history. The leaves (best chopped) and flower heads are used to enhance meals. Native peoples used wild onion with buffalo meat as we do in hamburger.

Onions (and garlic) are said to be antiatherosclerotic, antiseptic, candidicidal, fungicidal, hypoglycemic and hypotensive. Some people are seriously allergic to onions and may find them indigestable, so caution is advised and it is best not to consume them in large quantities.

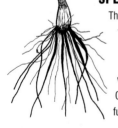

Allium geyeri S. Wats.

RELATED SPECIES

Allium schoenoprasum L., **Wild Chives**, is the only other onion of wet areas in the region. It has more or less hollow leaves which are round in cross-section. The flower head is very compact (vs. *A. geyeri*'s open umbel), flower segments are longer (8–14 mm), and are pink or purple with dark midveins. This is a circumpolar species which is found in the Rocky Mountains and boreal forest. It is not common. [syn. *A. sibiricum* L.]

Cypripedium calceolus (pp. 78–79)
Yellow Lady's-Slipper

JOAN WILLIAMS

Maianthemum trifolium (L.) Sloboda

LILIACEAE (Lily Family)

Three-leaved Solomon's-seal

Syn.: *Smilacina trifolia* (L.) Desf.

Other Common Names: Three Leaf False Solomon's-seal

Maianthemum is derived from the Latin *Maius* (May) and Greek *anthemon* (a flower). *Trifolium* pertains to its three leaves.

Wetland
Perennial
Native
Common
Hardiness Zone: 0
Flowering Season: early summer

DESCRIPTION

Stems (5–20 cm tall) arise from slender creeping rootstalks and bear 2–4 (usually 3) alternating oblong-lanceolate **leaves** (4–10 cm long by 1–4 cm wide) which clasp directly to stem. Leaves are glabrous, ascending and have parallel veins.

From 3 to 8 white **flowers** (1 cm wide) are loosely arranged along an unbranched raceme creating a zigzag pattern. Flowers are held above or equal to the height of the leaves. Flowers are composed of 3 sepals and 3 petals (sepals and petals are similar looking and spreading), 6 stamens, a 3-lobed stigma on a single style, and a 3-loculed ovary.

Fruit is a small (6 mm dia.), dark red berry which usually has 1–2 seeds.

HABITAT AND DISTRIBUTION

Three-leaved Solomon's-seal can be found growing in fens, swamps, bogs, and wet woods. It is often associated with sphagnum moss and is commonly encountered in the boreal forest region. This is a widespead plant scattered across the northern two thirds of Alberta, central to northernmost Saskatchewan and into southern to northernmost Manitoba. It extends beyond the Prairie provinces into northern British Columbia and eastern Asia to the west and throughout the Great Lakes area and Atlantic provinces to the east.

SPECIAL FEATURES

The berries are eaten by grouse, thrush and mice. Hares, deer and moose eat the leaves.

Although the berries are considered edible for humans, they can cause intestinal problems if eaten in quantity. Native peoples used them to treat headaches, back pains and coughs.

Two closely related species (see below), False Solomon's-seal and Star-flowered Solomon's-seal, were used considerably by Native peoples. The young shoots were edible after cooking. The starchy roots are bitter and require boiling in several changes of water before they are palatable. Roots and shoots can be pickled. Star-flowered Solomon's-seal is eaten by livestock.

Maianthemum trifolium (L.) Sloboda

RELATED SPECIES

Two other similar and closely related plants may be found in the Prairie provinces. Both prefer somewhat drier habitats.

Maianthemum racemosum (L.) Link., **False Solomon's-seal**, is much larger (30–90 cm tall with 15 cm long leaves) and has its flowers in a densely branched panicle. Its red berries sometimes have purple spotting. [syn. *Smilacina racemosa* (L.) Desf.]

Maianthemum stellatum (L.) Link., **Star-flowered Solomon's-seal**, is somewhat similar to *M. trifolium* but has 6 to 12 leaves (some hairiness below) per stem. The flower stalk is quite short (1.5–5 cm). Its berries are green with 6 black stripes and turn completely black as they mature. [syn. *Smilacina stellata* (L.) Desf.]

Maianthemum stellatum

HEINJO LAHRING

73

Tofieldia glutinosa (Michx.) Pers.

Sticky False Asphodel

LILIACEAE (Lily Family)

Other Common Names: Sticky Asphodel

Tofieldia is named in honor of the English botanist Thomas Tofield, 1730–1779. The species epithet, *glutinosa*, means viscidus or sticky and describes the sticky stems.

Wetland
Perennial
Native
Common
Hardiness Zone: 0
Flowering Season: early to mid-summer

DESCRIPTION

Rootstocks are short and vertical. The 10–50 cm tall stems are dotted with sticky glands or hairs, especially towards the top. A small, bract-like leaf is often formed near the middle of this stem. At the base are 2–6 linear **leaves** (8–20 cm long and less than 1 cm wide). These may sheath the stem at their base and are present, more or less, in two layers.

Clusters of 3 creamy white, tipped with deep red (which is the dominant colour before they open), long-pedicelled **flowers** are borne at the top of the stem in a short raceme (2–5 cm long). Each flower has 3 small bractlets just below it. The oblong/obovate perianth segments (4 mm long) are without glands and separate. Each flower has 6 stamens, and 3 short styles attached to a 3-loculed (many-ovuled) ovary.

Tofieldia glutinosa (Michx.) Pers.

BARRE HELLQUIST

Tofieldia glutinosa

JOAN WILLIAMS

Tofieldia glutinosa

Fruit is a red or yellowish red ovoid capsule (5–6 mm long) containing many seeds. Seeds have a comma-like appendage at each end.

HABITAT AND DISTRIBUTION

Sticky False Asphodel grows in rich fens, bogs, wet and recently dried meadows (especially at higher elevations), roadside ditches, and along shores and riverbanks. It is a plant of the boreal forest and is particularly common on calcareous soils in the northern and eastern edge of this region.

Plants can be found across the entire boreal forest region of the North American continent including the north and central Prairie provinces and reaching into the Great Lakes area and beyond. In Alberta it is especially common in the Rocky Mountains and along the foothills.

SPECIAL FEATURES

Tofieldia glutinosa is one of those rare treasures we sometimes come across on walks through the wetlands. It has a special magic to it in the early morning hours when dew is heavy and the water droplets cling like jewels to the glandular hairs and reddish flower buds.

RELATED SPECIES

The other *Tofieldia* species encountered in wet areas is *T. pusilla* (Michx.) Pers., **Dwarf** or **Bog Asphodel**. It differs in that it lacks glandular hairs and has single greenish white flowers on a very short raceme. Seed capsules are only half the size of the Sticky False Asphodel. The seeds have no appendages on the ends.

Tofieldia looks somewhat like Death Camas (*Zygadenus venenosus* S. Wats.). Death Camas always grows from bulbs, versus a short rootstock in *Tofieldia*, and has more and much heavier-looking flowers along its spike.

Tofieldia glutinosa

PAT PORTER

Iris missouriensis Nutt.   **IRIDACEAE (Iris Family)**

Western Blue Flag

Other Common Names: Rocky Mountain Iris, Missouri
Iris, Water Flag, Snake Lily

Iris is Greek for the goddess of the rainbow.
Missouriensis refers to Missouri (likely the river
drainage where it has been found).

Wetland
Perennial
Rare
Native
Hardiness Zone: 3
Flowering Season: spring to early summer

DESCRIPTION

Flat (0.5–1 cm wide), two-ranked, basal, sword-like
leaves stand erect (20–50 cm tall) from a thick, creeping rootstock.
Two to 4 large (5–8 cm long), showy, variegated blue-violet **flowers** are held
out from the main stalk (20–50 cm tall) on long pedicels (to 6 cm long). The
outer 3 perianth segments are strongly curved downwards and the inner three
stand erect. There are 3 petal-like style branches (2–4 cm long) which stand
upright towards the inside. Flowers have 3 stamens and a single, 3-cleft style
which is attached to an inferior, 3-loculed ovary.
Fruit is a 3-loculed capsule with many seeds.

HABITAT AND DISTRIBUTION

Western Blue Flag is a rare plant which grows in wet meadows, marshes,
swamps, occasionally fens, and along stream banks of southwestern
Alberta. It can be found from low to high elevations in the Rocky
Mountains.
Only the northernmost limit of the range occurs in Canada, with plants
preferring the heat of more southerly latitudes. Distribution extends into southwestern British Columbia and southward as far as South Dakota, New Mexico
and California.

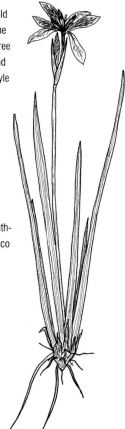

Iris missouriensis Nutt.

Iris missouriensis

BARRE HELLQUIST

Iris missouriensis

SPECIAL FEATURES

Flowers are bee-pollinated. Pollen from previously visited flowers is brushed from the bee's back as it enters for nectar. Nectar is also sought by the Ruby-throated Hummingbird.

This is generally considered a poisonous plant and should not be taken internally. Fresh roots are very toxic. The active ingredient, iridin (an oleoresin complex), is a cathartic and causes violent vomiting. The seeds will cause strong burning in the mouth and throat and will persist for hours.

Its toxic character was used in a couple of different ways by Native peoples. First, it was used as a poultice to sooth burns and treat skin infections. A half-inch of root was steeped and applied to boils to reduce them. Secondly, ground roots were mixed with animal fats and warmed near the fire for several days, after which arrow heads were coated in the blend and used for hunting (including enemies). Slightly wounded victims apparently died in 3 to 7 days. Western Blue Flag is an indicator of water being near the soil's surface.

Iris versicolor

(See additional photo of *Iris versicolor* on page 67.)

RELATED SPECIES

The non-native *Iris pseudacorus* L., **Yellow Water Iris**, has found its way into many wetland areas across Canada. It is taller than the blue irises, a fast colonizer (displacing native plants) and is heavily used in water gardening. It is very showy when in bloom with bright yellow to cream coloured flowers 7–9 cm in diameter. This iris is on the invasive plant list for many of the U.S. states.

Iris versicolor L., **Blue Flag** or **Fleur-de-lis**, is the Blue Iris of Manitoba. It occurs in marshes, swamps, and lakeshores of the parkland and boreal forest. It tends to be taller (to 80 cm) than *I. missouriensis* with broader leaves (1–2 cm). Flowers (6–8 cm across) range from pale blue to violet. Capsules are 3–6 cm long.

Iris versicolor

Cypripedium calceolus L.
Yellow Lady's-slipper

ORCHIDACEAE (Orchid Family)

Other Common Names: Golden-slipper, Large Lady's-slipper, Noah's-ark, Nerve-root, Venus's-shoe, Whip-poor-will-shoe, Yellow Indian-shoe, Moccasin-flower

Cypripedium is from the Greek *Cypris* (Venus) and *pedilon* (shoe). *Calceolus* means slipper-shaped. The Lady's-slipper term was used to describe this group over 200 years before Linnaeus described the genus.

Wetland
Perennial
Native
Rare
Hardiness Zone: 1
Flowering Season: spring to early summer

DESCRIPTION

A short, coarse, fibrous rhizome gives rise to a stem with 2–4 opposite (all cauline, none basal), elliptical **leaves** (6-20 cm long). Leaves have parallel veins with a few hairs.

One to 2 bright yellow (often purple-striped) **flowers** are held high on a 10–40 cm stalk. An erect, leaf-like bract is at the base of the flower. Flower consists of 3 yellow-green sepals (3–5 cm long) of which the lower two may be united under the lip. Two lateral petals are 3–6 cm long and taper to a narrow, often twisted point. The lower petal is modified to form a large, pouch-like lip with margins slightly rolled inward. Two fertile stamens form a central column with the style. One sterile stamen forms a thick triangular staminode above. One somewhat 3-lobed stigma is connected, via the column, to a long, twisted inferior ovary (1-loculed containing many ovules). **Fruit** is a many-seeded, brown, 3-ribbed capsule (opening by 3 slits). Seeds are very tiny and easily blown by the wind.

PAT PORTER

Cypripedium calceolus L.

HABITAT AND DISTRIBUTION

This moisture-loving orchid (only vaguely considered a wetland species) can be found in wet woods, along

Cypripedium calceolus growing on undeveloped road allowance.

stream banks and revegetating flood plains. It is often found growing in small clones in decaying leaf litter since it forms a symbiotic relationship with a fungus which assists it in absorbing

GLEN SUGGETT

(See additional photo of *Cypripedium calceolus* on page 71.)

Below and inset detail: *Cypripedium calceolus*

nutrients from the soil. This relationship also makes it a difficult plant to move from one location to another.

Cypripedium calceolus is a circumpolar orchid and is scattered across each of the three Prairie provinces. Its range extends well into the eastern United States.

JOAN WILLIAMS

SPECIAL FEATURES

This is a bee-pollinated flower in which the bee enters the pouch in search of its sticky nectar. In doing so it deposits pollen onto the stigma. Upon exiting, it brushes past the stamens where gummy pollen is deposited on its body and carried off to the next flower.

Native peoples considered this a sacred flower. It was wrapped in bundles and used to induce supernatural dreams.

After germinating it can take several years for it to flower.

RELATED SPECIES

Another *Cypripedium* species which is often found in wet areas is *C. passerinum* Richardson, **Sparrow's-egg Lady's-slipper** or **Northern Lady's-slipper**. This is a smaller, 3–5-leaved (all cauline, none basal), white to pale lilac flowered orchid (sometimes with purple spots). Sepals are rounded and 1–1.5 cm long. It is more of a woodland vs. wetland species and occurs in the boreal forest and Cypress Hills.

Cypripedium passerinum

JOAN WILLIAMS

Platanthera hyperborea (L.) Lindley
Northern Green Bog Orchid

ORCHIDACEAE (Orchid Family)

Syn.: *Habenaria hyperborea* (L.) R. Br.

Hyperborea is a compound word from *hyper* (over or above) and *boreas* (mythical seat of the North wind).

DESCRIPTION

Wetland
Perennial
Native
Common
Hardiness Zone: 0
Flowering Season: mid-summer

This small orchid has 3–6 leaves along its stem (10–70 cm tall) and a fleshy root. Narrow **leaves** range from 2–10 cm long by up to 3 cm wide, decreasing in size towards the top of stem.

Flowers are greenish yellow in a compact spike (6–20 cm long). Sepals are thick and green with the upper one shorter and rounder than the other two. The two erect lateral petals are slightly smaller, but similar in shape to the sepals. Lip is 4–7 mm long, gradually widening towards the base. A nonfringed spur (5–8 mm long) is present and about equal in length to the lip. Flowers have one stamen and exposed stigmatic discs. The discs (viscidia) are attached to stalks (caudicles) which, in turn, are attached to pollinia. **Fruit** is a capsule filled with tiny seeds.

HABITAT AND DISTRIBUTION

Northern Green Bog Orchid makes its home in fens, open swamps, wet meadows, woodlands, ditches, stream banks and bogs. It is closely associated with

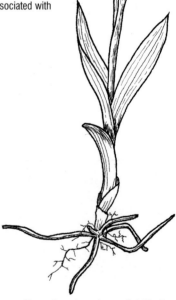

Platanthera hyperborea (L.) Lindley

Platanthera hyperborea

PAT PORTER

80

JOAN WILLIAMS

Platanthera hyperborea

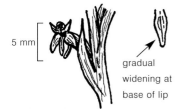

JOAN WILLIAMS

the boreal forest region and tends to be rare in the prairies.

Distribution is across all three Prairie provinces. The range extends up into the Territories and Alaska, south to New Mexico and California, and eastward to the Great Lakes, Newfoundland, and Iceland.

SPECIAL FEATURES

The *Platanthera* orchids are highly variable throughout their range which is believed to be a sign of active speciation. Numerous levels of evolution are apparent with variations in flower colour (from whitish green to deep bluish green), size, and shape of floral parts.

The tuber-like root is considered edible. However, they are very small and over-collection would certainly have disastrous results.

RELATED SPECIES

Platanthera dilatata (Pursh) Hook., **Tall White Orchid**, is similar to *P. hyperborea* but has strongly spicy-scented white (sometimes yellowish white or greenish) flowers. The lip is abruptly widened at its base. Very common orchid of wet areas.

Platanthera saccata Greene, **Slender Bog Orchid**, has non-scented, green flowers (may be tinged with purple or brown, especially the lip). The spur is shorter than the lip. Prairie province range is limited to southwestern Alberta.

Platanthera viridis (L.) R. Br. var. *bracteata* (Muhl.) Gray, **Bracted Bog Orchid**, is a small, green-flowered orchid with strongly ribbed stems, a 3-toothed lip (central tooth shorter than other two), short spur (2–3 mm long), and very noticeable bracts growing along stem.

Several other *Platantheras* can be found in the region but tend to prefer moist woodland locations versus actual wetland habitats of the above four.

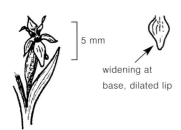

5 mm

gradual widening at base of lip

Platanthera hyperborea (L.) Lindley

5 mm

widening at base, dilated lip

Platanthera dilatata (Pursh) Hook.

Listera cordata (L.) R. Br.
Heart-leaved Twayblade

ORCHIDACEAE (Orchid Family)

Syn.: *Ophrys cordata* L.

Listera is dedicated to a celebrated English naturalist by the name of Martin Lister (1638–1711). *Cordata* means heart-shaped. Twayblade refers to the two opposite leaves.

> Wetland
> Perennial
> Native
> Rare
> Hardiness Zone: 0
> Flowering Season: early to mid-summer

DESCRIPTION

Listera cordata is a small, delicate orchid growing from slender rhizomes (at times fibrous). It has hairless stems 10–25 cm tall. Attached about halfway up the stem are two opposite heart to triangular-shaped **leaves** (1–3 cm long).

Several pale purplish green **flowers** (5–7 mm wide) are arranged in a spike at the top of the stem. Sepals and lateral petals are similar. Lip (up to twice as long as other two petals) is deeply notched at apex and has two teeth at its base. Spur is lacking. Flowers have one stamen (anther stands erect at top of column) and a stigma with a rounded beak.

Fruit is a small brown capsule filled with tiny seeds.

Listera cordata (L.) R. Br.

HABITAT AND DISTRIBUTION

Heart-leaved Twayblade is often found nestled in amongst carpets of moss in conifer swamps, moist conifer woods, thickets, and bogs of the boreal forest.

This is a circumpolar plant which ranges across all three Prairie provinces and, in particular, northern Alberta, central to northern Saskatchewan (Lake Athabasca), and southern Manitoba. Its range extends from Alaska to Newfoundland in the north, to New Mexico and California in the south, and to the Great Lakes and Appalachians in the southeast.

SPECIAL FEATURES

This is a wetland gem commonly hidden among the moss. Although widely distributed, it is a rare find and a true representative of wilderness areas. Care should be taken not to disturb sites in which it grows.

RELATED SPECIES

Listera borealis Morong, **Northern Twayblade**, is green-flowered with an oblong lip (constricted in middle and with 2 ear-shaped appendages at base). *L. borealis* is widespread (although rare and sporadic) across the southern mixed wood boreal forest of central Saskatchewan and Manitoba.

Listera caurina Piper, **Western Twayblade**, is green-flowered with a short lip (teeth at base).

The above two species are rare plants found on moist wooded mountain slopes (considered marginally wetland) in southern Alberta.

Listera convallarioides (Sw.) Torr., **Broad-lipped Twayblade**, can also be found in similar habitats as *L. cordata*. Its oval leaves are larger (3–5 cm). Stems have glandular hairs. Flowers are green or yellowish green (lacking purple tinge). The lip (ciliate along margin) is very broad at the tip, and the teeth are very small at base.

This species is very rare, and only known from Alberta within the Prairie provinces.

BARRE HELLQUIST

Listera cordata

Malaxis brachypoda (Gray) Fern.
White Adder's-mouth

ORCHIDACEAE (Orchid Family)

Syn.: *Malaxis monophylla* (L.) Sw., *Microstylis* (L.) Lindl.

Malaxis is from *malacos* (weak or delicate) and refers to the frail character of *M. paludosa* (L.) Sw. *Monophylla* describes the plant's single leaf. Adder's-mouth is from the lip of the flower which is relatively long and pointed and, in one species, forked.

> Wetland
> Perennial
> Native
> Rare
> Hardiness Zone: 1
> Flowering Season: early spring to mid-summer

DESCRIPTION

This small (5–15 cm tall) orchid grows from a corm. Its single elliptic to ovate clasping **leaf** (3–5 cm long) is located either near the base or part way up the stem.
Several tiny (2 mm long) white to greenish yellow **flowers** are arranged on a slender, upright spike. Sepals (3) are narrow and pointed. Lateral petals (2) are of similar shape but smaller and curved forward. The drooping lip tapers to a point. Spur is absent and the column is very small.
Fruit is a small capsule with several tiny seeds.

HABITAT AND DISTRIBUTION

Adder's-mouth occurs on wet soils in rich conifer swamps, cool damp woods, along stream banks and in bogs. It is known to grow under white spruce on damp, mossy slopes.
Although quite rare, it is circumpolar with its range closely associated with the boreal forest. Distribution includes central and northern Alberta, central Saskatchewan and southern Manitoba.

SPECIAL FEATURES

This small orchid looks very much like *Platantheras* (Bog Orchids) until one looks closely at the detail of the flower which is considerably different (check for the missing spur). The shiny green leaf and slender flower spike can easily go unnoticed within the dark and damp community of the conifer understory.

RELATED SPECIES

Two other *Malaxis* species may be encountered in similar habitats. Both are considered rare.
Malaxis paludosa (L.) Sw., **Bog Adder's-mouth**, has 2 or more basal leaves. At the base of the leaves is a small bulb and sometimes several small bulbils. The lip is erect and conspicuously green-nerved.
Malaxis unifolia (Michx.), **Green Adder's-mouth**, has one basal leaf. The flowers are greenish and the lip is deeply lobed. This species is found only in Manitoba in the Prairie provinces.

Malaxis brachypoda (Gray) Fern.

Spiranthes romanzoffiana Cham.
Hooded Ladies'-tresses

ORCHIDACEAE (Orchid Family)

Other Common Names: Beemsquandawish (Ojibway)

Spiranthes is a compound word derived from the Greek term *speira* (a coil or spiral) and *anthos* (a flower), and refers to the spirally twisted flower clusters. The species epithet was named by Chamisso in honor of his patron, Nikolai Rumiantzev, Count Romanzoff (1754–1826).

> Wetland
> Perennial
> Native
> Common
> Hardiness Zone: 0
> Flowering Season: mid- to late summer

DESCRIPTION

Narrow basal **leaves** are 7–35 cm long by 0.5–1 cm wide and slightly wider towards the tip. Stem leaves gradually get smaller towards apex. Leafy **flower** stems are 15–40 cm tall (sometimes to 60 cm). Stems are usually hairy towards the top. Tubular-appearing flowers are arranged spirally in 2–3 rows, forming a 10–12 cm spike. Small (0.7–1 cm) almond- or vanilla-scented flowers are yellowish white, spreading and nodding. The 3 sepals and 2 lateral petals are similar and may be partly united forming a hood. The wavy margined lip (9–12 mm) is constricted just beyond the middle and widens towards the outer end. Spur is absent. **Fruit** is small, many-seeded capsule.

Spiranthes romanzoffiana Cham.

HABITAT AND DISTRIBUTION

This fragrant and exotic-looking orchid grows in open woods, fens, bogs, lakeshores, streambanks, swamps, marshes, ditches and wet meadows. It is often associated with *Equisetum* (Horsetail) and *Triglochin* (Arrow-grass).
Distribution is scattered across the Prairie provinces. Range extends from Alaska south to New Mexico, Arizona and California in the west and from the Great Lakes to Newfoundland in the east. Relict populations are also found in Ireland and Scotland.

SPECIAL FEATURES

This is one of nature's masterpieces. Its beautifully arranged flowers are very characteristic, making this an easy orchid to identify. The flowers, when viewed from the side, look like an old-fashioned sunbonnet and often bloom well into September. It is commonly found growing in colonies.

RELATED SPECIES

Spiranthes lacera Raf., **Northern Ladies'-tresses**, is rare and found in open woods and bogs from Saskatchewan to Nova Scotia. Its flowers are arranged in a single spiral up the stem. Leaves are mostly basal and may wither away before the flower stalk appears.

HEINJO LAHRING

Spiranthes romanzoffiana

—SPERMATOPHYTA—
MONOCOTS
GRASSES, SEDGES, RUSHES

Herbaceous monocots of the following families:

GRASSES (POACEAE)

- flowers small, arranged in spikelets
- each floret composed of 1 ovary (2 styles and 1 plumose stigma), 3 stamens, 2 palea, 2 lemmas, 2 glumes (lowest bracts)
- perianth segments none or reduced to minute lodicule
- stems hollow, round in cross-section, jointed
- leaves 2-ranked (open leaf-sheaths)
- seed a grain (caryopsis)

SEDGES (CYPERACEAE)

- flowers small, solitary in axil of single scale
- each flower composed of 1 ovary (1 pistil), 3 stamens, 1 scale
- perianth segments reduced to bristles, scales or absent
- stems solid, often 3-sided, not jointed
- leaves 3-ranked (closed sheath)
- seed an achene

RUSHES (JUNCACEAE)

- flowers small, few to many in crowded cymes or heads
- each flower composed of 1 ovary (3 stigmas), 3 or 6 stamens, 3 scale-like sepals (calyx), 3 scale-like petals (corolla)
- perianth present as 6 scales
- stems round in cross-section, solid at nodes, not jointed
- leaves (sometimes reduced to scales) slender and either round in cross-section or grass-like; sheath open
- fruit a capsule (splitting at maturity); seeds 3 or many (often with appendages)

Alopecurus aequalis Sobol.   **POACEAE (Grass Family)**

Short-awned Foxtail

Syn.: *A. geniculatus* L. var. *aristulatus* (Michx.) Torr.
Other Common Names: Water Foxtail

Alopecurus is from the Greek *alopex* (fox) and *oura* (tail). The species epithet, *aequalis*, means equal and refers to the glumes and lemma.

Wetland
Perennial
Native
Common
Hardiness Zone: 0
Flowering Season: summer

DESCRIPTION

This wetland grass has erect to spreading stems either singly or in bunches forming small to large tufts. The flat, gray-green **leaf** blades are from 1 to 4 mm wide. Stems sometimes root at the nodes.

Flowers are held on stems 15–60 cm high in slender (about 5 mm wide by 2–7 cm long), soft, dense, spike-like panicles. Spikelets are single-flowered with glumes (2.5–3 mm), lemma (2.5 mm long with a short awn at the middle), and orange anthers.

Fruit is a seed-like grain called a caryopsis.

HABITAT AND DISTRIBUTION

Short-awned Foxtail grows in areas of moist to wet soil conditions as well as in the shallow water of lake margins, sloughs, and river flats.

Distribution is circumpolar. Its range extends across all three of the Prairie provinces.

SPECIAL FEATURES

Nearly all grasses bear seeds which are edible. Seed can be gathered in late summer and early fall. Removal of the outer husk is done by rubbing between the palms and then winnowing (tossing into the air and allowing the wind to blow away the lighter chaff). Always check for the dark purplish to black growth caused by ergot (a toxic fungus) and discard these seed heads. Some collectors recommend cleaning the grain and then parching it (some toxins can be eliminated with heat). Once processed the seed can either be left whole or ground into flour and used for baking.

RELATED SPECIES

Short-awned Foxtail spikes resemble those of Timothy (*Phleum* sp.), but Timothy favours drier habitats. Also, Timothy lacks the characteristic keeled and awned-tipped glumes found in Short-awned Foxtail. *Alopecurus aequalis* is the more commonly found of the three wetland *Alopecurus* species.

Alopecurus carolinianus Watt. is a tufted annual with a very narrow and dense panicle, 2–3 mm long spikelets, awns attached towards the base of the lemma (exserted at

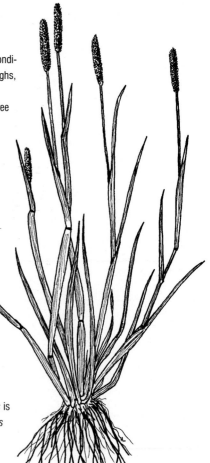

Alopecurus aequalis Sobol.

(See additional photo of
Alopecurus aequalis on page 89.)

Alopecurus aequalis

COLIN STONE

HEINJO LAHRING

least 2–3 mm), and anthers about 0.5 mm long. It is not known from Alberta but is reported to occur in southern Saskatchewan. [syn. *A. macounii* Vasey, *A. geniculatus* var. *caespitosus* Scribn.]

Alopecurus geniculatus L., **Water Foxtail**, is a Eurasian introduction. It is perennial with decumbent culms (rooting at the nodes), 2–3 mm long spikelets, awns are attached toward the base of the lemma, and anthers are about 2 mm long. It is transcontinental, occurring in ditches, pools and wet clearings. [syn. *A. pallescens* Piper & Beattie]

Alopecurus occidentalis Scribn. & Tweedy, **Alpine Foxtail**, has densely woolly, spike-like panicles (1 cm thick).

Alopecurus pratensis L., **Meadow Foxtail**, is a rare introduced species, with longer (5 mm) glumes than *A. aequalis*.

Hordeum jubatum L., **Foxtail Barley**, is a long-awned Foxtail found around saline sloughs, marshes and along streams. The soft foxtail-like plumes range in colour from green to silver, gold to bronze and at times purplish. It is very common throughout the region.

Hordeum jubatum

HEINJO LAHRING

Beckmannia syzigachne (Steud.) Fernald
Slough Grass

POACEAE (Grass Family)

Syn.: *B. syzigachne* var. *uniflora* (Scribn. ex Gray) Bovin
Other Common Names: American Slough Grass

Beckmannia is named after Johann Beckmann (1739–1811), a professer at Gottingen, Germany. The species epithet, *syzigachne*, means 'scissor-like glumes' and refers to this key feature used in its identification.

> Wetland
> Annual
> Native
> Common
> Hardiness Zone: 0
> Flowering Season: mid- to late summer

DESCRIPTION

Light green stems and leaves (0.5 to 1 m tall) grow in tufts from fibrous roots. **Leaf** blades are flat (5–10 mm wide) with overlapping sheaths and are rough to the touch. Ligules (5–8 mm long) can be found where the leaf blade meets the stem.

Flowers occur in elongate panicles made of many overlapping spikes (up to 2 cm long) which spread as the flower matures. Flattened, circular spikelets form 2 rows on one side of the spike stem. The spikelet consists of one flower and is concealed by 2 deeply keeled glumes (2–3 mm long).

Fruit is an oblong, seed-like grain falling free from the spikelets when ripe.

HABITAT AND DISTRIBUTION

Slough grass frequents the edges of marshes, sloughs, ponds, lakes, flooded stream-banks, wet fields and ditches. It rapidly establishes itself in wet disturbed areas stabilizing shorelines. Tolerant of drying-out of the landscape as the summer progresses, it drops its seed (which float with the paired glumes) and continues its life cycle when moistures levels permit (usually during spring run-off or June rains).

Distribution is widespread across the Prairie provinces. In Saskatchewan it tends to be more common in eastern and northeastern areas.

Beckmannia syzigachne (Steud.) Fern.

ALISON BAKKEN

SPECIAL FEATURES

Slough Grass makes good hay and pasture grass for livestock. Deer and moose are also known to feed on it. The seeds are good as a waterfowl food.

Beckmannia syzigachne often covers large areas. The grain is easily harvested when ripe and is suitable for human consumption. Its ability to establish stands in one season and reseed itself in subsequent years makes it valuable for wetland reclamation, wildlife enhancement and landscaping projects.

RELATED SPECIES

Beckmannia is the only multiple-spiked grass of wetlands areas which has spikelets on only one side of the spikelet stem (rachis) and does not resemble a comb in appearance. *Bouteloua* (Gramma Grass), found in dry areas, and *Spartina* (Cord Grass), of wet areas, have a similar spikelet arrangement but both have comb-like flower spikes.

Beckmannia syzigachne

Alopecurus aequalis (pp. 86–87)
Short-awned Foxtail

COLIN STONE

Calamagrostis canadensis (Michx.) Beauv.

POACEAE (Grass Family)

Bluejoint

Syn.: *C. nubila* Louis-Marie

Other Common Names: Canada Bluejoint, Marsh Reed Grass

The term *Calamagrostis* was used by the ancient Greeks to describe a plant which resembled a reed. *Calamus* means reed and *agrostis* is the name of a plant. *Canadensis* refers to its Canadian distribution.

Wetland
Perennial
Introduced
Common
Hardiness Zone: 0
Flowering Season: summer

DESCRIPTION

Strong creeping rhizomes give rise to densely clustered stems with swollen, purple-blue joints. Plants reach 1 m in height. **Leaves** are 4–8 mm wide, flat, slightly curving downward and rough to the touch. Blades have 3–8 mm long ligules at their base. Leaf tips are often somewhat ragged. Size and colour of plant are quite variable depending on genetics and the environment.

Flowers are held in open panicles (often purplish) 8–20 cm long. Spikelets are normally 1-flowered per pair of outer glumes. Glumes are 3–6 mm in

Calamagrostis canadensis (Michx.) Beauv.

Calamagrostis in bloom

HEINJO LAHRING

length. The lemma has a straight awn attached below mid-point, is shorter than palea, and has a tuft of straight white hairs (callus-hairs) attached at its base (about the same length as the lemma).

Fruit is a plump, elliptic grain (caryopsis).

HABITAT AND DISTRIBUTION

Bluejoint is tolerant of a wide range of moisture levels and grows in swamps, fens, marshes, moist woodlands and drier areas. It colonizes wet, open areas with mineral soil such as beaver meadows, ditches and shores.

This species is circumpolar in distribution and can be found throughout the Prairie provinces.

SPECIAL FEATURES

The young shoots are grazed by deer, moose, and muskrats. The stems are quite strong and held high in the winter providing cover for smaller wildlife. The seed bearing panicles are commonly held above the snow where birds and rodents can reach them during the winter months.

Calamagrostis is known by farmers as 'beaver hay,' being harvested from the wetter areas of fields.

RELATED SPECIES

Two other species of *Calamagrostis* can be found in *C. canadensis* habitat. *Calamagrostis stricta* (Timm) Koeler, **Narrow Reed Grass**, is a smaller grass than *C. canadensis* with smoother, softer and more lax leaves and stems. Its glumes are only 2–3 mm long. The callus hairs are of unequal lengths and shorter than the lemma. Flower panicles are more contracted than *C. canadensis*.

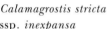

Calamagrostis stricta
ssp. *inexpansa*

PAT PORTER

Calamagrostis stricta (Timm) Koeler ssp. *inexpansa* (A. Gray) C.W. Greene, **Northern Reed Grass**, has rough, firm blades. The callus hairs are of unequal lengths and shorter than the lemma. Flower panicles are more contracted than *C. canadensis*.

PAT PORTER

Catabrosa aquatica (L.) Beauv.   POACEAE (Grass Family)

Brook Grass

Other Common Names: Water-hairbrush, Water Hairgrass

Catabrosa is from the Greek *catabrosis* (an eating) and refers to the erose or 'nibbled' glumes. *Aquatica* appropriately describes this water-loving grass.

> Wetland
> Perennial
> Native
> Common
> Hardiness Zone: 3
> Flowering Season: summer

DESCRIPTION

Prostrate stems root at the nodes. Upright stems (10–40 cm tall) grow from long rhizomes. Short, flat, light green **leaf** blades (4–8 mm wide) are somewhat drooping, smooth and without hairs.

Flower panicle is pyramidal in shape (10–30 cm long). Its fine branches are upright and spreading with some arching downwards. Spikelets (3 mm long) are 2-flowered with the glumes (1–1.5 mm long) being shorter than the lemmas (2.5–3 mm long). Lemma is strongly 3-nerved with an irregular tip. Palea is equal in length to the lemma.

Fruit is a small grain (caryopsis).

HABITAT AND DISTRIBUTION

This plant is an indicator of very wet soil conditions. It is found near springs, ponds, swamps, and along streams.

Catabrosa aquatica occurs in both the prairie and parkland regions of the Prairie provinces. It is more common in central to southern locations. The range extends across to Greenland, Iceland and Eurasia.

RELATED SPECIES

The creeping-growth form and water-inhabiting nature of this grass assist in making it quite unique and easy to identify. It is the only species of *Catabrosa* found in North America.

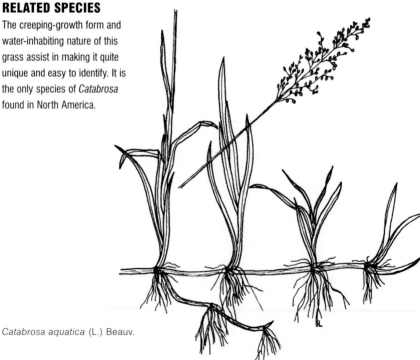

Catabrosa aquatica (L.) Beauv.

Dicanthelium acuminatum (Swartz) Gould & Clarke   POACEAE (Grass Family)

Hot-springs Millet

Syn.: *Panicum thermale* Boland, *P. ferventicola*
Schmoll var. *papillosum* Schmoll, *P. acuminatum* Sw.

The species epithet, *acuminatum*, means tapering to a
narrow point.

Wetland
Perennial
Native
Rare
Hardiness Zone: 2
Flowering Season: spring and early summer

DESCRIPTION

Three different seasonal phases occur. Spring gives
rise to the formation of flowering stems (Phase 1).
Summer is a period of vegetative growth. In autumn, plants
take on a bunched habit with some axillary culms and panicles (enclosed by leaf sheaths) branching off and spreading
(Phase 2). Over-wintering is in the form of a rosette of leaves
(Phase 3). Plants are densely tufted, or cushion forming, and
covered with velvety hairs. **Leaf** blades are flat, greyish green,
quite thick and 5–12 mm wide.

Flower panicles contain spikelets (2 mm long) with 2 florets. The
first floret is sterile or staminate and the second is fertile. The
florets are made of 2 unequal membranous glumes
and a several-nerved lemma which envelopes a
reduced or absent palea.

Fruit is a grain (caryopsis).

HABITAT AND DISTRIBUTION

Dicanthelium grows in marshy wetlands. It is known to occur in
the vicinity of hot springs.

Distribution is limited to mild and southern (warmer) locations of
the Prairie provinces. Its range extends beyond the Prairies into British
Columbia in the west and to Nova Scotia in the east.

SPECIAL FEATURES

This wetland grass's ability to inhabit hot springs is unique among the
grasses.

RELATED SPECIES

Of the three species of *Dicanthelium* found in the Prairie provinces, *D.
acuminatum* is the only one which prefers wet locations. Its tufted and
velvety appearance and three seasonal phases set this grass apart
from the others.

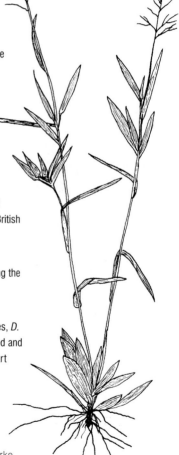

Dicanthelium acuminatum (Swartz) Gould & Clarke

Glyceria borealis (Nash) Batchelder
POACEAE (Grass Family)

Northern Manna Grass

Other Common Names: Small Floating Manna Grass, Float Grass, Sugar Grass

Glyceria is derived from the Greek word 'glykeros,' meaning 'having a sweet flavour' and refers to the edible grains of *G. fluitans* (found in eastern parts and similar to *G. borealis*). *Borealis* describes its northern home.

Wetland
Perennial
Native
Common
Hardiness Zone: 0
Flowering Season: mid-summer

DESCRIPTION

Medium to tall (50–100 cm), solitary or tufted stems rise upwards from creeping rhizomes. Stems often root at the lower stem nodes. **Leaves** are soft and spongy due to large air spaces. Non-wettable (i.e., water droplets bead and roll off) leaf blades are 2–5 mm wide, flat or folded, and sometimes floating. Distinctive of this genus are the closed sheaths at the base of the leafblades.

Large open and airy **flower** panicles (20–50 cm) are held above the foliage. Panicle branches, often drooping, are up to 10 cm long. Spikes are longer than their stalks. Linear, rounded spikelets are many flowered (6–12) and 7–14 mm long. Sterile florets (below the perfect ones) are absent. Glumes are unequal and shorter than the lemma (both are hairless at their base). Lemma (3–4 mm long) is prominently 5–9 parallel-nerved (i.e., not converging at apex). Palea is elliptic to obovate in shape.

Seeds are small grains (caryopsis).

HABITAT AND DISTRIBUTION

Northern Manna Grass is at home in either semi-aquatic or aquatic locations. It is known to form dense meadows around beaver ponds, marshes, sloughs, lakeshores and along slow moving streams. In deeper water it may form long, narrow, reddish floating leaves and usually will not flower.

Although distributed across the Prairie provinces, it tends to be more common in the boreal forest region and rather rare in the parkland and prairies. Its range extends up into the Territories and as far south as California.

Glyceria borealis (Nash) Batchelder

Glyceria borealis

HEINJO LAHRING

SPECIAL FEATURES

In general the manna grasses are palatable to livestock, although they are often somewhat out of reach due to their aquatic habitat. *Glyceria striata* (Fowl Manna Grass), also found in the region, may be toxic to grazing animals because the leaves are known to have a high cyanogenetic potential.

Grains are the most valuable of all sources of plant food for humans. Grains are used directly for cereals, flour, and meal and indirectly as fodder for livestock. This is one of the grasses used by Native peoples. The grain is harvestable and suitable for use as food. In the past it was handled in the same manner as wild rice (*Zizania* sp), in which the seeds were parched and ground up for flour, or boiled and eaten. Seeds were also used as a soup thickener.

RELATED SPECIES

Several other manna grasses occur in the area. *Glyceria borealis* stands out because of its narrow, erect panicle with long, linear spikelets (over 7 mm long and circular in cross-section).

Glyceria elata (Nash) A.S. Hitchc., **Tufted Tall Manna Grass**, considered rare. It is not quite as tall as *G. grandis* (60–150 cm) and has smaller flowers (first glume not more than 1 mm long vs. 1.5 mm for *G. grandis*). This species is strictly cordilleran in range.

Two species which are recognized by their broad, open, drooping panicles and somewhat flattened spikelets are *G. grandis* and *G. striata*:

Glyceria grandis S. Wats., **Tall Manna Grass**, reaches to 200 cm tall, has wide leaf blades (6–12 mm) and purplish spikelets.

Glyceria striata (Lam.) A.S. Hitchc., **Fowl Manna Grass**, is a considerably smaller grass in comparison to *G. borealis*, only reaching 30–80 cm in height with narrow leaf blades (2–4 mm). It has small flowers (first glume 0.5–0.8 mm long; lemma barely 2 mm long).

HEINJO LAHRING

Glyceria grandis

HEINJO LAHRING

HEINJO LAHRING

Muhlenbergia glomerata (Willd.) Trin.   POACEAE (Grass Family)

Bog Muhly

Other Common Names: Marsh Timothy, Muhly

This wetland grass is named after the American botanist G.H.E. Muhlenberg (1753–1815). *Glomerata* means 'aggregated into clusters' and refers to the closely spaced flowers and fruits.

Wetland
Perennial
Native
Common
Hardiness Zone: 1
Flowering Season: summer

DESCRIPTION

Bog Muhly is a medium-height (20–80 cm) grass which grows from creeping, hard and scaly rhizomes. Stems are in small clumps or solitary, sometimes branching near base. Leaf stems are puberulent between the nodes. **Leaves** are upright, flat, hairless, and 2–6 mm wide. Sheaths are open at their base.

Flower clusters are in narrow (almost cylindrical), solitary panicles (2–11 cm long x 3–15 mm wide). The spikelets (less than 3 mm long) are tight and start out purplish or blue then changing to pale yellow by late summer. Each spikelet has one flower. Glumes taper to a long scabrous awn. Glume awns are much longer than the lemma and hairy below the middle. **Fruit** is a small grain (*caryopsis*).

HABITAT AND DISTRIBUTION

Habitat varies from very wet to dry. Although the name Bog Muhly is indicative of boggy areas (in which it can be found), it is more often considered a fen indicator. It is common in water tracks of large peatlands and occasionally grows in floating mats along lakeshores.

Range extends across the Prairie provinces and is often associated with boreal forest areas.

SPECIAL FEATURES

Some varieties of *Muhlenbergia* are lightly browsed by deer and moose. Grains of the closely related Scratch Grass (*M. asperifolia*) were a food source for Native peoples.

RELATED SPECIES

Bog Muhly tends to be the most water-loving of the four *Muhlenbergias* occurring in the Prairie provinces.

Muhlenbergia asperifolia (Nees & Mey.) Parodi, **Scratch Grass**, grows on moist alkaline soil and has a more open panicle (4–12 cm wide). Spikelets are on long pedicels, whereas in *M. glomerata* the spikelets are on short pedicels.

Muhlenbergia glomerata (Willd.) Trin.

96

Scirpus validus (p. 127)
Softstem Bulrush or
Common Great Bulrush

HEINJO LAHRING

Phalaris arundinacea L.

POACEAE (Grass Family)

Reed Canary Grass

The name *Phalaris* has Greek roots and comes from *Phalaros*, an expanded form of *Phalos* ('white,' referring to a coot's white head), meaning 'dotted with white.' This is descriptive of the shiny, fertile flower scales (lemmas) in this genus.

Wetland
Perennial
Introduced
Common
Hardiness Zone: 0
Flowering Season: mid-summer

DESCRIPTION

Plants often form dense stands (60–200 cm tall) from creeping and spreading rhizomes. Leafy stems are hollow, stiff and swollen at the nodes. **Leaf** blades are flat, 10–20 cm long and up to 20 mm wide. Ligules (2–6 mm long) are blunt and membranous. Sheaths are open, hairless, and not overlapping.

Flower clusters are held above the foliage in a narrow and dense panicle (1–20 cm long). Panicle branches are spreading at maturity. Spikelets (5–6 mm long) may have a purplish tint, and consist of one perfect terminal floret with two sterile lemmas below. Glumes (not winged; 5 mm long) are longer than the lemma (3–4 mm long, covering palea). Sterile lemmas are no more than very small hairy scales. Fertile lemmas are shiny when in fruit.

Fruit is a grain (caryopsis), and is enclosed within a shiny flower scale (lemma) when shed.

Phalaris arundinacea L.

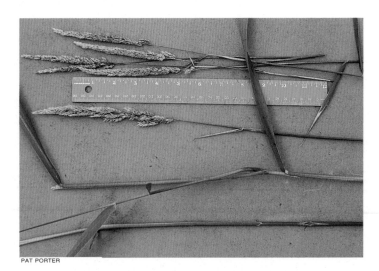

Phalaris arundinacea

PAT PORTER

98

HABITAT AND DISTRIBUTION

Reed Canary Grass is tolerant of both semi-aquatic and dry land conditions. It grows in muddy soil along the shores of lakes, rivers, streams, marshes, and in roadside ditches.

Distribution is circumpolar and the range extends across the Prairie provinces.

SPECIAL FEATURES

Phalaris seeds are a favorite of birds. *Phalaris canariensis* (occasionally found in the Prairie provinces) is grown commercially in the Mediterranean for domestic bird (e.g., Canary) seed.

As a result of the long Canadian summer days, and with abundant water, this grass can grow over 2 m by mid-summer and is known as 'beaver hay'. It was introduced as a wetland forage grass. When cut and bunched it makes an excellent roof-thatching material.

Young shoots can be eaten raw or cooked. The grain is harvestable and useful as a food source.

RELATED SPECIES

A horticultural variation, which rarely escapes gardens, is the green-and-cream-striped 'Ribbongrass' (*P. arundinacea* var. *picta*).

Phalaris canariensis L., **Canary Grass**, an introduced ornamental annual, may also be found in the area as an escape from cultivation. It is much shorter (30–80 cm) and its panicle (1.5–4 cm long) is very dense and ovoid in shape. Glumes and lemmas are longer (7–8 mm and 5 mm respectively). Glumes have a green stripe. Outer glumes are winged.

PAT PORTER

Phalaris arundinacea

COLIN STONE

Phragmites australis (Cav.) Trin. ex Steud. — POACEAE (Grass Family)

Reed Grass

Syn.: *P. communis* Trin.

Other Common Names: Common Reed Grass, Giant Reed Grass, Cane, Reed, Carrizo

Phragmites is derived from the Greek term *phragma* meaning 'fence,' and refers to its hedge-like growth along ditches.

> Wetland
> Perennial
> Native
> Occasional
> Hardiness Zone: 1
> Flowering Season: late summer

DESCRIPTION

This plant resembles a 'northern bamboo.' Its leafy stalks have well-defined and thickened nodes (internodes at times purplish), can reach from 2 to 4 m in height and form dense colonies. Rhizomes are very strong and creeping with sharp terminal shoots. **Leaf** blades (10–40 cm long by 1–3 cm wide) are spreading, flat and glabrous with loose overlapping sheaths (a few long hairs are present at the base).

Flower clusters are held high in many-branched, plume-like panicles (10–40 cm long). Spikelets are 3–7 flowered (12–15 mm long) with long, soft, silky white hairs attached to the base. These hairs persist throughout the winter giving a feathery appearance. Flowers are either bisexual or male only. Glumes (unequal) and lemma (8–12 mm, 3-nerved) are narrow and pointed. Palea is shorter than lemma.

Fruit is a grain (caryopsis) which at times is rarely produced.

HABITAT AND DISTRIBUTION

Common Reed Grass forms dense, spreading colonies in seasonally flooded areas. Stands can be found in roadside ditches, fresh and brackish marshes, sloughs, and lake margins (up to 2 m deep). Occasionally found in swamps, fens and sand dunes.

Phragmites australis is circumpolar in distribution with a preference towards southern boreal regions. This range suggests that most populations are likely introduced.

Phragmites australis (Cav.) Trin. ex Steud.

HEINJO LAHRING

Phragmites australis

SPECIAL FEATURES

Dense stands of *Phragmites* leafy stalks provide year-round shelter for wildlife. The thick rhizomes are a favorite food of muskrats.

The ability to translocate substantial volumes of water and produce large amounts of biomass during a short growing season make *Phragmites* an excellent plant for wastewater treatment.

HEINJO LAHRING

Native peoples harvested the nutritious seed in the autumn. The grain was boiled in their hulls or dried and ground into flour. Tender young shoots were pickled or eaten raw (strong, sweet taste is reminiscent of wheat grass). The stems (prior to blooming) are rich in sugars. They were dried and ground into a sweetish powder which was added to flour for making cakes and breads. Indians moistened the powder, roasted it and ate it as a delicacy. At times a sweet 'gum' exudes from the stem. This was gathered, rolled into small balls and eaten as a treat.

The rootstalks were also a food source. These were eaten raw, roasted, or boiled. One method was to crush and wash the roots in water to dissolve the starch. The water was filtered and poured into a container. The starch settled to the bottom. Then the water was poured off and the starch gathered.

The reeds were used for making arrow shafts, mats, screens, pipestems, thatching for huts, and cordage for items such as fishing nets.

RELATED SPECIES

Common Reed Grass is the only *Phragmites* species in North America. Because of its huge size and thicket-forming habit, it is easily recognized. When grown under poor conditions it may become stunted and resemble Reed Canary Grass (*Phalaris* sp), but only *Phragmites* has long, silky hairs at the base of its leaves (persisting in the panicle).

HEINJO LAHRING

Above, right, and below: *Phragmites australis.*

Note hairs at base of leaf, below.

HEINJO LAHRING

Poa leptocoma Trin.   POACEAE (Grass Family)
Bog Bluegrass

Syn.: *P. paucispicula* Scribn. & Merr.

Poa is of Greek origin meaning 'grass' or 'fodder.' *Leptocoma* is a combination of *lepto* (slender, narrow, thin) and *coma* (tuft of hairs).

Wetland
Perennial
Native
Occasional
Hardiness Zone: 1
Flowering Season: summer

DESCRIPTION

Creeping rhizomes are absent. Stems (20–50 cm tall; longer than basal leaves) are solitary or in loose tufts. Narrow (2–4 mm) **leaf** blades are soft, flat, and decumbent at base. Leaf tips end in the characteristic 'boat-shape' common to the bluegrass genus. Ligules on the upper leaves are 3–4 mm long.

Flowers are arranged in an open, spreading panicle 5–10 cm long. Spikelets are narrow (6 mm long) and pointed with 2–several flowers. Glumes (1–3-nerved) are unequal and keeled. Lemma (4 mm long, 3–5-nerved) has a cluster of crinkly white hairs at its base and may have pubescence on the keel and marginal nerves. Palea is equal to or shorter than the lemma.
Fruit is a grain (caryopsis).

HABITAT AND DISTRIBUTION

Poa leptocoma is one of the few bluegrasses which prefers very wet conditions and can be found in bogs and wet meadows.
It is somewhat restricted to the Rocky Mountain region of west central Alberta. Its range extends beyond the Prairie provinces in the north to include Yukon Territory, Alaska, and eastern Asia, and in the south to Montana and California.

SPECIAL FEATURES

The soft tender growth of bluegrasses are very palatable to wildlife and live-stock. Fowl Bluegrass (*P. palustris*) leaves are eaten by American Coots in large quantities, making up to 50% of the bird's diet. Leaves and seed heads are eaten by moose, deer, voles and other mammals. Seeds are eaten by gamebirds and songbirds.
The base of the stems and grains of various bluegrasses are known to have been used by Native peoples for food.

RELATED SPECIES

Three other bluegrasses also inhabit the Prairie provinces wetlands.
Poa canbyi (Scribn.) Piper, **Canby Bluegrass**, is somewhat less common and can be found in dry to moist (often alkali) meadows of

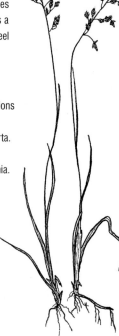

Poa leptocoma Trin.

the prairies and parklands. The lemmas have no webbing (cluster of crinkly hairs) at their base but may be somewhat hairy on lower part of the back.
Poa juncifolia Scribn., **Alkali Bluegrass**, is occasionally found. It grows in moist, open alkaline meadows. The panicle is dense and narrow (10–20 cm long). Lemmas are not webbed at base.
Poa palustris L., **Fowl Bluegrass** or **Fowl Meadow Grass**, is the most common, and prefers moist meadows and open woods. It has smaller spikelets and lemmas (less than 4.5 mm and less than 3 mm respectively) than *P. leptocoma*.

Puccinellia nuttalliana (Schlt.) A. S. Hitchc.
Nuttall's Salt-meadow Grass

POACEAE (Grass Family)

Syn.: *P. airoides* (Nutt.) Wats. & Coult.
Other Common Names: Alkali Grass

Puccinellia is named in honour of the Italian botanist B. Puccinelli, 1808–1850. The species epithet, *nuttalliana*, is named after the English-born botanist Thomas Nuttall (1786–1859).

Wetland
Perennial
Native
Common
Hardiness Zone: 1
Flowering Season: summer

Puccinellia nuttalliana (Schlt.) A.S. Hitchc.

DESCRIPTION

This low, tufted, sod-forming grass has slender stems 30–60 cm tall. Its smooth **leaf** blades are narrow (1–3 mm wide) and flat, or somewhat rolled, with a bluish white colouring.

Slender feathery panicles (sometimes ovoid or pyramidal in shape) are 10–20 cm long with erect to spreading branches. Spikelets are 4–7 mm long with 3 to 6 **flowers**. Florets are hairless at their base. Glumes are unequal (1–2 mm long) and shorter than the first lemma (2–3 mm long; narrowed to a broad tip; awnless). The palea is as long as the lemma. Anthers are 0.7–1.2 mm long.

Fruit is a small grain (caryopsis).

HABITAT AND DISTRIBUTION

Puccinellia favours moist alkali flats, hence the name Alkali Grass. It is tolerant of both very wet and very dry soils, a situation which occurs almost yearly with the seasonal drying-out of the prairie landscape.

This grass can be found throughout the prairie and parkland region of the Prairie provinces. The range extends beyond into British Columbia in the west, and California, Texas and Kansas in the south.

SPECIAL FEATURES

The grain of *P. nuttalliana* was used as food by Native peoples of central and western North America.

RELATED SPECIES

There are four other species of *Puccinellia* found in the area.

Puccinellia cusickii Weatherby, **Cusick's Salt-meadow Grass**, resembles *P. nuttalliana* except for having a larger second glume (2.0–2.8 mm) and longer anthers (1.5–2.0 mm long). Occasional to rare.

Puccinellia distans (L.) Parl., **Slender Salt-meadow Grass**, is circumpolar and is likely introduced. It has wider leaves (2–5 mm) than *P. nuttalliana*. Anthers are 0.6–0.8 mm long. Occasional to rare.

Puccinellia hauptiana (Krecz.) Kitagawa, **Haupt's Salt-meadow Grass**, is similar to *P. distans* but with narrower leaves (1–2 mm wide) and shorter anthers (0.3–0.6 mm). Rare.

Puccinellia pauciflora (Presl) Munz, **Few-flowered Salt-meadow Grass**, is taller than the others. Nerves on the lemma are conspicuous (obscure on the other species). Leaves are 4–12 mm wide. Rare. [syn. *Glyceria pauciflora* Presl., *Torreyochloa pauciflora* Church]

PAT PORTER

Puccinellia nuttalliana

Scholochloa festucacea (Willd.) Link
Spangletop

POACEAE (Grass Family)

Syn.: *Fluminia festucacea* (Willd.) A. S. Hitchc.
Other Common Names: Whitetop, Marsh Grass, Thatch Grass, Scotch Grass

Scholochloa is derived from the Greek *scolops* (a pickle) and *chloa* (grass). *Festucacea* means like *Festuca*.

Wetland
Perennial
Native
Common
Hardiness Zone: 0
Flowering Season: summer

DESCRIPTION

Tall (80-150 cm) stems stand erect from thick, creeping rhizomes. Leaf sheaths are closed, hairless and veined. **Leaf** blades (5–10 mm wide) are flat or rolled longitudinally, tapering to a fine point. Ligules are 3–5 mm long.

Flower panicles (10–20 cm long) are open and spreading. Branches are long with closely bunched florets on the tips. Spikelets (6–11 mm long) contain 3–7 flowers. The glumes are unequal and thin with the first (5–7 mm long) being 3-nerved and the second (6–8 mm long) 5-nerved. Lemma is lanceolate, awnless, densely hairy at the base, and about the same length as the glumes. Palea is two-toothed.

Fruit is a grain (caryopsis).

HABITAT AND DISTRIBUTION

Spangletop is a grass of marshes, sloughs, stream edges and shallow water. It is tolerant of fresh to brackish water conditions. *Scholochloa festucacea* can be found growing across the Prairie provinces from the boreal forest in the north to the prairies in the south. Its range extends into Eurasia as well as central and western North America (including Wyoming, Nebraska, Indiana, Oregon, and British Columbia).

SPECIAL FEATURES

When the oat-shaped seeds shed, the head bleaches out; thus the name Whitetop.

RELATED SPECIES

Scholochloa festucacea is the only species of *Scolochloa* found in North America. It may be confused with Manna Grass (*Glyceria* spp.), Bent Grass (*Agrostis* spp.), or Alkali Grass (*Puccinellia* spp.). *Scholochloa festucacea* looks much like the introduced pest *Bromus inermis* but this latter does not grow in water. Manna Grass has glumes which are shorter than the lemma. The lemma is not hairy at the base and has 5–9 parallel nerves (not converging towards the tip).

Bent Grass has spikelets with only one flower. The florets are not hairy at their base. The palea is often lacking or reduced in size.

Alkali Grass prefers saline habitats, has open leaf sheaths and the lemma is not prominently nerved or hairy at its base.

Scholochloa festucacea (Willd.) Link

Spartina pectinata Link
Prairie Cord Grass

POACEAE (Grass Family)

Other Common Names: Cord Grass, Freshwater Cord Grass, Slough Grass

In the past this grass was used to make cord, hence the name *Spartina* (Greek for 'cord'). The species epithet, *pectinata*, means 'in the form of a comb' and describes the comb-like arrangement of spikelets along the stem.

Wetland
Perennial
Native
Common
Zone: 1
Flowering Season: summer

DESCRIPTION

Tall (50–200 cm), smooth, shiny stems stand erect and are sometimes tufted from long, tough, scaly rhizomes. The **leaves** (5–15 mm wide) grow to 60 cm long, taper to a narrow whip-like point, and are flat or with inrolled edges (especially at emergence). Upper surface is rough while lower surface is smooth and shiny. Sheaths are hairless, strongly veined, with scarious margins. Ligules are 2–3 mm long.

Flower panicles (10–30 cm long) are narrow with 10–20 alternating spikes (2–10 cm long) closely paralleling the main stem. Spikes are flattened and consist of many closely spaced 1-flowered spikelets. Glumes are scabrous. Upper glume (8–12 mm long) has barbs along its keel and a 4-10 mm awn at the tip. Lemma (7–9 mm long) has a scabrous keel. Palea is longer than lemma. **Fruit** (one per spikelet) is a very small grain (caryopsis).

Spartina pectinata Link

HABITAT AND DISTRIBUTION

Prairie Cord Grass is at home in saline sloughs and marshes where it can grow in abundance. It is found growing in sand or among boulders along lakeshores and riverbanks. This grass is more common in the southern and eastern portions of the Prairie provinces. Distribution extends from the southern Northwest Territories to Newfoundland.

SPECIAL FEATURES

The vigorous, strong soil-binding rhizomes are very effective in providing erosion control and stabilizing sediments along shorelines and in shallow water. *Spartina pectinata* grows well on moist soils and can be harvested in large quantities for hay (in particular in wet, saline areas), although its coarse texture makes it less preferred over other more palatable grasses. *Spartina*'s fibrous nature and long length make it ideal for cordage. The large rhizomes are especially suited to this purpose.

RELATED SPECIES

Spartina gracilis Trin., **Alkali Cord Grass**, can also be found in the area. It is more common in the western portions of the district, whereas *S. pectinata* is more prevalent in the east. *Spartina gracilis* glumes have very short or non-existent awns and its ligules are only about 1 mm long. The comb-like appearance of the flower spikes sets this group aside from other grasses.

HEINJO LAHRING

Spartina pectinata

Zizania aquatica L.
Annual Wild Rice

POACEAE (Grass Family)

Other Common Names: Southern Wild Rice, Eastern Wild Rice, Indian Rice, Canadian Rice, Water Oats, Water Rice, Manomin

Zizania is from the Greek *Zizanion*, a weed of wheat fields. The species epithet, *aquatica*, refers to its watery habitat.

Emergent
Annual
Native
Occasional
Hardiness Zone: 2
Flowering Season: summer

DESCRIPTION

This aquatic grass grows to 3 m in height from fibrous roots. Adventitious roots sometimes grow from the stem nodes and assist in anchorage. There are short, horizontal rootlets but no true root-hairs, which is unusual among grasses. The light green **leaves** are 5–15 mm wide, soft, and occasionally branched. Sheaths are long. Ligules (8–15 mm long) are pointed.

There are 3 phases in its annual growth sequence: first is the 'floating-leaf phase' with long, ribbon-like surface leaves; second is the 'emergent phase' with stems growing above the water's surface; third is the 'flowering and fruiting phase' with panicles held well above the water's surface.

Flower panicle (30–60 cm long) is narrow and held erect with lower branches somewhat pendulous. Spikelets are 1-flowered and unisexual. Female flowers occur on the upper portion of the spike and male on the lower portion. There are no glumes. Male flowers have 6 stamens, a thin lemma (pointed or short-awned), and a palea. Female flowers have a club-shaped pistil, a long-awned (1–6 cm) 3-ribbed lemma, and a palea.

Fruit is a long, dark brown to purplish black, cylindrical grain (caryopsis) which drops off while tightly wrapped in lemma and palea. The long awn of lemma assists in guiding and orienting the seed while it is sinking to pond bottom.

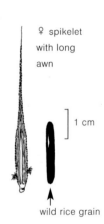

♀ spikelet with long awn

1 cm

wild rice grain

HABITAT AND DISTRIBUTION

Zizania aquatica inhabits marshes, lake margins, sloughs, and watercourses. It is tolerant of a wide range of environmental conditions. Water depth is usually shallow but ranges from 0.5–2.5 m. Abrupt changes in water levels result in poor stands. Soil type ranges from clay to peat. Stands tend to be concentrated near the inlet and outlet of lakes and ponds where there is a constant but slow current.

Distribution is generally between 30–56 degrees N latitude. The region west of Lake Superior to southern Manitoba and into Wisconsin and Minnesota is known as the 'Wild Rice Bowl' with optimal conditions supporting large stands. It becomes quite scarce, except for introduced populations, as one leaves the Canadian Shield and moves into the central and western sections of the Prairie provinces.

Zizania aquatica L.

SPECIAL FEATURES

Wild rice is a very important waterfowl food. It is often planted solely to attract ducks and geese. Dense stands make suitable nesting sites.

The Sioux and Algonquin were the traditional tribes which gathered wild rice. The Minomini Indians of Wisconsin, whose tribal name is derived from the Native name of wild rice, had sites which under favourable conditions harvested up to 20 kg of wild rice per day. The panicles were bent over the canoe edge with a paddle and a stick was used to knock off the seeds which dropped to the bottom of the boat. These were later spread out on hides to be thoroughly dried in the sun. In order to remove the chaff a 2-storied contraption was constructed of two hides:

> ...four poles (6 feet tall) were driven into the ground; then one hide was tied between the poles; another hide was placed on the ground to one side of the first; when a brisk wind was blowing, they raked the rice off of the edge of the upper and let it fall to the hide on the ground (the loose chaff blew away in the wind).

Another method of cleaning and removing the awns and husks was to first heat it in a dry kettle or skillet and then beat or trample the grains to loosen it. This was followed with winnowing in the wind (the heavier grain dropped down and the lighter material blew away). The rice was then washed and dried for storage for use at a later time.

The grain can be boiled, steamed or popped. If parched using wood heat, it takes on a smoky sweetness which is excellent with game and poultry. If the smoky flavour is too strong it should be washed in cold water first. The grain is very nutritious being mostly starch and low in fat. It is high in protein, rich in vitamin B, and richer in riboflavin than wheat, corn, oats or rye. Its thiamine content compares favourably to these. Tender shoots can be eaten raw.

RELATED SPECIES

Zizania aquatica is sometimes separated into two distinct species, *Z. aquatica* L., or **Southern Wild Rice** (including *Z. aquatica* var. *brevis* Fassett, **Estuarine Wild Rice**) and *Z. palustris* L., or **Northern Wild Rice** (including *Z. aquatica* var. *interior* (Fassett) Dore, **Interior Wild Rice**). See Aiken et al., 1988, for details.

HEINJO LAHRING

HEINJO LAHRING

Above and left, *Zizania aquatica* L.

Left, floating leaf stage

Carex aquatilis Wahlenb. CYPERACEAE (Sedge Family)

Water Sedge

Syn.: *C. stans* Drejer, *C. aquatilis* var. *stans* (Drej.) Boott
Other Common Names: Sheargrass

Carex is the Greek name, *keirein*, meaning to cut. The species name,
aquatilis, means 'growing in water' and refers to its watery habitat.

Wetland
Perennial
Native
Common
Hardiness Zone: 0
Flowering Season: summer

DESCRIPTION

Plants form tufts with stems (20–150 cm tall) growing from long, scaly
rhizomes. **Leaf** clumps are often reddish tinged at base. Blades (2–7
mm wide) are bluish white, hairless, and sharply 3-angled above.
Flowers are in two types of spikes (1.5–7 cm long). Male spikes (1 or 2) have purplish
black to brown scales. Male flowers have 3 stamens. Female spikes (2–4; sometimes
with a few male flowers at tips) are densely packed with flowers which are arranged
spirally and look 'corn cob-like.' Female flowers have 2 stigmas. Perigynia (2–3 mm
long) are flattened with a short beak. Scales are about as long as the perigynia and distinctly bicoloured with a light center and dark purplish black edge.
Fruit is a lens-shaped achene encased within the perigynium.

HABITAT AND DISTRIBUTION

Carex aquatilis is often found in abundance in marshes, wet fields, fens, ditches,
streambanks and lakeshores. It grows at the water's edge often forming tuft-like
islands and in time filling in the shoreline. It prefers habitats with at least some water
throughout the summer.

This is a circumpolar sedge which ranges across Canada from east to west and from the
Territories as far south as California and Arizona.

SPECIAL FEATURES

Water Sedge produces seeds in abundance and is an important food for waterfowl and
songbirds. It makes up the bulk of what is known as 'beaverhay' or 'slough hay' cut
from wetlands. It is eaten by cattle, although it can be quite tough at certain times
of the year.

The whitish leaf base can be eaten raw and has a very pleasant, mild, nutty
flavor remniscent of palm hearts. Water Sedge was eaten in Europe
where it is native as well. Ergot infections can be found on spikes in
the fall, so caution is advised in plant collection for consumption.
The ability to tolerate a wide range of growing conditions and its
beautiful bluish green foliage make it highly valuable as an ornamental plant for water gardens.

RELATED SPECIES

The sedges are a very complex group and require close examination for accurate identification. *Carex aquatilis* has very characteristic spiral-patterned spikes which appear beautifully bicoloured.
The foliage is a unique bluish green colour (especially in the early
spring). This is a sedge representative of Section *Phacocystis*.

Carex aquatilis Wahlenb.

perigynia

perigynia
behind
scale

scale

characteristic
pattern of perigynia
and scale

Carex aquatilis (facing page)

Water Sedge

HEINJO LAHRING

inflorescence

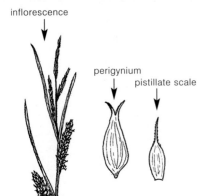

perigynium
pistillate scale

Carex atherodes Spreng.

Section: Paludosae
Awned Sedge

Carex aurea Nutt.

Section: Bicolores
Golden Sedge

Carex brunnescens (Pers.) Poir.

Section: Heleonastes
Brownish Sedge

Carex chordorrhiza Ehrh. ex L.f.

Section: Chordorrhizeae
Prostrate Sedge

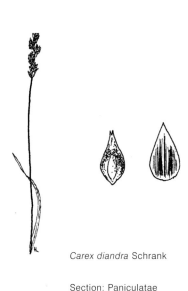

Carex diandra Schrank

Section: Paniculatae

Two-stamened Sedge

Carex lacustris Willd.

Section: Paludosae

Lakeshore Sedge

Carex limosa L.

Section: Limosae

Mud Sedge

Carex livida (Wahlenb.) Willd.

Section: Paniceae

Livid Sedge

Carex pseudo-cyperus L.

Section: Pseudo-cypereae
Cyperus-like Sedge

Carex retrorsa Schw.

Section: Vesicariae
Turned Sedge

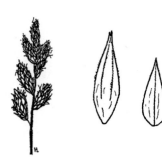

Carex scoparia Schk. ex Willd.

Section: Festucaceae
Broom Sedge

Carex utriculata Boott
(syn. *C. rostrata* var. *utriculata* (Boott) Bailey)

Section: Vesicariae
Beaked Sedge

Carex bebbii (Bailey) Fern.

Bebb's Sedge

CYPERACEAE (Sedge Family)

This wetland sedge is named in honour of Michael Schuck Bebb, a botanist of the 1800s who studied willows.

Wetland
Perennial
Native
Common
Hardiness Zone: 0
Flowering Season: summer

DESCRIPTION

The rhizome, if any, is vertical, producing a tufted plant. Stems are erect (20–80 cm tall), very slender and rough to the touch. Light green **leaves** are soft and flat (2–5 mm wide). Lowest leaves are reduced to scales. **Flower** clusters (1–3 cm long) are dense and oblong. They start out light green or straw-coloured and mature to brown. Clusters consist of 3–12 stalkless spikes. Spikes (broadly ovoid to rounded) are composed of a dense grouping of many flowers. Flowers (4–10 mm long) are of two types. Female flowers are above and male are below. Scales are brown and slightly shorter than perigynia. Perigynia (3–3.5 mm long; 2–2.5 times as long as wide) are narrowly egg-shaped with a two-toothed beak. **Fruit** is a lens-shaped achene which has a narrowly wing-margined perigynia with 2 stigmas at the top.

Carex bebbii (Bailey) Fern.

HABITAT AND DISTRIBUTION

Bebb's Sedge is found in wet meadows, marshes, sandy shores, stream-banks, ditches, clearings in damp woods, and tamarack swamps. This sedge is scattered across the Prairie provinces and in particular in openings of wooded regions such as the parklands and boreal forest. Range extends across North America from Alaska to Newfoundland and as far south as New Mexico, Nevada, and California.

HEINJO LAHRING

SPECIAL FEATURES

Sedges are important builders of soil in our northern wetlands. Over the course of hundreds of years they build up enough bio-mass to fill in what was once open water, allowing dryland plants to eventually replace them.

RELATED SPECIES

Bebb's Sedge is a member of Section *Ovales* Kunth. There are approximately 20 species within this section in the Prairie provinces.

Pointed Broom Sedge, *Carex scoparia* Schk. ex Willd., is another species of this group. It has narrow leaves and perigynia which are narrowly lanceolate (about 3 times as long as wide). *Carex scoparia* is somewhat rare with locations in the Rocky Mountain region of Alberta, boreal forest and a few locations in the parklands.

Carex bebbii

Carex lacustris Willd.

CYPERACEAE (Sedge Family)

Lakeshore Sedge

Syn: *C. riparia* var. *lacustris* (Willd.) Kuek.
Other Common Names: Lake Sedge, Lakebank Sedge, Rip-gut Sedge

The species epithet, *lacustris*, means 'inhabiting lakes' and is indicative of its association with open water areas.

Wetland
Perennial
Native
Common
Hardiness Zone: 1
Flowering Season: mid-summer

DESCRIPTION

Strong, triangular stems are tall (50–150 cm), grow from stout, scaly rhizomes, and are purplish to reddish at the base. Bluish green **leaf** blades (8–15 mm wide) are usually longer than stems, rough and hairless. Sheaths are usually cross-veined.

Flowers are in 4–8 well-separated spikes. Upper 2–4 spikes are male, and the lower (2–10 cm long) are female. Some spikes tend to be compound. Purplish scales are ovate and half the length of the olive green perigynia (4–7 mm long, oblong-ovoid, bidentate beak).

Fruit is a 3-sided achene with 3 stigmas.

HABITAT AND DISTRIBUTION

Lakeshore Sedge grows in water up to 50 cm deep. It is a plant of the boreal forest and can be found in marshes, swampy woods, ditches, along shores, and the edges of floating fen mats.

Its range extends from British Columbia to Newfoundland and southward into the central and eastern United States.

SPECIAL FEATURES

Carex lacustris is able to grow well in standing water, making it an excellent plant for shoreline revegetation projects.

The seeds are eaten by waterfowl and songbirds. The stems and leaves remain throughout the winter providing food and shelter for rodents and other small animals. In the spring the plants provide spawning habitat for pike and muskelunge.

RELATED SPECIES

Carex lacustris is an example of a sedge in section *Paludosae*. Another species in this group is the **Awned Sedge** (*C. atherodes* Spreng.). It differs in having a longer perigynium-beak (1.5–3.0 mm long) and pubescent leaf-blades and sheaths. Awned Sedge often forms a major part of slough hay and is very palatable to livestock.

Carex lacustris

HEINJO LAHRING

Carex vaginata Tausch

CYPERACEAE (Sedge Family)

Sheathed Sedge

The species epithet, *vaginata*, means 'sheathing' and refers to the long, loose sheaths of bracts.

Wetland
Perennial
Native
Common
Hardiness Zone: 0
Flowering Season: mid- to late summer

DESCRIPTION

Extensive, loose clumps of 10–60 cm tall stems arise from long, creeping rhizomes. The soft yellow-green **leaves** (1–5 mm wide) are shorter than the flowering stems. **Flower** clusters (2–4) are in widely separated elongate groups. Spikes are more or less spreading with one male terminal spike and 2–3 lateral female spikes below (lower peduncles are long). Female spikes may have some male flowers at top. The lowest spike bract has a loose 1–2 cm long sheath. Female flowers (8–30 per spike) have purplish brown scales which are shorter and narrower than perigynia. Yellowish green or brown perigynia (3–5 mm long) are arranged in two rows with each having a 1 mm long beak. **Fruit** is a triangular (3-sided) achene with 3 stigmas.

HABITAT AND DISTRIBUTION

Sheathed Sedge occurs in bogs, wet meadows, stream banks, and rich conifer (cedar or black spruce) swamps.

Distribution is circumpolar, with plants within the Prairie provinces tending to prefer the boreal forest, mountains and parkland areas.

SPECIAL FEATURES

Sedges are the equivalent in the north to grasses in the south. The poorly drained topography of northern Canada is favoured by sedges. Many species occupy these wetlands with much variation in floral and vegetative character-istics, each adapted to suit the local environmental conditions.

RELATED SPECIES

This is a sedge of section *Paniceae*. *Carex vaginata* can be confused with *C. livida* (Wahlenb.) Willd., **Livid Sedge**. The Livid Sedge is strictly confined to groundwater-fed fens. The foliage is blue-green with stiff leaf blades. In com-parison to *C. vaginata*, the bracts have shorter sheaths, female spikes are not widely spaced, the perigynia are beakless and the lower peduncles are rarely long.

Carex vaginata Tausch

Eleocharis erythropoda Steud.
Creeping Spike-rush

CYPERACEAE (Sedge Family)

Syn.: *E. palustris* var. *calva* (Torr.) Gray
Other Common Names: Spike-rush

Eleocharis is from the Greek terms *elos* (a marsh) and *charis* (grace).

Wetland
Perennial
Native
Common
Hardiness Zone: 0
Flowering Season: summer

DESCRIPTION

Dark green stems (10–100 cm tall) are circular in cross-section, wiry and erect, growing from stiff, creeping rhizomes. Stems are clustered, forming tufts. A collar-like sheath (a reduced **leaf** blade) wraps around the base of the leafless stems. The sheath is sometimes reddish towards base.

Narrow **flower** spike (5–20 mm long) is solitary on the top of a simple stem. From 1–3 broad sterile scales are at the base of the spike. Above these are fertile scales which have a distinct midrib and are usually narrower and sharper. Scales are overlapping in a spiralling pattern. Flowers consist of 4 bristles (the perianth), 1–3 stamens, and a 2-cleft style.

Fruit is a smooth, yellow to brown, lens-shaped achene (1.5 mm long) with a raised tubercle (an enlarged style) at the top.

Eleocharis erythropoda Steud.

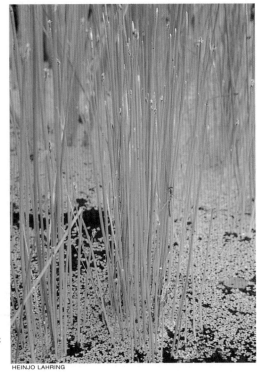

Eleocharis erythropoda

HEINJO LAHRING

HABITAT AND DISTRIBUTION

Eleocharis erythropoda is a very stiff and compact Spike-rush of aquatic and semi-aquatic locations. It can be found in areas which are seasonally wet such as ditches, mud flats and lake shorelines.

Distribution is circumpolar. The spike-rush's ability to tolerate a wide range of environmental conditions is reflected in fact that this plant can be found in wetlands throughout the Prairie provinces from east to west and north to south.

SPECIAL FEATURES

Creeping Spike-rush rapidly colonizes disturbed soils by the tillering nature of the rhizomes. For this reason, and its ability to withstand varying moisture levels, it is excellent for stabilizing shorelines and drainage channels. Over the long term it plays an important role in succession as ponds age and disappear.

Muskrats and birds will use the plants for food.

A related species (*E. dulcis*) of Rhodesia known as 'Masungu' was used for making salt.

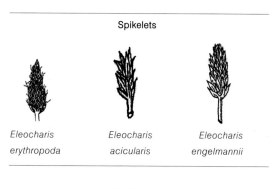

Eleocharis acicularis

RELATED SPECIES

Even at close inspection spike-rushes may look very much alike. *Eleocharis* species are best identified by using flower, achene and tubercle characters. *Eleocharis erythropoda* is one of the most commonly encountered species in the Prairie provinces. Another spike-rush with a '2-cleft style' is the **Engelmann's Spike-rush**, *Eleocharis engelmannii* Steud. This spike-rush is an annual. Its spikes are more oval than *E. erythropoda* and has 5–7 perianth bristles. It is very common in southern Saskatchewan in sloughs and tilled fields which dry up in midsummer (the crop either never having been sown for wetness or having been drowned out from summer rains).

A rush with a '3-cleft style' which is common in the region is the **Needle Spike-rush**, *Eleocharis acicularis* (L.) R. & S.. It forms short (up to 10 cm tall), dense mats and has small (2–7 mm long), flattened spikes.

Spikelets

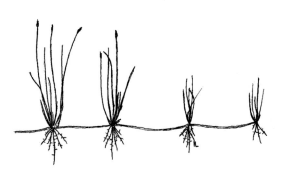

| *Eleocharis erythropoda* | *Eleocharis acicularis* | *Eleocharis engelmannii* |

Achenes

tubercle

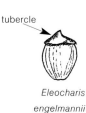

| *Eleocharis erythropoda* | *Eleocharis acicularis* | *Eleocharis engelmannii* |

Key to *Eriophorum*

(adapted from Crow and Hellquist, 2000)

1. Spikelet solitary, erect, not subtended by involucral bracts

  2. Plants with creeping rhizomes, stems solitary; sterile scales at base of spikelet 7 or fewer

    3. Perianth bristles bright white; scales narrow, tapering to tip,
    blackish green ....*E. scheuchzeri*
    ONE-SPIKE COTTON-GRASS

    3. Perianth bristles cinnamon brown to reddish (rarely white); scales broad,
    slightly rounded at tip, brownish to blackish ....*E. russeolum*
    RUSSET COTTON-GRASS

  2. Plants densely cespitose, not spreading by rhizomes; sterile scales at base of spikelet usually 10–15

    4. Cauline sheath with conspicuous white margin (becoming straw-coloured on drying); scale pale-margined, with pigmentation strongest near lower middle, divergent or reflexed; achenes 2.5–3.5 mm long ....*E. vaginatum*
    SHEATHED COTTON-GRASS

    4. Cauline sheath lacking white margin; scales with pigmentation stronger toward margin, weaker toward lower middle, ascending; achenes 2–2.3 mm long.

      5. Stems slender, 30–60 cm long; perianth bristles dull white; uppermost cauline sheath located above middle of stem, scarcely inflated....................*E. brachyantherum*
      CLOSE-SHEATHED COTTON-GRASS

      5. Stems thick, 6–20 cm long; perianth bristles bright white; uppermost cauline sheath typically located below middle of stem, conspicuously inflated ....*E. callitrix*
      BEAUTIFUL COTTON-GRASS

1. Spikelets 2–several, drooping or spreading, subtended by 1–several involucral leaves

  6. Involucral bracts 1, not extending beyond inflorescence, inflorescence appearing lateral; leaves triangular, channeled

    7. Uppermost cauline leaf with blade shorter than sheath; scales lead-coloured to blackish; achenes 1.5–2 mm long ....*E. gracile*
    SLENDER COTTON-GRASS

    7. Uppermost cauline leaf with blade as long as or longer than sheath; scales greenish to reddish brown; achenes 2.5–3 mm long ....*E. tenellum*
    FILIFORM COTTON-GRASS

  6. Involucral bracts 2 or more, extending beyond inflorescence, inflorescence appearing terminal; leaves flat (at least below middle)

    8. Spikelets densely crowded, spreading on short peduncles; perianth bristles tawny, at least at base; scales brownish to reddish, the lower with 3–5 nearly equally strong nerves ....*E. virginicum*
    VIRGINIA COTTON-GRASS

    8. Spikelets loosely clustered, nodding on slender, elongate peduncles; perianth bristles white or creamy to buff; scales drab to lead-coloured or blackish, with 1 strong nerve

      9. Scales with strong midrib extending to tip; upper leaf sheath lacking dark margin ....*E. viridicarinatum*
      THIN-LEAVED COTTON-GRASS

      9. Scales with strong midrib not extending to tip; upper leaf sheath with dark margin ....*E. angustifolium*
      NARROW-LEAVED COTTON-GRASS

Eriophorum gracile (p. 121)
Slender Cotton-grass
HEINJO LAHRING

Eriophorum angustifolium (p. 121)
Narrow-leaved Cotton-grass
HEINJO LAHRING

119

Eriophorum viridicarinatum (Engelm.) Fern.   CYPERACEAE (Sedge Family)
Thin-leaved Cotton-grass

Other Common Names: Cotton-grass

Eriophorum is Greek for wool (*erion*) bearing (*phero*) and is alluding to the aspect of the inflorescence. *Viridi* means green and *carinatum* is keeled.

Wetland
Perennial
Native
Common
Hardiness Zone: 0
Flowering Season: mid-summer

DESCRIPTION

The thin, flat, 2–7 mm-wide **leaves** of this Cotton-grass are mostly basal (some may be cauline) and grass-like (30–90 cm tall). The green culms are sometimes brownish at their base and may be either solitary or form small tufts.

The **flowers** are held in closely arranged spikelets which form a drooping head. Two to 3 leaf-like bracts extend from the base of the head. Flowers (in 6 parts), which are in the axil of a scale, contain both male and female parts. Long, slender bristles (modified sepals), attached at the base of the flowers, give the flower head the appearance of a 'cotton ball.'
Fruit is a long-bristled 3-sided achene.

Eriophorum viridicarinatum
(Engelm.) Fern.

HABITAT AND DISTRIBUTION

Thin-leaved Cotton-grass is found in boggy woods, wet meadows, and cold swamps. It is often found interspersed with sedges and wetland grasses in shallow standing water.

Eriophorum is definitely a plant of the north and becomes a very dominant part of the landscape the farther one heads into the boreal forest and on into the tundra. Distribution is from the parkland belt northward, across the boreal forest and into other regions where conditions are suitable.

SPECIAL FEATURES

In areas where large quantities of Cotton-grass grow, mice will gather it for nest building and put away significant amounts for winter reserves. Historically it is said that Native peoples would raid these caches to secure the seed and roots.

Eriophorum viridicarinatum

BARRE HELLQUIST

Scale

Eriophorum angustifolium

Eriophorum viridicarinatum

The Alaskan Inuit peeled the lower stem and rhizome of Slender Cotton-grass (*E. angustifolium*) and used it as food.

RELATED SPECIES

Several species of *Eriophorum* can be found across the Prairie provinces. Some are quite rare such as *E. callitrix* Cham., **Beautiful Cotton-grass** (restricted to alpine bogs). *Eriophorum angustifolium* Honck., **Narrow-leaved Cotton-grass**, can be mistaken for *E. viridicarinatum* but has slightly wider leaves (3–6 mm) and flower head bracts which often blacken at the base. *Eriophorum angustifolium* has anthers 3–4 mm long whereas in *E. viridicarinatum* they are only 1–1.5 mm long. Slender Cotton-grass extends into the prairie in groundwater bogs. [syn. *E. polystachion* L.]

Eriophorum brachyantherum Trautv. & C. A. Mey., **Close-sheathed Cotton-grass**, is found in calcareous bogs, and muskeg of the boreal forest. [*E. vaginatum* var. *opacum* Bjornstr.]

Eriophorum gracile Koch, **Slender Cotton-grass**, inhabits muskeg, swamps and bogs of the boreal forest.

Eriophorum russeolum Fries, **Russet Cotton-grass**, often forms extensive colonies on wet peats and is found across northern Canada including Alberta and Manitoba. [*E. chamissonis* C. A. Mey. pro parte; *E. chamissonis* var. *aquatile* (Norman) Fern.]

Eriophorum scheuchzeri Hoppe, **One-spike Cotton-grass**, is known from wet peats of arctic regions, muskegs and fens of the boreal forest. Range includes Saskatchewan and western Alberta.

Eriophorum tenellum Nutt., **Filiform Cotton-grass**, occurs in bogs, conifer swamps and peaty soils. Its range extends eastward from Saskatchewan to Labrador and Newfoundland, and as far south as Tennesee and Georgia.

Eriophorum vaginatum L., **Sheathed Cotton-grass**, flowers in very early spring and can be found in bogs and marshes of the boreal forest. [*E. spissum* Fern.]

Eriophorum virginicum L., **Virginia Cotton-grass**, is found in bogs and peaty meadows from Manitoba eastward to Labrador and Newfoundland, and as far south as Tennesee and Georgia.

Eriophorum angustifolium

(See additional photos of *Eriophorum* on page 119.)

HEINJO LAHRING

Kobresia simpliciuscula (Wahlenb.) Mack.
Simple Bog-sedge

CYPERACEAE (Sedge Family)

This plant was named in honor of Von Kobres, a nobleman of Augsburg and patron of botany in Willdenow's time. The undivided, unbranched habit of this plant gives rise to the epithet *simpliciuscula* (simple).

Wetland
Perennial
Native
Rare
Hardiness Zone: 0
Flowering Season: mid-summer

DESCRIPTION

Kobresia simplisciuscula has short (10–35 cm), green (cinnamon brown at base), filiform **leaf** blades which form dense tufts.

Flowers are either pistillate, and found at the top of the spike, or staminate (with 3 stamens) and found near the bottom. Both are often found on the same plant. These are arranged on a terminal, ovoid to compound spike atop a stiff, slender, triangular culm which is slightly higher than the leaves.

The **fruiting** body is an achene (2.5–3 mm long) with a short beak enclosed in a perigynium. These plants differ from *Carex* in that in *Kobresia* the perigynium is only partially fused (i.e., the perigynia is open along one side and looks like another scale).

HABITAT AND DISTRIBUTION

The Simple Bog-sedge is restricted to montane elevations of western Alberta. As the name implies it prefers boggy habitats and grows in calcareous bogs and muskegs as well as open mountain slopes.

Distribution is circumpolar. It is known to occur in the Rocky Mountains as well as near Hudson Bay.

RELATED SPECIES

A second species of Bog-sedge which can be found in the region is *K. myosuroides* (Vill.) F. & P., **Bog Sedge** or **Bellard's Kobresia**. It has more linear, undivided spikes. The enveloping glume is larger (3–3.5 mm) and the achene is slightly smaller (2.5 mm long) than *K. simplisciuscula*. Its range is restricted to the mountain slopes of the Rocky Mountains.

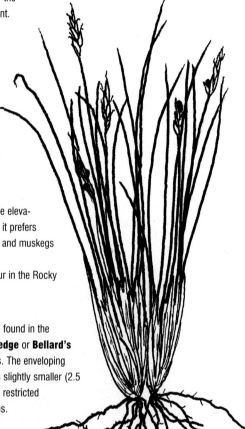

Kobresia simpliciuscula (Wahlenb.) Mack.

Rhynchospora capillacea Torr.　　　　　　**CYPERACEAE (Sedge Family)**

Slender Beak-rush

Other Common Names: Beak Rush

The 'Beak' of Beak-rush refers to the small tubercle on the end of the achene. *Rhynchospora* is composed of the Greek *rynchos* (snout) and *spora* (seed), referring to the beaked seed. The species epithet, *capillacea*, means 'slender as a hair' and describes the narrow, hair-like foliage.

Wetland
Perennial
Native
Rare
Hardiness Zone: 1
Flowering Season: early summer

DESCRIPTION

Rhynchospora grows in dense tufts with narrow bristle-like **leaves** 10–40 cm tall. Rhizomes are absent and the main spread is by narrowly linear, bud-like offsets (turions) at the base of the culm.

Flower stalks appear similar and equal to, or slightly shorter than, the foliage. Each flower stalk has 1–2 flower heads of which each contains 1–10 reddish brown spikelets (5–7 mm long). Spikelets have scales arranged in a spiral pattern. Each spikelet has 2–3 flowers which most often contain both male (with 3 stamens) and female flowers, but at times may be only male towards the top of the spike. The perianth is of 6 (rarely 12) barbed bristles.

Fruit is an achene 2–4 mm long with a granular surface. A long tubercle or beak on the top is almost the length of the fruit body.

HABITAT AND DISTRIBUTION

Slender Beak-rush is a rare plant. It grows in calcareous bogs, swamps and wet sands. It is known to occur in the boreal forest region of the Prairie provinces.

Rhynchospora capillacea Torr.

Plants range from Alberta to Newfoundland and as far south as Tennessee and Virginia.

SPECIAL FEATURES

Because of its rare nature, this plant does not seem to have been used in abundance by Native Americans. However, *R. cyperoides*, a related species growing in the Dominican Republic, was called wild quinine locally and used for curing fever. In Puerto Rico the same plant can be found. Here, the achenes are boiled and used to treat toothache by the local people.

RELATED SPECIES

Rhynchospora alba (L.) Vahl, **White Beak-rush**, is another Beak-rush found in the Prairie provinces. Its flower head is whitish and matures brown. Perianth bristles are 10–12 in number.

Rhynchospora fusca (L.), **Brown Beak-rush**, Ait. f. is known from northwestern Saskatchewan's Cliff Lake and Lake Athabaska (south shore) regions. Its deep brown flower clusters are terminal (often compound) from 1 or 2 upper axils. Three of its perianth bristles (usually 6 total) equal or exceed the tubercle.

BARRE HELLQUIST

Rhynchospora capillacea

Key to *Scirpus*

(Looman and Best, 1979; Moss, 1983; Crow and Hellquist, 2000)

1. Culms terete; leaf blades small or inconspicuous

  2. Inflorescence of 1 terminal spikelet; involucral bract reduced to small scale next to spikelet

    3. Plants wiry, forming short (10–30 cm) dense tussocks; rhizomes lacking; spikelet lanceolate (3.5–6 mm long); perianth bristles 6 (twice the length of achene); midvein of lowest involucral bract prolonged into a blunt awn........*S. cespitosus*
                                 TUFTED BULRUSH/ DEER-HAIR SEDGE

    3. Plants slender and loosely tufted (5–17 cm tall); rhizomes slender; spikelet ovate (2–3 mm long) and blunt-tipped; perianth bristles absent; outermost involucral bract prolonged to more than 1/2 length of spikelet ....*S. pumilus*
                                   DWARF BULRUSH

  2. Inflorescence of more than 1 spikelet; involucral bract from less than to extending beyond the spikelet cluster

    4. Style 3-cleft; bristles 2–4 (5); spikelets all pedunculate ....*S. heterochaetus*
                                   SLENDER BULRUSH

    4. Style 2-cleft; bristles 6; spikelets, at least some of them, sessile and glomerulate (rarely all pedunculate)

      5. Inflorescence once compound, stiff, not long and hanging; spikelets (3–40) narrowly ellipsoid (8–10 mm long), usually solitary or in clusters of 2–7; achenes hidden by scales; scales usually a dull grayish brown with conspicuous bright brown spots, sometimes dark reddish brown, awns usually contorted (0.5–1.5 mm long); culms dark olive green and firm............*S. acutus*
                                   HARDSTEM BULRUSH

      5. Inflorescence with some of the primary rays split into secondary rays, long and hanging; spikelets 12–125 ovoid (5 mm long), usually solitary or in clusters of 2 or 3; achenes usually visible beyond scales; scales bright orange-brown, with obscure darker spots, awns nearly straight (0.2–1 mm long); culms pale green, soft and easily compressed ....*S. tabernaemontani*
                                   SOFTSTEM BULRUSH

1. Culms 3-angled; leaf blades small or large

  6. Leaf blades broad (flat or V-shaped)

    7. Perianth bristles much longer than scales, giving spikelets a woolly appearance

      8. Scales pale brown, reddish brown, or sometimes blackish; achenes maturing in early August to September...*S. cyperinus*
                                   WOOL-GRASS

      8. Scales usually blackish; achenes maturing in late June and early July.....*S. atrocinctus*
                             BLACK-SCALED WOOL-GRASS

    7. Perianth bristles shorter than above, with spikelets not appearing woolly

      9. pikelets large (10–50 mm long and 5–11 mm wide) in short-peduncled clusters; culms sharpley 3-angled; rhizomes tuberous

        10. Style 2-branched; inflorescence appearing compact and congested; spikelets sessile or on peduncles to 5 cm long; achenes lens-shaped; preferring saline locations..*S. maritimus*
                                   PRAIRIE BULRUSH

        10. Style 3-branched; inflorescence comparatively open; spikelets sessile or on peduncles to 10 cm long; achenes triangular; preferring fresh to brackish water ....*S. fluviatilis*
                                   RIVER BULRUSH

Key (continued)

9. Spikelets small (2–25 mm long and 1–4(5) mm wide) in long-peduncled, large and spreading compound heads; culms obtusely 3-angled; rhizomes not tuberous

    11. Leaf sheaths and triangular culms with red-purple tinge; style 2-branched; achenes (1 mm) whitish and lens-shaped ....*S. microcarpus*
                          SMALL-FRUITED BULRUSH

    11. Leaf sheaths and triangular culms without red tinge; style 3-branched; achenes (1 mm) whitish and triangular shaped ....*S. atrovirens*
                          GREEN BULRUSH

6. Leaf blades narrow

    12. Inflorescence of 1 spike appearing terminal on stem; involucral bract equalling or slightly longer than spikelet

        13. Plants loosely tufted; rhizomes slender; spikelet ovoid (5–7 mm long); outer scale (bract) with blunt tip and shorter than to equalling spikelet, inner scale awnless; perianth bristles 6 (several times longer than achene); achenes 1.5 mm long, 3-sided and apiculate ....*S. hudsonianus*
                          ALPINE COTTON-GRASS

        13. Plants densely tufted; rhizomes short or absent; spikelet (4-5 mm long); outer scale (bract) prolonged with a blunt awn as long as spikelet, inner scales acute or obtuse; perianth bristles 3–6; achenes 1.2–2 mm long, obovoid and scarcely beaked ....*S. clintonii*
                          CLINTON'S BULRUSH

    12. Inflorescence of 2 (1) or more spikelets on side of stem; involucral bract relatively long and appearing as an extension of stem

        14. Culms tall (10–100 cm), sharply 3-angled

            15. Culms 10–80 cm tall; leaf blades 5–30 cm long, close to base, narrow, channeled (often spreading); flower head clustered with 1–5 reddish brown spikelets immediately next to stem; scales with apical notch; styles 2-cleft (rarely 3-cleft); involucral bract 5–20 cm long; perianth bristles 4; achenes (2) 2.4–3 mm long ....*S. pungens*
                          THREE-SQUARE RUSH

            15. Culms 40–100 cm tall; leaf blades 5–10 cm long, narrow and channeled; flower head clustered with 1–5 ovoid to cylindric spikelets (10–15 mm long); styles 3-cleft; involucral bract 3–15 cm long; perianth bristles 4; achenes 3–4 mm long...*S. torreyi*
                          TORREY'S THREE-SQUARE RUSH

        14. Culms shorter (10–50 cm), bluntly or less strongly angled than above

            16. Culms tufted; spikelets 2–5, flattened and arranged in two rows; chenes not appearing net-like..*S. rufus*
                          RED BULRUSH

            16. Culms stiffly erect, solitary or few-tufted; spikelets 2–10, not noticeably flattened or arranged in 2 rows; perianth bristles 1–3, minute; achenes net-like in appearance; rare ....*S. nevadensis*
                          NEVADA BULRUSH

Scirpus acutus Muhl. ex Bigel   **CYPERACEAE (Sedge Family)**

Hardstem Bulrush

Syn.: *Schoenoplectus acutus* (Muhl. ex Bigel) Love & Love

Other Common Names: Viscid Great Bulrush, Great Bulrush, Tule, Tules

Scirpus is Latin for rush. *Acutus* means sharpened into a narrow point, and describes the narrowly tapering leaves.

Emergent
Perennial
Native
Common
Hardiness Zone: 0
Flowering Season: summer

DESCRIPTION

The stiff, erect **leaves** of *S. acutus* are circular in cross-section, stand 0.5–3 m in height, and arise from a thick, spongy rhizome. The base of the olive green leaves are enclosed in a sheath which may have a short blade.

A 1–8 (to 15) cm long panicle forms near the top and to the side of the **flowering** stems. The involucral bract, at the base of the spikelets, appears as an extension of the stem. The inflorescence may be erect or spreading but rarely to the point of long and hanging as in *S. validus*. The inflorescence is once compound (2–7 sessile spikelets are borne at the ends of the primary rays of the inflorescence). The narrowly ellipsoid spikelets (to 8–10 mm long) are 3–40 flowered. Each flower consists of 2 or 3 stamens, a pistil with a 2–3 cleft style and a perianth of 1–6 bristles (variable in length).

Light brown **achenes** (1.5–3.0 mm long) become shiny black at maturity. Grayish brown flower scales have conspicuous bright brown spots (sometimes dark reddish brown), are narrowly ovate and much longer than the achenes (cf. *S. validus* below). Awns are usually contorted (0.5–1.5 mm long).

Scirpus acutus Muhl.

HABITAT AND DISTRIBUTION

Hardstem Bulrush grows in sloughs, marshes, lakeshores, and river banks. It is tolerant of fresh to moderately brackish waters. Bottom sediments may vary from organic mud to sand or gravel. The strongly growing rhizomes can extend into relatively deep water (1 m+).

This common plant of prairie, parkland, and boreal waterbodies is found across much of the Prairie provinces.

SPECIAL FEATURES

Seeds and rhizomes are eaten by waterfowl and muskrats. The stems are used by wildlife for nesting. In the shallows they provide shelter and spawning habitat for fish. Shoreline wave action and sediment movement are moderated by their presence.

It is a pioneering species in hard-bottom lakes.

All of the *Scirpus* group have rootstocks which were used for food by Native peoples. Young roots and shoots can be peeled and eaten raw. The pith (core) of

Scirpus acutus

HEINJO LAHRING

the rootstalk may be eaten throughout the year fresh, baked or dried (ground into flour). The thin rhizome has a pleasantly sweet taste and, when young, can be bruised and boiled in water to furnish a sweet syrup. Old rhizomes are very fibrous and less palatable. When in flower, the pollen can be gathered and used as is or mixed with flour for baking. Ripened seeds were prepared into a meal.

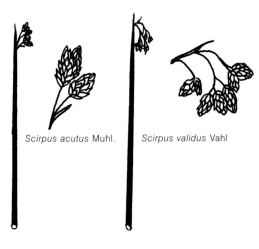

Scirpus acutus Muhl.   *Scirpus validus* Vahl

RELATED SPECIES

There are over 16 species of *Scirpus* found across the Prairie provinces; 5 of these have stems which are round in cross-section.

Scirpus acutus is easily confused with *S. validus*. At one time they were grouped taxonomically under one name, *S. lacustris* L. *Scirpus lacustris* is now used to describe only the Eurasian species.

Scirpus validus Vahl, the **Softstem Bulrush** or **Common Great Bulrush**, has soft spongy stems (easily compressed) which are light bluish green. The flower head is very long and drooping (1–6 cm long) with many of the primary rays of the inflorescence split into secondary rays before bearing spikelets. The spikelets (12–125) are ovoid (5 mm long) and in clusters of 2 or 3. The bright orange-brown flower scales are broad and slightly shorter than the achenes. The achenes are smaller in *S. validus* (1.4–2.2 mm) than in *S. acutus*. Awns are nearly straight (0.2 mm long). It tends to grow in shallower water (up to 0.5 m) than Hardstem Bulrush. [*Scirpus tabernaemontani* K. C. Gmel., *Schoenoplectus validus* (Vahl) Love & Love]

Scirpus cespitosus L., **Tufted Bulrush**, is a short (10–30 cm tall) boreal forest and tundra dweller which forms dense tussocks and lacks rhizomes. Its flower head consists of a single spikelet 3.5–6 mm long.

Scirpus heterochaetus Chase, **Slender Bulrush**, is known from calcareous shores of lakes, ponds and marshes of southern Manitoba. The range continues into Ontario and across the northern and central US. This plant is similar to the Eurasian *S. lacustris* L.
[*Schoenoplectus heterochaetus* (Chase) Sojak]

Scirpus pumilus Vahl, **Dwarf Bulrush**, is found in bogs and marshes of the boreal forest and parklands.

NOTE: *S. cespistosus* L. = *S. caespitosus* L.
   S. tabernaemontani K.C. Gmel. = *S. validus* Vahl

HEINJO LAHRING

HEINJO LAHRING

Above: *Scirpus acutus*
Left: *Scirpus validus*

(See additional photo of *Scirpus validus* on page 97.)

127

Scirpus microcarpus Presl
Small-fruited Bulrush

CYPERACEAE (Sedge Family)

Syn.: *S. rubrotinctus* Fern., *S. microcarpus* var. *rubrotinctus* (Fern.) M.E. Jones

The common name is a direct translation of the species epithet, *micro* (small) and *carpus* (fruit).

Wetland
Perennial
Native
Common
Hardiness Zone: 0
Flowering Season: mid-summer

DESCRIPTION

This is a flat-leafed bulrush with thick rhizomes. Blades (5–15 mm broad) are V-shaped towards base and 30–100 cm long. The **leaf** sheaths and triangular culms have a conspicuous red tinge.

The compound **flower** head is large, in contrast to other bulrushes. Below each spreading head are 3 leaf-like bracts, the lowest of which may extend beyond the head. Dark green to brown spikelets (3–6 mm long) are tightly grouped, with shorter clusters ascending and longer ones hanging. Perianth bristles are whitish and shorter than the scales. Style is 2-branched.

The **fruit** is a small (1 mm), whitish, lens-shaped achene.

HABITAT AND DISTRIBUTION

Small-fruited Bulrush grows in wet ditches, bogs, marshes, and swamps. It is tolerant of a wide range of growing conditions and, as such, may be found in prairie, parkland, and boreal forest wetlands.

Distribution extends beyond the Prairie provinces into the Territories, Alaska, and across to Kamchatka in the north, to Newfoundland in the east, California in the south, and West Virginia in the southeast.

Scirpus microcarpus Presl

SPECIAL FEATURES

Scirpus microcarpus is an important muskrat food and is used by birds for nesting. The roots can become quite interwoven and act as a soil binder along water courses preventing erosion. Seed heads are held above the snow and become an important winter food source for rodents and bird life.

HEINJO LAHRING

ALISON BAKKEN

Above inset: *Scirpus microcarpus* early flower head
Right: *Scirpus microcarpus*, later flower head

Scirpus cyperinus (L.) Kunth

RELATED SPECIES

Scirpus atrocinctus Fern., **Black-scaled Wool-Grass**, is known to grow and hybridize with *S. cyperinus* (also called Wool-grass). Its habitat includes disturbed areas as well as meadows, swamps, marshes and ditches. Its range extends across Canada.

Scirpus cyperinus (L.) Kunth, **Wool-grass**, has very scabrous flat (2–5 mm wide) and mostly basal leaves. It forms dense tufts to 1 m or more high. Spikelets (which have a woolly appearance, hence the name Wool-grass) are long-peduncled. Perianth bristles are longer than the scales. Its seeds are a favourite of waterfowl. Wool-grass is associated with sedge meadows, shallow marshes, bogs and roadside ditches.

Scirpus pallidus (Britt.) Fern.

Scirpus pallidus (Britt.) Fern., **Pale Bulrush** or **Green Bulrush**, is similar to *S. microcarpus* but differs in that it has a 3-branched style, lacks the conspicuous red-tinged sheaths, its leaf-like bracts are generally quite short, has long-peduncled spikelets and small, pale white triangular achenes. *Scirpus pallidus* tolerates seasonal flooding. [syn. *S. atrovirens* Willd. var. *pallidus* Britt.]

Two other commonly found species with flat blades are *S. fluviatilis* (Torr.) Gray, **River Bulrush** (rare in the west), and *S. maritimus* L. [syn. *S. paludosus* Nels.], **Prairie Bulrush**. These two differ from all of the above by having short peduncled-spikelets, the spikelets themselves are large (more than 10 mm long), and the rhizomes have swollen nodes. *Scirpus fluviatilis* has a 3-branched style (achenes are triangular) and *S. maritimus* a 2-branched style (achenes are lens-shaped). *Scirpus maritimus* does well in highly saline locations. Geese feed on the rhizomes and seeds of both species.

Scirpus maritimus L.

HEINJO LAHRING

Scirpus cyperinus

HEINJO LAHRING

Right: *Scirpus maritimus*
Below inset: *Scirpus maritimus,* roots

HEINJO LAHRING

Scirpus pungens Vahl

CYPERACEAE (Sedge Family)

Three-square Rush

Syn.: *Schoenoplectus pungens* (Vahl) Palla
Other Common Names: Three-square Bulrush

Pungens means sharp-pointed and refers to the sharp, stiff leaf culms.

DESCRIPTION

Three-square Rush has slender (at times twisted), 3-sided, green culms 10–80 cm tall. The shorter (5–30 cm) **leaf** blades are close to base, narrow, channeled and often spreading.

A single involucral bract appears to be continuous with the stem placing the **flower** head to the side of the culm. The tightly clustered flower head consists of 1–7 reddish brown spikelets (5–20 mm long) located immediately next to the stem. Perianth is of 4 bristles.

Grey to black **achenes** are smooth and 3 mm long.

HABITAT AND DISTRIBUTION

Three-square Rush is a food source for waterfowl and muskrats. It provides habitat for innumerable insect species and life stages as well as fish cover in shallow waters to 1 m. It has a preference for sandy areas such as lakeshores, streams and marshes. Stands occur in fresh to saline water conditions.

Distribution is throughout the Prairie provinces, beyond to Alaska in the west, Newfoundland in the east, and is common in the lower 48 states.

Emergent
Perennial
Native
Common
Hardiness Zone: 2
Flowering Season: mid–late summer

involucral
bract

Scirpus pungens Vahl

SPECIAL FEATURES

This rush is quite tolerant of brackish water conditions making it a suitable choice for shoreline plantings across the prairies. It is a rapid colonizer in the warmer parts of the region and develops into dense stands when conditions permit.

RELATED SPECIES

Scirpus clintonii Gray, **Clinton's Bulrush,** favors open woodland and woody shores. Its range includes Alberta and Saskatchewan, and extends from Ontario to New Brunswick and south to Minnesota, Michigan and New York.

Scirpus hudsonianus (Michx.) Fern., **Alpine Cotton-grass,** is closely related to *S. cespitosus.* Its habitat includes bogs, swamps, wet gravels and wet seepages. It prefers calcareous areas of the boreal forest and Rocky Mountains. [*Eriophorum alpinum* L.]

Scirpus nevadensis Wats., **Nevada Bulrush,** is similar to *S. pungens* but quite rare. It is found on riverflats and lakeshores (often brackish waters) of the western prairie and parklands. Its stiffly erect leaves (unlike the spreading leaves of *S. pungens*) stand solitary or few-tufted (30–50 cm high) from creeping rhizomes. Culms are not as strongly 3-angled as Three-square Rush. The flower head has 2–10 spikelets. Achenes have a net-like appearance.

Scirpus rufus (Huds.) Schrad., **Red Bulrush,** prefers saline marshes (although sometimes in freshwater areas rich in peat) of the boreal forest and parklands. It is known from the eastern Manitoba (Hudson Bay) and the Territories to the north. Its range extends eastward to the Atlantic provinces including P.E.I. [*Blysmus rufus* (Huds.) Link, *Schoenus rufus* (Huds.) Schrad.]

Scirpus torreyi Olney, **Torrey's Three-square Rush,** is found in sandy and peaty shoreline areas (fresh or brackish waters). Its range includes Manitoba and extends eastward to New Brunswick, south into the northeastern states and on to Virginia and Missouri.

Scirpus pungens

HEINJO LAHRING

Juncus arcticus Willd.

JUNCACEAE (Rush Family)

Arctic Rush

Syn.: *J. balticus* Willd., *J. arcticus* Willd. ssp. *balticus* (Willd.) Hyl.
Other Common Names: Baltic Rush, Wire Rush

Juncus is a classical name for this cosmopolitan genus. *Arcticus* describes its northern range.

Emergent
Perennial
Native
Common
Hardiness Zone: 0
Flowering Season: summer

DESCRIPTION

Narrow, wire-like and sharply pointed, deep green stems (20–60 cm tall) stand erect from thin, creeping rhizomes. The base of the stems have a brownish, paper-like sheath 8–15 cm long. The sheath is a very reduced **leaf** which is open without any tongue-like or blade-like extentions. The brown, somewhat drooping **flower** head is terminal with a single erect involucral bract. The bract is shorter than the stem and appears to be a continuation of the stem. The 2–4 cm head is loosely branched with many flowers. Each flower consists of 6 small, purplish brown scales in 2 similar-looking whorls (calyx and corolla), 3 or 6 stamens, 3 stigmas, and a superior ovary. Three or more **seeds** (0.8–1 mm long) are contained within a small chestnut brown capsule (5 mm long).

Juncus arcticus Willd.

HABITAT AND DISTRIBUTION

Arctic Rush is a true rush of wet meadows and bogs. It grows in ditches which seasonally flood and retain adequate moisture for much of the year.

This is the most frequently encountered rush of the Prairie provinces. Its distribution is circumpolar and can be found as far north as the tundra of the Territories eastward to Hudson Bay, northern Quebec and Newfoundland.

SPECIAL FEATURES

The thickened plant bases are used by muskrats for food and the seeds are eaten by upland birds. Stands, at times, cover large areas where it provides food and shelter for wetland wildlife. It is very tolerant of a wide range of soil and water conditions.

RELATED SPECIES

There are at least 23 different species of *Juncus* found in the Prairie provinces. Most species occur in wet areas and a few prefer woodland or grassland locations.

PAT PORTER

Only two *Juncus* species of low elevations appear to have the flower head on the side of the stem and with the leaves reduced to basal sheaths. These are *J. arcticus* and *J. filiformis.*

Juncus filiformis L., **Thread Rush**, is slightly smaller and thinner than the Arctic Rush, has green flowers and a flower head bract that is nearly as long as the stem or longer. Thread Rush is quite common in Saskatchewan.

Juncus arcticus

Juncus nodosus L.
Knotted Rush

JUNCACEAE (Rush Family)

Juncus is a classical name for this cosmopolitan genus. *Nodosus* means knotted or knobby and refers to the tuber-like thickenings on the roots.

DESCRIPTION

Emergent
Perennial
Native
Common
Hardiness Zone: 0
Flowering Season: summer

This short (10–40 cm) rush has erect, thin, pointed **leaves** which are circular in cross-section with septations (i.e., cross-partitioning) along its length. Leaves arise individually from slender creeping rhizomes. Rhizomes form tuber-like thickenings between nodes.

The spherical, light to mid-brown, prickly **flower** head (7–10 mm wide) appears to be terminal on the stem. Flower head, often more than one per stem, contains 8–20 flowers. Flowers are 3–4 mm long and pointed. Each consists of 3 sepals and 3 petals (both scale-like and similar).

Fruit is a small multi-seeded capsule which splits open when mature. Nonwinged seeds are about 0.5 mm across.

Seeds

◄— wing

Juncus nodosus L.

HABITAT AND DISTRIBUTION

Knotted Rush can be found in bogs, marshes, stream shallows and lakeshores. Water conditions vary from moist soil to several inches over the creeping rhizomes.

Juncus canadensis *Juncus nodosus*

Plants occur across all three Prairie provinces inhabiting prairie, parkland, and boreal forest regions.

SPECIAL FEATURES

This is a low growing rush which rapidly colonizes wet areas. As such, it is particularly useful in stabilizing sandy or muddy areas thereby helping to reduce erosion.

The tuberous growths on Knotted and Torrey's Rush assist the plant in surviving periods of drought and flooding. These are eaten by waterfowl. The large seed heads are also a source of food for birds and small mammals.

Juncus torreyi

HEINJO LAHRING

The flower heads are very attractive and make an excellent addition to floral bouquets.

RELATED SPECIES

Canada Rush, *J. canadensis* J. Gray, is similar to Knotted Rush but is taller (40–100 cm tall), has more flower heads (5–50), the mature fruit and perianth is 2.5–5 mm long, and the seeds are winged (two thirds to as long as body length). It is known from the northeastern parkland and boreal forest.

Torrey's Rush, *J. torreyi* Coville, is another rush taller (40–100 cm) than Knotted Rush. It has dark brown spiky flowerheads (10–15 mm wide). The roots also have tuberous thickenings. Torrey's Rush is found in warmer areas than Knotted Rush and therefore tends to be restricted to the southern prairies and parkland.

134

—SPERMATOPHYTA—
DICOTS
SHRUBS

- woody vascular plants reproducing by seeds
- embryo with 2 cotyledons (seed leaves)
- flower parts in 5s or 4s
- stems with central pith, vascular bundles in a ring (cambium present)
- leaves usually net-veined

Lonicera involucrata (p. 168)
Bracted Honeysuckle
HEINJO LAHRING

Salix amygdaloides Andersson
Peach-leaved Willow

Salix arbusculoides Andersson
Shrubby Willow

Salix brachycarpa Nuttal
Short-capsuled Willow

Salix candida Fluegge ex Willdenow
Hoary Willow

Salix commutata Bebb
Changeable Willow

Salix discolor Muhlenberg
Pussy Willow

Salix drummondiana Barratt in Hooker
Drummond's Willow

Salix lasiandra Bentham
Pacific Willow

Salix maccalliana Rowlee
Velvet-fruited Willow

Salix monticola Bebb
Mountain Willow

Salix pedicellaris Pursh
Bog Willow

Salix petiolaris J.E. Smith
Basket Willow

Salix planifolia Pursh
Flat-leaved Willow

Salix pyrifolia Andersson
Balsam Willow

Salix rigida Muhlenberg
Mackenzie Willow

Salix serissima (Bailey) Fernald
Autumn Willow

Salix bebbiana Sarg.

SALICACEAE (Willow Family)

Beaked Willow

Syn.: *S. rostrata* Richardson, *S. depressa* L. ssp. *rostrata* (Richardson) Hiitonen

Other Common Names: Bebb's Willow, Long-beaked Willow, Gray Willow

Salix is a classical Latin name. This willow is named after Michael Schuck Bebb (1833–1895), an Illinois *Salix* specialist and author of *Botany of Northern and Middle States—1853*.

Wetland
Deciduous Shrub
Native
Common
Hardiness Zone: 0
Flowering Season: spring

DESCRIPTION

Slender and intertangled branches grow vertically to 3.5 m tall.
Leaves (1–1.5 cm wide x 4–8 cm long) are green on top with a whitish, waxy bloom below, narrowly oblanceolate (tapering at both ends), hardly toothed, and edges more or less undulate. Petioled (more than 3 mm) leaves have some hairiness when young but soon become glabrous. Leaf bracts are tawny coloured.

Flowers are borne in ovoid to cylindrical catkins. Catkins are of two types, each occurring on separate plants before (or while) leaves appear in early spring. A few small leaves appear on the catkin stalk beneath the flowers. Male catkins (2–3 cm long) have light brown bracts and 2 stamens (hairy at base). Female catkins (3–5 cm long) consist of an elongated capsule held upon a thin 2–5 mm long stipe (longer than the bract). Stigma on top of capsule is short and often bifid.

Fruit is a hairy bivalved capsule (4–6 mm long), held on a slender stalk (half as long as capsule), containing several seeds. Seeds have a coma of fine hairs allowing for wind dispersal.

HABITAT AND DISTRIBUTION

Beaked Willow is a very common willow of wetland areas. It often grows into dense thickets in marshes, swamps, wet meadows, beaver ponds, ditches and along watercourses. It does well in lime-rich areas and is tolerant of drier locations such as upland forests.

This is a widely occurring willow found across the Prairie provinces, with distribution from the Atlantic to the Pacific and beyond into Eurasia.

Salix bebbiana Sarg.

SPECIAL FEATURES

Salix bebbiana is one of the better 'diamond willow' types. After being damaged, by browsers such as moose, fungal attack or heavy snowfalls, scarred wood heals over forming a characteristic diamond pattern. This wood is prized in making handicrafts and furniture.

Browsers such as hares, moose and deer use this willow extensively as a year-round food source. Thickets provide protection for nesting birds and smaller wildlife.

The Dene Indians used the inner bark for tobacco, the shredded bark for making cordage and fishing nets and lines. Peeled sticks were used for arrow-shaft and basket weaving. Tubes of willow bark were fashioned into drinking straws or children's whistles. Dried bark and catkins make excellent tinder for starting fires.

Young leaves, buds, and catkins, rich in vitamin C, are used in salads or boiled (to remove the bitterness) and used as cooked vegetables. Inner fibers of bark can be used as an emergency food.

RELATED SPECIES

In southern Saskatchewan, if a willow of good size has catkins before the leaves, the catkins being sessile on old wood, it is likely not Bebb's Willow but, rather, *S. discolor* Muhlenberg (**Pussy Willow**).

COLIN STONE

COLIN STONE

Salix bebbiana

Salix exigua ssp. *exigua* Nutt.

SALICACEAE (Willow Family)

Sandbar Willow

Syn.: *S. interior* var. *wheeleri* Rowlee

Other Common Names: Coyote Willow, Ditchbank Willow, Narrow-leaf Willow

Salix is a classical Latin name. *Exigua* comes from the term *exiguus* and means weak, feeble, or little.

Wetland
Deciduous Shrub
Native
Common
Hardiness Zone: 0
Flowering Season: early spring–late summer

DESCRIPTION

Plants form dense thickets of very long, thin, erect branches and may, at times, become tree-like. Short-petioled, green (above and below) **leaves** are very long (to 15 cm), narrow (5–20 times as long as wide) and often somewhat hairy on both sides. Leaf margins are more or less parallel to each other and smooth, or with evenly spaced, shallow teeth. Leaf ends are sharply tapered.

Flowers are borne in catkins on leafy side-branchlets and produced before spring leaf-buds open, at the time new leaves are formed, and later throughout the growing season. Catkins are of two types, each occurring on separate plants. Male catkins (2–4 cm long by about 1 cm wide) have hairy yellowish bracts and 2 stamens (hairy at base). Female catkins (3–5) consist of pear-shaped (wide at base and narrow towards the top) capsules (4–7 mm long) held upon short, 0.5–1 mm long stipes (shorter than the bract). Stigma on top of the capsule is short and stout.

Fruit is a 3–8 mm long, short-stalked, hairy capsule. Several seeds are contained within. Each has a coma of fine hairs on one end, assisting in wind dispersal.

HABITAT AND DISTRIBUTION

Sandbar Willow is an often-encountered, drought-resistant willow of sandy lakeshores, slough margins, and river and stream floodplains. It spreads extensively from shallow underground roots to form dense clumps or colonies. This willow has one of the greatest distributions of all willows. Plants occur in Alaska, Yukon, British Columbia, all three Prairie provinces, and on across to New Brunswick in the east and as far south as Louisiana, Texas, and California.

Salix exigua ssp. *exigua* Nutt.

Salix exigua

HEINJO LAHRING

SPECIAL FEATURES

Salix exigua is heavily browsed by moose, deer, beavers, snowshoe hares, and muskrats.

Although roots can easily clog drainage systems, the rapid growth of Sandbar Willow makes it especially suited for planting along watercourses to prevent erosion.

The long, straight stems are excellent for willow furniture, basket weaving, whistles, hotdog sticks, and flexible fishing poles.

The bark and leaves give a good rose-tan or yellow dye.

Willow wood charcoal was at one time used in making gunpowder and for artists crayons.

As with other species of willows it was used as a herbal in treating fever and headaches (see *S. myrtillifolia,* page 142).

RELATED SPECIES

This is a very easily recognized willow because of its long, narrow leaves with parallel sides and preference for riverine areas. Taxonomic treatment varies with the three subspecies recognized (see the following), or *S. exigua* ssp. *interior* and *S. exigua* ssp. *melanopsis* each considered separate species, or all three grouped as *S. exigua.*

Salix exigua ssp. *interior* (Rowlee) Cronquist has long (5–8 mm), more or less hairless capsules on a short stipe. Leaves are greater than 6 mm wide. Catkins are loose and long (up to 8 cm).

Salix exigua ssp. *melanopsis* (Nuttall) Cronquist is very much the same as *S. exigua* ssp. *exigua* but has relatively wider leaves which are hairless and glabrescent when mature. Bracts are blunt. Capsules are hairless.

Salix exigua ssp. *pedicellata* (Andersson) Cronquist has short (3–5 cm long), hairless capsules without a stipe. Leaves are less than 6 mm wide. Catkins are short (3–5 cm long).

Salix myrtillifolia Anderss.   **SALICACEAE (Willow Family)**

Myrtle-leaved Willow

Syn.: *S. pseudocordata* (Anderss.) Rydb.
Other Common Names: Blueberry Willow

Salix is a classical Latin name. *Myrtillifolia* is a compound word with *Myrtilli* meaning Myrtle-like and *folia* meaning leaf.

Wetland
Deciduous Shrub
Native
Common
Hardiness Zone: 0
Flowering Season: spring to early summer

DESCRIPTION

This low (10–100 cm) shrub has short, erect branches growing from trailing stems (rooting along their length). Green to reddish brown branchlets are sparsely covered with short, curved hairs. Finely toothed (often glandular) **leaves** are short (1–5 cm) and narrowly elliptic with a fairly blunt tip and rounded base. Upper leaf surface is green (some hairiness may be on midvein) and lower is pale green.

Catkins appear with the leaves and are of two kinds (male on one plant and female on another). Both are held noticeably upright on short, leafy branchlets. Male catkins are small (1.5–2.5 cm long) with 2 glabrous stamens per flower. Female catkins are slightly longer (2–3 cm) with short-stiped (0.6–1.6 mm) glabrous capsules. Bract at base of capsule and stamens is short (1 mm) and usually (but not always) hairy.

Fruit is a many-seeded capsule. Seeds have a coma of fine hairs on one end assisting in wind dispersal.

Salix myrtillifolia Anderss.

HABITAT AND DISTRIBUTION

Myrtle-leaved Willow is a plant of bogs, moist coniferous forests, floodplains, lake and stream banks, and fens.

Distribution is across the Prairie provinces. Range extends into the Territories and Alaska in the northwest and Ontario in the east. This is a frequently encountered willow of Alberta's foothills and mountain wetlands. It is a northern willow and does not range too far into the south.

SPECIAL FEATURES

Wildlife such as deer, moose, elk and hare browse on the twigs.

Leaves and buds are rich in vitamin C.

Willows are among the most important first aid plants of the wilderness. The value as a medicinal herb lies in the glucosides *salicin* and *populin* as well as the commonly present *tannin*. About 170 years ago salicin, a compound of salicylic acid (similar to the active ingredient in today's aspirin), was isolated and found to be the reason it worked so well in treating fevers, headaches, neuralgia, and hayfever. It can be obtained from the twigs, bark, leaves or roots. Most species are not particularily potent and a fair amount of bark or stem is needed. Native peoples chewed the bitter tasting bark. The bark and roots were used in a remedy to control bleeding. Willow bark is a strong, but benign, antiseptic. A strong wash or poultice was made from the fresh or dried leaves. For infected wounds, ulcerations, or eczema, the plant should be boiled in twice its volume of water in a covered pot for at least half an hour with some borax or boric acid added (1 teaspoon to a pint of water) and the resulting tea used externally as often as necessary.

RELATED SPECIES

There are two distinct varieties of *S. myrtillifolia*. Intermediates apparently occur in the western part of their range.

Salix myrtillifolia var. *myrtillifolia* Anderss. is a short (20–40 cm) form which grows in wet black spruce woods like an Ericoid.

Salix myrtillifolia var. *pseudomyrsinites* (Anderss.) Ball is a tall (100–150 cm) form which grows in calcareous groundwater bogs. [syn. *S. m.* var. *cordata* (Anderss.) Dorn.]

Myrica gale L.

MYRICACEAE (Bayberry Family)

Sweet Gale

Other Common Names: Meadow-fern, Sweet Willow, Dutch Myrtle

Myrica is derived from the Greek word *myrike*, meaning fragrant and is in reference to the scented leaves. *Gale* is from *galea*, meaning helmet-shaped.

Wetland
Deciduous Shrub
Native
Common
Hardiness Zone: 0
Flowering Season: spring

DESCRIPTION

This small (to 1.5 m tall) shrub has upright, brown branches. Stems are hairy and dotted with glands. Alternate, fragrant, wedge-shaped **leaves** (2.5–6 cm long) are dotted above and below with yellow glands. Leaf margins are smooth near base but gradually become toothed towards the tip.

Tiny **flowers** are borne in dense catkins which appear before leaves. Male and female catkins are usually (but not always) on different plants. Plants of one year may produce catkins of the opposite sex the next year. Male catkins (1–2 cm long) have closely arranged flowers and large, brown bracts. Male flowers have 4–16 stamens. Female catkins are about 1 cm long and round. Female flowers have two styles on a 1-loculed ovary, and 2 small bractlets at the base.

Fruit is a gland-dotted nutlet, subtended by two corky bracts. Nutlets are held in what resembles a tight ovoid cone (1 cm in diam.). Seeds are dispersed by water, floating on their 2 bracts.

Myrica gale L.

HABITAT AND DISTRIBUTION

Sweet Gale forms dense, low thickets in the boreal forest. It can be found growing in shallow water of peat bogs, muskeg, swamps, streams, and the stony margins of lakes.

Plants occur in northern Alberta, northern Saskatchewan, and northern to southern Manitoba. Range extends well across the north to Alaska and northeast Asia in the west, to Newfoundland and northwestern Europe in the east, and the Great Lakes and Appalachians in the south.

SPECIAL FEATURES

The dense growth provides cover for many species of wildlife. Deer browse on the leaves and twigs, and birds such as grouse, catbirds, chickadees, crows and blue birds eat the seeds.

Root nodules contain bacteria which live in symbiosis, fixing nitrogen for the plant.

The fragrance of the leaves is quite noticeable when the leaves are crushed. These can be used for making tea. Native peoples used the dried leaves and ground nutlets for seasoning stews and roasts (similar to sage). The boiled seeds and buds produce a yellow dye.

The aromatic resin contained in the leaves and fruits is known as an emetic and purgative. The Chipewyan used it as a laxative. An overdose can cause digestive and nervous disorders; therefore, it should be consumed in small amounts.

In western Europe it was traditionally employed for flavouring beer before hops came into use. In England it is still occasionally used for this purpose. The fruit is covered with a white wax. When boiled in water the wax was skimmed off of the surface and used in making candles. The dried plant was useful in storing linen, since it was found to repel flies and moths.

RELATED SPECIES

There is only one species of *Myrica* in Canada (the only other species in North America occurs in California). The catkin-bearing nature of the plant makes it similar to the willows, but it differs in having a 1-seeded nutlet (willows have a many-seeded capsule), seeds which are not hairy (willow seeds have a coma of hairs at their base), and multiple leaf-bud scales (willows have only one large bud scale).

Alnus tenuifolia Nutt.

BETULACEAE (Birch Family)

River Alder

Syn.: *A. incana* (L.) Moench ssp. *tenuifolia* (Nutt.) Breitung
Other Common Names: Thinleaf Alder, Mountain Alder,
Western River Alder

Alnus is an ancient Latin name. *Tenuifolia* describes the thin (*tenui*)
leaves (*folia*) of this shrub.

Wetland
Deciduous Shrub
Native
Common
Hardiness Zone: 0
Flowering Season: early spring

DESCRIPTION

This tall (4 m), densely growing shrub or small tree has twigs covered in white speckles (lenticels). Winter buds (with several bud scales) are
on short stalks. Twigs have a 3-sided pith. Dull green **leaves** are alternate, oval (6–10 cm long by 3–4 cm wide), veins are not deeply
impressed above, somewhat hairy on veins beneath, and double-
toothed along the margins. Leaf base is rounded or slightly
wedge-shaped.

Flowers are in dense male or female catkins, both
found on the same plant, developing before the
leaves. The male catkin is long, hanging, scaly, and
clustered at the end of branches. Each main bract
consists of 2–4 bractlets plus 3 flowers. Male flowers have a 4-parted
calyx and 4 stamens. The smaller, oval, female catkin has fleshy bracts.
Each bract has 4 bractlets and 2 flowers (1 pistil and a 1–2-loculed ovary).
Fruits are 1-seeded, flat, wing-margined nutlets contained in an oval or

Alnus tenuifolia Nutt.

Alnus tenuifolia

oblong woody cone. Female bracts become woody and persistant. Cones from previous years often remain on plant.

HABITAT AND DISTRIBUTION

This alder occurs where water is readily available. It localizes in swamps, and along stream banks and lakeshores.

River Alder is restricted in distribution to the western part of the Prairie provinces. It can be found from Alaska to western Saskatchewan and as far south as Colorado and California.

SPECIAL FEATURES

The seeds are very important for overwintering birds such as Redpolls, Goldfinches, and Pine Siskins. Grouse feed on the buds and seeds. Beaver and hare eat the twigs and leaves. Moose and deer will feed on them occasionally but it is not preferred. River Alder's dense growth provides important cover for wildlife.

There is a symbiotic relationship with bacteria in root nodules which allows for nitrogen fixation.

Alders have been used by Native peoples in creating dyes of yellow-green (leaves), yellow-brown to red (inner bark), and brown (roots).

RELATED SPECIES

Alnus rugosa (Du Roi) Spreng., **Speckled Alder** is commonly found where the River Alder leaves off (the two merging together rather imperceptibly in Saskatchewan). *Alnus rugosa* occurs from Saskatchewan eastwards to the Atlantic coast and southward into the Great Lakes region. The leaves are thick textured with the veins deeply impressed above. River Alder may be a geographic variation of the Speckled Alder.

Alnus viridis (Villars) Lam. & DC., **Green Alder**, is more of a shrub than a tree. At times it may also be found growing in similar habitats as *A. rugosa* and *A. tenuifolia*, although it is usually considered an upland species growing in sand or light till. A few differentiating features include: broadly winged nutlets, the leaf buds are not on a stalk, flowers develop after leaves are on the tree, and the singly serrate leaves are shiny. [syn. *Alnus crispa* (Ait.) Pursh]

Alnus viridis catkins

HEINJO LAHRING

Betula glandulosa Michx.
Bog Birch

BETULACEAE (Birch Family)

Syn.: *Betula nana* L. var. *sibirica* Led.

Other Common Names: Dwarf Birch, Scrub Birch, Resin Birch

Betula is derived from the Celtic *betul*. *Glandulosa* refers to the glandbearing character of the branches.

Wetland
Deciduous Shrub
Native
Common
Hardiness Zone: 0
Flowering Season: spring

DESCRIPTION

This short (to 2 m), densely branched shrub has gray to dark brown branches covered with small, whitish resin glands. Alternating, toothed (less than 10 teeth per side), dark green **leaves** are circular (1–2 cm in diameter on 3–5 mm long petioles) and usually slightly longer than wide. Shiny leaves are quite thick and stiff with glandular dots and hairs beneath.

Flowers are formed on catkins, appearing with the leaves in the spring. Catkins are of two types and occur on the same plant. Male catkins (up to 2 cm long) tend to hang. Male flowers occur in threes (along with small bractlets) next to a large bract.

Betula glandulosa Michx.

Each has a 2–3-lobed calyx and 2 stamens. Female catkins are short (about 1 cm long). Two or 3 female flowers are formed in the axils of thin 3-lobed bracts. Female flowers have an ovary and 2 linear stigmas.

Fruit is a flat, winged (less than half the width of fruit) nutlet or samara (2–4 mm long). They are formed on cone-like catkins and are shed along with the papery bracts in spring.

HABITAT AND DISTRIBUTION

Bog Birch is an indicator of fen-like habitats and is only rarely found in bogs. It also grows in open conifer swamps, seepage areas, alpine slopes, subalpine forests, and along lakeshores.

Plant distribution is linked to the boreal forest zone of northern and central Alberta, Saskatchewan and Manitoba. The range extends from Alaska to Newfoundland, and beyond to Greenland and eastern Asia.

SPECIAL FEATURES

Bog Birch is a very important food plant for wildlife. Deer, elk, moose, hare, porcupine, and beaver browse heavily on the foliage and twigs, often keeping them very stunted and densely branched. The seeds are eaten

HEINJO LAHRING

Betula glandulosa

148

by smaller creatures such as chickadees, finches, sparrows, songbirds, chipmunks, squirrels and woodrats. Birch is an important survival plant. The young leaves can be added to salads for flavouring. The scented leaves, buds, twigs, and peeled-off bark (about 1 handful per person) are good for tea. The Chippewa used bark tea for stomach aches. The inner bark (i.e., the cambium) can be dried and ground up into flour for making bark bread. Birch sap (half as sweet as Maple sap) can be used for a sweetener as is, or boiled down to produce a syrup. It is best used in early spring when nights are still freezing and sap is running clear. Later when it turns milky it also becomes bitter.

The twigs are handy in basket making. The wood is good for making items such as snowshoe frames, spoons, brushes (split wood into strips), furniture, bows and arrows. Birch bark dyes wool light brown without mordant and green with copper sulfate. Dried bark and twigs (in particular the resinous parts) make excellent fire-starter.

RELATED SPECIES

Betula pumila L., **Swamp Birch**, is very closely related. It can be recognized by its pubescent and less glandular twigs and overall taller size (to 3 m). The leaves are larger (usually more than 10 teeth per side), and nutlet wings more than half the width of the nutlet.

HEINJO LAHRING

Betula glandulosa
resinous twigs

Sarcobatus vermiculatus (Hook.) Torr.   CHENOPODIACEAE (Goosefoot Family)

Greasewood

Sarcobatus is from the Greek terms *sarx* or *sarcos* (flesh) and *bato* (spine or bramble), meaning fleshy-spined and describes the succulent and spiny habit. *Vermiculatus* means worm-shaped and refers to being marked with irregular or bent lines.

> Wetland
> Perennial
> Native
> Common
> Hardiness Zone: 3
> Flowering Season: summer

DESCRIPTION

Greasewood is a spiny, shrub-like plant growing to 3 m tall. Yellowish white stems (to 2.5 cm in dia.) become woody with age. Alternate, narrowly linear, pale yellow-green **leaves** (1–4 cm long) are fleshy.

Small **flowers** are yellowish green. Male flowers are on dense terminal spikes, with each flower consisting of a lower bract and 3 stamens. Individual female flowers are borne in leaf axils and include a calyx (united with ovary to form a broad wing), 2 stigmas, and a superior ovary with 1 ovule.

A single **seed** develops within the calyx (6 mm long) and has a membranous wing.

HABITAT AND DISTRIBUTION

Greasewood occurs in saline sloughs, mud flats, and dry buttes of clayey bedrock of the southern prairies. It is well adapted to suviving seasonal flooding and long periods of drought on alkaline soils.

Distribution in Canada is limited to southern Alberta and Saskatchewan. Plants occur as far south as California and Texas.

Sarcobatus vermiculatus (Hook.) Torr.

SPECIAL FEATURES

Sarcobatus vermiculatus contains hydrocyanic acid and oxalates of sodium and potassium. These compounds can become quite concentrated, especially during periods of drought, and have caused bloating and poisoning in livestock. Lambs seem to be particularly prone to Greasewood poisoning in the spring and summer.

The fresh leaves are edible in moderation. It is best to cook them in a change of water in order to detoxify the oxalates. The seeds have also been reported to be edible.

The presence of Greasewood is an indication of extreme soil salinity.

RELATED SPECIES

Greasewood can be confused with the sages (*Artemisia* spp.) which also grow under similar saline prairie conditions. The woody old growth, narrow cone or catkin-like flower spikes, and characteristic spines set this plant apart from the more herbaceous sages.

Sarcobatus vermiculatus

JIM ROMO

Ledum groenlandicum (pp. 162–163)
Labrador Tea
COLIN STONE

Elaeagnus commutata Bernh.

Silverberry

ELAEAGNACEAE (Oleaster Family)

Other Common Names: Wolf Willow

Elaeagnus is of Greek origin meaning 'sacred olive tree' (*Elaia*, olive tree and *agnos*, sacred). *Commutata* means changeable.

Wetland
Woody Shrub
Native
Common
Hardiness Zone: 0
Flowering Season: late spring

DESCRIPTION

This stoloniferous shrub grows to 4 m with grey bark and rusty brown twigs. Alternate, silver, smooth-margined **leaves** (2–10 cm long) are oblong to elliptic and covered with silvery scales above and below (sometimes dotted with brown scales beneath).

Clusters of 2–3 **flowers** are formed in leaf axils of the current year's twigs. Fragrant, short-petioled flowers (1.2–1.5 cm long) are silver with a yellow interior. They may be unisexual or have both sexes in the same flower. Flowers consist of 4 thick, spreading sepals (tube-forming towards the base), no petals, 4 stamens, and a 1-loculed superior ovary.

Fruit (1 cm across) resembles a silver berry (technically called a drupe) with a thick, papery outer layer (covered with silvery hairs), dry and mealy interior and a hard-stoned center (with 8 longitudinal grooves).

HABITAT AND DISTRIBUTION

Silverberry can be found growing on gravel bars of streams and rivers, in moist coulees, pond and lake shores, and flood plains. Its presence in the prairies usually indicates gravel or sand beneath the surface. It is quite common in the prairies and

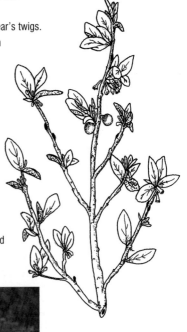

Elaeagnus commutata Bernh.

Elaeagnus commutata

HEINJO LAHRING

Elaeagnus commutata

parklands and frequents riparian areas of the southernmost boreal forest.

This shrub occurs across the Prairie provinces. The range extends from Alaska to the Gaspe on the east coast. Silverberry is considered a northern plant with distribution reaching Washington, Idaho, Utah, Colorado, North and South Dakota and western Minnesota.

SPECIAL FEATURES

The stoloniferous root system stabilizes stream and river banks. The roots form nitrogen-fixing nodules. Thickets of Silverberry offer valuable habitat for nesting birds, and cover for hares.

Native peoples used this plant in many ways. The hard seeds were dried and used to make necklaces and decorate clothing. The mealy part of the berry was eaten fresh or cooked. Northern peoples cooked them in moosefat. The berries were also added to soup or made into jelly. The dried twigs made excellent fire-starter, and the long, green branches were used in making baskets, shelters, fish hooks and assorted tools.

RELATED SPECIES

Elaeagnus angustifolia L., **Russian Olive**, is an introduced shrub to small tree which has escaped from cultivation. It differs in eventually becoming tree-like (to 7 m), has silvery twigs, narrower leaves, and yellow ellipsoid fruit (1 cm long). Although Russian Olive closely resembles Silverberry, it is found in drier locations and generally not considered a wetland plant.

Shepherdia argentea Nutt., **Thorny Buffaloberry**, also has silvery leaves and grows in moist valleys and along river banks. It differs in having opposite leaves, long thorns on the twigs, and 8 stamens. The sour, juicy fruit is scarlet or amber yellow. It is more heat-loving and is limited to the southern prairie regions.

Andromeda polifolia L.
Bog-rosemary

ERICACEAE (Heath Family)

Other Common Names: Dwarf Bog-rosemary

Andromeda shares its name with the Ethiopian Princess (daughter of King Cepheus and Queen Cassiopeia) of Greek Mythology whom Perseus rescued from a sea monster and then married, as well as the stellar constellation which is so prominant in the northern sky (below which this plant grows). *Polifolia* is from the Greek *poly* (many) and *folia* (leaved).

Wetland
Evergreen Shrub
Native
Common
Hardiness Zone: 0
Flowering Season: spring to early summer

DESCRIPTION

This dwarf (10–30 cm tall) evergreen with creeping roots is sparingly branched with thin, erect, woody twigs. The alternate, dark green, leathery **leaves** (1–5 cm long) are elliptic to linear and have smooth, downward, rolled margins. The hairless lower surface is white-glaucous.

Four to 5 nodding, pinkish white **flowers** (6 mm long) are clustered at the ends of branches. Flowers are composed of a 5-lobed calyx, 5-lobed corolla (urn-shaped), 10 stamens (2-awned and opening by pores), 1 pistil of 2–5 united carpels, and a superior ovary.

Fruit is a dry, loculed, spherical capsule with a persistent style. Each capsule contains numerous seeds.

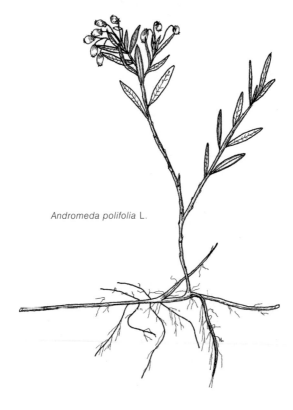

Andromeda polifolia L.

HABITAT AND DISTRIBUTION

As the name implies, it is a plant of wet bogs, fens, swamps, and muskegs. It is commonly associated with the boreal, arctic, and alpine zones.

Distribution is circumpolar. Plants range from Alaska in the north, to Idaho, the Great Lakes region and New Jersey in the south, and to northern Quebec and Newfoundland in the east. Although predominantly a northern plant, collections have been made in southern Saskatchewan and Manitoba.

SPECIAL FEATURES

Bog-rosemary's leaves and flowers contain *andrometoxin*, a poisonous glucoside which acts as a hypotensor. Consumption can result in digestive, nervous and respiratory disorders. Foraging on quantities of the foliage can have dangerous effects on livestock. In Europe, cases of poisoning from Bog-rosemary honey have been reported.

Fresh or dried plants were used as tea by Native peoples and is said to have inebriating effects.

RELATED SPECIES

Andromeda glaucophylla Link, **Glaucous-leaved Bog-rosemary**, a species of eastern North America, differs in being taller (30–100 cm) with pink flowers, short pedicels, and the undersides of the leaves are hairy. It grows in *Sphagnum* with roots creeping within the moss layer (usually not down into the underlying peat or subsoil). [A. *polifolia* ssp. *glaucophylla* (Link) Hult.]

HEINJO LAHRING

Andromeda polifolia

Chamaedaphne calyculata (L.) Moench   **ERICACEAE (Heath Family)**

Leatherleaf

Syn.: *Andromeda calyculata* L., *Cassandra calyculata* (L.) D. Don

Other Common Names: Cassandra

Chamaedaphne is from the Greek terms *chamai* (close to the ground or dwarf) and *daphne* (Laurel) and describes the creeping roots and resemblance to Laurel. *Calyculata* (Latin for calyx-like) refers to the bracts below the calyx.

Wetland
Evergreen Shrub
Native
Common
Hardiness Zone: 0
Flowering Season: late spring to early summer

DESCRIPTION

This branching evergreen shrub forms low (less than 1 m) dense clumps or thickets with creeping roots. Twigs are more or less erect and covered with short hairs. Green, leathery **leaves** are alternate, oblong to elliptic (1–5 cm long), smooth to slightly flat-toothed along the margins (mainly towards tip), and with white or brownish scales above and beneath (appearing dotted).

Nodding white **flowers** are in 1-sided leafy racemes at branch tips. Each flower rests upon 2 bractlets and consists of a deeply 5-parted calyx, a white 6–7 mm long urn-shaped corolla (slightly constricted at throat with 5 small teeth around its opening), 10 stamens, 1 pistil of 2–5 united carpels, and a superior ovary.

Chamaedaphne calyculata (L.) Moench

BARRE HELLQUIST

Chamaedaphne calyculata

BARRE HELLQUIST

Chamaedaphne calyculata

Fruit is a 3–5 mm wide, round and angular capsule containing a few chambers and several small seeds. Capsules tend to remain on branches for many years.

HABITAT AND DISTRIBUTION

Leatherleaf does well in moist, sandy soil and highly acidic conditions. It is associated with *Sphagnum* bogs and conifer swamps and often grows with *Kalmia polifolia* (Pale Laurel) and *Ledum groenlandicum* (Labrador-tea). It is known to contribute to the development of floating mats around the edges of ponds and lakes. In Massachusetts its rate of advancement has been recorded at over 1 foot per decade.

Distribution is circumpolar. In the Prairie provinces it occurs in the boreal forest zone of the northern half of Alberta, central to northernmost Saskatchewan and northernmost to southern Manitoba. Its range extends to the Yukon and Alaska in the north, the Great Lakes and Georgia in the south, and Newfoundland in the east.

SPECIAL FEATURES

This plant contains the same compound as *Andromeda polifolia* (Dwarf Bog-rosemary), *andrometoxin*, and is therefore somewhat toxic. Boiling the foliage extracts the toxin.

Native peoples made tea from the leaves and used it to treat fevers.

RELATED SPECIES

This is the only species of *Chamaedaphne* found in the Prairie provinces.

Several low evergreen heath-like plants occur in the same wetland habitats and it is easy to confuse them. Leatherleaf stands out with its erect habit, hairy and brown to white scaly leaves (not glaucous beneath), and 1-sided raceme of nodding white flowers with a 5-toothed corolla opening.

Gaultheria hispidula (L.) Bigel.   ERICACEAE (Heath Family)
Creeping Snowberry

Syn.: *Chiogenes hispidula* (L.) Torr. & Gray
Other Common Names: Teaberry, Capillaire,
Maidenhair-berry, Moxie-plum

Gaultheria is named after the Quebec physician, Jean
Gaulthier (1708–1756). *Hispidula* is of Latin origin and
means covered with coarse, erect hairs (bristly) and
refers to the hairy stems and lower leaves.

Wetland
Evergreen Shrub
Native
Common
Hardiness Zone: 1
Flowering Season: spring to early summer

DESCRIPTION
This low-growing (10–40 cm) evergreen shrub has horizontal rootstocks and prostrate twigs covered with
reddish hairs. Small (6–9 mm long), green, alternate **leaves** are ovate to elliptic with short (3–6 mm long)
petioles and brown hairs beneath. Leaf margin is smooth to slightly flat-toothed.
Single, white **flowers** (2–3 mm long) hang from leaf axils. Flowers are subtended by 2 bractlets. Each flower
has a deeply 4-parted calyx, a bell-shaped, white corolla (4 teeth-like lobes at the opening), 10 stamens with
awned anthers, 1 pistil of 2–5 united carpels and a superior ovary.
Fruit is a spherical white capsule (5–10 mm) which appears berry-like due to a fleshy calyx surrounding the
actual capsule.

HABITAT AND DISTRIBUTION
Creeping Snowberry is found in treed bogs, swamps, muskeg, and moist conifer forest (often on moss,
rocks and logs). It is generally associated with the boreal forest zone.
Plant range extends from Alaska to Newfoundland. It occurs in northern Alberta, central Saskatchewan and
southern Manitoba. The southern limit includes Washington, Idaho, the Great Lakes region, and along the
Appalachians to West Virginia, Maryland and Pennsylvania.

SPECIAL FEATURES
The white berries are eaten by grouse, mice, deer, and black bears.
Berries are good fresh or cooked, but dry and somewhat acidic, with a wintergreen-like scent and a lemony

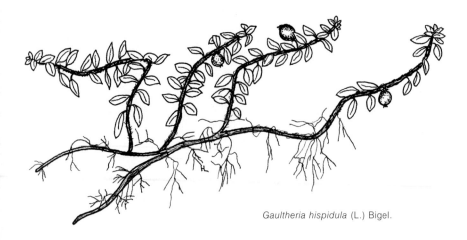

Gaultheria hispidula (L.) Bigel.

BARRE HELLQUIST

Gaultheria hispidula

evergreen flavour. In the early spring the leaves are often picked and chewed by hikers. The tender, young leaves are good in salads and to flavor deserts.

Gaultheria humifusa (see below) has edible, red fruit which are good fresh or cooked. *Gautheria procumbens* makes excellent tea and is the source of the true 'oil of wintergreen' used in flavoring foods. It contains methyl-salicylate (related to aspirin) and is used as a tonic, stimulant, astringent, aromatic and in the treatment of asthma and prevention of cavities.

RELATED SPECIES

Two other *Gaultherias*, not normally considered wetland species, may be found in wet locations in the Prairie provinces:

Gaultheria humifusa (L.) Bigel, **Alpine Wintergreen**, is found in moist subalpine slopes of the Rocky Mountains and differs in having non-hairy stems, longer-toothed leaves (10–15 mm long), flower parts in 5s, and red fruit.

Gaultheria procumbens L., **Wintergreen**, is a boreal forest species found west only to southeastern Manitoba (not west of Winnipeg or Lake Winnipeg). Its branches are more erect (10–20 cm high), the flowers hang on long pedicels (5–10 mm), and the fruit is bright red.

Kalmia microphylla (Hook.) Keller

ERICACEAE (Heath Family)

Mountain Laurel

Other Common Names: Swamp Laurel, American Laurel, Bog Wintergreen

Kalmia is named in honour of Pehr Kalm, a pioneer botanist who collected and recorded Canadian flora. *Microphylla* means small leaved.

Wetland
Evergreen Shrub
Native
Common (in west)
Hardiness Zone: 1
Flowering Season: late spring

DESCRIPTION

Low-growing (5–20 cm tall), matted to erect plants have creeping roots and branching stems with 2-edged branchlets. The evergreen **leaves** (1–1.5 cm long) are opposite, sessile, and elliptic to oblong (less than twice as long as wide) with smooth, downward-rolled margins. Leaves are leathery, green above and glaucous-white below.

Reddish stalked, rosy pink **flowers** (6–12 mm across) are in clusters on the branch tips. Flowers have a green and pink 5-parted calyx, an open plate-like corolla (pink) with 5 broad-pointed lobes, 10 stamens, 1 pistil of 5 united carpels, an elongated style and a superior ovary. The anther end of the stamen is held in a pouch on the inner surface of the corolla creating tension on the arching filament. Insect movement causes the anthers to spring inwards, with pollen directed towards the central pistil or insect.

Fruit is an ovoid to spherical capsule (6 mm long) containing several seeds.

HABITAT AND DISTRIBUTION

This western species of Kalmia frequents moist mountain meadows, coniferous wetlands and bogs. It is associated with *Ledum*, *Chamaedaphne* and other members of the heath family.

Distribution pattern follows the mountain regions and boreal forest areas from the Yukon south to Colorado and California. It is limited to the western part of Alberta (it is not reported to occur in Saskatchewan or Manitoba).

Kalmia microphylla
(Hook.) Keller

SPECIAL FEATURES

The showy flowers are attractive to numerous insect pollinators. The low-growing, woody and evergreen nature of this plant offers excellent shelter for small mammals and other animals during all seasons.

The leaves of *K. latifolia* (Mountain Laurel or Calico Bush) were used to make a yellow-tan dye.

Kalmia angustifolia (**Sheep Laurel** or **Lamb-kill**) and *Kalmia polifolia* (see below) of eastern North America are known to contain the poisonous compounds *arbutoside* (a glucoside) and *andromedotoxin* in their leaves. The Columbia College of Pharmacy Herbarium has a note on one specimen that reads "Die Pflanze hat giftig narkotische Eigenschaften," which refers to its narcotic-like effects. *Kalmia polifolia* leaves are reported to be especially poisonous to sheep. Honey made from its nectar is also noted to be poisonous. Effects include vertigo, loss of sight, coldness of extremities, nausea and vomiting.

RELATED SPECIES

Kalmia polifolia Wang., **Northern**, **Pale**, or **American Laurel**, is a common boreal forest species of sphagnum and spruce bogs across the Prairie provinces. It differs from *K. microphylla* in being a larger plant (mostly more than 30 cm) and by having longer leaves (2–4 cm).

Kalmia microphylla (facing page)
Mountain Laurel

JIM ROMO

DICOTS ■ SHRUBS

Ledum groenlandicum Oeder
Labrador Tea

ERICACEAE (Heath Family)

Other Common Names: Common Labrador Tea

Ledum comes from the Greek *ledos,* which is the name of a resin-producing rockrose (*Cistus ladaniferus*). *Groenlandicum* refers to its occurrence in Greenland.

Wetland
Evergreen Shrub
Native
Common
Hardiness Zone: 0
Flowering Season: early summer

DESCRIPTION

Labrador Tea grows as a low (30–80 cm), woody shrub with leathery, evergreen **leaves**. Young twigs are covered with woolly, orange-brown hairs. Short-petioled, dark green leaves are alternate, oblong to elliptic (1–5 cm long), densely covered with white to rusty-coloured hairs beneath, and have smooth, rolled-under margins.

Long-pedicelled, white **flowers** are in umbel-like clusters at the ends of twigs. Flowers (1 cm wide) consist of a small, 5-toothed calyx, 5 spreading oblong petals (5–8 mm long, narrowed at base), 5–7 stamens, and a 5-loculed superior ovary with an elongated (5–7 mm) style.

Oval **capsules** (5–6 mm long) are covered with short, soft hairs and a long, persistent style. Each capsule opens from the bottom to top, releasing many seeds.

Ledum groenlandicum Oeder

HEINJO LAHRING

PAT PORTER

Ledum groenlandicum

Ledum groenlandicum in mid-winter

162

Below: *Ledum groenlandicum* leaves: (at right, top of leaf; at left, underside of leaf)

COLIN STONE

HEINJO LAHRING

Ledum groenlandicum

(See additional photo of *Ledum groenlandicum* on page 151.)

HABITAT AND DISTRIBUTION

This northern evergreen prefers coniferous forests, bogs, and muskegs. It is often associated with deep, mossy locations with considerable shade. Labrador Tea is a plant of the boreal forest, Rocky Mountain and parkland areas.

It is is found over much of the three Prairie provinces excluding the south-central prairies. In the north the range extends from Alaska to Newfoundland (including parts of the tundra) and parts of Greenland. In the south it includes Oregon, Idaho, North Dakota, the Great Lakes region and the northeastern states.

SPECIAL FEATURES

Ledum groenlandicum is adapted to survive in harsh conditions. The leathery leaves, rolled margins, and furry undersides help to keep moisture loss to a minimum during times of water shortage (e.g., frozen roots well into spring, hot dry summers, etc.) The evergreen foliage allows the plant to minimize nutrient loss in nutrient-poor bogs.

The fresh or dried aromatic leaves make excellent tea, but should be used in moderation since they contain *arbutin* (a glucoside) and *tannin* which in quantity can irritate the digestive and nervous systems. Native peoples collected the dried leaves for use as a trade item.

As a herbal it was used to treat for lice and ringworm. A mix of crushed leaves with alcohol and glycerine is reported to act as a mosquito repellent and to relieve insect bites.

RELATED SPECIES

Ledum glandulosum Nutt., **Glandular Labrador Tea** or **Trapper's Tea**, has leaves which have only slightly under-turned margins and are pale and glandular-dotted beneath. It occurs in moist mountain woods of southwestern Alberta. This species is bitter tasting and considered poisonous.

Ledum palustre L. (Ait.) Lodd., **Northern** or **Marsh Labrador Tea**, is very similar to *L. groenlandicum* but not as common. It differs in having linear leaves (length to width ratio of 12:1) and 8–11 stamens.

Vaccinium oxycoccus L.
Small Bog Cranberry

ERICACEAE (Heath Family)

Syn.: *V. microcarpum* (Turcz.) Hook., *V. oxycoccus* var. *ovalifolium* Michx., *Oxycoccus palustris* Pers., *O. ovalifolius* (Michx.) Seymour, *O. quadripetalus* Gilib., *O. microcarpus* Turcz.

Other Common Names: Dwarf Bog Cranberry, Small Cranberry, Swamp Cranberry

Wetland
Evergreen Shrub
Native
Common
Hardiness Zone: 0
Flowering Season: early to mid-summer

Vaccinium is from the Latin term *Vaccinus* meaning dun (dull grayish brown) coloured. *Oxycoccus* is of Greek origin and stands for 'sourberry.' The common name was originally 'craneberries' because of the resemblance of the blossoms and stems to the head and neck of a crane.

DESCRIPTION
This low, trailing evergreen plant has alternate **leaves** and roots along thread-like stems (10–50 cm long). The small (4–10 mm long), elliptic-ovate, leathery green leaves have smooth edges, under-turned margins, and are whitish beneath.

Small (8 mm across), nodding, pink **flowers** are held in clusters (1–3) at the ends of branches. Pedicels (1–2 cm long) are hairless and often have a pair of red, scale-like bracts below the middle. Each flower consists of 4 sepals, a 4-parted corolla (divided nearly to base) with strongly reflexed lobes, 8 stamens, and a 4-loculed inferior ovary. With the turned-back petals and stamens which are arranged in a tube around the style, it has the look of a small shooting-star flower.

Fruit is a small (5–10 mm) and round, juicy, red berry (often spotted) containing several seeds.

HABITAT AND DISTRIBUTION
Small Bog Cranberry grows in wet acidic conditions in woods, fens, swamps, muskegs and peat bogs. It is often found growing within cool, wet moss carpets and *Sphagnum* moss hummocks.

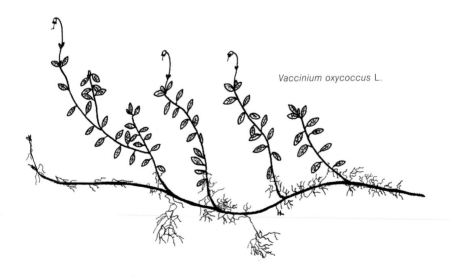

Vaccinium oxycoccus L.

BARRE HELLQUIST

Vaccinium oxycoccus

Distribution is circumpolar and follows the foothills, mountain, and boreal forest zones of the Prairie provinces. Range extends from Alaska to Newfoundland.

SPECIAL FEATURES

The bright red, acidic berries were much used by Native peoples. The berries start ripening in late August and remain on the creeping plants throughout the winter. The taste actually improves after the first frost.

Small Bog Cranberry fruits can be used in the same recipes as cultivated berries. Some uses include sauces, jellies, pie-fillings, bannock, muffins, and pancakes. A cold drink of the juice with sweetener and soda or ginger ale is excellent. The berries contain pectin and are high in vitamin C. When canned with sugar they will keep for years.

Berries can be cleaned as for blueberries. Stretch a woollen branket on a slant with a wide basin at the lower edge. Drop a handful of picked berries on at a time. The leaves and debris will remain on the blanket and the berries will roll into the basin. Rinse berries.

The leaves contain glucosides such as *arbutin* and are best not eaten.

Cranberry juice is well known for its use in treating urinary infections.

RELATED SPECIES

The unique shooting star–like flowers, slender branches, and very small evergreen leaves make this plant stand apart from other heathish plants of wet, mossy habitats.

Vaccinium vitis-idaea L.

ERICACEAE (Heath Family)

Bog Cranberry

Syn.: *Vitis-idaea punctata* Moench.
Other Common Names: Mountain Cranberry, Dry-ground Cranberry, Cowberry, Foxberry, Lingonberry, Alpine Cranberry, Partridgeberry, Red Whortleberry

Vaccinium is from the Latin term *Vaccinus* meaning dun (dull grayish brown) coloured. *Vitis-idaea* means 'Grape (vine) of Mount Ida.'

Wetland
Evergreen Shrub
Native
Common
Hardiness Zone: 0
Flowering Season: late spring to early summer

DESCRIPTION

Bog Cranberry is a low (10–20 cm), creeping, mat-forming evergreen with alternate, short-petioled **leaves**. Thick, shiny green leaves are elliptic to ovate (6–15 mm long), strongly indented along the midrib, have smooth, under-turned margins, rounded tips, and a pale green undersurface with black dots (hairs).
Bell-shaped, pink **flowers** (5–8 mm long) are held in clusters at the ends of branches. Each bloom consists of 4 sepals, an open, cup-shaped corolla with 4 lobes, 8 stamens, a slender style and an inferior ovary.
Many-seeded, round **berries** (5-10 mm) are dark red and acidic.

Vaccinium vitis-idaea L.

HABITAT AND DISTRIBUTION

This species is tolerant of drier habitats than the Small Bog Cranberry (*Vaccinium oxycoccus* L.) and often occurs with Bearberry (*Arctostaphylos uva-ursi* L.) and mosses. It is found in swamps, muskegs, sandy woodlands, wet and dry peat bogs, coniferous forests and alpine slopes. *Vaccinium vitis-idaea* is not actually a wetland plant per se, but will be encountered in very close proximity to forest seepages, often on mossy hummocks.
This is a very abundant ground-cover species found throughout the boreal forest and Rocky Mountains. Distribution is circumpolar. In North America plants occur from Alaska to Newfoundland including central and northern Alberta, central to northernmost Saskatchewan, southern to northernmost Manitoba, across to Ungava Labrador, Quebec, Minnesota, Wisconsin and the northeastern United States. Plants have been observed as far north as the High Arctic (Victoria and south Baffin Island).

SPECIAL FEATURES

Animals dig them up in winter and use them as a winter food source. They are a favourite of bears and a resource for flocks of waterfowl on their way to their breeding grounds.
This highly popular wilderness food was gathered in abundance by the northern tribes, such as the Dog-rib and Hare Indians, as well as by northern Eurasians. The juicy, but sour, berries maintain their edibility underneath winter snows until snowmelt the following June. It is said to be slightly less flavourful than Dwarf Bog

Cranberry in early autumn but superior to it after the first frost. It is very often used in place of commercial cranberry sauce. Sugar helps to reduce the tart taste.

The leaves contain a glucoside (*arbutin*) and are not recommended for use in teas.

Bog Cranberry juice acts as an antiseptic in the urinary tract as well as helping to reduce blood sugar levels. Berries will dye wool and cotton yellow with alum.

RELATED SPECIES

Vaccinium vitis-idaea is very often confused with *Arctostaphylos uva-ursi* (Bearberry). The former has shiny-surfaced, dark green leaves with black dots (hairs) beneath and sour, juicy berries whereas the latter has larger (1–2 cm long), leathery (reticulate-veiny), lighter green leaves lacking the conspicuous dots on the undersurface and dry, mealy berries.

HEINJO LAHRING

*Vaccinium
vitis-idaea*

Lonicera caerulea L.   **CAPRIFOLIACEAE (Honeysuckle Family)**

Blue Fly Honeysuckle

Syn.: *L. villosa* (Michx.) R. & S.

Other Common Names: Sweet-berry Honeysuckle, Water-berry, Mountain Fly Honeysuckle

Lonicera is named after the German physician and botanist Adam Lonizer (1528–1586). *Caerulea* means deep blue of the mid-day Mediterranean sky.

> Wetland
> Deciduous Shrub
> Native
> Common
> Hardiness Zone: 0
> Flowering Season: early summer

DESCRIPTION

This upright shrub (0.5 to 1 m) has brownish green branches with hairy young twigs. The opposite sessile **leaves** (2–4 cm long) are oblong with a blunt apex and hairy beneath.

Short-peduncled **flowers** occur in pairs in the leaf axils. Yellowish flowers (12 mm long) have a fused calyx (formed into a lobed-ring above ovary), 5-lobed corolla (2-lipped), 5 stamens (alternating with corolla lobes), and an inferior 2–3-loculed ovary (1–several ovules per locule). The ovaries of each pair of flowers are united and enclosed within a cup-like bract.

Fruit of paired flowers are united to form one several-seeded, bluish black berry.

Lonicera caerulea L. var. *villosa* (Michx.) T. & G..

HABITAT AND DISTRIBUTION

This moisture-loving honeysuckle can be found in swamps, bogs, and wet drainages in the Rocky Mountains and boreal forest. Distribution is circumpolar. Plants are found over much of the Prairie provinces, but are more or less absent from the central and southern plains. Range extends from British Columbia to Newfoundland, south to California, and eastward from Manitoba to beyond the Great Lakes. Occurs in northern half of Alberta.

SPECIAL FEATURES

The nectar-rich flowers are visited by hummingbirds, and long-tongued insects such as Hawkmoths. The berries are eaten by wildlife. Birds distribute the undigested seeds in their droppings. Native peoples used the berries to make juice and tea. In British Columbia the children of the Lillooet sucked the sweet-tasting nectar from the flowers. Pioneers made jams and jellies from the berries.

RELATED SPECIES

Other Honeysuckle species which may be found in wetland locations include:

Lonicera involucrata (Richards.) Banks, **Bracted Honeysuckle**, is a taller shrub (1–3 m) with more pointed leaves and very large leaf-like bracts at the base of the paired flowers; its 2 purple-black berries are separate.

Lonicera oblongifolia (Goldie) Hook., **Swamp Fly Honeysuckle**, is a low shrub (0.5–1.5 m) with densely pubescent leaves (at least below), yellow flowers (purple-tinged inside), and more or less united purplish red berries. It occurs in swamps and marshes of the eastern Boreal Forest.

Lonicera utahensis S. Wats., **Utah Honeysuckle** or **Red Twinberry**, is similar to *L. caerulea* but is somewhat taller (1–2 m), has hairless leaves (pale beneath), small bracts (not leaflike as in *L. involucrata*), pale yellow flowers, and twin red berries. This is a plant of the southern Rocky Mountains.

See photo on page 135.

—SPERMATOPHYTA—

DICOTS

HERBS

- non-woody vascular plants reproducing by seeds
- embryo with 2 cotyledons (seed leaves)
- flower parts in 5s or 4s
- stems with central pith, vascular bundles in a ring (cambium present)
- leaves usually net-veined

Nuphar variegata (pp. 186–187)
Yellow Pondlily

HEINJO LAHRING

Urtica dioica L.
URTICACEAE (Nettle Family)
Common Nettle

Syn.: *Urtica gracilis* Ait., *U. lyallii* S. Wats.
Other Common Names: Stinging Nettle, European Nettle, Slender Nettle, Tall Nettle

Urtica comes from the Latin word *uro*, meaning to burn. *Dioica* is from *dioecious* which refers to having male and female flowers on separate plants (European material is said to be more inclined to dioecism).

Wetland
Perennial
Native
Common
Hardiness Zone: 0
Flowering Season: early to mid-summer

DESCRIPTION
Growing in clusters from coarse roots are erect, straight stems up to 2 m tall. Outer stems tend to fall over if no support is available. Stems (often square in cross-section) and leaves have stinging hairs. Narrow-lanceolate to ovate (2.3–3 cm wide), pointed **leaves** (5–12 cm long) are opposite, mid-green and sharply toothed.

Flowers are in dense clusters (paniculate cyme) in leaf axils. The male flower cluster is equal to or longer than the leaf petiole. Male flowers have a deeply 4-cleft calyx and 4 stamens. Female clusters are smaller than the male. Female flowers have 4 sepals (of which the 2 innermost are larger) and a 1-loculed ovary (superior) with 1 ovule.

Fruit is a flattened, oblong achene held tightly between the two larger inner sepals.

Urtica dioica L.

HABITAT AND DISTRIBUTION
Common Nettle is a pioneering species which is tolerant of a wide range of growing conditions. It does well in sun or shade as well as rich or poor soil, often inhabiting disturbed areas. Some common areas in which it is found include damp woods, barnyards, compost piles, sloughs, streams, rivers, roadsides, beaver lodges, and on islands with bird nesting colonies. Distribution is circumpolar, in association with the boreal forest region. Found across the Prairie provinces.

SPECIAL FEATURES
This plant has long been utilized in Europe and continues to be one of the best wild vegetables available. It is one of the first greens to appear in the spring and can be gathered until early summer. Due to the stinging hairs, they must be collected with gloves and cooked prior to consumption. Always choose young leaves since old leaves can produce lesions on the kidneys, especially if consumed in large quantities.

The stinging properties are lost during boiling. The flavour and texture resembles beansprouts. The cooking water can be used as soup stock or tea concentrate. The young leaves and shoots are rich in protein, iron, and vitamins A and C. The dried plant makes excellent tea (Mountain Man Spring Tonic). In Russia, good yields of high quality hay are obtained. Nettle leaves saturated with salt have been used for curdling milk for making cheese.

The dried stalks can be soaked in water and the outer skin removed. The inner fibers can be twisted and made into cordage for fishing nets, rope and cloth. A yellow dye is obtained by boiling the roots.

The stinging properties, or burning sensation (urticating-effect), is due to histamin, acetylcholine, and 5-hydroxytryptamine. These compounds are contained within hollow hairs which easily break off and penetrate the skin on contact. The resulting effects, inflamed bumps and irritation, may last for several hours. The juice of Curly Dock (*Rumex crispus*) and Plantain (*Plantago* spp.) relieves the symptoms of stinging nettle, as well as the application of a tannin astringent or cold compress (i.e., mud or cold water). The stings apparently have a beneficial effect on arthritis and rheumatism.

RELATED SPECIES

Urtica urens L., **Annual English Nettle** or **Small Nettle**, is a small (10–50 cm), introduced weed found in the Prairie provinces. The male and female flowers are in mixed clusters which are shorter than the petioles. The fruiting calyx has bristles along the margins.

Urtica dioica

HEINJO LAHRING

Nuphar microphylla (p. 187)
Small Pondlily

BARRE HELLQUIST

Geocaulon lividum (Richards.) Fern.
Northern Comandra

SANTALACEAE (Sandalwood Family)

Syn.: *Comandra livida* Richards.

Geocaulon is from the Greek terms *gaia* (the earth) and *kaulos* (stem) meaning the stem that is found underground and is referring to the slender, red rhizomes.

Wetland
Perennial
Native
Common
Hardiness Zone: 0
Flowering Season: early to mid-summer

DESCRIPTION

Growing from slender, red rhizomes are 10–30 cm tall erect stems. Thin, hairless **leaves** (1–4 cm long) are oval with a rounded tip and smooth margins. The bright green (often mottled with yellow), alternating leaves have short petioles.

Small (2 mm diam.), bronze or greenish **flowers** are arranged in clusters of 2–4 (commonly 3) in the middle leaf axils. The lateral flowers of the cluster are often male. The middle flower has both male and female parts. There are 5 broadly triangular sepals (1–1.5 mm long), sometimes referred to as tepals, which are partially connected above the 1-loculed inferior ovary (few-ovuled) forming a short tube. This tube is lined with a fleshy disc. There are 5 stamens, sometimes connected to the sepals by tufts of hairs, and 1 style.

Fruit is a fleshy, single-seeded drupe, looking very much like an orange to scarlet berry (5–10 mm across), formed in late summer or early autumn.

HABITAT AND DISTRIBUTION

Geocaulon lividum (Richards.) Fern.

Northern Comandra, only remotely considered a wetland species, makes its home in the damp humus and moss of black spruce swamps, bogs, treed fens, and upland forests. It is often associated with the feather moss understory of coniferous forests.

Its range extends across the boreal forest region from Alaska to Newfoundland and includes each of the Prairie provinces. Its southern distribution extends into the western Rockies of Montana, Idaho and Washington. To the southeast the range includes the Great Lakes area and beyond to New York.

SPECIAL FEATURES

Geocaulon lividum is a partially parasitic plant living on the roots of ericaceous shrubs. The rootlets form sucker-like organs which attach themselves onto the host plant.

The juicy, berry-like drupe is edible but has an unpleasant flavour. The sweet-tasting leaves make a welcome addition to salads.

RELATED SPECIES

This is the only species of *Geocaulon* which might be found in wet areas.

Geocaulon lividum

BARRE HELLQUIST

173

DICOTS ■ HERBS

Polygonum amphibium L.   **POLYGONACEAE (Buckwheat Family)**

Water Smartweed

Other Common Names: Swamp Persicaria, Wild Rhubarb

Polygonum is from the Greek terms *polys* (many) and *gonu* (knee), referring to the many swollen joints on the stem. *Amphibium* describes the plant's ability to live in water and on land.

Wetland and Floating-leaved
Perennial
Native
Common
Hardiness Zone: 0
Flowering Season: mid–late summer

DESCRIPTION

This plant is quite variable and comes in two forms. The aquatic plant form has broadly oval (2–15 cm long), floating **leaves** (often reddish). The erect terrestrial form (up to 1 m tall) has alternate, short-petioled leaves (6–12 cm long) which are deep green and hairless above (often hairy below), lance-shaped and pointed. Leaves on both forms are smooth margined. Stems (up to 38 cm long) are weak and floppy with thickened joints surrounded by a papery sheath (ocreae). The submerged creeping rhizomes will root at the nodes.

A bright pink, cylindrical **flower** spike (1–3 cm long by 1.5 cm wide) is held at the end of a hairless stem. Flower colour tends to vary from light pink to reddish purple. The flowers within the clusters are 4–5 mm long and composed of 5 (4–6) sepals (pink and petal-like), no petals, 5 (3–9) stamens, 2–3 styles, and a 1-loculed (1 ovule) superior ovary. On some plants the stamens are long and the styles short; on others the stamens are short and the styles long.

Fruit is a small (2.5–3 mm long), lens-shaped achene with one brown to black seed formed in late summer or early autumn.

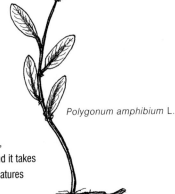

Floating leaves and flower spike

Polygonum amphibium L.

HABITAT AND DISTRIBUTION

Water Smartweed inhabits the shallow waters of ponds, sloughs, marshes, drainage ditches, streams, rivers, and lakes. In wet mud it takes on an upright habit. In water either floating leaves and/or erect features may be present.

This is a circumpolar wetland plant having a Canadian range from the Pacific to the Atlantic. It occurs as far north as the Territories and as far south as California, Colorado, Nebraska, and New Jersey.

SPECIAL FEATURES

When in full bloom, entire sloughs can be rose pink in July. This plant colonizes areas rapidly from underground stems.

The seeds are an important food for waterfowl such as black ducks, mallards, pintails, teals, wood ducks, rails, geese, sparrows and red polls. The seed heads are often available as a winter staple. Mammals, such as deer, squirrels, chipmunks, mice and voles, eat the plants and fruit.

Water Smartweed is an edible plant for people. Stems, shoots and roots can all be gathered for food. Young growth is preferred. Older plants are best peeled before using. Fresh material has a hot peppery taste when used in salads. It is high in vitamins K and C. The stems themselves are at times tart like rhubarb; however, they can be made into a jam or condiment with a little sugar added. They can also be served like spinach by boiling or steaming the stems and shoots for 5 minutes. Some wilderness cooks soak them several hours in water prior to boiling. Seeds were used whole or ground into flour by Native peoples and pioneers.

Medicinally, Native peoples applied it as an antiseptic for cleansing and healing wounds (the plant contains a coagulating substance) as well as for stomach pains (ulcers), headaches and hemorrhoids.

RELATED SPECIES

Two varieties are recognized:

Polygonum amphibium var. *emersum* Michx. has a long (greater than 5 cm), slender flower spike. Flowers are formed on terrestrial, or strongly emersed, plants. Peducles are glandular. Stipular sheaths are entire, or with dry, shredded margins. [*P. coccinium* Muhl., *P. muhlenbergii* S. Wat.]

Polygonum amphibium var. *stipulaceum* Coleman has a short (less than 5 cm), broad flower spike. Flowers are formed on aquatic plants (i.e., those with floating leaves). Peduncles are hairless. Stipular sheaths (on sterile terrestrial forms) have at least some flared, green collars. [*P. natans* Eat., *P. inundatum* Raf., *P. hartwrightii* Gray, *Persicaria amphibia* (L.) S.F. Gray]

Polygonum persicaria L., **Lady's-thumb**, is an annual, pink-flowering smartweed also found in wet areas. Its terrestrial form is shorter (10–60 cm) than *P. amphibium*. The leaves often have a dark blotch on the upper side. The papery sheaths around the joints (ochreae) have conspicuous hairs on the upper margins. Introduced from Eurasia.

Polygonum amphibium var. *stipulaceum*

HEINJO LAHRING

Rumex occidentalis S. Wats.   POLYGONACEAE (Buckwheat Family)
Western Dock

Syn.: *R. aquaticus* L. ssp. *occidentalis* (S. Wats.) Hult.,
R. aquaticus L. var. *fenestratus* (Greene) Dorn
Other Common Names: Dock, Indian Rhubarb

Rumex is an ancient Latin name. *Occidentalis* refers to its western distribution.

Wetland
Perennial
Native
Common
Hardiness Zone: 0
Flowering Season: early summer

DESCRIPTION

Western Dock is an easily recognized plant of wetland areas with its tall (up to 1.5 m), green-tinged-with-red stems standing well above most sedges and grasses. Plant colour changes from green in the summer to red or brown in the fall. **Leaves** are alternate, long (to 25 cm) and narrow, with smooth wavy margins and a pointed tip. Root is a prominant yellow or orange taproot.

Flowers are arranged in densely packed clusters on a long (20–50 cm) terminal spike. The small (1 mm) green flowers have 6 sepals (of which 3 are larger) but no petals. There are 6 stamens and attached to a 1-loculed (1-ovuled) ovary are 3 styles.

Fruit is a 3-sided achene enclosed in dry and papery (often veined), reddish brown sepals (known in fruit as valves). Valves have no tubercle on the back.

HABITAT AND DISTRIBUTION

Western Dock grows in damp soil which may be seasonally flooded for a part of the growing season. It is a common plant of fens, sloughs and roadside ditches.

Rumex occidentalis is scattered across the Prairie provinces. Its range extends to Alaska in the west, Quebec and Newfoundland in the east, and California, Nevada, Utah, New Mexico, South Dakota in the south.

SPECIAL FEATURES

Young spring leaves are suitable for salads; however, warm weather turns the plant bitter. In order to remove the strong taste, stalks and leaves can be boiled in two changes of water. The cooked greens can be used as you would spinach or in place of rhubarb in a pie. This plant is very rich in vitamin A and also contains vitamins B1, B2, and C, iron and other

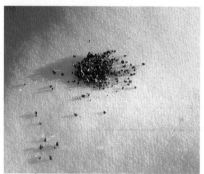

Rumex occidentalis S. Wats.

Rumex occidentalis seeds collected in winter

HEINJO LAHRING

minerals. The seeds were ground by Native peoples and made into cakes, with a taste similar to buckwheat. The seeds were rubbed between the hands to remove some of the three-bladed membrane, then winnowed and finally ground into flour or boiled for mush.

This is a wetland plant that should never be eaten in excess due to the high oxalic acid content of the leaves and the high concentration of tannic acid in the roots which may result in kidney problems. Also, unlike vitamin C, vitamin A is stored in the body and an overdose can occur if too much is consumed.

The roots of *Rumex* were used by the Navaho Indians to create a yellow dye. Northern tribes boiled the taproots for half an hour to prepare the dye for colouring moose hides.

Medicinally the roots of *Rumex* are valuable as a cure for skin infections and itches by using freshly washed and crushed leaves over the sore.

The rich brown, fall flower stalks are excellent for floral arrangements.

RELATED SPECIES

Several other species of moisture-loving docks may be readily encountered in the Prairie provinces.

Rumex crispus L., **Curly Dock**, has been introduced into the area from Eurasia. It is shorter (30–80 cm tall) than *R. occidentalis* with very strongly wavy-curled leaves. The flower spike is well branched. Three large (half the length of valve), round tubercles can be found on the back of the achene valves.

Rumex fennicus (Murb.) Murb., **Field Dock**, is an 80–150 cm high introduced perennial weed from Europe which spreads rapidly. It has no teeth or tubercles on the valves. *Rumex fennicus* is very common in Saskatchewan, taking the place of our native *R. occidentalis* in like habitats. [syn. *R. pseudonastronatus* Borbas]

Rumex maritimus L., **Golden Dock**, is a circumpolar annual of saline shores and disturbed locations (often dominating large areas). Plants are short (20–60 cm tall) with long, narrow, moderately wavy leaf margins (hairy beneath). The flower spike is golden brown at maturity. The achene valves have 1–3 bristle-like lobes on their margins and 3 narrow tubercles on the back.

Rumex triangulivalvis (Dans.) Rech. f. , **Narrow-leaved Dock**, is similar to *R. crispus* but lacks the waviness in the leaf margin as well having longer and more tapered leaf ends. It is known for its axillary tufts of leaves on the stem, sometimes developing into branches. The flower spike has very little branching. The valve tubercles are narrow (half to two-thirds the length of valve). [syn. *R. mexicanus* Meisn., *R. salicifolius* Weinm.]

HEINJO LAHRING

HEINJO LAHRING

Rumex occidentalis

Atriplex heterosperma Bunge
Two-scale Saltbush

CHENOPODIACEAE (Goosefoot Family)

Syn.: *A. micrantha* Ledeb.

Other Common Names: Orache

Atriplex is an ancient Latin name. *Heterosperma* means different (*hetero*) seed (*sperma*) and refers to the two varieties of fruit this plant produces.

Wetland
Annual
Introduced
Very Rare
Hardiness Zone: 3
Flowering Season: summer

DESCRIPTION

The silvery, erect stems grow to 150 cm tall. The **leaves** are alternate, triangular, sometimes have a pair of lobes (auricles), and when young are covered with a whitish, mealy powder below. Both sides of the leaves turn green as they mature.

Flowers are borne in clusters on the side or top of the flower stalk. The flowers are of two types, both found on the same plant. Male flowers have a 5-lobed calyx and 5 stamens. Female flowers lack sepals and petals but have two circular bracts around a single superior ovary containing 1 ovule. Some of the female flowers have small bracts (2–3 mm long), while others have large bracts (5–6 mm long).

Single seeds are encased within a thin outer covering (pericarp) which can be easily removed and are of two types. Small bracted flowers produce small, black **fruit** (1.5 mm) and large bracted flowers produce larger (2–3 mm), yellow-brown fruit.

HABITAT AND DISTRIBUTION

Saltbush, as the name implies, has a strong preference for saline habitats. This is a common plant of seashores and a colonizer of waste places, gardens, disturbed peat wetlands, and saline sloughs. Generally this is considered a coastal species. Over time plants have established themselves inland where conditions are favourable, particularly in the warmer parts of the prairies.

SPECIAL FEATURES

Atriplex heterosperma is a close relative of spinach or garden orach (*A. hortensis* L.). The leaves and young stems (especially the tips) can be used in the same manner as we would use common spinach. They can be boiled (or steamed) and added to soup or as greens. Changing the water when cooking helps eliminate the saponins the plant contains. The tender fresh parts can be used in making salads. Because of its salty taste, it is a good plant for flavouring food. Saltbush seeds can be ground and added to flour for use in making pancakes, cereals, soups and general baking. In the southern United States the seeds were parched, ground and added to pinole (corn flour).

RELATED SPECIES

Several *Atriplex* species can be found across the prairies but most prefer quite dry, saline conditions. The saltbush group tends to occur in the southern part of the Prairie provinces where the climate is warmer and extended periods of drought are common.

See also *Sarcobatus vermiculatus* on page 150.

Caltha natans (p. 195)
Floating Marsh-marigold

ALISON BAKKEN

Chenopodium rubrum L.   CHENOPODIACEAE (Goosefoot Family)

Red Goosefoot

Other Common Names: Coast-blite

Chenopodium is from the Greek *chen* (goose) and *podium* (small foot), referring to the web-footed shape of the leaves.

Wetland
Annual
Native
Common
Hardiness Zone: 0
Flowering Season: summer

DESCRIPTION

Fleshy, reddish green stems are branched and erect (20–80 cm tall). **Leaves** (3–10 cm long) are thick, coarsely toothed, pointed at both ends, and have only a slight (if any) amount of whitish, powdery coating beneath. Leaves of flower stalk are smaller, without the jagged margin.

Flowers (green becoming reddish) are produced in clusters along a leafy stem. Each flower has a 5-lobed somewhat fleshy calyx (eventually enclosing the fruit), no corolla, 2–5 stamens, 2–5 styles, and 1 pistil. The single ovary is superior and contains one ovule.

Brownish **fruit** is a single, dry, lens-shaped seed (0.7–0.8 mm long) covered by a thin and easily removed pericarp.

HABITAT AND DISTRIBUTION

Red Goosefoot is associated with lakeshores, moist saline mud flats, and dried slough beds across the prairies and parkland. It prefers sunny, open areas where soil conditions are often very poor and prone to periods of flooding followed by long periods of drought.

Distribution is circumpolar with plants found from Alaska to the southwestern Mackenzie district, down and across the central and southern reaches of the Prairie provinces and over to Newfoundland. Southern range extends from California to Missouri and up to New Jersey.

Chenopodium rubrum L.

SPECIAL FEATURES

This plant is rich in vitamins A and C. The young stems, leaves and fruits can be eaten raw or cooked (like spinach). Older plants become quite tough and unpalatable.

The bright red fruits of a closely related plant, Strawberry Blite (*C. capitatum*, see below), were used for dying porcupine quills. The Athapaskan Indians used the crushed fruit as an ink to mark beadwork patterns on moosehide. Cakes or mush were made by grinding up the small seeds.

RELATED SPECIES

Chenopodium capitatum (L.) Aschers, **Strawberry Blite**, can be confused with *C. rubrum*. It has large, spike-like flower clusters. The calyx is fleshy and bright red when in fruit. The pericarp does not easily come off of the seed. *Chenopodium capitatum* is a boreal forest plant of disturbed places.

Chenopodium fremontii S. Wats., **Fremont's Goosefoot**, is a tall (over 50 cm), slender annual of very southern areas. It grows in moist, shady locations among bluffs and bushes. It usually has longitudinal, dark green lines. Broad, triangular leaves are up to 5 cm long.

Chenopodium pratericola Rydb., **Goosefoot**, is a mostly erect plant of slough margins and open, disturbed saline locations. The primary leaves are long and narrow with 1 or 2 lobes near the base. Plants are covered in a whitish powder. The calyx lobes do not completely cover the seeds at maturity. The pericarp easily comes off of the fruit.

Chenopodium salinum Standl., **Oak-leaved Goosefoot**, is similar to *C. capitatum* and *C. rubrum*, but differs in having very short (2–3 cm), oak-like leaves which are densely covered with a whitish powder beneath, especially when young. Flower spikes are small and in the axils of leaves. Common in prairie and parkland. [syn. *C. glaucum* L.]

HEINJO LAHRING

Saline slough—
Chenopodium habitat

Salicornia rubra A. Nels.   **CHENOPODIACEAE (Goosefoot Family)**

Red Samphire

Syn.: *Salicornia europaea* ssp. *rubra* (A. Nels) Breitung
Other Common Names: Slender Glasswort, Saltwort, Prickly-weed, Pigeon's-foot, Chicken's-claws, Samphire

Salicornia is from *sal* (salt) and *cornu* (horn), referring to this saline plant with horn-like branches. *Rubra* refers to its red colour.

Wetland
Annual
Native
Common
Hardiness Zone: 0
Flowering Season: mid- to late summer

DESCRIPTION

Erect plants are low-growing from prostrate, succulent stems (often semi-woody at base). Jointed stems (round in cross section), up to 25 cm long, turn bright red at maturity. Dark reddish green **leaves** are opposite and reduced to fleshy, triangular, scale-like growths (3 mm long) attached at stem nodes.

Flowers (in groups of 3), sunk into the stem where upper scales join the stem, form a terminal spike (1–5 cm long). Male and female, or only female, flowers are present. The fleshy calyx (there is no corolla) has a small slit for an opening. Within are 1 or 2 stamens and/or 2 styles. Ovary is superior with 1 ovule.

The spongy calyx encloses the **fruit** at maturity. Fruit is a small (1 mm), flattened seed covered with microscopic hairs.

HABITAT AND DISTRIBUTION

Red Samphire, a common plant of ocean beaches and saltwater marshes, inhabits alkali lakeshores, sloughs and mud flats of the parkland and prairies. It can withstand the highest salt content of any of our halophytes, so it is seen nearest the center of the alkali slough.

This plant is restricted to moist, saline growing conditions within its overall range. It has a circumpolar distribution. In North America it can be found from Alaska to Newfoundland in the north and as far south as California, Nevada and Georgia.

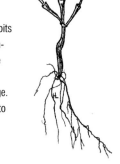

Salicornia rubra A. Nels.

Salicornia rubra

PAT PORTER

SPECIAL FEATURES

In summer the plants give the impression of a bright red carpet. Its presence is an indicator of strongly saline growing conditions.

Cattle relish it for its high salt content.

Red Samphire is edible. Due to the salty nature of this plant, it is recommended for pickling. It is rated as a good salad herb, or can be added to stews. The seeds are also edible and contain vitamin C and various other minerals.

Ashes of the plant, which have a high soda concentration, were mixed with animal fat to make soap. Glass makers of the past utilized its unique properties in their trade.

RELATED SPECIES

There is only one species of *Salicornia* in the Prairie provinces. Its succulent habit and preference for saline conditions make it an easy wetland plant to recognize.

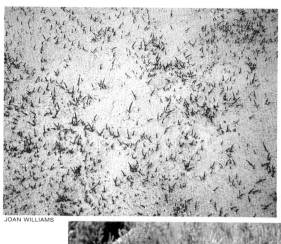

JOAN WILLIAMS

Salicornia rubra

PAT PORTER

Stellaria calycantha (Ledeb.) Bong.
Northern Stitchwort

CARYOPHYLLACEAE (Pink Family)

Syn.: *S. borealis* Bigel.
Other Common Names: Starwort, Chickweed

Stellaria is from the Latin *stella* (star) and describes the star-like shape of the flower. *Calycantha* means calyx-flowered.

Wetland
Perennial
Native
Common
Hardiness Zone: 0
Flowering Season: early to late summer

DESCRIPTION
The thin, trailing stems (10–40 cm long) grow from slender rootstocks. Green **leaves** (10–35 cm long) are thin, narrow, lanceolate to ovate in shape, and often ciliate at base. Lower leaves are directly attached to stem.

Flowers are either single on long, thin stalks (pedicels) or several along a leafy-bracted stem (cymes). Flowers consist of 5 sepals (2–4 mm long), 5 deeply 2-lobed white petals (at times absent or much reduced) which are shorter than sepals, 10 (or less) stamens, 3 styles, and a 1-loculed ovary.

Fruit is a dark, many-seeded capsule which opens by 6-valves.

HABITAT AND DISTRIBUTION
Northern Stitchwort grows in a low-trailing manner among the mosses and grasses of wet and shaded areas. Although often considered a forest understory plant, it tends to show up along seepages and drainages where light levels are low and humidity is high. This is a commonly encountered plant of the Rocky Mountains, foothills, boreal forest and Cypress Hills.

Its distribution is circumpolar occurs throughout Alberta, southern Saskatchewan and southern Manitoba. Range extends from the Yukon to Alaska in the north, to California, Utah and Wyoming in the south, and to Quebec, Newfoundland, the Great Lakes, and Appalachians in the east.

SPECIAL FEATURES
Stellaria calycantha is considered an edible plant. The young green leaves and stems can be used fresh in salads or boiled for 5 minutes in a small amount of water and served as a cooked green. 'Chickweed stew' tastes similar

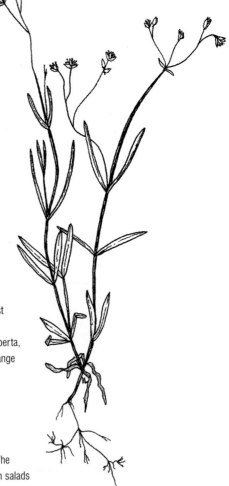

Stellaria calycantha (Ledeb.) Bong.

to okra. The plant is a winter source of vitamin C when most other greens are unavailable. Some recipes include Rabbit Stew with Chickweed, Fresh Chickweed Salad, and Chickweed Pancakes. Native peoples used the seeds for bread or to thicken soups, although they must have spent considerable time picking them as they are very small and the capsules not always very abundant in the wild.

The leaves contain vitamin C, a fixed oil, saponin, and are rich in iron. They are used in making hot and cold drinks. Chickweed tea is recommended as a laxative. Steep one spoonful per cup for 5 to 10 minutes.

RELATED SPECIES

The Chickweed family has several genera and many species which can be found in wet areas. Careful examination and a detailed flora are required to identify them correctly.

HEINJO LAHRING

Stellaria

DICOTS ■ HERBS

Nuphar variegata Engelm. ex Durand

NYMPHAEACEAE (Waterlily Family)

Yellow Pondlily

Syn.: *N. lutea* ssp. *variegata* (Engelm. ex Durand) Beal, *N. variegata* (Engelm. ex Durand) G. S. Mill., *Nymphozanthus variegatus* (Engelm. ex Durand) Fern.

Other Common Names: Spatter-dock, Cow-lily, Water-collard, Marsh-collard, Wokas, Bullhead Lily

Rooted Floating-leaved
Perennial
Native
Common
Hardiness Zone: 0
Flowering Season: early summer

top of leaf

bottom of leaf

flower

fruit

Nuphar variegata
Engelm. ex Durand

Nuphar, apparently of Arabic origin, is the name used by the Greeks, Egyptians and Persians to describe the plant. *Variegata* means to be varied or different, and in botany is usually used to describe a difference in colours, streaks or blotching pattern. It likely describes the purple blotch on the inside of the sepals of most plants.

DESCRIPTION

Arising from thick (4–10 cm), horizontal, at times branching, rhizomes are long, flattened (winged) petioles and peduncles growing towards the water surface. Often attached directly to rhizome are thin, translucent and wavy underwater foliage (especially on young plants). Thick, green surface **leaves** (10–40 cm long) are heart-shaped and pinnately veined below.

Solitary, yellow, cup-shaped **flowers** (4–7 cm wide) are held on or just above the water surface. Flowers consist of six showy sepals (usually with a purple blotch on the inside), many scale-like petals which merge towards center with numerous stamens, and a large compound pistil with 8–30 locules (many ovules). On top of pistil is a prominent green or yellowish stigmatic disc.

Fruit is a swollen (4 cm long), leathery berry (white spongy on the inside when young and turning mucilaginous at it decays) containing many seeds. The tan to dark brown seeds are hard and round (2–4 mm dia.).

HABITAT AND DISTRIBUTION

Yellow Pondlily can be found in ponds, lakes, and slow moving streams. On rare occasions it has been found growing in damp mud (rather than submerged) with short, upright stems and leaves. However, the tubers can freeze-out if too shallow, so plants tend to survive where they can overwinter beneath the ice at depths from 0.5 to 3 m. Water clarity is a limiting factor in water depth.

It occurs throughout the Prairie provinces. The range extends to the Territories and Alaska in the north (usually staying below tree-line), Montana, Idaho, Nebraska, Ohio, Delaware in the south, and across to Newfoundland in the east.

Nuphar variegata

JOAN WILLIAMS

HEINJO LAHRING

HEINJO LAHRING

Nuphar variegata: far left: cross-section through petiole; left: seed; below: cross-section through seed pod

SPECIAL FEATURES

Muskrats and beavers feed heavily on the rhizomes. Moose prefer the leaves of *Nuphar* vs. *Nymphaea*. Lily pads provide shelter and food for fish and invertebrates. Seeds are eaten by waterfowl such as Black Ducks, Mallards, Pintails, Ring-necked Ducks, Teals, Wood Ducks, Bitterns, and Soras.

HEINJO LAHRING

Nuphar leaves can be cooked and eaten like spinach. The leaves are handy as a wrapper for cooking other vegetables, or as a plate to hold food. The starchy rhizomes are best peeled and boiled in several changes of water to remove the extreme bitterness. The seeds were gathered, roasted and ground into flour for bread making or kept dry and stored for later use. The seeds, rich in oil, protein and starch, can be boiled and added to soups. At high temperatures and with a little oil or fat the seeds will crack open (somewhat like popcorn) and can be eaten as a snack sprinkled with a little salt. Medicinally the rhizomes were used to heal cuts and swellings.

RELATED SPECIES

Nuphar variegata is the dominant *Nuphar* of the Prairie provinces. *Nuphar advena* (Ait.) Ait. f., a pondlily of the southern Great Lakes region, may possibly be found in the southeastern areas of Manitoba (although yet unrecorded). It has leaves which tend to be raised out of the water, the petioles and peduncles are not as flattened or winged, the sepals lack the conspicuous purple blotch on the inside, and they bloom slightly later than *N. variegata*. [*N. fluviatile* (Harper) Standl., *N. lutea* ssp. *advena* (Ait.) Kartesz & Gandhi, *N. lutea* ssp. *macrophylla* (Small) Beal, *N. ovata* (Mill. & Standl.) Standl., *N. puteora* Fern., *Nymphaea advena* Ait., *Nymphozanthus advena* (Ait.) Fern., *Nymphozanthus advena* var. *macrophyllus* (Small) Fern.]

Nuphar microphylla (Pers.) Fern.

Nuphar advena

Nuphar microphylla (Pers.) Fern., **Small Pondlily**, has small (1.5–2.5 cm dia.) yellow flowers with an orangy red stigmatic disc, and small leaves (5–10 cm long) which often stand out of water. It is found in the boreal forest of central to southern Manitoba. [*Nymphaea microphylla* (Pers.) Robins. & Fern., *Nymphozanthus microphyllus* (Pers.) Fern.]

(See photo of *Nuphar microphylla* on page 172.)

Nymphaea odorata ssp. *odorata* Aiton

NYMPHAEACEAE (Waterlily Family)

Fragrant White Waterlily

Syn.: *Castalia odorata* (Ait.) Woodville & Wood

Nymphaea is from the Greek *nymphe* (nymph), the goddess of water. The strong fragrance of this waterlily gave it the name *odorata* (odorous or fragrant).

Rooted Floating-Leaved
Perennial
Native
Rare
Hardiness Zone: 1
Flowering Season: summer

DESCRIPTION

Horizontal rhizomes (2–6 cm dia.) produce side branches which are not noticeably constricted at base. Long, green, ascending petioles and peduncles are not strongly red-striped. Thin, translucent, submerged **leaves** are sometimes present. Surface leaves, green above and usually purple (not always) beneath, are orbicular (5–40 cm across) with the sinus about one third the length of the blade (typically narrow or closed).

Floating on the water surface are strongly scented white (rarely pinkish) **flowers** 6–19 cm across. Flowers open in the morning and close later in the day over a 3-day period (longer during poor weather). Each flower consists of 4 green sepals, 17–43 white petals (inner are transitional to stamens), numerous stamens, a compound pistil with many joined locules (numerous ovules), and a radiate stigma on a stigmatic disc. All of these are connected to a central, fleshy receptacle. Petals are more or less pointed at the tip. Upon successful fertilization, the peduncle becomes spiralled and pulls the developing fruit under water where the seeds ripen and are released.

Fruit is a many-seeded, globe-like berry. Small (1.5–2.3 mm), round to oval seeds are enveloped by a membranous sac-like structure (aril) which allows for flotation for a period of time.

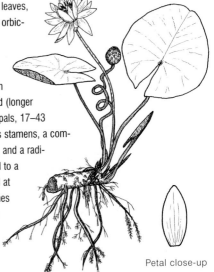

Petal close-up

Nymphaea odorata ssp. *odorata* Aiton

HABITAT AND DISTRIBUTION

The Fragrant White Waterlily grows in sloughs, pools in marshes, ponds, ditches, canals, swamps, slow moving streams, and lakes of the southeastern boreal forest. It tends not to be found in alkaline water bodies. Distribution in Canada corresponds in part to Canadian Shield water bodies and includes northern and central Saskatchewan, and central and southern Manitoba. Range extends eastward to Newfoundland and south to Florida, eastern Texas and Arizona.

Nymphaea odorata
ssp. *odorata*

BARRE HELLQUIST

Nymphaea odorata var. *tuberosa:* red stripes on peduncle and petiole

SPECIAL FEATURES

Leaf stomata (tiny openings where gas exchange occurs) are on the upper leaf surface rather than on the lower surface as in land plants. The round petioles have 4 large air passages used to pump oxygen to the roots (which are very buoyant when uprooted).

Rhizomes are eaten by muskrats, beavers, deer and porcupines.

HEINJO LAHRING

Nymphaea odorata ssp. *tuberosa*

Moose also eat them but prefer *Nuphar* tubers. Waterlilies shade the water and offer food and shelter for fish and invertebrates. The fruit, seeds and rhizomes are eaten by waterfowl such as teals, wood ducks, and scaups. By late summer, large areas will often have had their fruits eaten off by birds and muskrats leaving only peduncles sticking out of the water.

The Ojibway ate the flower buds. Leaves were used for wrapping food in for cooking. The rhizomes themselves are very bitter and require several changes of water to make them palatable.

Tea made from the rhizome was used to treat diarrhea and sore throats (and baldness!). Powdered, dried rhizome was used to treat boils, ulcers, sores and cough medicine. It has also been used as a heart tonic (due to the presence of the glucoside nymphaline).

RELATED SPECIES

Nymphaea odorata ssp. *tuberosa* (Paine) Wiersema & Hellquist, **Tuberous White Waterlily** or **Magnolia Waterlily**, may be encountered in the southeastern portion of the district and southward as far as Kansas. Its range extends eastward to southern Quebec and New England. This species is found in more alkaline waters than *N. odorata* ssp. *odorata*. It differs in having very little (if any) fragrance, strong reddish striping on petioles and peduncles, petals which are more rounded at the tips, larger seeds (2.8–4.4 mm long), leaves that are green above and below (sometimes pale purplish below), and rhizome branches which are constricted at the base (readily breaking off). [syn. *N. tuberosa* Paine, *Castalia tuberosa* (Greene) Paine] Where the two subspecies grow in close proximity to each other they are difficult to separate and may interbreed.

Petal close-up

HEINJO LAHRING

Nymphaea odorata var. *tuberosa*

Nymphaea leibergii Morong
Leiberg's Waterlily

NYMPHAEACEAE (Waterlily Family)

Syn.: *Castalia leibergii* Morong, *Nymphaea tetragona* Georgi ssp. *leibergii* (Morong) Porsild

Other Common Names: Pygmy White Waterlily

Nymphaea is from the Greek *nymphe* (nymph), the goddess of water. *Leibergii* is named after John Bernhard Leiberg, 1853–1913, known to have collected in Idaho in 1887 and founder of the botanical garden Baden-Baden, Germany. He introduced numerous ornamental species.

Rooted Floating-leaved
Perennial
Native
Rare
Hardiness Zone: 1
Flowering Season: summer

DESCRIPTION

Slender rhizome is erect or slightly horizontal and has few or no side branches. Surface leaves and flowers are at the end of very long, thin petioles and peduncles (up to 2 m in deeper water). Green, leathery **leaves** (5–12 cm long by 3–7 cm wide) have no leaf mottling on upper surface and are maroon to purple, without prominent veining, beneath. Leaf sinus is usually longer than midrib. Leaf lobes are divergent (not overlapping) with acute apices. The small (2.4–4 cm wide), non-fragrant, white **flowers** have 8–15 petals, 21–39 stamens, small (0.6–1.5 mm long by 0.8–1.4 mm wide) carpellary appendages, and a yellow stigmatic disc. The receptacle is slightly square to rounded when viewed from beneath.

Fruit is a many-seeded, globe-like berry. Small (3 mm), round to oval seeds are enveloped by a membranous sac-like structure (aril) which allows for flotation for a period of time. Fruit becomes mucilaginous as it decays and releases the seeds.

Nymphaea leibergii Morong

BARRE HELLQUIST

Nymphaea leibergii

HEINJO LAHRING

Right: *Nymphaea tetragona*
Below: *Nymphaea leibergii* pod
(left) and *Nymphaea tetragona*
pod (right)

HEINJO LAHRING

HEINJO LAHRING

HABITAT AND DISTRIBUTION

Nymphaea leibergii occurs in ponds, lakes
and slow moving streams. It has been noted to grow in acidic water bodies. Although this is a small waterlily,
it can be found in relatively deep water (1–2 m).

In the Prairie provinces the range is from northwestern Saskatchewan south-eastward through central and
southern Manitoba. Plants have been collected in northern Alberta, but are considered rare. Range extends
beyond Manitoba into southern Ontario and western Quebec. Populations also occur in British Columbia,
northwestern Montana, northern Idaho and northern Michigan and Minnesota.

SPECIAL FEATURES

The fruit is eaten by waterfowl. Floating leaves offer shade in the heat of summer. The plants offer food and
shelter for fish and invertebrates.

Small flowers provide nectar and pollen to flying insects during the
flowering period.

Nymphaea tetragona
Georgi

Flowers open in the late morning to early afternoon (noticeably later
than *N. odorata*), and close in the late afternoon. This opening and clos-
ing cycle normally lasts 3 days (in poor weather this is sometimes longer).
The stigma is receptive on day 1 (with a pool of liquid on the stigmatic
disc). On days 2 and 3 the liquid is gone and the pollen is released.
Fertilized flowers will form a characteristic bend just below the
receptacle. At this stage the peduncles coil, pulling the developing fruit
down into the water where the seeds ripen and are later released.

RELATED SPECIES

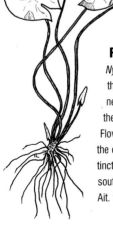

Nymphaea tetragona Georgi, **Small White Waterlily**, also occurs in the region. Its
thin leaves are often mottled or variegated on the upper leaf surface and prominently veined and purplish brown to green beneath. The leaf sinus is shorter than
the midrib. Leaf lobes are overlapping to divergent with rounded to acute apices.
Flowers have 10–16 petals, 30–69 stamens, a reddish to purple stigmatic disc, and
the carpellary appendages are 2–4 mm long by the same wide. The receptacle is distinctly square (very noticeable when observed from below). Only known to occur in
southeastern Manitoba. [*Castalia tetragona* (Georgi) G. Lawson, *N. pygmaea* (Salisb.)
Ait. f., *N. fennica* Mela]

Ceratophyllum demersum L.   CERATOPHYLLACEAE (Hornwort Family)

Hornwort

Other Common Names: Coontail, Coon's-tail

Ceratophyllum means horned (*cerato*) leaved (*phyllum*). *Demersum* means submerged in water and refers to its underwater habit.

Free-floating
Perennial
Native
Common
Hardiness Zone: 0
Flowering Season: mid- to late summer

DESCRIPTION

Although this plant may be imbedded in muddy pond sediments, it does not grow roots. The green stems, sometimes forming large colonies, are long, slender and much branched. **Leaves** are in whorls of 5–12 around the stem. Each leaf is stiff and 2–3 times forked into 2 equal segments with sharp teeth on the margin. Leaf whorls become increasingly more dense towards the ends of branches, giving the appearance of a Raccoon's tail (hence Coontail).
Unisexual **flowers**, appearing as tiny, red cylinders, are solitary and without stalks in the axils of the submerged leaves. There are no sepals or petals but 8–12 bracts subtend each flower. Male flowers consists of 12–16 stamens. Female flowers have a thin style, and 1 ovary containing a single ovule.

close-up of small teeth on a leaf

Fruit is a dark olive green, elliptical achene (5 mm long) with two spines near the base and a persistent style slightly longer than the achene (appearing as a spine) on top. Fruit is smooth or somewhat warty.

HABITAT AND DISTRIBUTION

Hornwort often occurs in water deeper than other submerged aquatic macrophytes (up to 7 m). It is found in ponds, quiet rivers, streams, and lakes.
This is a circumpolar water plant with a wide distribution across the Prairie provinces. It ranges from Alaska to Nova Scotia, is widespread in the northern United States and reaches as far south as Florida.

SPECIAL FEATURES

In alkaline waters the foliage often becomes encrusted with marl, a white precipitate composed of calcium and various salts. Under such conditions the plants are quite hard and brittle, easily fragmenting when handled.
Waterfowl eat the seeds and leaves. Muskrats occasionally eat the leaves. The dense foliage is an ideal refuge for invertebrates and fish fry.
Overwintering buds form late in the season at the ends of the branches. In the spring these buds (densely packed leaves and shoots) grow into new plants.
Hornwort is very sensitive to water quality changes. Once they have grown accustomed to certain water conditions they are difficult to

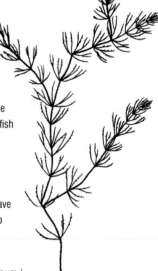

Ceratophyllum demersum L.

move successfully. When transported to a new aquatic environment they often lose all of their old growth and must readjust to the new water conditions by growing new branches and leaves.

RELATED SPECIES

Ceratophyllum can easily be confused with *Myriophyllum* (Water-milfoil) (see pages 232–234).

The spiny, forked leaves which are rough to the touch set the Hornwort apart. In Water-milfoil the leaves look like a miniature antenna (pinnately branched, not dichotomously forked), and true roots are formed.

Ceratophyllum echinatum Gray, the only other species in the region, occurs in southeasternmost Manitoba. Its leaves have more forks per leaflet (3 or 4 consecutive forkings vs. 1 or 2 for *C. demersum*) and the teeth on leaf segments are mostly absent, fruit has small, marginal spines and a warty surface. It prefers more oligotrophic and acidic waters (ave. pH 6.6 vs. 7.4 for *C. demersum*).

HEINJO LAHRING

Ceratophyllum demersum

MYRNA PEARMAN

193

Caltha palustris L.

Marsh-marigold

RANUNCULACEAE (Crowfoot Family)

Other Common Names: Cowslip, King's Cap, May-blob, Meadow-bright, Waterdragon, Meadow-bouts, Palsywort

Caltha is derived from the Latin name of a yellow-flowered plant (originally *Calendula* sp). *Palustris* (swampy or marshy) describes the habitat in which it is found.

Wetland
Perennial
Native
Common
Hardiness Zone: 1
Flowering Season: spring

DESCRIPTION

Plants grow as a compact clump (20–50 cm tall) with young, vegetative plantlets forming around the central mother plant. Broad (5–10 cm across), thick, round to kidney-shaped basal **leaves** are dark green, heart-shaped at base and have long petioles. Leaf edge is smooth to round-toothed. Erect stems are hollow and branching. Flowering stem leaves are smaller and short-petioled to clasping (towards the top).

Bright orange to yellow spring **flowers** (1.5–4 cm wide) are on short to long peduncles in loose and spreading clusters. Each flower consists of 5–9 showy oval to elliptic sepals, no petals, numerous stamens, 6–12 carpels and numerous ovules arranged in 2 rows in the ovary.

Fruit is a small, wedge-shaped and recurved pod (follicle) opening along the ventral side and containing many seeds. Pods are borne in dense heads.

HABITAT AND DISTRIBUTION

Marsh-marigold inhabits swamps, marshes, ditches, streambanks, lakeshores, wet meadows, seepages, and woods. It appears as a reduced form in the sub-arctic. It has a preference for slightly moving water. It is associated with the

Caltha palustris L.

GLEN SUGGETT

JOAN WILLIAMS

Caltha palustris

parkland, boreal and tundra areas of the Prairie provinces. Distribution is circumpolar with populations spread from Alaska to Newfoundland, as far north as Melville Island in the Arctic and as far south as Tennessee and the Appalachians.

SPECIAL FEATURES

Deer and moose feed on it and livestock will occasionally eat it. Grouse are known to eat the seeds. Although this is an edible plant, it should be cooked before being eaten since the toxins *helliborin* and *protoanemonin* are present which cause heart problems and inflammation of the stomach. Dried plants lose much of the poisonous properties. Handling the fresh plant may cause skin irritation.

Plants are best collected in spring before flowers appear or have finished blooming. This plant grows in the same habitat as the poisonous Water-hemlock and care must be taken during gathering. The bitter taste and volatile toxic compounds are removed by boiling for 30–60 min. in two changes of water. The long, white roots can be cooked and look like sauerkraut.

Pickled flower buds make a good substitute for capers. Soak in saltwater, cook in 2 changes of water and pickle in hot vinegar.

Teas were made for medicinal purposes such as a counter-irritant to relieve rheumatic pain. Large quantities must never be consumed and not more than 3 or 4 days in a row or mild kidney or liver inflammation may result. The caustic juice was dripped onto warts.

RELATED SPECIES

Two other Caltha species occur in the Prairie provinces:

Caltha leptosepala DC., **Mountain Marsh-marigold** or **Elk's Lip**, is a plant of wet alpine meadows of the Rocky Mountains. The cluster of oval or oblong basal leaves are coarsely toothed, heart-shaped at base and have long petioles. Single-leafed (or leafless) flower stems (10–40 cm tall) have one or two flowers (2.3–3.3 cm broad). Flowers have 6 or more white (sometimes bluish white on outside) sepals.

Caltha natans Pallas, **Floating Marsh-marigold**, is found in ponds, woodland lakes and slow moving streams of the parkland and boreal forest. It can be recognized by its small (2–4 cm across), floating, waterlily-like leaves and white or pinkish flowers (1 cm broad). Stems creep on mud, rooting at nodes, when water levels are low.

MYRNA PEARMAN

HEINJO LAHRING

Above: *Caltha leptosepala*

Left: *Caltha natans*

(See additional photo of *Caltha natans* on page 179.)

Ranunculus aquatilis L.   RANUNCULACEAE (Crowfoot Family)

White Water-crowfoot

Syn.: *R. trichophyllus* Chaix.
Other Common Names: White Water Buttercup, Large-leaved Water-crowfoot

Submerged
Perennial
Native
Common
Hardiness Zone: 0
Flowering Season: early to mid-summer

Ranunculus originates from the Latin term *rana* meaning frog and refers to the amphibious nature of several of the species. *Aquatilis* describes the plant's association with water.

DESCRIPTION

Rooted in mud are long, slender, branching stems. These rise to the water's surface, often forming a floating mat. **Leaves** are all submerged, alternate, petioled, finely divided (hair-like and not noticeably coiled) and collapse when taken from the water.

White **flowers** (1–1.5 cm across) are either floating or held just above the surface. Each flower consists of 5 sepals, 5 white petals, numerous yellow stamens, and 5 or more carpels (1-ovule each).

Fruit is an achene borne in a dense head. Each achene has a short (less than or equal to one third the length of the achene) beak on the top.

HABITAT AND DISTRIBUTION

White Water-crowfoot grows in shallow water of sloughs, ponds, ditches, lakes, and slow moving streams.

Distribution is circumpolar and scattered across the Prairie provinces. Range extends into the Territories and Alaska in the north, to California and Minnesota in the south, and to Newfoundland in the east.

Ranunculus aquatilis L.

HEINJO LAHRING

HEINJO LAHRING

Ranunculus aquatilis, left and above inset; above, submerged leaves

Ranunculus aquatilis

HEINJO LAHRING

SPECIAL FEATURES

The submerged foliage is excellent habitat for aquatic invertebrates and fish. The seeds are occasionally eaten by moose and waterfowl. Petals have a nectariferous spot or pit at their base and are a nectar source for pollinating flies and bees.

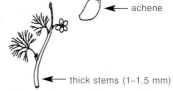

Ranunculus aquatilis var. *capillaceus*

The Crowfoots contain the toxins *anemonin* and *protoanemonin* and should not be eaten. Although *Ranunculus* is known to poison cattle in the fresh stage, hay containing dried buttercups is harmless.

In the past it was used as a rheumatism treatment as well as an antiseptic against bacteria.

RELATED SPECIES

Ranunculus aquatilis is quite variable. It is considered an Old World species by some authors. In the Prairie provinces we can further subdivide it into 4 varieties:

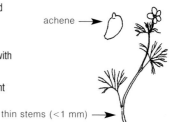

Ranunculus aquatilis var. *eradicus*

Ranunculus aquatilis var. *capillaceus* (Thuill.) DC. is a large plant with thick stems 1–1.5 mm in diameter. [*R. trichophyllus* Chaix]

Ranunculus aquatilis var. *eradicatus* Laest. is a small, reduced plant with slender leaves less than 1 mm in diameter. [*R. trichophyllus* Chaix]

Ranunculus aquatilis var. *longirostris* (Godr.) Laws., **Curly White Water-crowfoot**, has an achene beak which is longer than 0.5 mm (all other varieties have beaks less than 0.5 mm long). [*R. longirostris* Godr.]

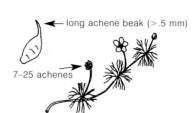

Ranunculus aquatilis var. *longirostris*

Ranunculus aquatilis var. *subrigidus* (Drew) Beit., **Firm White Water-crowfoot**, has leaves which are stiff with a short (or sometimes absent) grayish green petiole included in the sheath. It is also known as *R. circinatus* Sibth., and is noted for its coiled leaf blades which do not collapse when removed from water. [*R. subrigidus* W.B. Drew, *R. circinatus* var. *subrigidus* (W.B. Drew) Brietung]

Other water-loving *Ranunculus* include:

Ranunculus cymbalaria Pursh, **Seaside Crowfoot**, is an amphibious, creeping, yellow-flowered crowfoot. Its leaves are simple and cordate-ovate to reniform in shape. The head of achenes is columnar. Found in saline or calcareous muds of marshes and streams across the region.

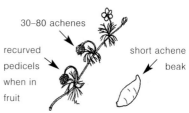

Ranunculus aquatilis var. *subrigidus*

Ranunculus flabillaris Raf., **Yellow Water-crowfoot**, is an amphibious crowfoot of shallow water and muddy shores of southern Alberta. It is distinguished from *R. gmelinii* in having finely, triternately divided leaf segments (1–2 mm wide) and longer petals (7–15 mm). [*R. delphinifolius* Torr.]

Ranunculus flammula var. *ovalis*

Ranunculus flammula var. *ovalis*

Ranunculus flammula var. *reptans*

HEINJO LAHRING

Ranunculus flammula

Ranunculus flammula L., **Creeping Spearwort**, has filiform [*R. f.* var. *reptans* (L.) E. Meyer D. Benson] or lance-shaped leaves [*R. f.* var. *ovalis* (J. M. Bigel.) L.]. The stems are creeping and root at the nodes. Flowers are yellow. Both are found across the Prairie provinces with *R. f.* var. *ovalis* being more southern. Found on muddy or marshy shores and wet sands.

Ranunculus gmelinii DC., **Gmelin's Crowfoot**, is a semi-aquatic plant common in the area. Its submerged leaves are circular and finely divided. Surface leaves are thicker and smaller with wider lobes (15–25 mm wide). A number of varieties are recognized and separated by hairiness, sepal and petal size.

Ranunculus hyperboreus Rottb., **Boreal Buttercup**, is a rare, yellow-flowered, semi-aquatic plant of the Rocky Mountains. It differs from *R. gmelinii* in having kidney-shaped leaves slightly to deeply 3-lobed.

Ranunculus gmelinii DC

Ranunculus gmelinii

HEINJO LAHRING

Cardamine pensylvanica Muhl. ex Willd.   BRASSICACEAE (Mustard Family)
Bitter Cress

Syn.: *C. scutata* Thunb.
Other Common Names: Pennsylvania Bitter Cress

Wetland
Biennial
Native
Common
Hardiness Zone: 0
Flowering Season: summer

Cardamine is the Greek name of a cress, *Kardamon* (probably the garden cress *Lepidium sativum*). *Kardamon* is from *Kardia* (heart) and *damao* (to overpower or to calm) with reference to heart medicine, poison or sedative. *Pensylvanica* is indicative of where the type specimens were collected (i.e., Pennsylvania).

DESCRIPTION
Growing from a taproot are erect or spreading stems (somewhat hairy at base) 10–50 cm tall. Compound **leaves** (2–8 cm long) have 1–6 pairs of rounded leaflets and one larger elliptical terminal leaflet.
Short, stalked, white **flowers** are arranged on a leafy terminal raceme. Flowers (3–5 mm across) consist of 4 sepals, 4 white petals, 6 stamens (outer 2 inserted lower down than the inner 4), 1 pistil (of 2 united carpels), and a 2-loculed ovary.
Straight, narrow and flattened **fruit** is an upright, pod-like capsule (silique; 1–3 cm long) which opens from the base. Pod sections curl back after discharging seeds at maturity. Each locule has one row of 12–20 wingless seeds (1–1.5 mm long).

HABITAT AND DISTRIBUTION
Bitter Cress grows on wet, muddy shores, riverbanks, beaver dams, wet woods, and rich swamps of the boreal forest, Rocky Mountains and Cypress Hills.
Plants may be found in each of the Prairie provinces. The range extends into the Territories, to California, Colorado, Oklahoma, and Florida in the south, and to Newfoundland in the east.

SPECIAL FEATURES
Ducks and muskrats feed on *Cardamine* as well as other cress species; however, plants are usually not found in abundance. Although listed as a biennial, it is sometimes considered a short-lived perennial.
The leaves are edible, fresh or cooked. On the East Coast they are called "creasy greens". The foliage is rich in vitamin C and a glucoside.

RELATED SPECIES
This is one of the most commonly encountered *Cardamine* species in the region. *Cardamine pratensis* L., **Meadow Bitter Cress**, also inhabits similar wetland locations (especially northern bogs and along the Peace River drainage in Alberta). It is circumpolar in distribution but considered rare in the Prairie provinces. It has long (8–13 mm), pink, rarely white, petals. Basal leaves and flowering stem leaves are usually long-petioled.
Bitter Cress may be confused with Watercress (see *Nasturtium officinale,* pages 200–201).

Cardamine pensylvanica Muhl. ex Willd.

Nasturtium officinale R. Br.   **BRASSICACEAE (Mustard Family)**

Watercress

Syn.: *Rorippa nasturtium-aquaticum* (L.) Schinz & Thell.

Nasturtium is derived from the Latin terms *nasi* (nose) and *tortium* (to twist) or a distortion of the nose and refers to the plant's strong smell and taste. *Officinale* (officinal or medicinal) indicates its use in herbal medicine.

Wetland
Perennial
Introduced
Rare
Hardiness Zone: 2
Flowering Season: summer

DESCRIPTION

Creeping stems (at times branching and hollow) root along their length (10–60 cm long) and are upright, reclining or floating.
Peppery **leaves** are pinnate with oval, smooth-margined leaflets.
White **flowers** are held up on widely spreading stems.
Flowers have long pedicels (1–2 cm long), 4 sepals (1.5–2 mm long), 4 white petals (3–4 mm long), 6 stamens, 1 pistil of 2 united carpels, and a 2-loculed ovary.
Fruit is a 1–2 cm long, curved, pod-like capsule (silique) which contains many seeds (arranged in two rows). Silique valves do not curl at maturity.

HABITAT AND DISTRIBUTION

Watercress is a European introduction finding its way into watersheds across North America. It grows either as a terrestrial plant on moist soils, or semi-aquatic in marshes, deciduous swamps, along streams and rivers, and at springs.

This popular plant is found across the continent from Alaska to Newfoundland.

Nasturtium officinale R. Br.

Nasturtium officinale

HEINJO LAHRING

SPECIAL FEATURES

Ducks and muskrats are known to eat Watercress.

Although highly sought-after for its strong taste and high nutrient content, caution is advised in collecting for food since it may grow in polluted water. If gathered in a healthy environment it can be used in several ways but should be consumed in moderation since excessive amounts may lead to urinary troubles (cystitis). Leaves can be cut off and eaten fresh in a salad (try birch sap as a salad dressing). It can be mixed with mild-tasting greens or added to stews and roasts to enhance the flavour (also good with wild onions). Tea is made by steeping the leaves. The juice should always be diluted with water to avoid irritation. Watercress can be fermented like sauerkraut.

Plants are rich in iron, calcium, copper, magnesium, iodine, niacin, and vitamins A, B, B_1 (thamine), B_2, C, and E. One hundred grams of fresh leaves is said to give 4900 I.U. of vitamin A and 80 mg of vitamin C.

RELATED SPECIES

This plant may be confused with *Cardamine pensylvanica* (Bitter Cress). Watercress is noted for its strong scent and peppery taste. The fruit of Watercress is curved (with seeds in 2 rows) and that of Bitter Cress is straight (with seeds in one row).

Nasturtium microphyllum Reichenb. is known from Saskatchewan. It is a smaller-leafed plant with longer, more slender fruits (16–26 mm) which have seeds in one row (versus 2 rows for *N. officinale*). [*N. officinale* var. *microphyllum* (Reishenb.) Thell., *N. uniseriatum* Howard & Manton]

HEINJO LAHRING

Nasturtium officinale

HEINJO LAHRING

Rorippa palustris (L.) Besser
Marsh Yellow Cress

BRASSICACEAE (Mustard Family)

Syn.: *R. islandica* (Oeder) Borbas

Rorippa suggests a plant which occurs in wet places, from *roridus* (covered with dew drops) and *ripa* (frequenting banks of streams or rivers). *Palustris* means marshy or swampy. Islandica refers to Iceland.

Wetland
Annual/Biennial
Native
Common
Hardiness Zone: 0
Flowering Season: summer

Rorippa palustris (L.) Besser

DESCRIPTION

Branching (above the base), erect stems (20–60 cm) have long-petioled, deeply lobed (almost pinnate) **leaves** (6–15 cm) near the base. Smaller, slightly lobed and petioled leaves (may be clasping stem) are near the top. In shallow water the lower leaves are sometimes submerged.

Long-pediceled (4–8 mm; spreading at maturity) **flowers** are held in a terminal raceme or on side branches of the main stem. The sepals (4) are longer than the 2 mm long yellow petals (4). Stamens are 6 or less. The single pistil is of 2 united carpels, and a 2-loculed ovary.

Fruit is a curved, elliptical to spherical pod (3–7 mm long) containing 2 irregular rows of seeds in each locule.

HABITAT AND DISTRIBUTION

Marsh Yellow Cress is common in marshes, sloughs, lakeshores and wet places of the prairie, parkland, boreal forest, foothills, mountains and tundra. This circumpolar species is distributed across the Prairie provinces. Range extends from Alaska to Newfoundland and is probably the most widely spread *Rorippa* species in the eastern and western United States.

SPECIAL FEATURES

Young shoots and leaves are edible either fresh or cooked. Plants have a pleasant taste.

RELATED SPECIES

The *Rorippa* group is commonly associated with wet locations. The yellow flowers and upright growth habit help to distinguish it from the more prostrate, white-flowered Watercress (*Nasturtium officinale*).

Rorippa tenerrima Greene, **Slender Cress**, looks quite similar to *R. palustris* but differs in that it branches from the base, and has shorter petals (less than 1 mm) and pedicels (less than 3 mm). Slender Cress is a rare plant of the southern Rocky Mountains and prairies of southern Alberta and Saskatchewan.

BARRE HELLQUIST

Rorippa palustris

Glycyrrhiza lepidota (pp. 218–219)
Wild Licorice

DICOTS ■ HERBS

Sarracenia purpurea L.

SARRACENIACEAE (Pitcher-plant Family)

Purple Pitcher-plant

Other Common Names: Southern Pitcher-plant, Sweet Pitcher-plant, Huntsman's Cap, Indian Cup Plant, Side-saddle Flower

Sarracenia, named by Linnaeus, is after Sarrazin, an early 1700s Quebec physician who used it to treat small pox. *Purpurea* is a botanical term for purplish and describes the colour of the leaves and flowers.

Wetland
Perennial
Native
Rare
Hardiness Zone: 0
Flowering Season: early summer

DESCRIPTION

Plants are insectivorous with a short root-stock and hollow, tubular, pitcher-like leaves. The bluish green **leaves**, patterned with red and purple veins, are formed in basal rosettes (10–20 cm tall). Each leaf has a narrow wing on one side and a partial hood over the top opening. The tube is covered in downward-pointing hairs on the inner surface and is often partly filled with water where insects are trapped, drowned and absorbed by the plant's enzymes. A solitary purple to dark red or maroon **flower** is held above leaves (20–40 cm). The large (5–7 cm wide), nodding flower consists of 5 spreading sepals, 5 incurved petals, numerous stamens,

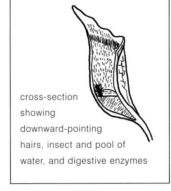

cross-section showing downward-pointing hairs, insect and pool of water, and digestive enzymes

and a pistil of 5 united carpels. Ovary is superior and 5-loculed with numerous ovules. Style is narrow at base but becomes large and umbrella-like at top with many small stigmas. **Fruit** is a capsule with 5 locules and many seeds.

Sarracenia purpurea L.

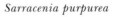

Sarracenia purpurea

Sarracenia purpurea

HEINJO LAHRING

HABITAT AND DISTRIBUTION

The Pitcher-plant dwells in amongst moisture-loving mosses (especially *Sphagnum* spp.) of the boreal forest. It is usually associated with acid and nutrient-poor conditions in peat bogs, muskegs, and coniferous woods. Populations have also been found in fens and old bogs which have become basic.

Plants occur in the northern and central portions of the Prairie provinces. Range extends into the Territories, eastward from Manitoba to Newfoundland, and south into the northeastern United States.

SPECIAL FEATURES

The musty odor and reddish colour of the leaves attract insects. Once they start down the tube the downward-pointing hairs prevent an upward retreat. After entering into the pool of liquid, a wetting agent and digestive enzymes dissolve the prey. This supplimental source of nitrogen assists the plant in surviving in a nutrient-poor (and often highly acidic) environment.

Not all small organisms succumb to a tragic ending. The larva of *Wyeomyia smithii*, a small mosquito, specializes in living only in the water of this plant. As well, the larvae of certain moths burrow into the leaves and feed on it.

Native peoples used the plant to hasten childbirth and treat dysentery.

RELATED SPECIES

The unique insect-trapping features of this plant make it easy to recognize. *Sarracenia purpurea* is the only Pitcher-plant found in the Prairie provinces.

Sarracenia purpurea

BARRE HELLQUIST

205

Drosera rotundifolia L.
Round-leaved Sundew

DROSERACEAE (Sundew Family)

Drosera is from the Greek *droseros* (glistening or covered with dew) and refers to the sticky droplets on the leaves. *Rotundifolia* describes the circular leaves: *rotundi* (rounded or almost circular) and *folia* (leaved).

Wetland
Perennial
Native
Common
Hardiness Zone: 0
Flowering Season: early to mid-summer

DESCRIPTION

This low-growing, insectivorous and fibrous-rooted plant has a rosette of basal **leaves** (to 10 cm across). Petioled leaves (3–10 cm long) are more or less round (1 cm wide) and covered with sticky, gland-tipped hairs. Margin of leaf is fringed with long-stemmed, reddish hairs. The tips of these hairs (tentacles) have sticky, dewdrop-like glands.
Flowers (3–10) are held above basal foliage (10–20 cm high) on a 1-sided flower spike (nodding towards top). Each flower is white (rarely pink) with 5 (4–8) sepals, 5 (4–8) petals (4–6 mm long), 5 (4–8) stamens, a pistil of 3–5 united carpels, and a 1-loculed ovary with numerous ovules. There are 3–5 deeply parted styles.
Fruit is a 3–5-loculed capsule containing many seeds.

HABITAT AND DISTRIBUTION

Round-leaved Sundew occurs in nitrogen-poor conditions in bogs, black spruce and tamarack swamps, and mossy locations along ponds and lakeshores. It is almost always associated with *Sphagnum* moss.
This circumpolar plant is scattered primarily across the boreal forest, tundra and mountain region of the Prairie provinces. Range extends into the Territories and Alaska in the north, to California, Alabama, and Florida in the south, and to Newfoundland in the east.

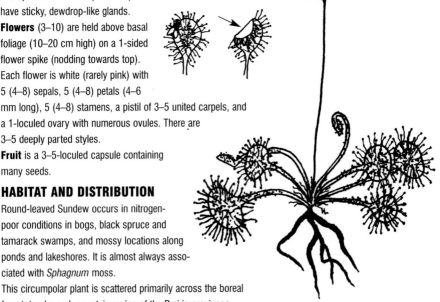

Drosera rotundifolia L.

SPECIAL FEATURES

Insects become trapped on the leaf's sticky hairs. The movement causes digestive enzymes to be secreted and pool around the victim. The organism is slowly dissolved, and the resulting nutrient solution is absorbed into the leaf.
The plant juice, when added to lukewarm milk, will cause it to curdle in a day or two.
Wool will dye yellow when boiled with sundew and ammonia. This is a rare plant and should not be collected in quantity.
Sundew contains *plumbagon* (a compound known for its antibiotic properties), resin, tannin, organic acids,

glucose, and various minerals. It has been used to treat whooping cough and asthma. The juice extract was applied to pimples and corns.

RELATED SPECIES

Two other species are often found growing in similar habitats:

Drosera anglica Huds., **Oblong-leaved** or **English Sundew**, has somewhat spoon-shaped (3–4 mm wide) leaves. White flowers are solitary (or up to 9) on a 1-sided raceme. It is found in similar habitats as *D. linearis*. This species is likely a hybrid between *D. rotundifolia* and *D. linearis*, since the three have been found growing together. Rare.

Drosera linearis Goldie, **Slender-leaved Sundew**, differs in having long, narrow (2 mm wide) leaves. White flowers are solitary (or up to 4) on a 1-sided raceme. Found in calcareous bogs, marly shores, and other lime-rich sites. Rare.

Drosera anglica Huds.

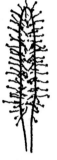

Drosera linearis Goldie

BARRE HELLQUIST

| *Drosera anglica* | *Drosera linearis* | *Drosera rotundifolia* |

A rare example of three Drosera species growing in close proximity: the shiny circles in the slide above are nickels indicating the location of each species, distinguishable here by their distinctive leaf shapes.

Chrysosplenium iowense Rydb.   **SAXIFRAGACEAE (Saxifrage Family)**

Golden Saxifrage

Chrysosplenium is of Greek origin (*chrysos*, gold; *splen*, spleen) and refers to the colour of the flower and its ancient medicinal usage. *Iowense* means of the state of Iowa or the Iowa Indian Tribe.

Wetland
Perennial
Native
Common
Hardiness Zone: 0
Flowering Season: early to mid-summer

DESCRIPTION

Plants are low growing, rooting along leafy stolons and producing bulbils. The petioled **leaves** are round to kidney-shaped (0.5–2 cm across) with veins. Margins have rounded teeth. Leaves often have some coarse, erect, white hairs above and below. **Flower** stems (3–15 cm tall) have 1–3 small leaves. Flowers (5–12) at top of stem are surrounded by small, spreading, yellow, leaf-like bracts. Each saucer-shaped flower (2.5–5 mm across) is composed of 4 golden yellow sepals (outer pair wider then the inner pair), no petals, 2–8 stamens, 2 carpels, and a 1-loculed ovary with numerous ovules. Center flowers tend to be larger than the outer (lateral) flowers.

Fruit is a flattened, 2-lobed capsule containing many seeds. Light brown seeds are smooth, thick-walled and more or less round (0.7–0.9 mm) with a keel on one side.

HABITAT AND DISTRIBUTION

Golden Saxifrage inhabits very wet ground in marshes, coniferous woods, and along streams. It is associated with the boreal forest zone and is often found in shade.

Chrysosplenium iowense Rydb.

Plants occur in Alberta, central Saskatchewan and southwestern Manitoba. Distribution also includes sections of the Territories, and just into the northeastern United States.

SPECIAL FEATURES

This low, creeping wetland plant is an indicator of water close at hand. It requires a dependable water source and is often found growing on hummocks with mosses and moisture-loving grasses and sedges.

Golden Saxifrage is a delicate and easily uprooted plant. It is quite sensitive to moves from one location to another and is best left in place.

The leaves of *Chrysosplenium* species from other areas (*C. americanum*, *C. alternifolium* and *C. oppositifolium*) are known to be edible either fresh or cooked.

RELATED SPECIES

Chrysosplenium americanum Schwein. ex Hook., **Water-mat** or **Water-carpet**, is of eastern distribution and known to occur in Saskatchewan and Manitoba. It is mat-forming with small and slightly succulent leaves. Flowers have stamens with orange-red anthers. There are two styles. Inhabits shallow, cool, often shady, springy waters.

Chrysosplenium tetrandrum (Lund) T. Fries., **Green Saxifrage**, differs from *C. iowense* in having smaller flowers (2–3 mm across), green, erect sepals (rather than gold and spreading), and 4 stamens versus 2–8. A frequently encountered plant of Saskatchewan wetlands.

Potentilla palustris (pp. 214–215)

Marsh Cinquefoil

HEINJO LAHRING

DICOTS ■ HERBS

Parnassia palustris L.   **SAXIFRAGACEAE (Saxifrage Family)**

Northern Grass-of-Parnassus

Syn.: *P. montanensis* Fern. & Rydb., *P. multiseta* (Ledeb.) Fern.

Other Common Names: Bog-stars

This was named in honour of Mount Parnassus in Greece (first named by Dioscorides). It was likely dedicated or sacred to the Muses who were believed to live on the snow-capped mountain. *Palustris* means marshy or swampy.

Wetland
Perennial
Native
Common
Hardiness Zone: 0

DESCRIPTION

Upright plants (5–30 cm tall) grow from a short rhizome. Long-petioled basal **leaves** are heart-shaped (2–4 cm long) and smooth margined.

Flower stem has a single, clasping heart-shaped leaf at or below the middle. Often there are several stems per plant. There is one large (2.5 cm across), white flower. It consists of 5 green sepals (0.5 cm long, partially united at base and alternating with petals), 5 white petals (1–2 cm long with 5–9 greenish or yellowish veins), 5 stamens, 5 scales with 7–15 gland-tipped staminodia (just opposite the petals), 4 united carpels with 4 stigmas, and a 1-loculed superior ovary.

Fruit is an oval capsule (1 cm long) opening with 4 valves and containing many winged seeds.

HABITAT AND DISTRIBUTION

Grass-of-Parnassus is often associated with calcium-rich soils. It is found in marshes, fens, ditches, shoreline meadows and wet, shady places. Common in the boreal forest, parkland and Rocky Mountain regions.

This circumpolar plant is spread from Alaska to Newfoundland in the

Parnassia palustris L.

Parnassia palustris

PAT PORTER

210

north and to California, Colorado, North Dakota, and the Great Lakes region in the south.

SPECIAL FEATURES

The veins on the petals act as runway lights to lead insect pollinators to the attractive, nectar-tipped staminodia.

The stamens ripen and shed their pollen one after the other.

Plants contain tannin.

Parnassia palustris

JOAN WILLIAMS

RELATED SPECIES

Parnassia fimbriata Konig, **Fringed Grass-of-Parnassus**, has fringed sides on its petals and the leaves are more or less kidney-shaped. It is generally considered a mountain species with distribution limited to the Rocky Mountains.

Parnassia kotzebuei Cham. & Schlecht., **Small Grass-of-Parnassus**, has only 3 veins in its white petals. The petals are shorter than the sepals and the flowering stem is leafless, or perhaps with a leaf close to the base. It is a plant of cool wetlands. Range includes Alberta's foothills and mountains, northern Saskatchewan, central Manitoba, northern Quebec, Newfoundland, and as far north as Baffin Island and Greenland.

HEINJO LAHRING

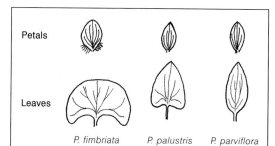

Petals			
Leaves			
	P. fimbriata	*P. palustris*	*P. parviflora*

Parnassia parviflora (DC.) Boivin, **Small** or **Northern Grass-of-Parnassus**, is very similar to the *P. palustris* but has narrowed leaf bases, 5–7 staminodia per scale and the flower stem leaf is small and narrow towards its base.

Parnassia fimbriata

JIM ROMO

Geum rivale L.

ROSACEAE (Rose Family)

Purple Avens

Other Common Names: Water Avens, Chocolate-root, Indian-chocolate

The species epithet, *rivale*, means 'pertaining to brooks.'

Wetland
Perennial
Native
Common
Hardiness Zone: 1
Flowering Season: summer

DESCRIPTION

This tall (40–100 cm) herb has long (to 30 cm) basal **leaves** which are lyrately pinnate with several smaller leaves along the length and 1–3 large, broad, toothed leaflets at the tip. Plants are usually quite hairy. The flowering stem has several small alternate leaves which are lobed and toothed. Few to several **flowers** (1.5–2 cm across) are in nodding clusters (becoming erect in fruit). Purplish to flesh-coloured (often yellow with purple veins) flowers are composed of a cup-shaped receptacle having 5 calyx-lobes (alternating with 5 bractlets), 5 petals, many stamens, many carpels, a superior ovary, and long styles (jointed at middle; upper half feathery). Flower heads consist of several spreading **achenes**. Each achene retains its long style (becoming hooked). The portion of style above the joint sometimes breaks off.

HABITAT AND DISTRIBUTION

Purple Avens inhabits wet meadows, swamps, fens, marshes, and stream banks. It is generally associated with the boreal forest but also grows in the foothills, mountains, parkland and Cypress Hills. Range extends across the country from British

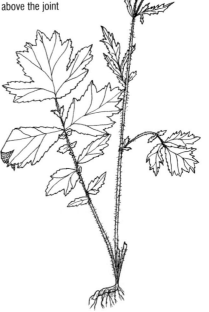

Geum rivale L.

Geum rivale

HEINJO LAHRING

Columbia to Newfoundland. Plants occur as far south as Washington, New Mexico, Missouri, Indiana and eastward to New Jersey. *Geum rivale* is also found in Europe and Asia.

SPECIAL FEATURES

The long, feathery style assists in wind dispersal of the seeds. The hooked feature inables the seeds to attach themselves to a passing animal or anchor themselves upon landing.

The aromatic roots can be boiled to make a beverage with a taste somewhat like chocolate, although the connection may be somewhat remote.

This dark-coloured drink was used as a tonic.

Native people were well aware of the powerful astringent action of the roots. It was a much-used medicinal plant for the treatment of dysentry.

RELATED SPECIES

The following two Yellow Avens species may also be found in wet meadows and damp woods in the area. Both can be recognized by their yellow flowers and turned-back sepals. Hybrids between the Yellow and Purple Avens are known to occur.

Geum aleppicum Jacq., **Yellow Avens**, has a hairy style. The basal-leaf terminal segments are tapered toward the petiole.

Geum macrophyllum Willd., **Large-leaved Yellow Avens**, has only a few or no hairs on the style. The basal-leaf segments are heart-shaped or non-tapering toward the petiole. [syn. *G. perincisum* Rydb.]

Left: *Geum* seed heads in winter

Below: *Geum rivale*

HEINJO LAHRING

JOAN WILLIAMS

Potentilla palustris (L.) Scop.
ROSACEAE (Rose Family)

Marsh Cinquefoil

Syn.: *Comarum palustre* L.
Other Common Names: Marsh Five-finger

Potentilla is a Latin diminutive form of *potens* (powerful). It originally applied to *P. erecta*, a powerful herb used during the Middle Ages. *Palustris* means marshy or swampy.

Wetland
Perennial
Native
Common
Hardiness Zone: 0
Flowering Season: summer

DESCRIPTION

Red, erect stems (20–60 cm) grow from creeping, woody rhizomes.
Green **leaves** (pale and fine-hairy beneath) are pinnately compound with 5–7 oblong to oval, coarsely toothed leaflets (5–10 cm long), tapered towards the base. Red to purple petioles have 2 sheathing stipules.

The open **flower** cluster of a few reddish purple or maroon flowers (2 cm across) is held erect on a leafy stem (smaller leaves and with fewer leaflets than the basal leaves). Reddish petals (5) are shorter and narrower than the 5 purplish sepals. Sepals alternate with 5 bractlets. There are many stamens, numerous carpels and a superior ovary. Red to golden brown, hairless **achenes** (1 mm long) are formed in a head and enveloped by the persistent hypanthium.

HABITAT AND DISTRIBUTION

This sprawling cinquefoil inhabits swamps, marshes, fens, bogs, stream banks, and lakeshores. It is associated with the boreal forest and occasionally the parkland (in particular the northern and eastern parts).
Marsh Cinquefoil is a circumpolar plant with populations found across the Prairie provinces. It ranges northward as far as the Arctic coast, southward to California, Wyoming, Indiana, and eastward to New Jersey.

Potentilla palustris (L.) Scop.

HEINJO LAHRING

Potentilla palustris

(See additional photo of *Potentilla palustris* on page 209.)

SPECIAL FEATURES

The plants and seeds are eaten by wildlife. Grouse consume the seeds while rabbits and hares are known to occasionally eat the leaves.

Potentilla palustris is the most aquatic of the *Potentillas* and is often found with stems floating in shallow water.

Potentilla anserina (see below) has long, narrow, edible roots. They can be boiled or roasted to produce a food similar to parsnips or sweet potatoes.

RELATED SPECIES

The reddish purple flowers of *P. palustris* set it apart from other moisture-loving *Potentilla* species including the following yellow-flowered varieties:

Potentilla anserina L., **Silverweed** or **Indian Sweet Potato**, is a low, tufted plant spreading by runners like strawberry plants. It has pinnate leaves (10–45 cm long; 7–25 leaflets) which are green above and silky white woolly beneath. Flowers are solitary on leafless stems. Very common across the region.

Potentilla diversifolia Lehm., **Mountain** or **Smooth-leaved Cinquefoil**, is a common mountain species (up to alpine) with palmately lobed leaves (5–9 leaflets, green and non-hairy above and below) which are toothed on the upper two-thirds of their margins. Flowers are few to several with petals longer than the sepals.

Potentilla drummondii Lehm., **Drummond's Cinquefoil**, is an alpine or subalpine species of the southern Rocky Mountains (15–50 cm tall) with pinnate basal leaves which are short (5–10 cm long), deeply toothed and have a few hairs along the veins. Petals (6–11 mm long) are much longer than the sepals.

Potentilla norvegica L., **Rough Cinquefoil**, an upright (15–60 cm tall) annual or biennial of moist meadows (and often a common weed of gardens) is upright with hairy, toothed, 3-foliate leaves. Numerous light yellow flowers form a dense cluster on a very leafy stem. Sepals are only slightly longer than the petals.

Potentilla paradoxa Nutt., **Bushy Cinquefoil**, has spreading or somewhat erect stems (20–50 cm tall) with short-petioled pinnate leaves (5–11 mostly hairless leaflets). Petals are about equal to the sepals. Flower stalk is leafy with many flowers. This is a prairie species found on shores of lakes and rivers.

Potentilla rivalis Nutt., **Brook Cinquefoil**, is an annual or biennial species very much like *P. norvegica*. It has leafy stems (20–40 cm tall) with digitate (5–9 divisions) basal leaves (green above and green to brownish below). Light yellow petals are shorter than the sepals (a feature separating it from *P. norvegica*).

HEINJO LAHRING

HEINJO LAHRING

Potentilla palustris

DICOTS ■ HERBS

Rubus arcticus L.   ROSACEAE (Rose Family)
Northern Dwarf Raspberry

Syn.: *R. acaulis* Michx.
Other Common Names: Crimson-berry, Crimson
Blackberry, Arctic Bramble, Nagoonberry

Rubus is named after the colour red (most likely repre-
senting the fruit colour of many species in this genus).
Arcticus means the Arctic or Far North.

Wetland
Perennial
Native
Common
Hardiness Zone: 0
Flowering Season: spring to early summer

DESCRIPTION

This low-growing (5–10 cm), tufted herb has a slender, underground rootstock with
annual shoots. Each non-prickly shoot has 2–4 **leaves** with 3 leaflets. Unevenly
toothed leaflets are broadly ovate (1.5–3.5 cm long) with a rounded to slightly
pointed tip. Stipules are oval and somewhat sheath-like.

fruit

Solitary, light to dark pink **flowers** are held up on long, thin pedicels. Each
flower (2 cm across) consists of a saucer-like receptacle, 5 sepals, 5–7
pink petals (1–1.5 cm long), numerous stamens, and numerous carpels.
Petals of *Rubus arcticus* var. *acaulis* are distinctly clawed whereas
those of *R. arcticus* var. *arcticus* are not.
Bright red **fruit** is a cluster of 20–30 fleshy drupelets held
together by the receptacle. Fruit ripens in late summer to early
fall.

HABITAT AND DISTRIBUTION

Dwarf Northern Raspberry grows in wet meadows and woods, muskegs,
black spruce swamps, bogs, fens, marshes, alder thickets, and along creek
and river banks. It is associated with the boreal forest and tundra.
This circumpolar raspberry occurs in each of the Prairie provinces. Its range
extends across northern Canada from the Yukon to Newfoundland. In 1795,
Hearne found it growing as far north as Marble Island. To the south it occurs in
Oregon, Montana, Colorado, Minnesota, Michigan.

Rubus arcticus L.

SPECIAL FEATURES

Grosbeaks, robins, sparrows, thrushes, orioles, catbirds, grouse, bears, chipmunks, squirrels, racoons, mice
and hares are all known to feed on the fruit.

The fragrant, sweet, juicy fruit (high in vitamin C and some vita-
min A) is considered the choicest of all the wild fruits and is
easily recognized by everone. Even the Swedish botanist
Linnaeus considered the fruit of this species a personal favorite.
It has been enjoyed by native North Americans, Laplanders and
Scandinavians to name a few. The fruit can be eaten fresh, with
cream, made into jams and pies or preserved by freezing.
Tea can be made from the fresh or dried leaves. The tender,
young shoots are edible and pleasant to chew on.
The root-bark was used in preparing a medicine for treating

Raspberryade recipe

1. put berries into sealer jar and fill
   spaces with white vinegar
2. seal jars and let stand 1 month
3. strain off juices through fine sieve
4. pour into sterilized jars or bottles
5. to serve, sweeten to taste with
   sugar and dilute with ice water

216

diarrhea and intestinal upsets.

A dark grey or almost black dye can
be produced from the young shoots of
R. chamaemorus (Cloudberry).

RELATED SPECIES

♀ flower

Other low-growing, moisture-loving
Rubus species include:

Rubus chamaemorus L., **Cloudberry** or **Baked-apple
Berry**, has leaves which are merely lobed (5–7 lobes)
vs. divided into three separate leaflets as in *R. arcticus*.
Flowers are white (1 cm long). Fruit is red becoming gold-
en yellow as it ripens. This is a boreal forest species
found in raised peat bogs on acid substrates, like
Sphagnum.

Rubus pedatus J.E. Smith, **Dwarf Bramble**, is a
low-growing, white-flowered herb with compound
leaves divided into 5 definite lobes. Each of the lateral lobes
are almost cleft to the base. Red fruit is small with 1–6 drupelets.
Tends to prefer wet woods rather than wetlands. Plant of the Rocky
Mountains, western boreal forest and western parkland.

Rubus chamaemorus L.

Rubus pubescens Raf., **Dewberry** or **Running Raspberry**, is very similar to *R. arcticus* but has small, white
to pale pink blooms (petals 4–8 mm long and erect; not spreading at maturity as in *R. arcticus*). The trailing
stems are long and semiwoody. The fruit has only a few loosely coherent, juicy, red drupelets. Prefers moist
woods. This species produces a hybrid with *R. arcticus* [*R. x paracaulis* Bailey].

Rubus pubescens in fruit

HEINJO LAHRING

Glycyrrhiza lepidota (Nutt.) Pursh FABACEAE (Pea Family)

Wild Licorice

Other Common Names: American Licorice, Sweet-root

Glycyrrhiza is from the Greek terms *glycys* (sweet) and *rhiza* (root) and refers to the root's sweet taste. *Lepidota* means covered with small scales.

Wetland
Perennial
Native
Common
Hardiness Zone: 1
Flowering Season: summer

DESCRIPTION

Growing from a thick rootstock are tall (30–100 cm), erect stems. Pinnately divided **leaves** have 11–19 elliptic to oblong, smooth-margined leaflets (2–4 cm long) with tapering bases and sharp tips. Leaves are pale green and glandular dotted.

Flowering stem, attached at leaf axil, is a raceme with 20 or more closely spaced yellowish white **flowers** (1–1.5 cm long). Flowers are pea-like with a 5-toothed tubular calyx, 5 petals (uppermost is the standard, two laterals are wings, and the lower two form the keel), 10 stamens, 1 pistil, and a superior ovary with 1 locule.

Fruits are reddish brown, oblong pods (1–2 cm long) covered with hooked prickles. Pods are in clusters with each containing 3–5 large (4 mm) seeds.

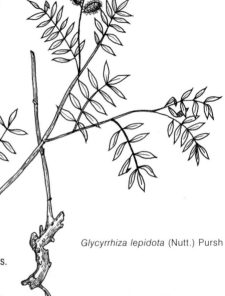

Glycyrrhiza lepidota (Nutt.) Pursh

HABITAT AND DISTRIBUTION

Wild Licorice is tolerant of very wet to moderately dry sandy soils. This is a prairie and parkland plant found in slough margins, coulees, moist grasslands, river and stream banks, and pond and lake shores.

Plants inhabit the southern and western half of the Prairie provinces. Range extends into southeastern British Columbia, southward to California, Arizona and Texas, and eastward from Missouri up to Minnisota and Ontario.

SPECIAL FEATURES

Glycyrrhiza lepidota is the North American equivalent of the European and cultivated licorice. The thick root-stocks (milder than the cultivated version) were chewed, baked and roasted by Native peoples. The slightly bitter outer part of the root was usually scraped off.

The sweet taste is due to *glycyrrhizin*, a saponin about 50 times sweeter than white sugar (saccharose). Roots contain 5% glycyrrhizin, 6% sugars (3% saccharose and 3% glucose), 30% starch, 15% resinous oil, plus flavoids, asparagin, estrogen and other miscellaneous compounds.

Root extracts are used by the confectionary and tobacco industries. The thick, black extract is obtained by slowly boiling the filtered liquid. This extract was used to give beer its head of foam. Pulverized roots were used in flavorings for candy, root beer, and medicines to name a few.

Consumption should not be in excess since it can cause hypertension if used over a long period of time.

RELATED SPECIES

This plant is easily recognized by the hooked prickles on its pods, stout upright stem, and fragrant rootstocks. It is the only species of *Glycyrrhiza* which is native to the region.

PAT PORTER

Glycyrrhiza lepidota

PAT PORTER

(See additional photo
of *Glycyrrhiza lepidota*
on page 203.)

DICOTS ■ HERBS

Callitriche verna L.
Vernal Water-starwort

CALLITRICHACEAE (Water-starwort Family)

Syn.: *C. palustris* L.
Other Common Names: Common Water-starwort

Callitriche is from *calli* (beautiful) and *tricho* (hair-like) and describes the thread-like submerged leaves and stems. The Latin term, *Verna*, pertains to spring.

Rooted Floating-leaved
Perennial
Native
Common
Hardiness Zone: 0
Flowering Season: late spring to summer

DESCRIPTION

Light green, tufted plants root in shallow water or mud. Branches can be up to 30 cm long. Submerged **leaves** are short (1–1.5 cm long), very narrow, and 1-nerved with a cut or notch at the point. Surface leaves are oval to spoon-shaped (3-nerved) and form a densely leaved rosette at branch ends, spreading out on the water surface creating a star-like pattern. A narrow membraneous wing exists at the point where the leaves meet the stem.

Tiny, greenish **flowers** (1–3 per leaf axil) are unisexual and subtended by 2 bracts (1 mm long). Male flowers have no sepals, no petals, and one stamen. Female flowers consist of 1 pistil of 2 carpels (4-loculed), 2 styles and a superior ovary.

The small, elongated, narrowly winged **fruits** (1 mm wide) are in pairs (separated by a wide groove). Each nut-like fruit is 4-lobed, splitting into 4 one-seeded units.

HEINJO LAHRING

Callitriche verna

MYRNA PEARMAN

220

DISTRIBUTION AND HABITAT

Water-starwort makes its home in shallow ponds, streams, ditches, and puddles where water persists for much of the growing season. Plants often end up growing on mud in the summer and fall due to decreasing in water levels. It has a preference for cold, clear water and does best in open areas with lots of light.

This circumpolar plant occurs over much of the Prairie provinces. Its range extends well into the Territories, westward to Alaska, eastward to Newfoundland, and from California to Virginia in the south.

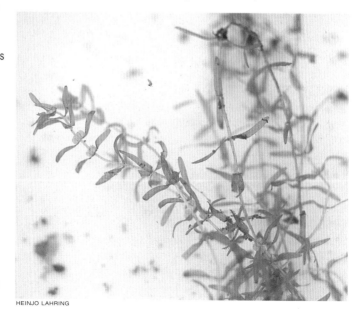

Callitriche verna L.

SPECIAL FEATURES

Callitriche verna is an important food for waterfowl. Its intertwining stems provide homes for invertebrate life, and small fish.
Callitriche hermaphroditica has been used in the aquarium trade as an oxygenating plant.

Plants reproduce vegetatively from sections of broken-off stems, rooting at the nodes. It is used in water gardening as an ornamental plant and is especially showy when the surface leaves develop their star-like arrangement later in the season. It is very hardy and will usually survive in shallow waters which are frozen solid for the winter, starting up fresh the following spring.

RELATED SPECIES

Callitriche hermaphroditica L., **Northern Water-starwort**, is an entirely submerged plant with stems reaching 40 cm in length. The dark green leaves are shorter (0.5–1.5 cm) than *C. verna*, usually crowded on stem, and lack the narrow wings where leaf meets stem. Leaves have a slight notch in the apex. Floral bracts are absent and fruits are more circular. This northern species is found in shallow lakes and flowing water across the Prairie provinces. [syn. *C. autumnalis* L.]

Callitriche hermaphroditica

HEINJO LAHRING

DICOTS ▪ HERBS

Impatiens noli-tangere L.

BALSAMINACEAE (Touch-me-not Family)

Western Jewelweed

Syn.: *I. occidentalis* Rydb.

Other Common Names: Touch-me-not, Yellow Balsam

Impatiens is Latin for impatient and refers to the fruit which explodes at maturity. *Noli-tangere*, short form of the Latin *noli me tangere* (a warning without meddling), describes the ripe seed cases which burst when touched.

Wetland
Annual
Native
Common
Hardiness Zone: 1
Flowering Season: summer

DESCRIPTION

This herbaceous plant has upright, succulent, straw-coloured or light green stems (50–150 cm tall). The oval to ovate, pale green, coarsely toothed **leaves** are alternate, petioled and lack stipules. Submerged leaves have a silvery look.

Downward-hanging blooms are held in axillary racemes. **Flowers** are large (2 cm long) and golden yellow, sometimes with red or purple spots on the inside of the long-spurred pouch (spur under but not parallel to sac as in *I. capensis*). Each flower consists of 3 sepals (2 are small and green, the third is formed into the pouch), 3 lobe-like petals (2 of which are considered to be pairs of united petals), 5 stamens, 1 pistil (5-loculed), and no style.

The **fruit** is a pod-like capsule which opens explosively (central column of fruit is under tension) when mature by 5 valves and ejects the seeds up to several meters. Many of the seed capsules are formed from self-pollinated, smaller flowers which do not fully open.

HABITAT AND DISTRIBUTION

This is a shade plant of wet woodlands, fens, valleys, canyons, stream banks, and occasionally in moist coniferous forests. It is known to do well in wet loam, sandy soil, and semi-emergent on stream banks. Plant distribution is closely correlated with the boreal forest zone of the Prairie provinces. Range extends westward to southern Alaska, south to Oregon and Idaho, and east to central Manitoba. It is also a resident of Europe and Asia.

SPECIAL FEATURES

The flowers are an important source of nectar for hummingbirds. Bees and butterflies are important pollinators. Capsules are eaten by grouse and mice. Hares and rabbits feed on the stems and leaves. Western Jewelweed was used as food by Native peoples.

Impatiens capensis Meerb.

The juice of *I. capensis* (see below) makes an effective wash in treating poison ivy and stinging nettle irritations, as well as an antifungal treatment for athlete's foot.

RELATED SPECIES

The **Spotted Touch-me-not**, *Impatiens capensis* Meerb., is similar to the above but has bright orange to reddish or pale yellow flowers heavily spotted with red or purple. The corolla abruptly contracts to the spur (the spur being bent back parallel to the pouch). In *I. noli-tangere*, the corolla tapers gradually into the spur (the spur being only slightly bent back). This is the most common species of *Impatiens* in Saskatchewan. It tends to put forth the showy flowers only in standing water, or at least where the ground is spongy with water. In mesic habitats only cleistogamous flowers appear (abundantly seed-bearing), making it difficult to assign these plants to a species. [syn. *I. biflora* Walt.]

GLEN SUGGETT

Impatiens capensis

Hypericum majus (Gray) Britt.   CLUSIACEAE (St. John's-wort Family)

Large Canada St. John's-wort

Other Common Names: Goat Weed

Hypericum is a compound word derived from the Greek *hypo* (almost) and *ereike* (heather). *Majus* means greater. The common name of St. John's-wort is from a European species which blooms around June 24th (St. John's Day).

Wetland
Perennial
Native
Occasional
Hardiness Zone: 0
Flowering Season: early summer

DESCRIPTION

Plants grow erect (10–50 cm tall) from short, leafy rhizomes. The oval to elliptic **leaves** (1–3.5 cm long) are opposite and sessile to stem. Leaves are 5–7-nerved and have translucent dots when emergent. Lower leaf margins meet or overlap, tending to clasp around the stem.
Flowers (0.5 cm long) are held in loose clusters (cymes). Each flower has 15–35 stamens, 3 styles, and a 1-loculed superior ovary with numerous ovules.
Fruit is a many seeded, blunt-tipped capsule (6–8 mm long).

HABITAT AND DISTRIBUTION

St. John's-wort grows in damp, sandy to mucky soils of marshes, fens, wet meadows, stream borders, and lakeshores.
Distribution is associated with the boreal forest. It is rare in Alberta but more frequent in Saskatchewan and Manitoba. Range is from British Columbia to Nova Scotia. To the south, populations occur in Washington, Colorado and across to New Jersey.

SPECIAL FEATURES

St. John's-wort is used as food by wildlife such as birds (ducks) and browsing animals (hares).
In England, *Hypericum* was hung over doorways in hopes of bringing prosperity to the household. The plants were also used to produce a dark yellow dye. As a herbal it was blended with olive oil for *touch and heal* medicine (the healing was through astringency). When employed in preparing various medicines, the juices from the flowers were red and the terms 'St. John's blood' and 'Mary's sweat' were used to describe them.

Hypericum majus
(Gray) Britt.

RELATED SPECIES

Three other Hypericums are noted to be present in Prairie province wetlands:
Hypericum canadense L., **Canada St. John's-wort**, is a smaller version of *H. majus*. It grows up to 40 cm tall with narrow, 1–3-nerved, pointed leaves. The margins of opposite leaves do not meet around the stem (in *H. majus* they do). Distribution is within the eastern boreal forest (southern Manitoba). *Hypericum canadense* and *H. majus* are sometimes classified as annuals.
Hypericum formosum HBK, **Western St. John's-wort**, is a yellow-flowering perennial (15–60 cm tall) with horizontal rootstocks and broad, almost circular, leaves with black dots along the edge. Petals (7–14 mm long) are twice the length of sepals. Sepals and petals may have black glandular dots along their edges. Plants are restricted to alpine locations in Alberta.
Hypericum virginicum var. *fraseri* (Spach) Fern., **Marsh St. John's-wort**, is similar to *H. formosum* but has pink to greenish flowers with sepals to 5 mm long and styles to 1.5 mm long. The foliage has translucent glands. This is a rare plant of wet sands, boggy or swampy ground and wet shores in the eastern boreal forest. It occurs in southern Manitoba and, very rarely, in east-central Saskatchewan. [syn. *Triadenum fraseri* (Spach) Gleason]

Elatine triandra Schk.
Waterwort

ELATINACEAE (Waterwort Family)

Other Common Names: Long-stemmed Waterwort, Mud-purslane

Triandra means 3 stamens and refers to the 3-parted flowers.

Emergent
Annual
Native
Occasional
Hardiness Zone: 1
Flowering Season: late summer

DESCRIPTION

These somewhat limp and matted aquatic plants have creeping, branching stems (5–10 cm long) which root at the nodes. On land, the plants form 1–4 cm diameter tufts (1 cm high). The smooth-margined, linear to obovate **leaves** (2–8 mm long, often widened above the middle) are arranged opposite each other.

The small **flowers** arise singly, without a pedicel, from the leaf axils. Each flower consists of 3 sepals, 3 petals, 3 stamens, 1 pistil, and a 2–3-loculed superior ovary con-taining numerous ovules.

Fruit is a 2–3-parted, membraneous capsule containing many seeds. Seeds are straight or slightly curved (less than 0.8 mm long) with 9–25 shallow pits in longitudinal rows on the surface.

Elatine triandra Schk.

HABITAT AND DISTRIBUTION

Waterwort is an aquatic to terrestrial plant which grows submerged in shallow water or as an emergent on wet mud. It is found on mud flats, drying cultivated slough bottoms, pond margins, and along muddy shores of slow moving streams and rivers. Although noted to be associated with the boreal forest it is also present in the warmer, southern drainages of the prairies.

The range extends across the country from New Brunswick to British Columbia, southward to California, and from Texas eastward to Virginia. *Elatine triandra* is also found in Eurasia.

SPECIAL FEATURES

Ducks are known to feed on the plant.

Elatine triandra is a northern representative of the *Elatine* genus.

Elatine americana (Pursh) Arnott, **American Waterwort**, is a common plant of tidal estuaries. It shows up to the east and south of the Prairie provinces (particularily in the St. Lawrence region) and is much more com-mon from an overall North American perspective. *Elatine americana*, as well as selected European species (e.g., *E. macropoda* Gussone), has been used in aquarium culture where the plant forms a thick, matted, green carpet on the tank bottom.

RELATED SPECIES

Waterwort may be confused with Vernal Water-starwort (*Callitriche verna*). *Callitriche* and *Elatine* are easiest told apart in fruit, which is borne much of the summer. *Callitriche* has fruit of 4 nutlets, like a Mint. *Elatine* has a semi-transparent spherical capsule through whose walls the striate seeds may be seen. Also, in *Elatine*, male and female parts are both included on the same flower, sepals and petals are present, and there are 3 stamens. In *Callitriche*, male and female flowers are on separate flowers, sepals and petals are absent, and there is only 1 stamen. *Elatine* plants appear branched and matted whereas *Callitriche* surface leaves form a flat rosette pattern when viewed from above.

Viola renifolia A. Gray
Kidney-leaved Violet

VIOLACEAE (Violet Family)

Other Common Names: Kidney-shaped Violet, Northern White Violet

Violet comes from *viola*, the purplish blue colour of many of the group's flowers. *Renifolia* is derived from the Latin *reni* (kidney-shaped) and *folia* (leaved), and refers to the characteristic leaf shape.

Wetland
Perennial
Native
Common
Hardiness Zone: 0
Flowering Season: spring–summer

DESCRIPTION
Alternate leaves grow directly from short, thread-like rhizomes.
Leaves are kidney-shaped (more than 3 cm wide and wider than long), rounded or slightly pointed at tip, heart-shaped at base, often hairy (especially below), with flat-toothed margins (somewhat wavy).

Viola renifolia – kidney-leaved

This stemless plant has flower peduncles (often shorter than leaves) attached to rhizome. Early spring **flowers** are showy (encouraging pollinators to visit) while later flowers have little or no corolla and are largely self-fertilizing (cleistogamous). Nodding white flowers are composed of 5 sepals (auricled at base), 5 petals (2 laterals are bearded at base while the lowest one is bearded in the throat, forming a basal spur; sometimes purplish veined), 5 stamens, 1 pistil, and a 1-loculed capsule containing numerous ovules.

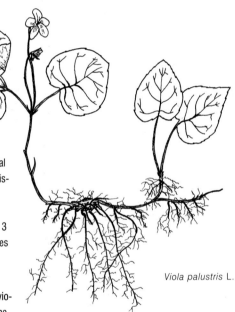

Viola palustris L.

Fruit is an oval, purplish capsule which opens by 3 valves, projecting numerous brown seeds. Capsules are held erect at maturity.

HABITAT AND DISTRIBUTION
Viola renifolia is one of the most moisture-loving violets (however, less so than *V. palustris*) found in the Prairie provinces. It inhabits cold, wet woods and forests, bogs, and swamps.
Range extends from Alaska to Newfoundland. Plants occur south to Colorado and New Mexico in the west and from the Great Lakes eastward. It is only rarely found in the drier southern parts of the Prairie provinces.

SPECIAL FEATURES
Pollinators seek the nectar found in the spur of the lowermost petal. Although the plants are usually spread apart from each other, wildlife commonly eat the plants when they come across them.
The edible flowers, leaves and buds are good in salads and as decorations on ice cream and cakes. Cooked plants are good as a pot-herb or used to thicken soups.

Violet leaves are rich in vitamin C and contain significant quantities of vitamin A and salicylic acid. Leaves were used during medieval times to treat heart attacks, strokes, pain, and skin and fungal infections. Ancient European herbalists and North American medicine men claimed it to have anti-cancer properties.

RELATED SPECIES

Viola cucullata Ait., **Blue Marsh Violet**, occurs in slough margins, bogs and wet locations across the Prairie provinces. It can be recognized by its thick rhizome, basal leaves, and large violet flowers. Lateral petals have knob-tipped hairs at the base.

Viola macloskeyi Lloyd, **Macloskey's Violet**, is a rare violet very similar to *V. renifolia* and *V. palustris* but with narrower leaves (1–3 cm long), the presence of stolons, and has 3 purple lines on its lower petal. *Viola macloskeyi* can be distinguished from *V. palustris* in that the former usually has several leaves per node on the rhizome.

Viola nephrophylla Greene, **Northern Bog Violet**, is a very common, large, blue purple-flowered violet of wetlands. It has a thick, fleshy, vertical rhizome with stems attached directly onto it. Glabrous leaves are heart-shaped. The short-spurred (4 mm or less) lower petal is hairy, and the laterals are bearded.

Viola palustris L., **Marsh Violet**, is a common wetland plant similar to *V. renifolia* but differs in having short-spurred pale violet to white (purple-veined) flowers. The leaves are without hairs (2.5–5 cm long by 2.5–3.5 cm wide). *Viola palustris* has long-creeping rhizomes, thin and thread-like, with seldom more than 1 leaf per node on the rhizome.

Viola cucullata

PAT PORTER

Lythrum salicaria L.
Purple Loosestrife

LYTHRACEAE (Loosestrife Family)

Other Common Names: Spike Loosestrife, Bouquet-violet

Salicaria is from the Latin terms *sali* (salt) and *caria* (a region of SW Asia Minor), referring to its ability to live in salty habitats. *Salicaria* is an old generic name meaning 'like a willow.'

Wetland
Perennial
Introduced
Rare
Hardiness Zone: 1
Flowering Season: summer

DESCRIPTION

Upright, branching, angular stems (50–150 cm tall) grow from long, thick, woody taproots. The opposite **leaves** (sometimes in whorls of 3) are 3–10 cm long, narrow and pointed with a heart-shaped base clasping the stem. Showy, purple flower spikes (10–40 cm long) have flowers clustered in the leaf axils. Each **flower** (1.5–2 cm across) consists of a tubular receptacle, 4–7 sepals, 4–7 magenta purple (rarely white) petals, twice as many stamens as petals, 1 pistil, and a 2-loculed ovary.

Fruit is a 2-celled subcylindrical capsule with about 100 seeds. One healthy plant can have as many as 900 capsules.

HABITAT AND DISTRIBUTION

Purple Loosestrife grows in wet meadows, shallow marshes, flood plains, roadside ditches, and along stream banks. Its introduction has resulted in expanding colonies across the prairies and parkland (especially near cities and in the southeastern part of the region).

A native of Eurasia, it is found in isolated sites across the Prairie provinces. Its range extends south into much of the central and eastern United States, where it has become the dominant plant in many wetlands. This plant is heat-loving and requires at least an 80-day growing season to bloom and produce seed, so its northern spread is limited to vegetative reproduction.

SPECIAL FEATURES

Purple Loosestrife contains tannins and was used as a herbal remedy to stop bleeding.

The showy spikes are used in flower arranging, water gardening, and by beekeepers.

The cultivation of the plant is now being discouraged because of its ability to crowd out native aquatics valuable to wildlife. Purple Loosestrife is rarely eaten by North American wildlife.

It is now classed as a noxious weed and in many locations laws are in place banning its importation and cultivation in hopes of providing measures for its control. It was originally introduced into the eastern United States in the early 19th century by seeds carried in ship's ballast. Importation and distribution of seeds and plants for ornamental use contributed significantly to the spread of the plant and by the 1930s it had reached the west coast.

Lythrum salicaria L.

Research is being conducted into the use of two species of leaf-eating beetles and one species of root-eating weevils for biological control. Hand removal of the plants as well as cutting and burning helps to exterminate the plant.

RELATED SPECIES

Lythrum salicaria is easily confused with the slightly shorter (30–100 cm tall) *Mimulus ringens* (**Blue Monkey-flower** or **Lavender Musk**). *Mimulus ringens* has indented or toothed leaves, irregular petals which are united making the corolla appear 2-lipped (in *L. salicaria* they are separate), and only 4 stamens.

HEINJO LAHRING

Lythrum salicaria

HEINJO LAHRING

Epilobium palustre L.
Marsh Willowherb

ONAGRACEAE (Evening-primrose Family)

Syn.: *E. lineare* Muhl.

Epilobium is from the Greek terms *epi* (upon) and *lobos* (pod or capsule). It refers to the flower being attached to the top of the long ovary which later becomes a capsule. *Palustre* is Latin for swampy or marshy.

Wetland
Perennial
Native
Common
Hardiness Zone: 0
Flowering Season: early to mid-summer

DESCRIPTION

Upright simple or branching plants (80 cm tall) grow from long, slender stolons. Some stolons form dark, fleshy turions (small bulb-like offsets) at the ends. Long (1.5–7 cm), narrow (0.2–1.9 cm) **leaf** blades are sparsely hairy above and attached directly and opposite to each other on the stem (at least towards base of stems). Margins are smooth or slightly dentate and have a downward roll (revolute). Flower spike is often nodding in bud. White (rarely pink) **flowers** are relatively small (4–6 mm wide) in comparison with other *Epilobiums*. Each flower has 4 sepals (1.4–4.5 mm long), 4 petals (twice the length of sepals), 8 stamens (alternate stamens are shorter), and a 4-loculed inferior ovary containing many ovules.
Fruit is a long (3–5 cm), slender, 4-valved capsule containing many seeds. Capsules split open from top to bottom. Elliptic, sometimes tapered at both ends, seeds (1.4–2.2 mm) have a tuft of white hairs (5–7 mm long) at one end.

HABITAT AND DISTRIBUTION

Marsh Willowherb is found in bogs, fens, marshes, and swamps. It tends to be more common in the western portion of the Prairie provinces.
Distribution is circumpolar with plants being found from Alaska to Newfoundland, north into the tundra of Manitoba, Quebec and the Territories, south as far as California and Nevada, and from Colorado eastward to the Great Lakes and New England states.

SPECIAL FEATURES

Willowherbs play an important role as a food source for wildlife. The soft, early summer shoots are particularly favored. Numerous butterflies and insects complete their life cycles on the plants.

Epilobium palustre L.

Epilobium palustre

HEINJO LAHRING

The long-haired seeds are easily gathered and make excellent tinder for starting fires. Young, tender shoots can be used fresh in salads or cooked for greens. The pith of more mature stems is good in soups. Dried or fresh leaves make excellent wilderness tea.

As a medicinal plant, the leaves and roots were used as a demulcent, tonic and astringent.

Below: *Epilobium ciliatum*
Inset: *Epilobium ciliatum* flower

HEINJO LAHRING

HEINJO LAHRING

RELATED SPECIES

There are over 15 different *Epilobiums* (including the popular Fireweed, *E. angustifolium* L.) found across the Prairie provinces. Most of these may be found in moist habitats. Many are rare and specific to habitats such as alpine meadows, tundra, or gravel bars. *Epilobium leptophyllum* and *E. ciliatum* are two which are widespread and may be encountered in very wet locations.

Epilobium ciliatum Raf., **Northern Willowherb**, has leaves which are narrow to ovate (3–12 cm by 0.5–4.5 cm), toothed, without inrolled margins, and pointed at tip. The erect (rarely nodding) inflorescence is glandular-hairy. Flowers (6 mm across) are pink and sometimes rose purple or white. The larvae of the Bedstraw Hawkmoth are often found eating *E. ciliatum* plants. [syn. *E. glandulosum* Lehm.]

Epilobium latifolium L., **River-beauty**, has showy pink zygomorphic flowers (petals 1–3 cm long) on a short open raceme. Leaves are broadly lanceolate to elliptic (1.0–5.5 cm by 0.5–2.5 cm wide) with smooth to broadly toothed margins. Plants often form colonies along gravel bars, river and stream banks and scree slopes to alpine elevations. It is found throughout the Rocky Mountain region. The range extends from Alaska south and eastward to Newfoundland.

HEINJO LAHRING

Above and inset: *Epilobium latifolium*

Epilobium leptophyllum Raf., **Narrow-leaved Willowherb**, is very similar to *E. palustre* but has slender, more linear leaves (0.2–0.7 cm wide). Upper leaf surface is hairy (sometimes glandular). Petals are white to pink (3.5–7 mm long). As in *E. palustre*, the ovary looks white or greyish because of a dense covering of short hairs. In Saskatchewan *Epilobium leptophyllum* tends to be more southern in distribution while in Alberta it occurs throughout the province.

HEINJO LAHRING

DICOTS ■ HERBS

Myriophyllum sibiricum Komarov   **HALORAGACEAE (Water-milfoil Family)**
Northern Water-milfoil

Syn.: *M. exalbescens* Fern., *M. spicatum* var. *exalbescens* (Fern.) Jepson, *M. magdalenense* Fern.

Myriophyllum means many or countless (Greek; *myrios*) leaf or leaf segments (Latin; *phyllus*), and refers to the many finely divided leaves. *Exalbescens* is of Latin origin meaning 'becoming whitish,' a trait showing up as the plants dry. *Sibiricum* pertains to Siberia.

**Submerged
Perennial
Native
Common
Hardiness Zone: 0
Flowering Season: summer**

DESCRIPTION

Long (30 to 150 cm long), submerged and rooted stems are densely covered with finely divided foliage. Dark green to purplish pinnate **leaves** (1–4 cm long) are attached to the stem in whorls of 4. Each short-petioled leaf has a thin central midrib with 5–12 thread-like leaflets per side. The leaf segments have a feathery appearance and look like miniature radar antenna. Leaves usually do not collapse when taken out of water. In alkaline water they often become covered with a white coating of lime. After drying, the stems appear white.

Flowers form on a terminal spike (2–8 cm long) which is held just above the water's surface. Flowers are in whorls (separated by a space on the stem) and subtended by smooth, or slightly toothed, ovate bracts shorter than the flowers. The uppermost flowers of the spike are often male. Flowers consist of 4 sepals, 4 petals (soon falling off), 8 stamens, 1 pistil, and an inferior 4-loculed ovary. Spikes lie in water when in fruit. **Fruit** is a small nutlet which splits into 4 parts, each with 1 seed.

HABITAT AND DISTRIBUTION

Water-milfoil grows in ponds, lakes, marshes, sloughs, fen pools, streams and quiet rivers.

This species is widespread across the Prairie provinces. Its range extends from Alaska to Newfoundland with plants growing well into the High Arctic (Victoria Island, Baffin Island, western Greenland) and as far south as California, Texas, and West Virginia.

Myriophyllum sibiricum Komarov

HEINJO LAHRING

Myriophyllum sibiricum – in flower

232

Key to *Myriophyllum*

(adapted from Crow and Hellquist, 2000)

1. Uppermost leaves alternate; leaves 3–12 (22) mm long ....*M. alterniflorum*
   ALTERNATE-FLOWERED WATER-MILFOIL

1. Uppermost leaves opposite; leaves mostly 8–45 mm long

   2. Flower bracts usually more than twice as long as pistillate flowers..................*M. verticillatum*
      BRACTED WATER-MILFOIL

   2. Flower bracts usually less than twice as long as pistillate flowers

      3. Middle leaves with 12 or more segments on each side of rachis; many of the
         uppermost leaves truncate at apex; stem diameter below inflorescence greater
         than, up to twice the diameter of, lower stem; stem tips usually reddish; winter
         buds not formed ....*M. spicatum*
         EURASIAN WATER-MILFOIL

      3. Middle leaves with 11 or fewer segments on each side of rachis; uppermost leaves
         rounded at apex; stem diameter below inflorescence the same diameter of lower
         stem; stem tips usually green; winter buds formed in fall ....*M. sibiricum*
         NORTHERN WATER-MILFOIL

HEINJO LAHRING

Myriophyllum sibiricum

HEINJO LAHRING

SPECIAL FEATURES

Myriophyllum sibiricum is a very important aquatic plant providing food and shelter for invertebrates and fish. The seeds, and small amounts of leaves, are eaten by waterfowl. Moose and muskrats feed on the long strands. Muskrats will use them in building pushups on the winter ice, helping to keep holes open. Water-milfoils act as water purifiers, using nutrients and releasing oxygen into the water.

Winter buds (turions; densely packed leaves at stem tips) form in the fall and can survive freezing into the ice. Old foliage usually decays through the winter and the buds commence growing the following spring.

Eurasian Water-milfoil, *M. spicatum* L., is introduced and has become a problem in irrigation canals of southern Alberta. It does not produce overwintering buds or die back each winter, as in native milfoils, but continues to grow longer with each season (rooting along the bottom as well as fragmenting and starting new colonies). Studies show that most of its nitrogen and over 70% of its phosphorus are taken in through the roots from bottom sediments with the remainder through the foliage allowing it to grow well even in nutrient-poor water conditions.

RELATED SPECIES

Other water-milfoils found in the Prairie provinces include:
Myriophyllum alterniflorum DC., **Alternate-flowered Water-milfoil** or **Little Water-milfoil**, which is characterized by its alternately arranged flowers and bracts. Stems are very thin with leaves about half the length (0.5–1 cm) of Northern and Whorled Water-milfoils, requiring close inspection to observe their feather-like appearance. Male flowers are either solitary or in pairs. The lowermost female flowers are whorled. It is associated with the boreal forest. In Saskatchewan it only occurs in the Precambrian regions of the north.
Myriophyllum spicatum L., **Eurasian Water-milfoil** (Spiked Water-milfoil) grows to 4 m in length with considerable branching near the surface, often forming dense floating mats, with tan to brown coloured stems. Leaflets are more (12–16 per side), longer and wider-spaced than in *M. sibiricum* or *M. verticillatum*. Floral spikes can reach 15 cm long. Flowers are in whorls in bract axils (upper are male and the lower are female). Winter buds are not formed in the fall. This introduced species easily outcompetes native species.
Myriophyllum verticillatum L., **Whorled** or **Bracted Water-milfoil**, has feather-like (pinnately divided) floral bracts usually twice the length of flower. The stems are green or brown and most leaves lack petioles. Leaf nodes are closer together than *M. sibiricum*, nearly hiding the stem. The overwintering buds are club-shaped. Plants are scarcely white once dried. It is found across the Prairie provinces, but not as commonly as *M. sibiricum*.

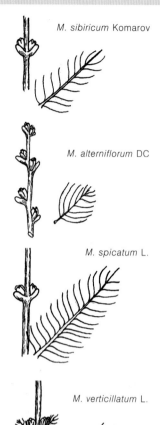

M. sibiricum Komarov

M. alterniflorum DC

M. spicatum L.

M. verticillatum L.

Left and above: *Myriophyllum sibiricum;* above, flowers

Mimulus lewisii (pp. 268–269)
Red Monkey-flower
JIM ROMO

DICOTS ■ HERBS

Hippuris vulgaris L.

HIPPURIDACEAE (Mare's-tail Family)

Mare's-tail

Other Common Names: Common Mare's-tail

This was originally a Greek name for the plant which somewhat resembles horsetail (*Equisetum* sp); *hippos* (horse) and *oura* (tail). *Vulgaris* means common.

Submerged/Emergent
Perennial
Native
Common
Hardiness Zone: 0
Flowering Season: summer

DESCRIPTION

Growing from spongy rhizomes, erect (5–30 cm tall), unbranched plants start out submerged when young and become emergent later in the season. Underwater stems are soft, thick, and brownish green with thin strap-shaped **leaves** attached in whorls of 6–12. Narrow (1–2 mm), smooth-margined, hairless leaves (1–5 cm long) flop when taken out of water. Green, emergent stems are stiff with whorls of flat, needle-like leaves.

Small, inconspicuous, green **flowers** are located in the axils of the leaves. Each flower consists of a non-divided calyx, no petals, 1 stamen (1 filament and a large 2-loculed anther), and a 1-loculed inferior ovary (2 mm long at maturity) containing 1 ovule. The style is thread-like with the stigma along one side (placement is between the anther lobes).

Nut-like, ellipsoid **fruit** (1.7–2.5 mm long) is non-splitting at maturity.

HABITAT AND DISTRIBUTION

Common Mare's-tail is found in shallow water of marshes, bogs, ponds, streams, lakes, calm or slow moving streams and rivers, on mossy banks, and sometimes on peat in fens. This is a cold water species and one of the few aquatic plants found in arctic pools and lakes.

This circumpolar species occurs across the Prairie provinces. The range extends to the High Arctic (Banks, northern Baffin, and Ellesmere islands) in the north, to California, New Mexico, the north-central Great Plains in the south, and to the Great Lakes and New England states in the east.

SPECIAL FEATURES

Stands of *H. vulgaris* create important underwater habitat for invertebrates and fish. The submerged foliage acts as a water purifier (utilizing nutrients, and providing natural aeration and circulation).

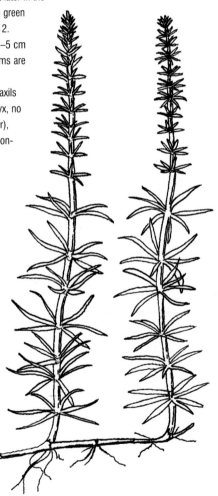

Hippuris vulgaris L.

DICOTS ■ HERBS

Waterfowl occasionally feed on leaves and stems. Alaskan Inuit cook the plant in soups. It is often available during cold weather since the plants stick out of the ice and are easily gathered.

RELATED SPECIES

Hippuris montana Ledeb., **Mountain Mare's-tail**, is found in the western part of North America with some populations occurring in Alberta's foothills and Rocky Mountain region. It has shorter stems (1–10 cm), only 5–8 whorls of leaves per stem, and narrower underwater leaves (less than 1 mm) than *H. vulgaris*. Its flowers are mostly unisexual (occasionally some have both sexes in the same flower) with the female being above the male. It is associated with mossy banks and mountain streams.

Hippuris tetraphylla L., **Four-leaved Mare's-tail**, is a plant of brackish waters found in coastal areas along the Hudson's Bay and James Bay. It is noted for its thicker and broader leaves arranged on the stem in whorls of four.

HEINJO LAHRING

Hippuris vulgaris
Inset left: aerial foliage
Below: submerged foliage

HEINJO LAHRING

237

Cicuta maculata L.
Spotted Water-hemlock

APIACEAE (Carrot Family)

Syn.: *C. occidentalis* Greene, *C. douglasii* (DC.) Coult. & Rose
Other Common Names: Beaver-poison, Muskrat-weed, Musquash-root, Poison Parsnip, False Parsley, Children's Bane, Spotted Cowbane

Cicuta is an ancient Latin name of the poisonous Hemlock, a deadly Old World herb. *Maculata* is of Latin origin meaning spotted or blotched and refers to the purple blotches which sometimes occur on the stem.

Wetland
Perennial
Native
Common
Hardiness Zone: 0
Flowering Season: summer

DESCRIPTION
This plant grows from thick, fleshy rhizomes containing hollow chambers separated by thin partitions. The branching stem is upright, (0.5–2 m tall) with several twice-pinnate **leaves**. Side branches form a sheath around the main stem (swollen where they connect). Lanceolate leaflets (5–8 cm long by 1–2 cm wide) are sharply toothed. Veins on the lower leaf surface form square patterns.

Small, white **flowers** are held high in dense, compound umbels (3–10 cm across). The primary umbel is composed of 18–25 branches while secondary umbels are of 12–25 branches. Each flower consists of several narrow bractlets, 5 triangular sepals, 5 petals, 5 stamens, 2 styles, and a 2-loculed inferior ovary (1 ovule per locule).

The oval **fruit**, a schizocarp, is as long as broad or broader (2–4 mm long) and splits into two mericarps, each containing a yellow or dark brown ribbed seed.

Cicuta maculata L.

Cicuta maculata root stalk showing interior air chambers

HABITAT AND DISTRIBUTION
Spotted Water-hemlock is a plant of wet drainages and swales of marshes, streams, ditches, thickets and swamps. It is often found growing with other species of the *Apiaceae*.

Cicuta maculata

HEINJO LAHRING

HEINJO LAHRING

Cicuta maculata

Plants occur from Alaska to Nova Scotia with collections having been made throughout the Prairie provinces. Range includes the Territories in the north to the Gulf of Mexico in the south.

SPECIAL FEATURES

Cicuta maculata is considered the most violently poisonous plant in North America. The roots are particularly toxic. Even small amounts can in minutes result in convulsions, abdominal pain, diarrhea, vomiting, respiratory depression, paralysis, delirium, unconsciousness and, ultimately, death. The cause is an oily, yellow liquid called *cicutoxin* which is exuded from the cut stock. The juice of crushed plants can cause poisoning if transferred from hand to mouth.

Water-hemlock is known to cause livestock poisonings. Drinking-water with crushed water-hemlock leaves can become contaminated.

RELATED SPECIES

This plant can easily be confused with other wetland species and careful identification is necessary if collecting wild foods where water-hemlock grows. The roots have a celery-like smell and sweet taste so one must be especially cautious. Some similar-looking, but edible, plants include Cow-parsnip (*Heracleum lanatum*) and Water-parsnip (*Sium suave*). In Saskatchewan, *C. maculata* grows only where the water is permanent and fresh, while *S. suave* can survive the drying-up of sloughs.

Cicuta bulbifera L., **Bulb-bearing Water-hemlock**, is a small plant which hides itself amongst the grasses and sedges of fens, marshes and swamps. In bloom it can reach 30–80 cm tall. The basal leaves are 2–3 times pinnate with thin, linear leaflets. The upper leaf axils have small vegetative bulblets. Cicutoxin is present.

Cicuta virosa L., **Poisonous Water-hemlock**, is a rare plant of the boreal forest which is very similar to *C. maculata* but has narrower and longer leaflets, veins on the lower leaf surface form a long rectangular pattern, only 9–21 branches in the primary umbel, up to 50 branches in the secondary umbels, and the fruit is longer than broad. Cicutoxin is present. [syn. *C. mackenzieana* Raup]

Cicuta bulbifera L.

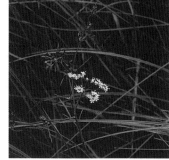

Cicuta bulbifera

HEINJO LAHRING

Conium maculatum L.

APIACEAE (Carrot Family)

Poison Hemlock

Other Common Names: Deadly Hemlock, Poison Parsley, Spotted Hemlock, California Fern, Nebraska Fern, Winter Fern, Stickweed, Snakeweed, Wade-whistle, Mother Die

Conium is the Greek name of the Hemlock by which Socrates and various criminals were put to death in Athens. *Maculata* is of Latin origin meaning spotted or blotched, and refers to the purple blotches on the stem.

Wetland
Biennial
Introduced
Rare
Hardiness Zone: 3
Flowering Season: summer

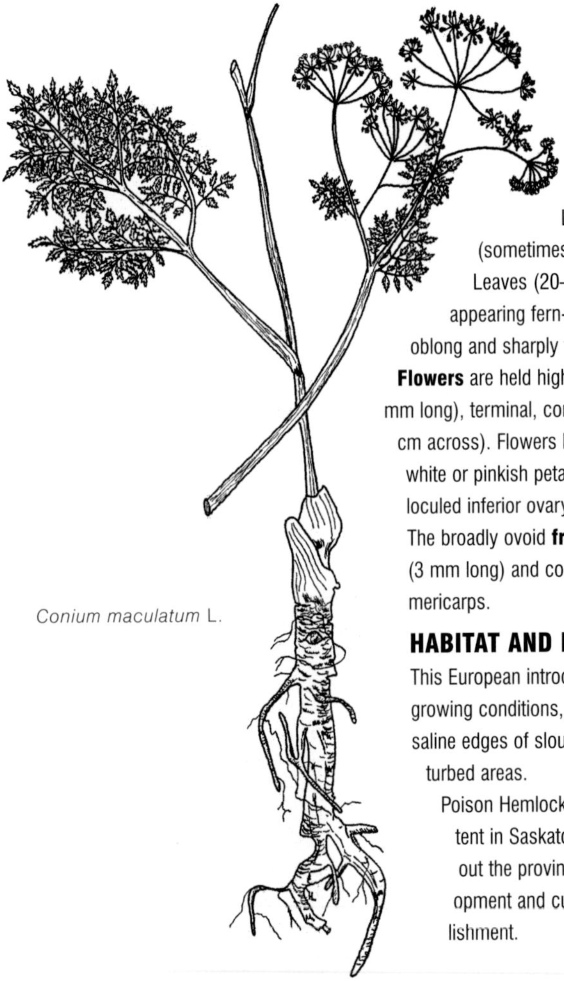

Conium maculatum L.

DESCRIPTION

Furrowed stems are upright (to 3 m), branched, and purple-blotched on the lower stems. The cut or damaged stem has a foul odor (some say like mice). Lower stem **leaves** are alternate (sometimes opposite on upper flower stalk). Leaves (20–40 cm long) are 2–4 times pinnate appearing fern-like. Leaflets are glabrous, ovate-oblong and sharply toothed.

Flowers are held high in numerous bracted (bracts 2–5 mm long), terminal, compound umbels (10–15 branched; 5 cm across). Flowers have short bractlets, no sepals, 5 white or pinkish petals, 5 stamens, 2 styles, and a 2-loculed inferior ovary (1 ovule per locule). The broadly ovoid **fruit**, a schizocarp, is laterally flattened (3 mm long) and contains 2 thick-ribbed seeds called mericarps.

HABITAT AND DISTRIBUTION

This European introduction prefers moist soil and warm growing conditions, establishing itself in moderately saline edges of sloughs, marshes, ditches, fields and disturbed areas.

Poison Hemlock is extremely rare (probably non-existent in Saskatchewan). Range is sporadic throughout the provinces, generally occurring where development and cultivation have encouraged its establishment.

SPECIAL FEATURES

All parts of this plant contain the very poisonous alkaloid *coniine*. The seeds, lower stems and roots concentrate especially high amounts of this compound. Consumption can result in gastrointestinal dysfunction, pain, muscular weakness, respiratory paralysis, death of tissue, convulsions, and possible death. Children have been known to die from sucking on the stems, leaves, or roots. Treatment should always include keeping air passages clear.

A potion made of Poison Hemlock is what killed Socrates over 2,400 years ago. Ancient Greeks would prepare a drink made from the unripe seeds and give it to those the State had sentenced to death.

RELATED SPECIES

This highly poisonous plant must never be confused with edible plants such as fiddlehead ferns, or parsnip look-alikes such as *Sium suave* (Water-parsnip).

Cicuta (Water-hemlock) and *Conium* (Poison Hemlock) are closely related but in *Cicuta* the foliage is only 1–3 times pinnate (less fern-like), stems are not as purple blotched, umbels have few or no bracts as well as being more branched (12–28), plants are sweet scented, and the roots are chambered. Both are highly poisonous.

Conium maculatum

BARRE HELLQUIST

DICOTS ■ HERBS

Heracleum lanatum Michx.　　　　　　**APIACEAE (Carrot Family)**

Cow-parsnip

Syn.: *H. maximum* Bartr.

Other Common Names: Woolly Parsnip, American Masterwort, Yerba del Oso, Mouthwort, Hogweed, Cow Cabbage

Heracleum is the name of a plant first used by Hercules as medicine. *Lanatum* means woolly.

Wetland
Perennial
Native
Common
Hardiness Zone: 0
Flowering Season: summer

DESCRIPTION

This hollow-stemmed herb grows to 2.5 m from a thick, fleshy rootstock. Stems are usually hairy (woolly) with longitudinal ridges. Compound **leaves** clasp stem with dilated sheaths. Leaf blades are very large (10–30 cm across), have 3 coarsely toothed lobes (rarely pinnate), and are hairy below.

Flowers, in slightly rounded, compound umbels (3–10 cm across), are held upright on sturdy stems. The small (2 mm), white flowers have no sepals, 5 petals (corolla somewhat irregular, being larger in outer flowers of umbel), 2 styles, and a 2-loculed inferior ovary with 1 ovule per locule.

The flat (winged on edges), oblong-ovate **fruit** is about 1 cm long marked with narrow ridges and dark lines (oil-tubes) running lengthwise from the tip halfway to the base.

HABITAT AND DISTRIBUTION

Cow-parsnip is found in moist woods, beaver meadows, clearings, ditches, and along drainages. It is particularily common in the aspen parkland and often prefers partial shade.

Plants are spread across the Prairie provinces, although it is less prevalent in the southwest and far north. Range extends into the Territories, westward to eastern Asia, as far south as the southern United States and eastward to Newfoundland.

SPECIAL FEATURES

Heracleum lanatum is one of the fastest growing perennial herbs. Virtually all parts of the plant are edible, fresh or cooked, with young stalks and roots being the most tender. Stems are peeled (hairs may cause skin irritation) and should be boiled in 3 changes of water. Roots are prepared like parsnips (cook until tender). Young flower stems can be

Heracleum lanatum Michx.

stewed like celery. Seeds make a welcome addition to soups or stews for seasoning. Strongly flavored basal parts can be dried (as well as burned dry leaves) and used as a salt substitute. The taste is different from sodium chloride since it contains mostly potassium chloride.

Tea made from the roots or seeds is said to be good for colds and asthma, and as a nerve stimulant and stomach treatment.

RELATED SPECIES

It is possible to confuse this plant with *Cicuta* (Water-hemlock) and *Conium* (Poison Hemlock) so care must be taken when collecting it for food. Both of these species have thinner stems, finer and more divided foliage, and purple spotting on the stem (*Conium* in particular).

There is only one species of *Heracleum* in the Prairie provinces.

Heracleum lanatum (seed head, inset above)

DICOTS ■ HERBS

Sium suave Walter
Water-parsnip

APIACEAE (Carrot Family)

Syn.: *S. cicutaefolium* Schrank.
Other Common Names: Hemlock Water-parsnip, False Hemlock

Sium is from the Greek name of a paludal plant called *Sion*. *Suave* is from the Latin *suavis* meaning sweet or pleasant and refers to the aromatic leaves.

Wetland
Perennial
Native
Common
Hardiness Zone: 0
Flowering Season: mid- to late summer

DESCRIPTION

Fibrous roots are fusiform shaped. The branching, ridged and hollow stem is erect (growing to 2 m). Submerged **leaves** are 1–3 times pinnate with thin, thread-like leaflets. Emergent leaves (5–10 cm long) are alternate, linear to lanceolate, 7–17-toothed and only once-pinnate. A sheath wraps around the junction where the leaf meets the stem.

Flat-topped compound umbels are held high and contain many small (3–4 mm wide), white **flowers**. Each umbel (3–12 cm across) has 6 or more branches. Small pointed bracts are present at the base of the umbels and umbellets. Each flower consists of 5 very small or absent sepals, 5 petals (2–3 mm long), 2 styles, and a 2-loculed inferior ovary (1 ovule per locule). The slightly flattened, oval **fruit** is 2–3 mm long with corky ridges.

HABITAT AND DISTRIBUTION

Water-parsnip grows in marshes, sloughs, wet meadows, swamps, ditches, and along stream and lake shores. It is found either emergent or submersed in standing water.

Sium suave Walt.

Sium suave

COLIN STONE

244

Siam suave

Plants occur across the Prairie provinces. Range extends to Alaska in the northwest, California, Texas, Missouri, and South Carolina in the south, and Newfoundland in the east.

SPECIAL FEATURES

Native peoples ate the leaves fresh or cooked. The fibrous roots were also eaten and were best in late fall or before the new leaves appeared.

Some reports indicate that livestock have been poisoned by this plant, but these reports are poorly documented and the plants may have been misidentified as *Cicuta maculata*.

Identification must be done carefully since this plant can easily be confused with the poisonous water-hemlocks which grow in similar habitats.

RELATED SPECIES

This is the only species of *Sium* found in the Prairie provinces. *Cicuta* and *Conium* are easily misidentified as this plant. *Sium* differs in having leaves which are once-pinnate, fibrous roots (lacking tuberous roots with hollow chambers) and its stems are not purple-blotched.

Glaux maritima L.   PRIMULACEAE (Primrose Family)

Sea Milkwort

Glaux is based on the name of a sea plant which is *glaukos* or bluish green. *Maritima* means seaside.

Wetland
Perennial
Native
Common
Hardiness Zone: 0
Flowering Season: summer

DESCRIPTION

This short-stemmed (5–10 cm tall) herbaceous to woody plant grows from a slender, creeping rootstock. Branching stems are erect or spreading. Whitish green succulent **leaves** (6–12 mm long) are oppo-site, sessile, linear to oblong and smooth margined. The tight clustering of the leaves along the stem gives it a bushy appearance.

Single, white to deep pink **flowers** (3 mm long) rest in the leaf axils. The showy flowers have 5 basally connected sepals, no corolla, 5 stamens which alternate with the sepals, 1 pistil, and a superior ovary.

The calyx encloses a small (2–3 mm), 5-valved (opening at top) ovoid **capsule** containing 2–5 seeds.

HABITAT AND DISTRIBUTION

This salt tolerant plant is found in brackish tidal flats along the coast and saline flats across the Prairie provinces. It occurs on moist soil of meadows, marshes, slough margins, ditches and saline flats in the prairies and parkland as well as along river drainages further north.

Distribution is circumpolar. Range goes from the southern parts of Alaska to Newfoundland. Southern limit includes California, New Mexico, North Dakota, Minnesota, Nebraska and Virginia.

Glaux maritima L.

SPECIAL FEATURES

Sea Milkwort is able to withstand saline conditions. The grey, succulent foliage and low, creeping habit are moisture-conserving features which allow it to survive during periods of drought common to seasonally flooded areas.

The young shoots can be eaten raw, and the fleshy stems and leaves pickled.

Although widespread, it is not usually common or abundant and should be protected.

RELATED SPECIES

This is the only species of the genus found in North America. The small, but showy, pinkish flowers arranged along the short, erect stem (appearing as a leafy spike), the absence of a corolla and the sage-like appearance of the foliage make it easy to distinguish from other wetland species of saline areas.

Glaux maritima

BARRE HELLQUIST

Menyanthes trifoliata (pp. 254–255)
Bogbean

JOAN WILLIAMS

Lysimachia thyrsiflora L.

Tufted Loosestrife

PRIMULACEAE (Primrose Family)

Syn.: *Naumbergia thyrsiflora* (L.) Duby

Other Common Names: Swamp Loosestrife

Lysimachia is Greek for loose (*lysis*) strife (*mache*). *Thyrsiflora* means a plant (*flora*) with a flower head like an ovoid or ellipsoid panicle with cymose branches (*thyrse*).

Wetland/Emergent
Perennial
Native
Common
Hardiness Zone: 0
Flowering Season: summer

DESCRIPTION

Upright stems (20–60 cm tall), sometimes branching, grow from creeping rhizomes. Plants often tend to fall over unless supported by other vegetation. Light green **leaves** are opposite (rarely alternate or whorled; lower leaves reduced), linear-lanceolate, tapered at base, 3–15 cm long, smooth edged, and have short petioles (sometimes absent). They are densely dotted with dark glands, often with a fringe along the basal margin of the petiole.

Showy **flowers** look like bristly, yellow balls (0.6–1.5 cm across) located on spike-like racemes. The racemes are long-stalked, and either terminal or from leaf axils. Flowers (4–5 mm diam.) have a 5-toothed calyx, 5–6 parted yellow corolla (deeply cleft into linear segments; often purple-spotted), 5 or 6 stamens (longer than corolla), 5 or 6 teeth-like staminodia (alternating with corolla segments), 1 pistil with a slender style, and a superior 1-loculed ovary.

The spherical, gland-dotted **capsule** opens by 5 longitudinal valves releasing several seeds.

HABITAT AND DISTRIBUTION

Tufted Loosestrife grows in wet meadows, marshes, shores, swamps, ditches, wet woodlands and moist thickets. Plants may be in several inches of water or on wet ground. It is

PAT PORTER

Lysimachia thyrsiflora L.

HEINJO LAHRING

generally found in the parkland and boreal forest zones. Distribution is circumpolar. Its range extends from the Prairie provinces to Alaska and the Territories in the north, California, Colorado, Missouri, and West Virginia in the south, and Newfoundland in the east.

SPECIAL FEATURES

Lysimachia thyrsiflora is finding its way into the world of watergardening because of its hardiness and showy, yellow flowers. The tillering roots help to bind soil and stabilize pond edges.

The flowers are attractive to pollinators, in particular in mid-summer when many of the early blooming wetland species have finished for the season.

RELATED SPECIES

Early stages of plant growth look somewhat similar to Fireweed (*Epilobium angustifolium*) and Purple Loosestrife (*Lythrum salicaria*). Fireweed is a dryland plant with showy, purple flowers. Purple Loosestrife, an introduced plant now listed as a noxious weed, differs in having 4-sided stems, leaves with a rounded or heart-shaped base, and showy, purple flower spikes.

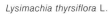

Lysimachia thyrsiflora L.

Lysimachia ciliata

PAT PORTER

Other *Lysmachias* found in wetlands across the Prairie provinces include:
Lysimachia ciliata L., **Fringed Loosestrife**, and *L. hybrida* Michx. [syn. *L. lanceolata* Walt.], **Lance-leaved Loosestrife**, differ from the above by having broad corolla lobes, petiolate leaves and the absence of long flower racemes (instead the flowers are long-stalked and appear in whorls of four in the leaf axils). *Lysimachia ciliata* has ciliate leaf petioles and creeping rhizomes, whereas *L. lanceolata* lacks each of these two features. *Lysimachia terrestris* (L.) BSP., **Swamp Candles**, is very much like *L. thyrsiflora* but has a loose open terminal flower spike and elliptic petals. Late in the season it produces small, elongated, purplish bulblets in the upper leaf axils. It is occasionally found in the southeastern boreal forest of Manitoba.

PAT PORTER

Primula incana M. E. Jones   **PRIMULACEAE (Primrose Family)**

Mealy Primrose

Primula is from the Latin term *primulus*, meaning 'the very first' and refers to its early spring blooms. *Incana* stands for 'hoary or white' and describes the plant's mealy surface.

Wetland
Perennial
Native
Common
Hardiness Zone: 0
Flowering Season: late spring

DESCRIPTION

Compact plants form a basal rosette of leaves and an erect flower stalk. **Leaves** are elliptic to oval (2–10 cm long), tapering towards the base. Leaf margins sometimes have a few broad, shallow teeth. Plant surface is covered with a white to sulfur yellow powder (farinose), particularly on the undersides of leaves, towards leaf base on upper surface and towards top of peduncle.

Lilac **flowers** (10–20) are borne in a tight umbel at the top of a stiff stem (10–40 cm). Umbel is just above several narrow, pointed bracts (0.5–1 cm long). Each flower (6–10 mm across) consists of a 5-cleft tubular calyx, a 5-lobed corolla (each lobe 2-cleft and spreading; bases joined to form a tube the length of the calyx), 5 stamens, 1 pistil with a slender style, and a superior ovary.

Several **seeds** (0.5–0.7 mm long) are contained within a short, elliptical capsule opening at the top by 5 valves. Dried sepals often envelope the capsule.

HABITAT AND DISTRIBUTION

Mealy Primrose inhabits open, moist slopes, slough margins, marshes, shores and saline meadows. It is found across the prairies and parkland.

Distribution includes Alberta, central to southern Saskatchewan (Cypress Hills and southeastern Parklands), and southern Manitoba. Range extends to the Territories and Alaska in the north, and Utah and Colorado in the south.

SPECIAL FEATURES

This is an indicator species for calcareous groundwater coming to the surface and is often found growing near the outflow of mineral springs.

Although widespread it is generally in low abundance. Efforts should be made to protect habitats where it grows.

RELATED SPECIES

Several other wetland primulas can be found in the region, but none has as dense of a farinose coating over its stems and leaves as *P. incana* has.

Primula egaliksensis Wormskj., **Igaliko Primula**, is a rare species of marshy ground known from a small area of the

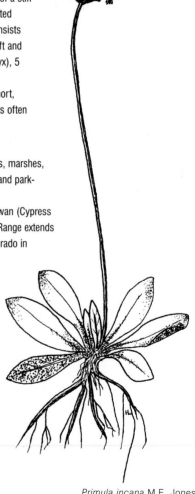

Primula incana M.E. Jones

Rocky Mountains. It is shorter (to 18 cm tall) than *P. incana* and lacks the mealy coating. Its leaves have long, slender petioles. Flowers are lilac to deep violet. It is named after a collection site in Greenland.

Primula mistassinica Michx., **Dwarf Canadian Primrose**, is a short (to 12 cm tall) plant of the boreal forest and mountains. It has slender stems and green leaves (perhaps some mealiness below). Flowers are white, pink or purple with a yellow throat.

Primula stricta Horn., **Erect Primrose**, is similar to *P. incana* except for slightly shorter flower stalks (to 30 cm), shorter leaves (1–3 cm) and the lack of a farinose coating (although sometimes it may have some beneath the leaves). It is found in moist alpine meadows and wet areas of the northeastern boreal forest.

Primula mistassinica Michx.

JOAN WILLIAMS

Primula incana

251

DICOTS ■ HERBS

Gentianella crinita (Froel.) G. Don GENTIANACEAE (Gentian Family)
Fringed Gentian

Syn.: *Gentiana crinita* Froel., *Anthopogon crinitus* (Froel.)
Raf.

The name is derived from *Gentius*, King of Illyria, who,
according to Pliny, discovered the plant's medicinal virtue.
The species name, *crinita,* is Latin for 'tufts of hairs' and
describes the fringed corolla lobes.

Wetland
Annual
Native
Common
Hardiness Zone: 2
Flowering Season: mid- to late summer

DESCRIPTION

This upright herb (5–50 cm tall) has opposite leaves and erect, leafy side branches. The narrow, tapering **leaves** lack petioles (2–5 cm long) and are somewhat clasping onto the stem.
Basal leaves are broader and shorter. Stipules are absent.
Single, large (2–6 cm long), showy, blue (rarely white) **flowers** are held erect on long pedicels.
Each flower has a 4-lobed calyx (1.5–2.5 cm long), a 4-lobed corolla (2–4 cm long), 4 stamens (alternate with corolla lobes), a pistil of two united carpels, and a 1-loculed superior
ovary. Calyx has small papillae on the outer surface. Corolla is tubular at base with broad,
spreading, fringed lobes above. Throat is often white, yellowish or light blue with some veining.
Many **seeds** are contained within a small, urn-shaped, 2-valved capsule.

Gentianella crinita
(Froel.) G. Don

HABITAT AND DISTRIBUTION

This showy wildflower can be found in damp woods, wet meadows, saline flats, moist shores
and calcareous bogs. It is associated with the parkland and boreal forest zones.
Distribution is limited to the central and southern portions of the Prairie provinces. Plants have
been found as far north as southern Yukon. This species is more common in the east including
the region from the Great Lakes to North Carolina.

SPECIAL FEATURES

The Fringed Gentian's showy flowers encourage insect pollination, especially later in the season
when other flowers have finished blooming. At the base of the corolla tube, and alternate with them, are nectaries. The inner-veining of the corolla assists in guiding insects in to reach them.

RELATED SPECIES

Several *Gentiana* (Gentians) and *Gentianella* (Fringed Gentians) species are found in
wetland locations. *Gentiana* has corolla lobes with thin, membranous folds between 3-
veined lobes. Its nectaries are at the base of the ovary. *Gentianella* lacks the folds, has
5–9 veined lobes and has nectaries on the base of the corolla tube.
Gentiana aquatica L., **Marsh** or **Moss Gentian**, is a rare biennial of sloughs and
marshes of the prairies, parklands, and alpine slopes. In can be found in grazed, thus
hummocky, marl flats due to groundwater seepage. It is quite short (3–10 cm tall) with
small, white-margined leaves (less than 6 mm; tightly arranged on stem), and solitary
purplish green flowers (5–8 mm long) at the stem ends. [syn. *G. prostrata* Haenke]
Gentianella detonsa Rottb., **Northern Fringed Gentian**, is similar to *G. crinita* but differs in having less-pointed upper leaves and a smooth, non-papillate calyx. This is a
circumpolar species found in the northeastern corner of Alberta.

BARRE HELLQUIST

*Gentianella
crinita*

Lomatogonium rotatum (L.) Fries
Marsh Felwort

GENTIANACEAE (Gentian Family)

Syn.: *Pleurogyne rotata* (L.) Griseb.

Lomatogonium is from the Greek terms *lomato-* (fringed or bordered) and *gonium* (small angled). The species name, *rotatum*, means wheel-shaped, and refers to the shape of the corolla.

Wetland
Annual
Native
Rare
Hardiness Zone: 0
Flowering Season: mid- to late summer

DESCRIPTION

Slender, erect (10–45 cm tall) plants arise from a short rootstock. Unbranched (sometimes branched above) stems have non-petioled opposite **leaves** (1–5 cm long). Upper leaves are narrow and pointed, while lower leaves are broader and pointed.

Star-shaped white or bluish **flowers** (solitary or a few in a group) are either terminal or on short pedicels attached at leaf axils. Each flower (1–2 cm across) consists of a deeply 5-cleft calyx (each segment alternating with corolla lobes), a 5-lobed corolla (appearing as 5 pointed petals; each lobe with a small scale at base), 5 stamens (alternating with corolla lobes), a 2-loculed pistil (style absent), and a 1-loculed superior ovary (with stigmas on the side). Several smooth **seeds** are contained within a 2-valved ovoid capsule (6–10 mm long).

HABITAT AND DISTRIBUTION

Marsh Felwort occurs in saline marshes, wet drainages, and slough margins. It is often scattered in amongst the reeds, sedges and grasses making it difficult to see until it blooms.

Distribution is circumpolar. Range extends from Alaska across the Territories to northern Quebec, Newfoundland and Greenland. Southern limit reaches New Mexico and Wyoming.

SPECIAL FEATURES

Its slender, stem-hugging foliage blends in well with the grasses and sedges it often grows with. Its narrow habit (allowing it to fit in tight spots) and annual cycle (encouraging seedlings to grow in new locations) give it a competitive advantage over many wetland perennials. The unique star-like flowers are an added attraction when many other flowers have finished blooming. The flowers provide insects with a mid- to late summer pollen source.

RELATED SPECIES

The white to bluish white, star-like flowers are unique among the *Gentian* group and permit easy identification. It is the only species of *Lomatogonium* found in the Prairie provinces.

Lomatogonium rotatum (L.) Fries

Menyanthes trifoliata L.

Bogbean

MENYANTHACEAE (Bogbean Family)

Other Common Names: Buckbean, Marsh-trefoil, Bog Myrtle, Bitterworm, Marsh Clover, Water Shamrock, Butter-root, Bog Hop

Menyanthes is from the Greek terms *minutho* (to diminish) and *anthos* (flower) and reflects the plant's short-lived flowers. The three (*tri*) leaved (*foliata*) foliage is described in the species epithet, *trifoliata*.

Emergent/Wetland
Perennial
Native
Common
Hardiness Zone: 0
Flowering Season: late spring

DESCRIPTION

Two to three leaves grow from the ends of long, spongy rhizomes (sometimes floating on water surface). Roots and side branches develop at intervals along the root's length, with the new growth moving forward and the old eventually decomposing. Long-petioled, thick, deep green **leaves** (3–8 cm long) are compound with 3 oval to elliptic, smooth-margined leaflets. A short, many-flowered spike (10–30 cm high) is held up on a leafless stalk. White (sometimes pinkish purple) **flowers** are short-pedicellate and have a 5-cleft calyx (shorter than corolla), 5-parted corolla (tubular at base, spreading and star-like at top), 5 stamens (alternate with corolla lobes), 1 style with a 2-lobed stigma, and a superior ovary. The corolla lobes have soft, white hairs on the inside surface. Several long (10 mm), shiny **seeds** are contained within an ovoid capsule (6–10 mm long). Capsule opens irregularly.

Menyanthes trifoliata L.

MYRNA PEARMAN

Menyanthes trifoliata

(See additional photo of *Menyanthes trifoliata* on page 247.)

HABITAT AND DISTRIBUTION

Bogbean occurs in marshes, swamps, fens, sphagnum bogs, and along pond edges. It is generally associated with the foothills, Rocky Mountains, and boreal forest areas.

Distribution is circumpolar. It is found in each of the three Prairie provinces. The range extends to include Alaska, the Territories, northern Quebec and Newfoundland in the north, and California, Colorado, Missouri, Indiana and Delaware in the south.

SPECIAL FEATURES

Muskrats feed on the fleshy rhizomes. The showy flowers are visited by insects. The foliage is often eaten by wetland invertebrates.

Bogbean has a long history of use both in northern Europe and North America. The alkaloid-containing foliage and roots are strongly bitter. The roots were used in making beer. By drying, grinding, rinsing, and drying

PAT PORTER

(repeated several times), a relatively non-bitter flour was made. This was mixed with cereal flours to make bread. The foliage was dried, prepared into a tea and used as a tonic.

Laplanders fed the roots to cattle.

RELATED SPECIES

The large, 3-parted leaves look very much like a large clover. The flowers are very unique with their bearded corollas. This is the only species of *Menyanthes* occurring in North America.

Menyanthes trifoliata

HEINJO LAHRING

Polemonium acutiflorum Willd.
Tall Jacob's Ladder

POLEMONIACEAE (Phlox Family)

Syn.: *P. caeruleum* L. ssp. *occidentale* (Greene) Davidson, *P. occidentale* Greene

Other Common Names: Greek Valerian, Western Jacob's Ladder

Polemonium is by some thought to be derived from the Greek *polemos* (war), and others suggest it is named in honor of *Polemon* (an early Athenian philosopher). The specific epithet, *acutiflorum*, means sharp-angled (*acuti*) flowers (*florum*). The evenly spaced leaflets appear as a small ladder and give it the name Jacob's Ladder.

Wetland
Perennial
Native
Common
Hardiness Zone: 0
Flowering Season: early summer

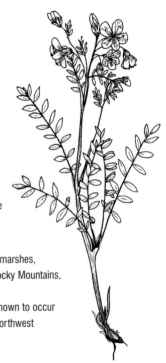

DESCRIPTION

Horizontal rootstocks give rise to a tall (40–100 cm), erect, solitary stem with alternate leaves. Stem is glandular hairy towards top.
Pinnate **leaves** have 15–27 narrow, pointed leaflets.
Dark blue **flowers** (rarely white) are in a flat-topped flower cluster in which the central flowers bloom first. Each flower consists of a 5-lobed cup-shaped calyx, 5-lobed bell-shaped corolla (petals hairy), 5 stamens (attached to corolla; filaments often hairy at base), 1 pistil with a 3-lobed elongated style, and a 3-loculed superior ovary (3–several ovules per locule).
Black spindle-shaped **seeds** are contained within a 3-loculed capsule which opens by 3 valves.

HABITAT AND DISTRIBUTION

This moisture-loving Jacob's Ladder can be found in wet meadows, marshes, bogs, open woods, and valleys. It is generally associated with the Rocky Mountains, foothills and boreal forest.
Distribution includes central and northern Alberta. This plant is not known to occur east of central Alberta. Its range extends into British Columbia, the Northwest Territories, Yukon, Alaska and across to Asia and Europe.

SPECIAL FEATURES

Polemonium acutiflorum is usually considered an arctic or alpine Jacob's Ladder. It is the tallest of the *Polemoniums* in the region. We often think of our garden cultivars, *P. caeruleum* (60 cm tall) and *P. reptans* (15 cm tall), when we see this plant in the wild.

Polemonium acutiflorum Willd.

RELATED SPECIES

Polemonium acutiflorum is the most likely species to be encountered in wet areas. The following two species are found in the Rocky Mountain region on moist open slopes to alpine meadows:
Polemonium pulcherrimum Hook., **Showy Jacob's Ladder**, is shorter (10–30 cm tall) and lacks hairs on the petals.
Polemonium viscosum Nutt., **Skunkweed**, **Sticky Jacob's Ladder**, or **Sky Pilot**, is 10–40 cm tall, has very short corolla lobes and densely glandular-hairy leaflets which are grouped in small clusters (appearing whorled on the leaves).

Myosotis laxa Lehm.
Small Forget-me-not

BORAGINACEAE (Borage Family)

Myosotis is of Greek origin and means 'mouse ear.' The species epithet, *laxa* (open or loose), refers to the loosely flowered raceme.

Wetland
Perennial
Native
Rare
Hardiness Zone: 3
Flowering Season: late spring to mid-summer

DESCRIPTION

Erect stems (15–30 cm) have spreading branches which often root at nodes touching the ground. The alternate oblong-lanceolate **leaves** are 2–6 cm long. Bright blue **flowers** are in terminal, open raceme-like flower clusters (to 20 cm long) in which the central flowers bloom first. Each flower is on a pedicel longer than the calyx. Flowers consist of a 5-parted calyx (3–4 mm long), a corolla-tube broading into 5 lobes(4–8 mm wide), 5 stamens inserted on the corolla, and a deeply 4-lobed superior ovary with 4-locules. Calyx outer surface has appressed straight hairs and its lobes are twice the length of the tube. Corolla is blue with yellow throat and its lobes are equal in length to the calyx lobes. **Fruit** is of four 1-seeded nutlets.

HABITAT AND DISTRIBUTION

Small Forget-me-not grows in shallow water or very wet locations such as ditches, marshes, and disturbed areas. It is sometimes considered a weed. It is found in scattered locations across the Prairie provinces and, as yet, unrecorded as naturalized in either Saskatchewan or Manitoba.

SPECIAL FEATURES

Birds are known to eat the numerous dark seeds.

As every gardener knows, true blue flowers are a rare find. Forget-me-nots fit into this category. From natives on isolated mountain slopes to non-natives in developed lowland areas, they all add an unforgettable touch to our landscape. The name Forget-me-not has truly been applied correctly. The garden cultivars are primarily *M. alpestris* (native to Alberta's Rocky Mountains), *M. sylvatica* and *M. scorpioides* [syn. *M. palustris*]. These species all produce seed in abundance and we, no doubt, will one day start to see them appear in the Canadian wild.

RELATED SPECIES

This is the most likely species to be found in wetland areas.

Myosotis scorpioides L., **Marsh Forget-me-not** or **Scorpion Grass**, the Forget-me-not of Europe and Asia, is a rare weed which has escaped cultivation and may be found on wet disturbed sites. It differs from *M. laxa* in being a perennial with spreading, hooked hairs on the outside of the calyx and the corolla lobes (6–8 mm across) are much longer than the calyx lobes. In England it is called Scorpion Grass because of the twisted stems which resemble a scorpion's tail.

Myosotis laxa Lehm.

Lycopus asper Greene

Western Water-horehound

LAMIACEAE (Mint Family)

Syn.: *L. lucidus* ssp. *americanus* (Gray) Hult.
Other Common Names: Rough Bugleweed

Lycopus is from the Greek terms *lykos* (wolf) and *pous* (foot), being interpreted as wolf's foot and is a reference to the flower's lobed lip. *Asper* (rough) describes the roughly edged leaves.

Wetland/Emergent
Perennial
Native
Common
Hardiness Zone: 2
Flowering Season: summer

DESCRIPTION

This plant looks very much like mint and smells of freshly sawn spruce lumber. Erect 4-angled stems (to 80 cm) grow from underground tuber-bearing stolons. Narrow, pointed **leaves** (2–8 cm long) are opposite (pairs at right angles to each other), sessile, and have 6–12 outward projecting teeth on the margins. Small, white to lavender flowers are in dense clusters where the leaf meets the stem. **Flowers** have a cup-shaped calyx with 4–5 sharp teeth (1–2 mm long or longer), a 4-lobed hairy-throated corolla (more or less symmetrical), 2 stamens (sometimes with 2 sterile staminodia), a 2-cleft style, and a deeply 4-lobed, 2-carpellate superior ovary.
Fruit consists of 4 nutlets, each with one erect seed. Nutlets are triangular with thick margins (upper margin is truncate and often wavy). Calyx lobes are longer than the nutlets.

HABITAT AND DISTRIBUTION

Western Water Horehound grows in shallow water or very moist soil in marshes, and along shorelines. It is generally found in the parkland and prairie regions.
Plants occur in the central to southern half of the Prairie provinces. The range extends southward throughout the western United States, the Great Plains as far as Texas and eastward throughout the northeastern states.

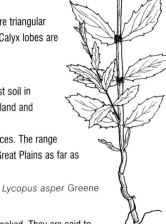

Lycopus asper Greene

SPECIAL FEATURES

Muskrats feed on the tubers.
The tubers (also formed on *L. uniflorus*) can be eaten raw or cooked. They are said to taste like a mild radish. The fleshy, pleasant-tasting rhizome is also edible.
Western Water Horehound is often found growing where Wild Mint and Skullcap are found.

RELATED SPECIES

This species may be confused with Wild Mint (*Mentha* spp.) but lacks the strong odour and the flowers have only 2 stamens (versus 4 in mint flowers).
Lycopus americanus Muhl., **American Water-horehound**, is also found in the region but differs from *L. asper* in having much more deeply incised leaves, nutlets with upper margins rounded and non-wavy, and the absence of tubers. Calyx lobes are longer than nutlets as in *L. asper*.
Lycopus uniflorus Michx., **Northern Water-horehound**, stands apart from the previous two species in having calyx teeth which are broader and short (less than 1 mm), leaves have a tapering base, margins are not as deeply toothed, and calyx lobes are shorter than nutlets. Stolons produce tubers. As the name implies, it has a more northern distribution. [*L. virginicus* var. *pauciflorus* Benth.]

Aster borealis (pp. 286–287)
Marsh Aster

HEINJO LAHRING

Mentha arvensis L.

LAMIACEAE (Mint Family)

Wild Mint

Syn.: *M. canadensis* L.
Other Common Names: Canada Mint, Field Mint, Corn Mint

Mentha is from Minthe, a classical Greek name. *Arvensis* means field or cultivated land.

Wetland
Perennial
Native
Common
Hardiness Zone: 0
Flowering Season: early to mid-summer

DESCRIPTION

Underground stolons give rise to erect (20–50 cm tall), aromatic, 4-angled stems. Stems are covered with downward-pointing hairs (especially along each angle). Short-petioled, ovate to lanceolate **leaves** (1–5 cm long) are opposite (pairs at right angles to each other) with small glandular dots on both surfaces and small teeth along the margins.

Flowers (3 mm long) are borne in dense clusters (appearing whorled) in leaf axils. Pinkish, purple or white flowers consist of a symmetrical or weakly 2-lipped 5-lobed calyx (2–3 mm long; teeth as long as tube), 4-lobed corolla (twice the length of calyx; upper lobe slightly wider than the others), 4 long stamens, and a deeply 4-lobed (but 2-carpellate) superior ovary.

Fruit is of 4 ovoid nutlets. Each nutlet contains a single seed.

HABITAT AND DISTRIBUTION

The strong fragrance of mint is usually noticed before the plant is actually seen (in particular when they have been stepped on). The plants are often hidden amongst grasses in moist meadows, sloughs, marshes, and along streams.

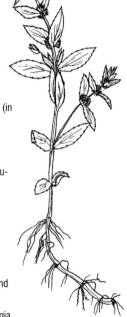

Although plants are often found growing in water, usually they establish themselves just next to it. Its distribution is circumpolar and occurs throughout the Prairie provinces. The range extends from Alaska to Newfoundland and from the Territories to California, Texas and Georgia.

Mentha arvensis L.

Mentha arvensis

HEINJO LAHRING

Mentha arvensis

HEINJO LAHRING

SPECIAL FEATURES

Wild mint was much used by Native peoples and pioneers. The young leaves can be eaten raw or cooked like a vegetable. Indians made wild vinegar from mint. It is popular in sauces, salad dressings, jellies, fruit, beverages and with new potatoes.

Green or dried leaves can be used to make mint tea which is said to be good for digestion and a soothing drink for colds. Plants can be harvested when flowers are open, tied in bunches and hung in a well-ventilated, shady location to dry. Once dry they can be stored in air-tight jars.

Wild mint propagates freely by underground runners. Slips are easy to transplant into a moist, shady garden location.

HEINJO LAHRING

RELATED SPECIES

The unmistakable scent of wild mint makes it easy to identify. If the plant you've found lacks the characteristic mint-smell, perhaps you have *Lycopus* (Water Horehound) instead.

Mentha spicata L., **Spearmint**, a non-native escape from cultivation, prefers drier habitats. It differs from the above in having several terminal flower spikes, sessile leaves, larger flowers (5 mm long), and floral bracts longer than the calyx. It is somewhat taller (30–90 cm tall) than *M. arvensis*. [*M. crispa* L., *M. longifolia* sensu auctt. non (L.) Huds.]

Physosteyia parviflora Nutt.

LAMIACEAE (Mint Family)

False Dragonhead

Syn.: *Dracocephalum nuttallii* Britton., *Physostegia virginiana* (L.) Benth. var. *parviflora* (Nutt.) Boivin

Other Common Names: Western False Dragonhead

Physostegia is from the Greek terms *physo-* (bladdery) *stege* (shelter). *Parviflora* describes the small (*parvi*) flowers (*flora*).

Wetland
Perennial
Native
Occasional
Hardiness Zone: 0
Flowering Season: summer

DESCRIPTION

This tall (30–90 cm), rarely branching herb has erect, smooth, 4-angled stems and opposite **leaves** (each pair placed at right angles to the next pair). Dark green, sessile, elliptic-lanceolate to oblong-lanceolate leaves (2–10 cm long) have coarsely toothed margins. Leaves midway down the stem are larger than above and below.

Large (1–1.5 cm long), rose-pink to purple **flowers** are closely arranged in long (2.5–7.5 cm) terminal and secondary spikes. Flowers are held individually in the axils of bracts and mature from the bottom up. Flower bracts are sharp (spined) and leaf-like. Each flower consists of a 5-toothed somewhat inflated calyx (4–8 mm long; 5–10 nerved), a 2-lipped (upper erect; lower spreading and 3-lobed) funnel-shaped corolla (8–16 mm long), 4 stamens (upper pair short; lower pair long), and a deeply 4-lobed (but 2-carpellate) superior ovary.

Fruit, held loosely by dried calyx, is of 4 smooth, ovoid nutlets. Each nutlet contains a single seed.

HABITAT AND DESCRIPTION

False Dragonhead can be found in moist woods, ditches, swales, stream banks, and along weedy or grassy lake margins. It is often located in shady sites. Plants occur primarily in the parkland region across the Prairie provinces. The range extends into the Northwest Territories, British Columbia, Oregon, Wyoming and Nebraska. Eastern distribution includes western Ontario, the Great Lakes region and along the St. Lawrence River in Quebec.

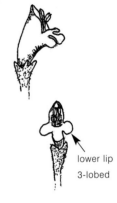

lower lip
3-lobed

Physostegia parviflora Nutt.

SPECIAL FEATURES

The flowers are bee pollinated. Bumblebees will make a slit in the calyx and corolla in order to gain access to the nectar.

Under certain conditions, such as rain driven by strong winds, the flowers will orient themselves into a more favorable position on the spike. Flower movement of up to 180 degrees can be achieved by the plant moving its pedicels. This control had been noticed as early as 1712.

RELATED SPECIES

This is a close relative to our garden cultivars (*P. virginiana* L.) and was at one time named *P. virginiana* L. var. *formosior* (Lunell) Boiv. It is quite possible that in time we will see more of the cultivated varieties begin to appear in the wild.

PAT PORTER

Physostegia parviflora

Scutellaria galericulata L. LAMIACEAE (Mint Family)
Marsh Skullcap

Syn.: *S. epilobiifolia* A. Hamilton
Other Common Names: Common Skullcap, Marsh Skullwort

Scutellaria is derived from the Latin term *scutellum* and means shaped
like a shield. *Galericulata* originates from *galerum,* meaning provided
with a little helmet-like skull-cap. The hump on the upper lobe of the
calyx resembles a helmet and the white markings on the blue flowers
look like skulls.

Wetland
Perennial
Native
Common
Hardiness Zone: 0
Flowering Season: summer

DESCRIPTION

This erect, simple or branching rhizomatous herb is 30–80 cm tall. Four-sided stems
have opposite **leaves** (2–6 cm long, each pair placed at right angles to the next pair).
Short-petioled leaves (upper are sessile) are oblong-lanceolate, heart-shaped at base
and have short, rounded teeth along the margins.

Short-pediceled, blue **flowers** occur either singly or in pairs at leaf axils. Flowers
have a 2-lipped cup-shaped calyx (lips are equal in length but upper has a
helmet-shaped projection), a 2-lipped corolla (12–20 mm long, widening at
throat), 4 stamens (lower pair longer), and a deeply 4-lobed (but 2-carpellate)
superior ovary. The reverse curve of the corolla-tube, as seen from the side, is a
notable feature.

Fruit is of 4 papillae-covered nutlets. Each nutlet contains a single seed.

HABITAT AND DESCRIPTION

Marsh Skullcap inhabits wet meadows, swamps, marshes, swales, and
stream banks. They seem to hide
themselves amidst tall wetland grasses, sedges and cattails, but once
found they usually appear in abundance. Sites often have true mints
growing nearby.

Distribution is circumpolar. This species
occurs throughout the Prairie provinces but
less so in the southern prairie region. Range
extends from Alaska to Newfoundland and
from California and Texas to West Virginia.

Scutellaria galericulata L.

Scutellaria galericulata

HEINJO LAHRING

SPECIAL FEATURES

Marsh Skullcap was used medicinally and contains *scutellarin*, a crystalline glucoside. This compound was employed in treating nervousness, headaches and heart problems. The plants are bitter in taste.
Once the plants have been cut back they soon return by growing from underground rhizomes.

RELATED SPECIES

In wet locations of the southeastern parklands *Scutellaria lateriflora* L., **Blue Skullcap** or **Mad-dog Weed**, is quite common. It differs from the above in having ovate leaves, smaller flowers (6–10 mm long) and several flowers in the leaf axils or on terminal racemes.

Scutellaria parvula Michx., **Small Skullcap**, is a dwarf version of Marsh Skullcap. It is 10–20 cm tall, has small (7–10 mm long), blue flowers, and the rhizomes are deeply constrict-ed between bead-like segments. It is rare in the southeastern Boreal forest of Manitoba, but becomes increasingly more common as one moves eastward from the Prairie provinces towards Ontario and Quebec, where it occurs on sandy soils and calcareous shores.

HEINJO LAHRING

Scutellaria galericulata

HEINJO LAHRING

DICOTS ■ HERBS

Gratiola neglecta Torr.   SCROPHULARIACEAE (Figwort Family)
Clammy Hedge-hyssop

Other Common Names: Neglected Hedge-hyssop

Gratiola is based on the diminutive of the Latin *gratus* or *gratia*, meaning pleasing or agreeable, apparently for the plant's supposed medicinal properties. *Neglecta* means missing or omitted. Clammy refers to the glandular hairiness of the plant which gives a moist and clinging sensation when touched.

Wetland/Emergent
Annual
Native
Occasional
Hardiness Zone: 3
Flowering Season: summer

DESCRIPTION

This short (10–30 cm) herb has widely spreading branches. The upper parts are glandular hairy. The sessile, opposite **leaves** (2–4 cm long) are linear to oblong-lanceolate, tapering towards the base. Margins are smooth or slightly wavy with some outward-pointing teeth.

In the leaf axils, and on long (1–2 cm) pedicels, are single, pale yellow to whitish **flowers** (6–10 mm long). Each flower consists of a 5-lobed calyx (4–6 mm long), a 2-lipped corolla (8–10 mm long; upper lip 2-lobed and lower lip 3-lobed), 2 stamens, 1 pistil, and a 2-loculed superior ovary. Corolla throat is bearded. Sepals have 2 bractlets. The flowers look very much like that of a Penstemon, but smaller.

Fruit is a 4-valved capsule (3–5 mm long) containing many seeds (0.5 mm long).

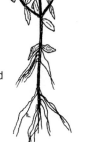

HABITAT AND DISTRIBUTION

These somewhat straggly plants grow in shallow water or wet mud of ditches, shores, river flood plains, and other wet sites of the prairies and parklands. Distribution is limited to southern parts of the Prairie provinces. Range extends to southern British Columbia in the west, Texas and Georgia in the south, and eastward to Quebec and Nova Scotia. It becomes more common as one moves south of the Prairie provinces into the United States.

SPECIAL FEATURES

Hedge-hyssop (*Gratiola officinalis*), a closely related species, is reported to be poisonous to cattle. As a herbal it was used as a strong cathartic, diuretic and emetic.

Gratiola neglecta Torr.

The showy flowers resemble miniature snapdragons.

RELATED SPECIES

This is the only species of the genus found in the Prairie provinces.

Gratiola aurea Muhl. ex Pursh (**Golden-pert**) has a range which includes Wisconsin to Newfoundland. It may possibly be found in the southern extremities of Manitoba. It can be recognized by its golden yellow flowers, presence of sterile swollen-tipped filaments (very small or absent in *G. neglecta*), and broad-based leaves (not strongly tapering). This species can be easily overlooked since it can grow in several feet of water. In this situation it may only be 2–6 cm high, have small, sharp-tipped leaves (versus blunt-tipped when grown out of the water) and lack flowers. [*G. lutea* Raf.]

Limosella aquatica L.

Mudwort

SCROPHULARIACEAE (Figwort Family)

Other Common Names: Mudweed

Limosella is from the Latin term *limosus*, meaning growing in muddy places. *Aquatica* pertains to its watery habitat.

Submerged/Emergent
Annual
Native
Occasional
Hardiness Zone: 0
Flowering Season: summer

DESCRIPTION

This dwarf (4–12 cm tall) amphibious plant produces tufts of leaves and fibrous roots at nodes along above-ground, horizontal, white runners (similar to a strawberry plant). Submerged **leaves** of aquatic plants have long petioles (6–12 cm) while terrestrial plants have short petioles (4–5 cm). The fleshy, hairless leaves (2–6 mm wide) are elliptic to oblong with smooth margins and rounded tips.

Single white or purplish **flowers** are held above the crown on a short, slender and recurving peduncle. Three or four flowers are usually produced per plantlet. Flowers have a 5-lobed cup-shaped calyx, cup-shaped 2-lipped corolla (2–3 mm long), 4 stamens (anther sacs formed as one), and a single 2-loculed superior ovary with numerous ovules.

Fruit is a many-seeded capsule (usually 2-valved) which resembles a rounded pod.

Limosella aquatica L.

HABITAT AND DISTRIBUTION

Mudwort makes its home on land as well as in water. At times it is grows floating on water. It usually can be found along wet shores, mud flats and in shallow water of lakes and streams. It is generally associated with the prairie and parkland regions, but some collections have also been made in the boreal forest and mountain regions. Distribution is circumpolar. Plants occur across the Prairie provinces. Its range extends from Alaska to Newfoundland (including the Territories and northern Quebec), and south to California, New Mexico, Nebraska, Missouri and Minnesota. In the United States, it is absent inland east of the Mississippi.

SPECIAL FEATURES

Limosella aquatica is quite tolerant of a wide range of water conditions including brackish coastal waters as well as fresh inland waters. In the prairies it is known to grow in cultivated slough bottoms where *Eleocharis engelmannii* might grow.

Being of small size and with tiny flowers and inhabiting locations most people would rather not walk, it is an easily missed aquatic plant. The plant's runners give it a competitive advantage, allowing it to travel and colonize recently exposed shorelines within a single season.

BARRE HELLQUIST

Limosella aquatica

RELATED SPECIES

This is the only species of the genus presently recognized as occurring in the Prairie provinces.

Limosella can be confused with the early stages of *Sagittaria* (Arrowhead). Later stages of development allow for easy separation of the two genera by vegetative and reproductive features.

Mimulus lewisii Pursh

SCROPHULARIACEAE (Figwort Family)

Red Monkey-flower

Other Common Names: Lewis Monkey-flower

Mimulus is from the Latin term *mimus* (mimic or actor), and refers to the flower which resembles the grinning masks used by actors in the early days of theatre. *Lewisii* was named after the explorer Captain Meriwether Lewis.

Wetland
Perennial
Native
Rare
Hardiness Zone: 2
Flowering Season: summer

DESCRIPTION

Soft, upright, branching stems (30–70 cm tall) are covered in sticky hairs. Opposite **leaves** (3–7 cm long) are thin, lanceolate to oblong, and smooth-edged or with a few shallow, irregular teeth.
Several large (3.5–5 cm long), rose red **flowers** are borne in leaf axils or on leafy racemes. Flowers are held out beyond the subtending leaf on long pedicels. Each flower consists of a 5-angled calyx, tubular 5-lobed and 2-lipped corolla (upper lip erect and 2-lobed; lower lip spreading and 3-lobed; throat 2-ridged with 2 bright yellow patches in red throat), 4 stamens in 2 pairs (anthers bearded), 1 pistil and a superior 2-loculed ovary with numerous ovules.
Fruit is a 2-valved capsule containing many seeds.

HABITAT AND DISTRIBUTION

Red Monkey-flower can be found growing in sunny to deep forest locations along mountain stream banks, mossy sides of springs and as dense, sprawling plants within moss-lined hollows and amongst moss-covered stones.

Overall distribution is large, being from Alaska to California, but generally it is only found in a few locations in Alberta's Rocky Mountains (including the Waterton Lakes–Crowsnest Pass area). It is not known to occur in Saskatchewan or Manitoba.

Mimulus lewisii Pursh

SPECIAL FEATURES

The plants are only occasionally eaten by sheep, deer, and elk. Muskrats will feed on the soft stems and leaves. The *Mimulus* group is certainly one of the showiest of the wetland species, and is worth an extra moment to stop and admire them.

The closely related Yellow Monkey-flower has been used

Mimulus lewisii

JIM ROMO

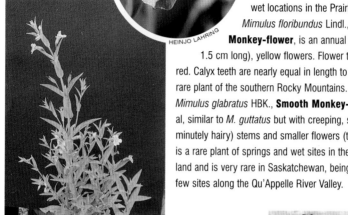

Mimulus ringens

HEINJO LAHRING

by Native peoples and pioneers alike. The slightly bitter-tasting fresh leaves were added to salads. Native peoples burned the dried plants and used the ashes as a salt substitute.

RELATED SPECIES

Several other *Mimulus* species are found in wet locations in the Prairie provinces:

Mimulus floribundus Lindl., **Small Yellow Monkey-flower**, is an annual with small (less than 1.5 cm long), yellow flowers. Flower throat is marked with red. Calyx teeth are nearly equal in length to each other. This is a rare plant of the southern Rocky Mountains.

Mimulus glabratus HBK., **Smooth Monkey-flower**, is a perennial, similar to *M. guttatus* but with creeping, smooth (or only minutely hairy) stems and smaller flowers (to 2.5 cm long). This is a rare plant of springs and wet sites in the southeastern parkland and is very rare in Saskatchewan, being recorded from only a few sites along the Qu'Appelle River Valley.

HEINJO LAHRING

Mimulus guttatus DC., **Yellow Monkey-flower**, is an erect annual or perennial similar to *M. floribundus* but has larger flowers (1.5–4 cm long, with some red speckling) and the calyx teeth are quite unequal in length. It is occasionally found in running streams of the southern Rocky Mountains and Cypress Hills.

Mimulus ringens L., **Blue Monkey-flower**, is a tall (30–100 cm), non-hairy perennial with blue to violet flowers (2–3.5 cm long). It is a common plant of swamps and streams of the southeastern parkland and boreal forest. Having been recorded only from several sites along the Red Deer River of west-central Saskatchewan, it is considered very rare in this province.

JOAN WILLIAMS

Mimulus guttatus

JIM ROMO

(See additional photo of *Mimulus lewisii* on page 235.)

Pedicularis groenlandica Retz.   SCROPHULARIACEAE (Figwort Family)
Elephant's-head

Other Common Names: Little Red Elephant, Fernleaf, Lousewort

Pedicularis is of Latin origin and describes a plant used to treat lice (*herba pedicularis*; derived from *pediculus* which means louse). *Groenlandica* means from Greenland (although first collections were probably from Labrador).

Wetland
Perennial
Native
Occasional
Hardiness Zone: 0
Flowering Season: late spring to summer

Description

Erect, nonbranching stems (20–60 cm tall) are hairless, green to reddish purple, and have clusters of fern-like **leaves** near the base. Pinnately incised leaves (5–20 cm long) are lanceolate in outline. Upper leaves are sessile and lower leaves have a long petiole. Each leaflet is coarsely toothed.
Flower spike (3–15 cm long), usually one per plant, holds many pink to reddish purple flowers. Each **flower** has a 2–5 lobed calyx, a 2-lipped corolla (upper lip 2-lobed; lower lip 3-lobed), 4 stamens in 2 pairs, 1 pistil, and a 2-loculed superior ovary with numerous ovules. The corolla upper lip (galea) has compressed sides, arches over (resembling an elephant's head) and has a long, curving beak (resembling an elephant's trunk).
The flattened and curved **fruit** is a 2-valved capsule containing many rough-surfaced seeds.

HABITAT AND DISTRIBUTION

Elephant's-head can be found among grasses, sedges and mosses in boggy meadows, marshes, swamps, alpine slopes, stony river bottoms, and stream banks. At times it grows in shallow water. Plants occur in the Alberta foothills, Rocky Mountains and boreal forest, as well as the west-central parts of Saskatchewan (53–54° latitude) and northern Manitoba (west of 106° longitude). Range extends from the Yukon and British Columbia to northern Quebec and Labrador. *Pedicularis groenlandica* is very northern and alpine in distribution (including southwestern Greenland). Collections have been made as far south as New Mexico and California.

SPECIAL FEATURES

Without a doubt the unique elephant's head, with curved forehead, ears, trunk, and tusks, makes this plant very characteristic and easily recognized. Elk will feed on Elephant's-head in early summer.
This genus is known to be semiparasitic on other plant roots; therefore, it is best not to transplant it.

Pedicularis groenlandica Retz.

The Inuit use the young stems and leaves fresh or cooked. The roots are dug up and prepared as a vegetable. The sweet nectar can be sucked out of the flowers as a treat. The people of Kurile Island use *Pedicularis* leaves for a tea sustitute.

Historically, an extract from this plant was used as a treatment for animal lice (hence, the name Lousewort). In fact, the plant contains the acrid glycoside *aucubin* which is reputed to have insecticidal properties and presumed to be poisonous to warm-blooded animals as well.

RELATED SPECIES

A few other moisture-loving *Pedicularis* species which may be encountered in the region include:

Pedicularis labradorica Wirsing, **Labrador Lousewort**, is a very low (1.5–30 cm), short-lived perennial found in bogs and tundra. Stems are branched. The yellow flowers (sometimes red-tinged or fading purple) are in few-flowered spikes. Common in the northern parts of the region including the High Arctic (south Baffin Island). Rare in Saskatchewan.

Pedicularis parviflora J. E. Smith, **Swamp Lousewort**, is a tall (30–60 cm), branched annual or biennial. The purple flowers are solitary in leaf axils or a few in short spikes. It is associated with the boreal forest. It is known to occur in calcareous fens in Saskatchewan.

Pedicularis sudetica Willd., **Purple Rattle**, is short (10–40 cm) and unbranched. Its flower stalk is usually leafless (sometimes 1 or 2 leaves may be present). Flowers are violet purple with a pale pink, purple-dotted lower lip. It has a circumpolar distribution within boreal forest and tundra habitats. Not known for Saskatchewan.

HEINJO LAHRING

Pedicularis groenlandica

Below: Wet meadow with
Pedicularis groenlandica in bloom

HEINJO LAHRING

Veronica americana (Raf.) Schwein. ex Benth.   **SCROPHULARIACEAE (Figwort Family)**

American Brooklime

Other Common Names: American Speedwell, Common Speedwell

Veronica comes from *veronikon* (true image), and was used to describe the flower. Its shape suggests the imprint of Christ's face left on the Sindon (the cloth used by St. Veronica to swab Jesus's face while on the climb to Calvary). *Americana* means from America.

Emergent/Wetland
Perennial
Native
Common
Hardiness Zone: 0
Flowering Season: late spring to summer

DESCRIPTION

This branched, spreading herb (10–70 cm long) roots at nodes and has opposite leaves. Short-petioled **leaves** (2–7 cm long) have oblong-lanceolate to obovate blades with small, widely spaced teeth.

Small (4–6 mm wide), short-stalked (0.5–1 cm), blue to pale violet (rarely white) **flowers** are held in short racemes attached to the leaf axil. Each flower consists of a 4-cleft calyx, 4-lobed corolla (lobes flat, spreading, and slightly irregular), 2 stamens, 1 pistil and a short, flattened, 2-loculed superior ovary with numerous ovules.

The heart-shaped **fruit** is a flattened, 2-valved capsule containing many seeds.

Veronica americana (Raf.)
Schwein. ex Benth.

HEINJO LAHRING

Veronica americana

HABITAT AND DISTRIBUTION

This semi-aquatic plant inhabits streams, springs, sandy slough edges, marshes, and pond margins. American Brooklime is a plant of the grasslands, southern boreal forest, riparian woodlands, mountains, and Cypress Hills.

Veronica americana occurs over much of the three Prairie provinces, but is restricted to creek and river valleys in the southern prairies of Alberta and Saskatchewan. Range is broad and includes eastern Asia, Alaska to Newfoundland, and south to California, Texas and South Carolina.

SPECIAL FEATURES

American Brooklime has a spicy taste similar to Watercress (*Nasturtium officinale*). The stems and leaves are excellent in a salad and best harvested before the flowers appear. Once in bloom they should be boiled to remove the slightly bitter taste.

The green foliage is very high in vitamin C and was used in the past to prevent scurvy.

Medicinally, root extracts were used as a cathartic and emetic. Tissues contain the glucoside *aucubine* and should be consumed in moderation.

Veronica americana L.

Veronica scutellata L.

RELATED SPECIES

Veronica catenata Pennell, **Water Speedwell**, is a succulent perennial of prairie areas. It is similar to *V. americana* but the leaves lack petioles and clasp the stems. The corolla is white or nearly so. [syn. *V. comosa* Richt.]

Veronica peregrina L., **Hairy Speedwell**, is a short (10–30 cm) annual with glandular-hairy stems, small (1–2.5 cm long) alternate (at least above) leaves, and whitish flowers located singly in leaf axils. It is common across the Prairie provinces. [syn. *V. xalapensis* HBK]

Veronica scutellata L., **Marsh Speedwell**, resembles *V. catenata* but its leaves are more linear and do not clasp the stem. This is a common plant of springs, marshes and shores. Distribution is circumpolar.

HEINJO LAHRING

Veronica americana

DICOTS ■ HERBS

Pinguicula vulgaris L.   **LENTIBULARIACEAE (Bladderwort Family)**

Common Butterwort

Pinguicula is from the Latin term *pinguiculus* (a diminutive form of *pinguis*, meaning fat) and refers to the buttery feel and look of the leaves. At one time it was thought that if cows ate the plant, milk production, and its relative butter yield, would improve. *Vulgaris* means common or ordinary.

Wetland
Perennial
Native
Rare
Hardiness Zone: 0
Flowering Season: spring to early summer

DESCRIPTION

This low, compact, semi-carnivorous herb has sticky, yellowish green **leaves** in a basal rosette. Inward rolled, oval to elliptic leaves (2–5 cm long by 1–2 cm wide) have shallow teeth on margins.
Plants bear 1–4 flowers per plant, each blooming one at a time in succession. The single, pale bluish violet **flowers** (12–18 mm long) are held above the leaf cluster on a somewhat glandular-hairy, 3–12 cm pedicel. Each flower consists of 5 sepals, a 2-lipped corolla (upper 2-lobed; lower 3-lobed, under 12 mm long) with a straight, nectar-filled spur (6–8 mm long), 2 stamens, and a 1-loculed superior ovary with numerous ovules.
The flower resembles a blue violet, except that the petals are united into a 1-piece corolla.
Fruit is a 2-valved capsule containing numerous wrinkled seeds.

HABITAT AND DISTRIBUTION

Common Butterwort grows on moist soil or in shallow water in bogs, cold swamps, lakeshores, springs, and among damp rocks and ledges. It is found in nutrient-poor, calcium-rich wetlands in the foothills, Rocky Mountain (up to alpine), and boreal forest regions.
Distribution is circumpolar. Plants are occasional in western Alberta but rare in Saskatchewan and Manitoba. Its range extends from Alaska to Newfoundland, with populations reaching as far north as south Baffin Island. The southern limit includes Oregon and Montana in the west, and the Great Lakes region, New York and Vermont in the southeast.

SPECIAL FEATURES

The sticky excretions on the leaf surface entrap small insects. Their presence causes the leave margins to roll over them. Proteolytic and rennin-like enzymes are secreted which assist in slowly digesting the organism, thereby providing supplemental nitrogen to the plant.
After the fruit has formed, a bud appears in the last leaf axil, forming an autumn rosette. As winter approaches the bud looses its outside leaves and scales. In the central bud-like portion which remains, next season's floral parts can be distinguished.

Pinguicula vulgaris L.

In Denmark the peasants used it to make a hair pommade (conditioner) to nourish their hair. In the Alps, herders used it to heal sore and cracked cows' udders.

RELATED SPECIES

Pinguicula macroceras Willd., **Western Butterwort**, is much like *P. vulgaris* but has a slightly recurving spur on the flower, dark purple flowers which are larger (2–3 cm long; lower lip over 12 mm long), and somewhat hairy petals (in particular near the mouth of corolla tube). Western Butterwort is a rare plant of bogs and swamps of the southern Rocky Mountains and Cypress Hills (replaced by *P. vulgaris* to the north and east).

Pinguicula villosa L., **Small Butterwort**, a plant of sphagnum bogs, differs from *P. vulgaris* in having smaller flowers (corolla less than 10 mm long) and a glandular-hairy flower stem. It is found in the northern boreal forest and tundra of the Prairie provinces.

HEINJO LAHRING

Pinguicula vulgaris

HEINJO LAHRING

DICOTS ■ HERBS

Utricularia vulgaris L.   LENTIBULARIACEAE (Bladderwort Family)
Common Bladderwort

Syn.: *U. vulgaris* var. *americana* Gray, *U. macrorhiza* Le Conte

Utricularia originates from the Latin term *utricularis* (possessing bladders). *Vulgaris* means common.

Submerged
Perennial
Native
Common
Hardiness Zone: 0
Flowering Season: late spring to summer

DESCRIPTION

This non-rooted (although stems are often anchored in mud), submerged aquatic plant forms long (30–80 cm), many-leaved, branching stems (at least 0.5 mm thick) bearing animal trapping bladders (3–5 mm long). Stems sometimes form a floating mat as the season progresses. Plants are often coated with epiphytic algae. Alternate or whorled brownish green **leaves** (2–5 cm long) are dichotomously divided into thin, hair-like segments. Bright yellow, snapdragon-like **flowers** (15-25 mm long) are held above the water on a 1–15-flowered raceme. Small bracts are at the base of the peduncle. The flower consists of a 2-lipped calyx (divided to base), 2-lipped corolla (yellow with short spur-like sac at base), 2 stamens, and a 1-loculed superior ovary containing several ovules. Many **seeds** are contained within a round, 2-valved capsule (5 mm long) which is held on a short, curved pedicel.

Utricularia vulgaris L.

HABITAT AND DISTRIBUTION

Plants occur in lakes, ponds, sloughs, ditches, and slow-moving streams and are tolerant of a wide range of water conditions.

Distribution is circumpolar. Common Bladderwort is spread across the Prairie provinces. Its range extends from Alaska to Newfoundland, as far north as the Territories and northern Quebec, and southward to California, Texas and Florida.

SPECIAL FEATURES

The small bladders on this plant (sometimes abundant and other times scarce) have evolved to catch small aquatic invertebrates. Each bladder has trigger-hairs at its entrance. When a small crustacean touches these, a trapdoor-like flap of tissue swings open, the bladder

Utricularia vulgaris

HEINJO LAHRING

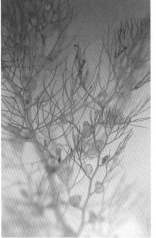

HEINJO LAHRING

HEINJO LAHRING

Utricularia vulgaris
Far left: empty
bladders
Left: filled bladders
Below: in flower

HEINJO LAHRING

quickly expands and the creature is sucked inside. Enzymes are then secreted. The prey is slowly dissolved and absorbed to supplement the plant's nutritional needs. The bladders are translucent and green while empty and turn dark purple to black as they become filled with trapped organisms.

Each flower blooms for scarcely one day. Once fertilized, the peduncle pulls down the developing pod into the water where they ripen and release their seed. Developing seeds, however, are almost always aborted. The plant compensates for this sterility by producing over-wintering buds (turions) at the ends of the branches in the autumn. The old branches eventually die, but the buds detach, float freely (often to a new location), and finally drop into the mud and debris of the pond bottom to grow into new plants the following spring.

RELATED SPECIES

Utricularia may be confused with *Myriophyllum* (Water-milfoil) and *Ceratophyllum* (Hornwort) but only *Utricularia* has the unique bladders.

Other Bladderworts found in the Prairie provinces include:

Utricularia cornuta Michx., **Horned Bladderwort**, is a rare wetland plant of the boreal forest growing on muddy shores, bogs, and the wetter parts of fens. Its slender stems and minute linear leaves are underground. One to three golden yellow flowers (15–25 mm long; spur 7–12 mm long) are held up on a 3–25 cm stem.

Utricularia intermedia Hayne, **Flat-leaved Bladderwort**, is similar to *U. vulgaris* but differs in having the bladders (relatively large, 5 mm long) and leafy stems on separate branches, flattened leaflets (margins with small teeth), and smaller flowers (10–15 mm long). Winter buds are 3–10 mm long. It is circumpolar with widespread regional distribution.

Utricularia minor L., **Small Bladderwort**, is a rare small version of *U. vulgaris* with stems less than 0.5 mm thick and few bladders (2 mm long or less). The somewhat flattened leaf blades are not toothed. The pale yellow flowers are small (4–8 mm long). Distribution is circumpolar and associated with the boreal forest region of the Prairie provinces.

Plantago maritima L.   PLANTAGINACEAE (Plantain Family)

Seaside Plantain

Plantago is derived from the Latin *planta* (sole of the foot) and refers to the leaf shape of some of this genus's species. *Maritima* means growing by the sea.

Wetland
Perennial
Native
Rare
Hardiness Zone: 1
Flowering Season: summer

DESCRIPTION

Rising from a short taproot is a basal cluster of prominently 3–5 ribbed leaves. Thick, fleshy, linear to lanceolate **leaves** (to 22 cm long by 1.5 cm wide) are smooth margined or distantly toothed.
There are 1–several (5–30 cm tall) flower stalks per plant. At the top of the stalk is a 1–8 cm long densely flowered spike. Small white or green **flowers** have a long (1.5–4 mm), broad bract equalling the calyx, 4-lobed calyx, 4-lobed corolla (1–1.5 mm spreading lobes; tube is hairy inside), 4 stamens, and a 2-loculed ovary.
Fruit is a many-seeded, 2-loculed capsule (pyxis) which opens by removal of the conical top. Wet seeds have a mucilaginous coating.

HABITAT AND DISTRIBUTION

Seaside Plantain, as the name implies, occurs in saline locations such as salt marshes, shores, and mud flats of the boreal forest and parkland. It tends to be restricted to saltwater wetlands where the salt in the water is NaCl.
Distribution is circumpolar but is considered rare in the Prairie provinces. It is known to occur in Saskatchewan's Nitenai Salt Marshes and Manitoba's Hudson Bay shore, Dawson Bay and the Lake Winnipegosis shore (in the area of the subcrop of the Prairie Evaporites). The range extends down the west coast to California and from northern Quebec south to New Jersey.

SPECIAL FEATURES

Seaside Plantain is not abundant in our region and Is therefore best lcft alone. Along with more dry-land plantains such as *P. major* and *P. lanceolata*, it is also known to be edible. Young leaves can be

Plantago maritima L.

eaten fresh, cooked, or pickled. The leaves are excellent mixed with dandelion greens and are best used before the ribs get tough. Tea can be made from the dried leaves. The seeds are easily harvested from the spike by drawing upwards with fingers. These can be crushed and used in baking. Their mucilagenous qualities make them good for hair lotions. The leaves and roots are a source for a green dye.

RELATED SPECIES

This plant can be confused with *Alisma triviale* (Water-plantain). *Alisma* has wider leaf blades (2–6 cm) with well-defined petioles, and an open flower panicle with 3-parted, white flowers.

Plantago eriopoda Torr., **Saline Plantain**, a common species of the prairie and parkland, can be found in alkaline locations on river flats and slough margins. It differs from *P. maritima* in having a mass of reddish or brownish wool at the leaf bases, wider (oblanceolate to ovate) leaves, and loosely flowered spikes. *Plantago eriopoda* grows on ground where the salt is Na_2SO_4, the typical salt of saline places on the dry prairies.

Plantago eriopoda

PAT PORTER

DICOTS ■ HERBS

Galium triflorum **Michx.**   **RUBIACEAE (Madder Family)**

Sweet-scented Bedstraw

Other Common Names: Catchstraw

Galium is a derivation of the Greek term *Galion*, or *Gala*, meaning milk. It was originally applied to *G. verum* (Yellow Bedstraw) which contains the enzyme rennin (1g per 100 gm of leaf tissue) and was used to curdle milk in cheesemaking. *Triflorum* means 3-flowered.

Wetland
Perennial
Native
Common
Hardiness Zone: 0
Flowering Season: summer

DESCRIPTION

Growing from slender, creeping rootstocks are thin, reclining to erect (30–100 cm long), square stems with whorls of 5–6 leaves. Sessile **leaves** are narrowly elliptic (2–8 cm long) with tapering tip and base, rough margined with short stiff hairs, and have a sharp, pointed tip. Tiny white **flowers** (3 to several) are in open clusters (cymose) from the leaf axils or ends of branches. Each flower lacks a calyx but has a 4-lobed corolla, 4 stamens, 2 styles, and a 2-loculed inferior ovary.

Fruit consists of a pair of round nutlets (2–3 mm long; 1 seed per nutlet) covered with small, hooked bristles.

HABITAT AND DISTRIBUTION

Sweet-scented Bedstraw grows in moist woods, mossy seepages, swamps, and wet hollows. It is associated with the boreal forest, parklands, foothills and mountains. In Saskatchewan it also is known from riverine woodlands in the grassland region.

Distribution is circumpolar. Plants occur across the Prairie provinces but are scarce in the drier prairie regions. The range extends from Alaska to Newfoundland and from the Territories southward to California, Oklahoma and Florida.

SPECIAL FEATURES

This species becomes very fragrant when dried and was collected by the Blackfoot women for use as perfume.

Dried plants of this and other species of Bedstraw were mixed with bedding straw to give a fresh fragrance. The scent is the result of coumarin compounds, which have also been found to be of importance in herbal medicine to prevent blood from clotting.

The roasted seeds of *Galium* are one of the best coffee substitutes found in the north. *Galium boreale* L., **Northern Bedstraw**, has more seeds in a head and is a better choice for collection. *Galium* is in the same family as the tropical coffee plant.

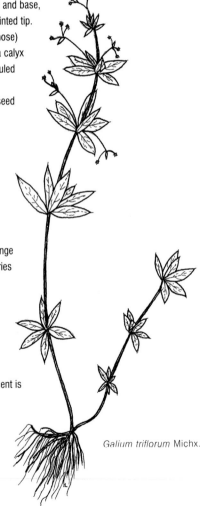

Galium triflorum Michx.

HEINJO LAHRING

Left: *Galium triflorum*

Below: *Galium labradoricum*

HEINJO LAHRING

By gathering handfuls of Bedstraw's bristly foliage, an effective backcountry sieve can be made to strain liquids through.

A permanent red to purple dye can be made from the roots of most bedstraws.

RELATED SPECIES

Galium labradoricum Wieg., **Labrador Bedstraw**, is a small (10–30 cm tall) boreal forest plant found in bogs and open marshes. It differs from *G. triflorum* in having leaves in whorls of 4 (8–14 mm long), the stems and leaf midrib are usually without bristly hairs, and flowers are at the ends of branches in groups of 3. Each flower has 4 corolla-lobes. [*G. tinctorium* var. *labradoricum* Wieg.] *Galium trifidum* L., **Small Bedstraw**, is similar to *G. labradoricum* but the stems and leaves are moderately hairy, the flowers are in terminal and axillary clusters and each flower has 3 corolla-lobes.

Galium trifidum L.

281

DICOTS ■ HERBS

Valeriana dioica L.   **VALERIANACEAE (Valerian Family)**

Northern Valerian

Syn.: *V. septentrionalis* Rydb., *V. sylvatica* Soland.
Other Common Names: Tobaccoroot, Wild Heliotrope

Wetland
Perennial
Native
Common
Hardiness Zone: 0
Flowering Season: late spring
to summer

Valeriana, from the Latin *valeo* (to be healthy), refers to the medicinal properties of *V. officinalis*, a European species popularly used back to the seventeenth century. *Dioica* means to have 2 sexes of flowers.

DESCRIPTION

Scented rootstocks give rise to slender, erect, nonbranching stems (30–70 cm tall). **Leaves** are of two kinds. Basal leaves (2–5 cm long) are petioled, elliptic to spatulate, and smooth margined. The stem has 2–4 pinnate (3–7 pairs of smooth margined leaflets each) leaves which are sessile or short petioled, and opposite to each other.

Many small, white (occasionally pinkish) **flowers** are held in spreading clusters (panicled cymes). Flowers (sometimes unisexual) consist of a ring of inrolled bristles (calyx), a 5-lobed corolla (1–3 mm long, equalling or slightly longer than the spreading lobes), 3 stamens (extending beyond corolla), and a 1-ovuled inferior ovary.

Fruit is a dry, flat, 1-seeded achene with a ring of bristles at the top (becoming feathery and dandelion-like).

HABITAT AND DISTRIBUTION

Northern Valerian inhabits wet meadows and bogs of the mountains and boreal forest.
Distribution is European as well as North American. It is found in Alberta, Saskatchewan and southern Manitoba. Range extends from the Yukon and Northwest Territories to Washington, Idaho and Wyoming. Eastward it reaches into southern Ontario, the Gaspe and Island of Anticosti in the Gulf of St. Lawrence.

SPECIAL FEATURES

Northern Valerian is eaten by elk, deer, sheep and livestock.
Historically, as medicinal plants, the Valerians were an important group. The roots of *V. officinalis* contain ethereal oils, alkaloids, a glucoside, and a compound called *valerian*. In moderation it is said to strengthen the nervous system (acting as a mild stimulant and antispasmotic) and create a calming effect. The Plains Indians used it to treat stomach problems. High dosages, if used frequently and over long periods of time, can cause digestive, cardiac and nervous problems. The scent of the rootstocks is due to isovaleric acid, the active principle in the smell of unwashed feet. The smell is relatively mild in *V. dioica* but quite memorable in *V. sitchensis*. When dried the strong smell, especially the roots, will last for years. The plant attracts cats (and rats) like catnip. "It is said that the secret of the Pied Piper of Hamelin was the roots of *Valeriana* which he carried in his pocket" (Coon, 1974). Valerians were an important food for many Native western tribes. It was used fresh, in soup, and dried and ground into flour for bread.

Valeriana dioica L.

RELATED SPECIES

Valeriana dioica is the most likely species to be found in our wetlands.
Valeriana sitchensis Bong., **Mountain Heliotrope**, may be encountered on moist mountain slopes, along streams and in wet woods. It differs in having larger flowers (5–8 mm long; corolla tube much longer than lobes), a 3–5-lobed stem and basal leaves. It occurs throughout Alberta's Rocky Mountains up to the subalpine zone.

Downingia laeta Greene
Downingia

CAMPANULACEAE (Bluebell Family)

Syn.: *Bolelia laeta* Greene
Other Common Names: Calico-flower, Bright Downingia

Laeta is from the Latin *laetus*, meaning cheerful, pleasant and bright and refers to the colourful flowers.

Wetland
Annual
Native
Rare
Hardiness Zone: 3
Flowering Season: summer

DESCRIPTION

Plants are low (5–20 cm) with simple to branched stems, sometimes rooting at the nodes. Alternate sessile **leaves** (to 15 mm long) are narrowly oblong with smooth margins.

Flowers (1 cm long) are on the upper portion of the stem and subtended by a leaf-like bract (longer than the leaves). Each flower has 5 leaf-like sepals (partly united and shorter than irregular corolla), 5 joined petals (4–7 mm long), 5 stamens (filaments and anthers wholly united to form a tube around the stigma; 2 anthers are tipped with bristles), and a long, thin, inferior ovary (resembling the flower stalk). The tube-like corolla is white to light blue with darker blue veins. The corolla throat is white with yellow spots.

Fruit is a 1-loculed, pod-like capsule containing many small seeds.

HABITAT AND DISTRIBUTION

This moisture-loving plant of the southern prairies can be found on muddy alkaline shores, slough margins, and in shallow water.

Distribution in the Prairie provinces is limited to the extreme southern parts of Alberta and Saskatchewan. *Downingia laeta* is becoming common on tilled sloughs in southwestern Saskatchewan, particularily around Rosetown and Leader. The range continues southward to western Montana, Wyoming, Utah and California.

Downingia laeta Greene

SPECIAL FEATURES

This is one of those species that few will ever see. So if you find it consider yourself fortunate and take a photograph but leave the plant alone. Its ability to survive under saline conditions, and reproduce annually by seeds, allows it to survive in the harsh prairie environment with its hot dry summers, long cold winters, and unpredictable water availability.

RELATED SPECIES

This is the only species of *Downingia* found in the Prairie provinces. It resembles Lobelia in flower shape but in *Lobelia* the corolla tube is split to near the base on the upper side and the capsule is 2-loculed. The wetland Lobelias generally occur further north.

DICOTS ■ HERBS

Lobelia kalmii L.   CAMPANULACEAE (Bluebell Family)

Kalm's Lobelia

Syn.: *L. strictiflora* (Rydb.) Lunell.
Other Common Names: Brook Lobelia

Lobelia was named in honour of Matthias de L'Obel (1538–1616), a
French physician-turned-botanist. Linnaeus named the species *kalmii*, in
honour of the plant's discoverer, Pehr Kalm, one of his favourite pupils.

Wetland
Biennial/Perennial
Native
Occasional
Hardiness Zone: 1
Flowering Season: summer

DESCRIPTION

From fibrous roots grow slender, erect stems (10–50 cm tall). Petioled
basal leaves (1–3 cm long) are spatulate to obovate with some hairiness. The
flower-stem **leaves** (1–7 cm long) are alternate, linear to lanceolate and erect.
First-year plants may only have a basal rosette, while second-year plants produce the floral spike.

A few light blue/purplish with white- or yellow-centered **flowers** (rarely all
white; 8–15 mm long) are held by short pedicels on a terminal raceme (often
one-sided). Flowers have 5 partly united sepals (3 mm long), a 5-lobed corolla (2
small, backwards-bent upper lobes or wing petals and 3 larger, downward-spread-
ing lower lobes), 5 stamens united into a tube around the style, and a 2-loculed
inferior ovary.

Fruit is a many-seeded, 2-celled, pod-like capsule (4–8 mm long). The rough-
surfaced seeds are very tiny and pointed at each end.

HABITAT AND DISTRIBUTION

Kalm's Lobelia is found in bogs, wet meadows, shores, stream banks, ditches, calcareous mud, and around cold mineral springs. Plants are found throughout the
boreal forest and mountain regions, and rarely in the parklands.
Distribution includes the central and northern parts of Alberta and Saskatchewan and
central to southern Manitoba. *Lobelia kalmii* occurs from British Columbia to
Newfoundland with the distribution reaching into the southwestern Northwest
Territories, and southward to Colorado, South Dakota, and New Jersey.

SPECIAL FEATURES

The Lobelias are generally considered poisonous, and therefore should not be consumed.
The milky juice of some species is said to be very poisonous to livestock
(Hutchens, 1973). The Lobelia group has long been known to have strong
medicinal properties and was used extensively by herbalists.
The Water Lobelia (see below), a true aquatic Lobelia, lacks the latex bearing
canals of other Lobelias. It tolerates acid conditions and reproduces vegetatively by
small plantlets or offshoots from the basal rosette. In Ontario and points east, it
grows in a similar manner to, and often with, the commonly encountered *Eriocaulon
aquaticum* (Hill) Druce [syn. *E. septangulare* With.], Seven-angled
Pipewort, with its short, linear basal leaves and emergent flower stalk.

Lobelia kalmii L.

BARRE HELLQUIST

RELATED SPECIES

Lobelia dortmanna L., **Water Lobelia**, is a perennial aquatic *Lobelia* named after Dortmann, a Dutch pharmacist. It is recognized by its cluster of submerged, fleshy, linear (2–8 cm long) basal leaves, long (40–70 cm), emersed, leafless flower stem (thread-like scales sometimes present), and pale lavender-mauve flowers (10–20 mm long). It grows in shallow water of ponds and lakes in scattered locations across the boreal forest of the Prairie provinces. Distribution also includes northern Europe, British Columbia, Washington, Oregon, the Great Lakes states and, in Canada, as far east as Newfoundland.

Above and right: *Lobelia kalmii*

HEINJO LAHRING

Aster borealis (T. & G.) Prov.　　　ASTERACEAE (Composite Family)

Marsh Aster

Syn.: *A. junciformis* Rydb., *Symphotrichum boreale* (T. & G.) A & D. Love

Other Common Names: Northern Aster, Rush Aster, Frost-flower, Starwort

Aster is a Greek term meaning star and refers to the star-shaped flowers. *Borealis* is Latin for northern.

Wetland
Perennial
Native
Common
Hardiness Zone: 0
Flowering Season: summer

DESCRIPTION

Upright, green stems (10–80 cm) arise from a slender (2 mm thick), creeping rhizome. Stems are little-branched and have lines of hairs above the upper leaf-bases (hairless below). Alternate sessile **leaves** (2–8 cm long) are very narrow (2–5 mm) with a tapering tip and base. Base of leaf is slightly clasping onto the stem. Margins are more or less smooth.

White or light rose **flower** heads (15–20 mm across) are 1–few in an open panicle. Involucre is 5–7 mm high, with overlapping, slender and pointed bracts (more or less without hairs). The ray (ligulate) florets (15 or more) are female and fertile with a bristle-like calyx, a showy, strap-shaped corolla, and a 2-carpelled (1-loculed) inferior ovary with 1 ovule. The discoid (tubular) florets consist of a bristle-like calyx, a tubular corolla, 5 stamens (united to form a tube), and an ovary as in the ray florets.

Fruit is a small achene with a cluster of bristles at the top end.

HABITAT AND DISTRIBUTION

Marsh Aster grows in swamps, marshes and bogs of the parkland and boreal forest. Distribution is from Alaska to Nova Scotia. It is generally found throughout the Prairie provinces but is somewhat scarce in the central and southern prairies. In the north it reaches into the western part of the Territories and in the south as far as Idaho, Colorado, Minnesota and New Jersey.

SPECIAL FEATURES

Historically asters played a variety of roles. *Aster xylorrhiza* (**Woody Aster**) is known to contain a poisonous resinous substance. This species, plus *A. adscendens* (**Western Aster**) and *A. commutatus* (**White Prairie Aster**), can absorb enough selenium to be toxic to cattle.

Aster lectophyllus and *A. macrophyllus* (**White Wood Aster**) of the Appalachians were eaten raw or cooked by the Cherokee Indians. The leaves of *A. engelmannii* (**Elegant Aster**), a Rocky Mountain species, were boiled and eaten by Native peoples. Big game and livestock are known to feed on most aster species of the Prairie provinces.

In Asters the pollen ripens before the stigma is ready to receive pollen, encouraging cross-pollination. They are considered generalist plants, being attractive to a host of pollinators including bumblebees, flies, butterflies, and many other insects.

Aster borealis (T. & G.) Prov.

RELATED SPECIES

Other asters of wet areas include:

Aster brachyactis Blake, **Rayless Aster**, is an annual aster which lacks (or are very inconspicuus) the colourful rays common to other asters. Leaves are linear (3–5 cm), smooth edged and clasping to the stem. It occurs on moist, saline ground across the region. [*Brachyactis angusta* (Lindl.) Britt.]

Aster hesperius A. Gray, **Western Willow Aster**, is similar to *A. borealis* but has wider and longer (5–15 cm) linear to broadly lanceolate leaves, there are more than 10 flower heads per cluster, the panicle is usually quite leafy and the corolla is white to often purplish. It is found in ditches, on moist ground, and along stream banks. [*A. lanceolatus* Willd.]

Aster modestus Lindl., **Large Northern Aster**, is 30–80 cm tall and glandular hairy (at least above). Leaves are lanceolate (4–8 cm long) with smooth to sharply toothed margins. The purple to violet flower heads (2–3 cm wide; 20–40 rays) are in a short leafy cluster. This is an aster of moist woods and bogs of the western parkland and boreal forest. It is rare in Saskatchewan.

Aster puniceus L., **Purple-stemmed Aster**, is 50–150 cm tall with a stout, reddish purple, non-hairy stem. Leaves (6–16 cm long) are lanceolate to oblong and at times sharply toothed (often with a hairy midrib). Light violet to pale purple (sometimes white) flower heads (2.5–3.5 cm across) have 30 to 60 rays. Common in marshes and swamps of the boreal forest.

HEINJO LAHRING

Aster umbellatus Mill., **Flat-topped White Aster**, is 60–200 cm tall and hairy throughout. The lanceolate to ovate leaves (6–15 cm long) are short-petioled, smooth margined and hairy beneath. The numerous white flower heads (1–2 cm across; 4–7 rays) are in a flat-topped cluster (corymb). Inhabits moist forests and swamps of the eastern parkland and boreal forest. It is rare in Alberta and Saskatchewan but more common in Manitoba.

(See additional photo of *Aster borealis* on page 259.)

GLEN SUGGETT

Above, inset: *Aster borealis*

Left: *Aster* sp.

DICOTS ■ HERBS

Bidens cernua L.
Nodding Beggarticks

ASTERACEAE (Composite Family)

Syn.: *B. glaucescens* Greene

Other Common Names: Smooth Beggarticks, Nodding Bur-marigold, Smaller Bur-marigold, Pitchforks, Stick-tights, Spanish Needles, Beggar's Tick, Devil's Pitchfork

Wetland
Annual
Native
Common
Hardiness Zone: 0
Flowering Season: late summer

The generic name, *Bidens*, means with 2 teeth and refers to the two barbed awns on top of the achenes. *Cernua*, from the Latin *cernuus* (slightly drooping), describes the flower's tendancy to nod with age.

DESCRIPTION

Upright branching stems (10–100 cm tall) arise from a decumbent base. Sessile and clasping, opposite **leaves** (5–15 cm long) are linear lanceolate. Margins are smooth to coarsely toothed.

Showy, yellow, sunflower-like **flower** heads (20–35 mm across) with dark centers are terminal or on stems from leaf axils. Flower heads are comprised of 2 flower types. Outer ray flowers (6–8) are neutral with a bristle-like calyx and a yellow (often red-tinged), strap-shaped corolla (to 1.5 cm long). The inner disc flowers have a bristle-like calyx, tubular corolla, 5 stamens (united into a tube), and a 2-carpeled inferior ovary (1-loculed) with 1 ovule.

Fruit is an achene (5–7 mm long) with 4 (rarely 2) downward pointing barbed awns (2–3 mm long).

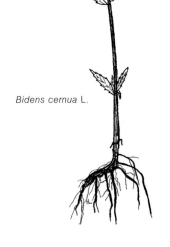

Bidens cernua L.

HEINJO LAHRING

Bidens cernua

288

HABITAT AND DISTRIBUTION

Nodding Beggarticks grows in marshes, ditches, swamps, beaver meadows, shallow waters, and along pond edges of the parkland and boreal forest.

Plant distribution is from British Columbia to Nova Scotia. It is common throughout the Prairie provinces.

Range includes the Territories and south as far as California, New Mexico, Oklahoma, Louisiana, Georgia and North Carolina.

SPECIAL FEATURES

The abundant seeds are eaten by birds; however, the seed's barbed awns can cause physical injury to some animals.

The common names refer to the hooked achenes which attach themselves to passersby and are carried to new locations.

The leaves are known to have been used as a pot-herb (although somewhat bitter) by Native peoples.

In Russia, Tall Beggarticks has been used medicinally as a tea to treat colds, headaches, bladder inflammation and help one relax and fall asleep. In commercial production, a seeding of 12–14 lb. per acre yields a harvest of up to 2,500 lb. of dried herb (Hutchens, 1973). Plants are cut just before the flowers open. Only the leaves and tops are used.

RELATED SPECIES

Bidens frondosa L., **Common Beggarticks**, taller (30–150 cm) than *B. cernua*, is reddish with coarse, furrowed stems. Stalked leaves (5–10 cm long) have 3–5 pinnately arranged leaflets. Flower heads are 12–20 mm across. The ray flowers are small and inconspicuous (sometimes absent late in the season). Disc flowers are pale yellow to orange. It is found in the southern prairies, eastern parklands and boreal forest.

Bidens tripartita L., **Tall Beggarticks**, is 20–80 cm tall. Its leaves (3–15 cm long) are elliptic to lanceolate and coarsely toothed or 3-lobed. Petioles are wing-margined. Flower head is 10–25 mm across. Ray flowers are absent. This is a rare introduced species of the southwestern prairies.

Bidens cernua

Erigeron elatus Hook.

Tall Fleabane

ASTERACEAE (Composite Family)

Syn.: *E. acris* L. var. *elatus* (Hook.) Cronq.

Erigeron is derived from the Greek *eri* (early) and *geron* (old man) and means to become old early. It was used to describe the flowers which once picked soon withered and formed white-haired seeds. *Elatus* means tall.

Wetland
Biennial/Perennial
Native
Occasional
Hardiness Zone: 0
Flowering Season: mid- to late summer

DESCRIPTION

Upright stems (5–20 cm) have alternate leaves. The lightly hairy, oblanceolate basal **leaves** (2–7 cm long) are smooth to remotely toothed on the margin. There are 3–8 somewhat narrower stem leaves.

The 1–8 short-petalled, pink (sometimes white) **flower** heads are held in a flat or round-topped cluster. Flowers are of two types. The outer ray flowers are pistillate and have a bristle-like calyx, a ligulate corolla (ligule 3–5 mm long), and a 2-carpeled inferior ovary (1-loculed) with 1 ovule. The yellow disc flowers have a bristle-like calyx, tubular corolla, 5 stamens and an ovary as in ray flowers. Between the outer ray flowers and the inner disc flowers are a few pistillate flowers missing rays or ligules.

Fruit is a bristle-topped achene.

Erigeron sp.

HEINJO LAHRING

HABITAT AND DISTRIBUTION

Erigeron elatus grows in marshes, shores, and wet, open meadows. It inhabits the parklands and boreal forest.

This species occurs across the Prairie provinces but is scarce in the drier prairie areas and northern Saskatchewan and Manitoba. The range extends from Alaska to Newfoundland and reaches as far north as the western Northwest Territories and Yukon.

SPECIAL FEATURES

The common name, Fleabane, indicates it was once considered a repellent for fleas. The plants were burned and resulting smoke kept gnats and fleas away. Another story relates the name to the little seeds which look like fleas.

Erigeron tea was used by the Cree to treat diarrhea.

An infusion of the whole dried plant was taken as a tonic, diuretic astringent and even to help reduce pimples. Several species tended to be used in the same way.

In Japan, leaves of introduced species (e.g., *E. annuus*, Whitetop) were boiled and eaten as a pot-herb.

RELATED SPECIES

Most species of *Erigeron* are associated with dryland habitats. The genus closely resembles the Asters; however, Fleabanes are often short, the rays are very narrow and abundant (usually more than 50), and the floral bracts are in 1 or 2 series. Asters are often taller, the rays are broader and fewer (10–50), and the floral bracts are usually in several series.

Erigeron acris L., **Northern Daisy Fleabane**, is a common species of the southern boreal forest, parkland and prairies and tolerates wet conditions. It is similar to *E. elatus* but is taller (30–80 cm), has a glandular involucre, the peduncle tends to arch, and there is usually a basal rosette of leaves. Distribution is circumpolar.

Erigeron lonchophyllus Hook., **Hirsute Fleabane**, is an occasionally found species widespread across the Prairie provinces. It also resembles *E. elatus* but is distinguished by its taller size (10–50 cm), linear stem leaves, raceme-like flower cluster (head sometimes solitary), and the absence of a band of rayless pistillate flowers between the outer ray and inner disc flowers. Distribution is across Canada and reaches as far as Asia.

DICOTS ■ HERBS

Eupatorium maculatum L.

ASTERACEAE (Composite Family)

Spotted Joe-pye Weed

Syn.: *E. bruneri* Gray, *E. purpureum* L. var. *maculatum* (L.) Darl.

Other Common Names: Purple Boneset, Tall Boneset, Trumpet-weed, Smoke-weed

Eupatorium is named in honour of Mithridates Eupator, the king of Pontus in Antiquity who apparently used this plant. *Maculatum* means spotted.

Wetland
Perennial
Native
Occasional
Hardiness Zone: 3
Flowering Season: summer

DESCRIPTION

This tall (50–200 cm), stout herb has branching, purplish or purple-spotted stems and whorls of 3–6 leaves. The petioled **leaves** (6–20 cm long) are lanceolate to ovate, hairy below, and have sharply toothed margins.

Flower heads are grouped in rounded to flat-topped clusters (15–20 cm across). Heads (10 mm high by 6 mm across) are composed of pink to purple disc flowers.

Each flower consists of a calyx of bristles, a tubular corolla, 5 stamens, and a 2-carpeled inferior ovary (1-loculed) with 1 ovule.

Fruit is a glandular-dotted achene (3–4.5 mm long) with a tuft of white hairs on one end.

Eupatorium maculatum L.

HABITAT AND DISTRIBUTION

Spotted Joe-pye Weed inhabits moist woodland clearings, stream banks, and marshes in the southeastern parkland and boreal forest. This is a heat-loving species and requires a long, warm growing season to do well.

Distribution is from British Columbia to Newfoundland. It is generally absent in the western part of the Prairie provinces, but common from Manitoba eastward. Range extends southward to New Mexico, Nebraska, and North Carolina. Rare in Kansas and Missouri.

SPECIAL FEATURES

Historically, a New England Indian by the name of Joe Pye made extractions from the roots to treat an outbreak of typhoid fever; thus the common name Joe-pye Weed. The plant is known to produce sweating and assist in breaking fever. In the early days, fevers were known as breakbone fevers.

Native peoples had many uses for the plant including preparing a cold wash for complexion improvement, as a diuretic, an astringent, and as a poultice for burns and scalds.

Eupatorium maculatum is the largest plant of the genus. The crystalline compound *euparine* has been

292

BARRE HELLQUIST

isolated and thought to be an important active ingredient to its medicinal properties. The distinctive odor of the flowers is from a very small amount of a volatile oil. *Eupatorium perfoliatum* is the most widely used herbal species. Its roots contain *inuline*, and the aerial portions have the volatile glucoside *eupatorine*.

Preparations made from this plant are said to act as an antidote for the poison of *Cicuta maculata* (Water-hemlock).

RELATED SPECIES

Eupatorium perfoliatum L., **White Boneset**, is found in the eastern part of the Prairie provinces. It differs from *E. maculatum* in being quite hairy overall, having opposite lanceolate leaves (each pair set at right angles to the previous pair). The leaves are wrinkled-looking and their bases are united around the stem (connate). Flowers are white.

Eupatorium maculatum L.

BARRE HELLQUIST

Gnaphalium palustre Nutt.   **ASTERACEAE (Composite Family)**

Western Marsh Cudweed

Other Common Names: Everlasting

Gnaphalium, from the Greek *gnaphalon* (lock of wool), was used to describe a downy plant. *Palustre* means swampy and refers to its wetland habitat.

> Wetland
> Annual
> Native
> Occasional
> Hardiness Zone: 3
> Flowering Season: summer

DESCRIPTION

Woolly stems are erect and low growing (5–20 cm). Later they become considerably branched near the base. Sessile **leaves** are alternate, linear-lanceolate to oblong (1–3 cm long), smooth margined and white-woolly below.

Yellow or whitish **flower** heads (3–4 mm high) are in terminal clusters. Heads are subtended by leafy bracts. White-tipped involucral bracts (woolly below) are in several overlapping series. Ray flowers are absent. Discoid flowers consist of a bristle-like calyx, a tubular corolla, 5 stamens, and a 2-carpeled inferior ovary (1-loculed) with 1 ovule.

Fruit is an achene with a tuft of white hairs on one end.

flower head
subtended by
leafy bracts

Gnaphalium palustre Nutt.

HABITAT AND DISTRIBUTION

Western Marsh Cudweed is tolerant of alkali and frequents prairie and parkland sloughs, marshes, and moist open areas. It is often found in dry basins of vernal pools.

This is a plant of the southwestern Prairie provinces. In Saskatchewan it is limited to west of longitude 104° west, and relatively common in the southwestern part of the province. It is absent in Manitoba. The range extends from British Columbia to California and across to New Mexico and Nebraska.

SPECIAL FEATURES

The woolliness of this species sets it apart from most wetland plants. It is an adaptation to the hot, dry prairie summers. Moisture availability along slough margins during the growing season often has periods of very wet followed by very dry. The long hairs assist in protecting it from excessive moisture loss. The white colour reflects the strong solar rays in its exposed environment.

Little has been documented on our local species; however, *Gnaphalium obtusifolium* L. (Obtuse-leaved Everlasting), a common plant of more southern areas, was used as a herbal to treat for intestinal problems, diarrhea, and as a fomentation for bruises. Another species which grows in Columbia (South America) was used to treat fever.

RELATED SPECIES

Most *Gnaphalium* species prefer dry open areas.

Gnaphalium uliginosum L., **Low Cudweed**, is an introduced species similar to the *G. palustre* but differs in having narrower leaves, the woolly hairs are more appressed, and the involucral bracts are green or brown at the tips. It tends to be found occasionally in the prairie and parklands. When the two species grow in the same area they tend to grade into one another, possibly through hybridization.

Iva xanthifolia Nutt.   ASTERACEAE (Composite Family)

False Ragweed

Syn.: *Cyclachaena xanthifolia* (Nutt.) Fresn.
Other Common Names: Big Marsh-elder, Burweed Marsh-elder

Iva originates from the name of an old medicinal plant. *Xanthifolia* means
yellow leaf.

Wetland
Annual
Native
Common
Hardiness Zone: 1
Flowering Season: summer

DESCRIPTION

Sturdy, erect, branching stems (50–200 cm) are rough and hairy. The
opposite long-petioled **leaves** (5–15 cm long) are heart-shaped, coarsely toothed, rough textured above and downy hair below. Lower and younger leaves
are often 3-lobed.

Small **flower** heads are on drooping axillary and terminal spike-like panicles.
Involucre (1.5–3 mm high) consists of 5 outer and 5 inner bracts. Heads are
composed of disc flowers with female on the outside and male on the
inside. Female flowers have a tubular corolla, and a 2-carpeled inferior
ovary (1-loculed) with 1 ovule. Male flowers have a tubular
corolla and 5-stamens.

Fruit is a flattened obovoid achene.

HABITAT AND DISTRIBUTION

Marsh-elder can be found in river and stream beds, wet
ditches, irrigation canals, open fields, and along roadsides in
the prairie and parkland.

Distribution includes the central to southern Prairie provinces.
Range extends south to Arizona, New Mexico, Texas and Missouri.

SPECIAL FEATURES

This plant is tolerant of both wet and dry growing conditions. Its ability to produce
abundant amounts of seed allows it to become quickly established on disturbed sites
and in some localities, such as southern Saskatchewan, is considered a weed.
The overall look of the plant reminds one of a sunflower with its large, heart-
shaped leaves. However, the long, upright clusters of drooping flower heads are
considerably different and help to set this plant apart.

Marsh-elder produces considerable pollen when in bloom and is known to cause 'hayfever' to susceptible individuals.

This western plant has been moving eastward with human activities and is
colonizing new areas, expanding its former range.

RELATED SPECIES

Iva axillaris Pursh, **Povertyweed**, a deep-rooted perennial with small leaves
and axillary flower heads, also occurs in the region but is not considered a wetland plant. It is a plant of eroded buttes and saline clays.

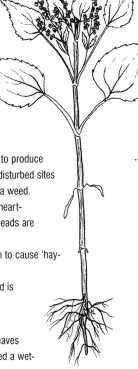

Iva xanthifolia L.

295

Megalodonta beckii (Torr.) Greene

Water-marigold

ASTERACEAE (Composite Family)

Syn.: *Bidens beckii* Torr. ex Spreng.

Megalodonta is from the Greek *Megalo* (with large) and *odontus* (toothed).

DESCRIPTION

Long (to 2 m) underwater strands have whorls or clusters of leaves. Submerged **leaves** (2–3 per node) have fine dichotomous divisions (hair-like and smooth margined). Sessile emergent leaves (2–3 pairs) are lanceolate (sometimes partially divided) with toothed margins.

Solitary **flower** head (1 cm across) is emergent and terminal. Involucre is of several ovate bracts. Flower head consists of an outer band of yellow ray flowers (rays 10–15 mm long) and an inner group of disc flowers.

Fruit is an achene with 3–6 awns on the top end.

Submerged
Perennial
Native
Rare
Hardiness Zone: 3
Flowering Season: summer

HABITAT AND DISTRIBUTION

Water-marigold is found in ponds, lakes, and slow streams. It commonly grows in shallow water of the eastern parkland and boreal forest but is able to grow as a terrestrial plant on wet ground.

Megalodonta beckii (Torr.) Greene

Distribution is limited to Saskatchewan and Manitoba. It is not known to occur in Alberta. Range extends to Nova Scotia and New Jersey in the east and includes Oregon and Washington in the west.

SPECIAL FEATURES

This is a freshwater species which is becoming increasingly rare because of water pollution.

The showy yellow flower head, held above the water, makes *M. beckii* an attractive water gardening plant. The underwater foliage acts as an 'oxygenator' and water purifier by removing nutrients from the water and releasing oxygen into the water.

The feathery nature of the underwater foliage is excellent for aquatic invertebrates to find food and shelter in.

RELATED SPECIES

This is the only species of the genus in North America.

Water-marigold is easily confused with *Myriophyllum*, *Ceratophyllum* and *Utricularia* in the pre-flowering stages. *Myriophyllum* has leaves which have pinnate divisions (like a feather). *Ceratophyllum* also has forking leaf-divisions, as in *Megalodonta*, but they feel rough to the touch due to sharp teeth along the margin. Utricularia has small bladders either within its foliage or on separate strands. Only *Megalodonta* has the showy, yellow flower head.

Megalodonta is closely related to *Bidens* (Beggarticks) and has the same small, yellow flower heads characteristic of that group. In *Bidens* spp. the heads range between 1–3 cm wide and in *M. beckii* they are only 1 cm wide.

HEINJO LAHRING

Megalodonta beckii

Petasites sagittatus (pp. 298–299)
Arrow-leaved Colt's-foot

HEINJO LAHRING

Petasites sagittatus (Banks ex Pursh) Gray   ASTERACEAE (Composite Family)
Arrow-leaved Colt's-foot

Syn.: *P. dentatus* Blank., *Petasites frigidus* var. *sagittatus* (Banks ex Pursh) Cherniawsky

Other Common Names:
Sweet Colt's-foot

Petasites is from the Greek *petasos* (large-brimmed hat) and refers to the large leaves. *Sagittatus* describes the leaf's arrowhead shape.

Wetland/Emergent
Perennial
Native
Common
Hardiness Zone: 0
Flowering Season: early spring

Petasites sagittatus (Banks ex Pursh) Gray

DESCRIPTION

Long-petioled leaves grow from a spongy, creeping rhizome. The triangular-ovate **leaves** (10–30 cm long by 10–20 cm wide) have toothed margins and are grayish green. Leaf surface is sparsely white woolly above and densely white woolly beneath.

Plants flower before the basal leaves appear. **Flower** heads, either male or female (usually on separate plants), are grouped in a tight cluster at the top of a bracted stalk (20–50 cm tall). Sheathing flower-stalk bracts are narrow and pointed. Flower head bracts are scale-like and in one series.

Female flower heads contain flowers with a bristle-like calyx, a white tubular or ray-bearing (ligulate) corolla, and a 2-carpeled inferior ovary (1-loculed) with 1 ovule. Male flower heads are predominantly male but often have a single row of female ray flowers on the outside. Male flowers have a tubular corolla and 5-stamens.

Fruit is a linear achene with a tuft of long, white hairs on one end.

HEINJO LAHRING

HABITAT AND DISTRIBUTION

Arrow-leaved Coltsfoot is found in wet meadows, slough margins, ditches, swamps, fens and bogs. It is abundant in the parkland, boreal forest, Rocky Mountain foothills, and wet grassland areas.

Distribution is from Alaska to Quebec, including much of the Prairie provinces. Range extends from the Territories south to Idaho, Colorado, Minnesota and Wisconsin.

Petasites sagittatus
Above: seed heads
Left: flowers

(See additional photo of *Petasites sagittatus* on page 297.)

HEINJO LAHRING

SPECIAL FEATURES

The young leaves, shoots, and roots of Coltsfoot can be eaten fresh, cooked, or roasted but should be consumed in moderation (strong doses are said to cause abortions). Because it is such an early blooming plant (often before the snow melts), it is highly valued as a wild food source in the spring. Tea can be made from the roots and was used by Native peoples for sore throats, rheumatism and respiratory ailments.

A salt substitute for seasoning foods was obtained by burning the leaves and gathering the ash in a similar manner as *Heracleum lanatum* (Cow-parsnip). In N.E. Asia (especially Japan) the closely related *P. japonicus* was collected and cultivated to produce a food known as *fuki*. The flower stalks, leaves and peeled petioles were cooked and eaten as a potherb or candied. It was also preserved in salt or *shouyu* (soya sauce).

Petasites palmatus (Ait.) A. Gray

Arrow-leaved Coltsfoot is becoming increasingly popular in water gardening because of its ability to overwinter well and produce showy, large, taro-like foliage.

RELATED SPECIES

Petasites frigidus (L.) Fries var. *nivalis* (Greene) Cronq., **Snowleaf Colt's-foot**, has 5–7-lobed leaves divided halfway to midrib. Distribution is limited to the Rocky Mountains in moist alpine to subalpine banks. [syn. *P. f.* ssp. *nivalis* (Greene) Cody, *P. hyperboreus* Rydb., *P. nivalis* Greene, *P. warrenii* St. John, *P. frigidus* auct. p.p. non (L.) Fries, *P. palmatus* var. *frigidus* auct p.p. non Macoun, *P. vitifolius* auct. non Greene]

Petasites palmatus (Ait.) Gray, **Palmate-leaved Colt's-foot**, occurs in boreal woodlands and is more or less absent in the grasslands. It is distinguished by its 5–7-lobed leaves almost divided to the midrib. [syn. *P. frigidus* (L.) Fries var. *palmatus* (Ait.) Cronq., *P. f.* ssp. *palmatus* (Ait.) Cody, *P. f.* ssp. *arcticus* (Pors.) Cody, *P. arcticus* Pors., *P. hookerianus* (Nutt.) Rydb., *P. speciosus* (Nutt.) Piper, *Nardosmia arctica* (Pors.) A. & D. Love]

Petasites x *vitifolius* Greene, **Vine-leaved Colt's-foot**, is claimed to be a hybrid between either *P. frigidus* var. *nivalis* and *P. sagittatus*, or *P. palmatus* and *P. sagittatus* (the more likely, since their distributions overlap). It has features which are intermediate between the two. [syn. *P. nivalis* ssp. *vitifolius* (Greene) Toman., *P. trigonophylla* Greene, *P. frigidus* var. x *vitifolius* (Greene) Cherniawsky, *P. frigidus* (L.) Fries var. *nivalis* auct. non (Greene) Cronq., *Nardosmia vitifolia* (Greene) A. & D. Love].

Petasites x *vitifolius* Greene

Petasites x vitifolius

HEINJO LAHRING

GLOSSARY

Achene: a small, one-seeded, dry, hard fruit that does not open when ripe.

Adaxial: on the inner face, between the leaf and its stem.

Anther: the pollen-bearing portion of a stamen.

Appressed: lying close to, or flat against.

Auricle: ear-shaped lobes.

Awn: a bristle-like appendage.

Basal: at the base of, such as leaves at the base of a plant.

Bidentate: having two teeth.

Bifid: forked.

Bulbil: a bulb-like vegetative reproductive structure.

Calyx: the outer floral ring or sepals.

Capitate: collected into the shape of a head or cluster.

Capsule: a dry, splitting or gaping fruit, composed of more than one carpel.

Carpel: a seed-bearing chamber at the base of a pistil.

Caryopsis: fruit of grasses where the seed coat is joined to the pericarp.

Ciliate: with a fringe of hairs.

Cleistogamous: self-fertilizing.

Corm: a solid, fleshy, thickened, underground stem at the base of a plant.

Corolla: the petals of a flower.

Culm: a plant stem.

Cyme: a loose, and often flat, flower cluster in which the central flowers open first.

Decumbent: a stem with the base on or near the ground, and its tip or main stem erect.

Dichotomous: branching in two equal parts.

Dioecious: unisexual, having flowers with pistils or with stamens on separate plants.

Drupe: a fleshy or pulpy fruit containing a single stony-covered seed.

Farninose: plant leaf or stem covered in a fine powder.

Filiform: threadlike.

Follicle: a dry fruit, derived from one carpel, that splits on one side.

Gametophyte: the gamete-producing generation of a plant species that reproduces by alternation of generations.

Glabrous: stems and leaves that are hairless.

Glaucous: covered with a bloom (i.e., a waxy, bluish-white powder).

Glumes: two empty bracts at the base of a grass spikelet.

Hypanthium: cup-shaped receptacle bearing the sepals, petals, stamens, and carpels.

Involucre: the bracts located below the inflorescence.

Lemma: the lower of the two bracts of a single grass flower.

Lenticel: a raised pore on a root or a stem.

Ligule: a flat tongue-like projection at the upper edge of a grass leaf sheath.

Locule: the single compartment of a pistil or anther.

Megaspore: a spore that produces a female gametophyte.

Mericarp: dry, seed-like fruit derived from an inferior ovary.

Microspore: a spore that produces a male gametophyte.

Ochreae: a sheath around the stem, above the base of the leaf.

Oligotrophic: low nutrient and organic levels.

Ovary: the enlarged basal portion of the female reproductive organs.

Ovary inferior: where the floral organs are attached above the ovary.

Ovary superior: where the floral organs are attached below the ovary.

Palea: the upper of the two bracts of a single grass flower.

Palmate: divided, hand-like.

Panicle: a flower cluster in which the lower branches are longer.

Papilla: short and rounded projections.

Pedicel: the stalk of a single flower of a flower cluster.

Peduncle: the stalk of a flower or flower cluster.

Perianth: the calyx and corolla together, normally when they cannot be distinguished.

Pericarp: a thin, outer covering encasing seeds.

Perigynium: vase-shaped membrane enclosing the ovary in sedges (*Carex* spp.).

Petiole: leaf stalk.

Pinnate: a compound leaf with leaflets opposite to each other on each side of the stalk.

Pistil: the ovary, style and stigma that develops into a fruit.

Pistillate: having only female reproductive parts.

Puberulent: covered in fine, short down.

Pyxis: a circumscissile capsule with the upper portion falling off like a lid.

Raceme: a flower cluster with each flower borne on a short stalk arising from different points on the common stem.

Rachis: the axis of a compound leaf, spike or raceme, bearing close-set organs.

Receptacle: the end of the flower stalk that bears the flower parts.

Revolute: rolled inwards to the underside from both sides.

Rhizome: an underground root-like stem.

Scape: a flowering stem that grows from a root crown and bears no proper leaves.

Scarious: dry and thin, translucent, not green in colour.

Schizocarp: fruits that derive from a simple, two-or-more locular compound ovary in which the locules separate at fruit maturity.

Sepals: green and leaf-like part of a calyx.

Sessile: being without a stalk.

Silique: an elongate pod-like fruit.

Spadix: a spike of small flowers on a thick, fleshy stalk.

Spathe: a large, solitary bract surrounding the spadix.

Sporangium: a specialized structure in which spores are produced.

Sporocarp: a case containing reproductive spore bodies.

Sporophyll: a leaf-like structure which bears sporangia.

Stamens: the male reproductive structure of a flower that produces pollen.

Stigma: the part of the female reproductive organ that receives the pollen.

Stipe: a short stalk or supporting structure; the leaf stalk of a fern.

Stipule: the paired leaf-like appendages located at the base of leaves in certain plants.

Stolons: creeping above ground stems.

Stoma: openings in the epidermal layer of a leaf.

Strobilus: a cluster of sporophylls and sporangia forming a conelike structure.

Style: the slender stalk connecting the stigma to the ovary.

Thallus: undifferentiated plant body.

Truncate: with the tip or base appearing to be cut off.

Tubercles: small swellings, projections.

Turion: a bulb-like growth from a bud on a rhizome.

Umbel: a flat or convex flower cluster in which the peduncles or pedicels are of about equal length and arise from the same point on the flower stalk.

Utricle: a sac or bladder-like structure.

Velum: a thin, protective membrane.

BIBLIOGRAPHY

FLORAS AND DESCRIPTIVE REFERENCES

Aichele, D. 1976. *A field guide in color to wild flowers.* Cathay Books, London, England.

Aiken, S.G., P.F. Lee, D. Punter, and J.M. Stewart. 1988. *Wild rice in Canada.* New Canada Publishers, Toronto.

Alberta plants and fungi—master species list and species group checklists. 1993. Alberta Environmental Protection, Edmonton.

Argus, G.W., and K.M. Pryer. 1990. *Rare vascular plants in Canada; our natural heritage.* Canadian Museum of Nature, Ottawa.

Best, K.F., J. Looman, and J.B. Campbell. 1971. *Prairie grasses—identified and described by vegetative characters.* Canada Department of Agriculture, Ottawa.

Boivin, B. 1972. *Flora of the prairie provinces.* Universite Laval, Quebec.

Brako, L., A.Y. Rossman, and D.F. Farr. 1995. *Scientific and common names of 7000 vascular plants in the United States.* APS Press, St. Paul, Minnesota.

Brayshaw, T.C. 1976. *Catkin bearing plants (Amentiferae) of British Columbia.* Occasional Paper No. 18. British Columbia Provincial Museum, Victoria.

Buckley, A.R. 1977. *Canadian garden perennials.* Hancock House Publications, Saanichton, British Columbia.

Burland, G.R. *An identification guide to Alberta aquatic plants.* Alberta Environmental Protection, FEESA, An Environmental Education Society, Edmonton.

Carmichael, L.T. *Common marsh plants of Saskatchewan.* Saskatchewan Museum of Natural History, Regina.

Catling, P.M., and W. Wojtas. 1986. The waterweeds (*Elodea* and *Egeria*, Hydrocharitaceae) in Canada. *Canadian Journal of Botany* 64: 1525–41.

Clark, L.J. 1974. *Lewis Clark's field guide to wild flowers of marsh and waterway in the Pacific Northwest.* Gray's Publishing Ltd., Sidney, British Columbia.

Conard, H.S. 1995. *The Waterlilies.* Lark Publications, Thetford Norfolk, United Kingdom.

Cook, C.D.K., B.J. Gut, E.M. Rix, J. Schneller, and M. Seitz. 1974. *Water plants of the world.* Dr. W. Junk b.V., Publishers, The Hague.

Cook, C.D.K., and Urmi-Koenig 1985. A revision of the genus *Elodea* (Hydrocharitaceae). *Aquatic Botany* 21: 111–56.

Coombes, A.J. 1985. *Dictionary of plant names.* Timber Press: Portland, Oregon.

Cormack, R.G.H. 1977. *Wildflowers of Alberta.* Hurtig Publishers, Edmonton.

Craighead, J.J., F.C. Craighead Jr., and R.J. Davis. 1963. *A field guide to Rocky Mountain wildflowers from northern Arizona and New Mexico to British Columbia.* Houghton Mifflin Co., Boston.

Crow, G. E., and C. B. Hellquist. 2000. *Aquatic and wetland plants of Northeastern North America.* Vols. 1 & 2. The University of Wisconsin Press.

Davy, A.J., and G.F. Bishop. 1991. Biological flora of the British Isles: Triglochin maritima L. *The Journal of Ecology* 79: 531–55.

Fernald, M.L. 1950. *Gray's Manual of Botany.* Eighth (Centennial Edition) D. Van Norstrand Co., Toronto.

Fisher, R.M. 1980. *Guide to the orchids of the Cypress Hills, including the most common orchids of Alberta and Saskatchewan.* Robert Fisher, Olds, Alberta.

Fleurbec 1987. *Plantes savages des lacs, rivieres et tourbieres—guide d'identification fleurbec.* Quebec.

Flora of North America Editorial Committee. 1997. Flora of North America. Oxford University Press.

Ford, B.A., and P.W. Ball. 1988. A reevaluation of the *Triglochin maritimum* complex (*Juncaginaceae*) in eastern and central North America and Europe. *Rhodora* 90: 313–37.

Gleason, H.A., and A. Cronquist. 1963. *Manual of vascular plants of northeastern United States and adjacent Canada.* Van Nostrand Co., New York.

Hallowell, A.I. 1935. Notes on the northern range of Zizania in Manitoba. *Rhodora* 37: 302–04.

Hallworth, B., and C.C. Chinnappa. 1997. *Plants of Kananaskis Country in the Rocky*

Mountains of Alberta. University of Calgary Press, Calgary.

Harms, V.L. 1983. The swamp saxifrage, *Saxifraga pensylvanica*, a rare plant in Canada, newly discovered in Saskatchewan. *Canadian Field-Naturalist* 97: 91–93.

Hellquist, C.B., and J.H. Wiersema. 1996. Observations on native *Nymphaea* of North America and their use in water gardening. *The Water Garden Journal* XII(4): 9–15.

Hermann, F.J. 1970. *Manual of the Carices of the Rocky Mountains and Colorado Basin*. Agriculture Handbook No. 374. Forest Service. U.S. Dept. of Agriculture.

Hitchcock, C.L., A. Cronquist, M. Ownbey, and J.W. Thompson. 1969. *Vascular plants of the Pacific Northwest*. University of Washington Press.

Hotchkiss, N. 1972. *Common marsh, underwater, and floating-leaved plants of the United States and Canada*. Dover Publications, New York.

International Water Lily Society. 1993. *Identification of hardy* Nymphaea. Stapeley Water Gardens Ltd., United Kingdom.

Johnson, D. L. Kershaw, A. MacKinnon, J. Pojar. 1995. *Plants of the western boreal forest and aspen parkland*. Lone Pine Publishing, Edmonton.

Looman, J. and K.F. Best. 1979. *Budd's flora of the Canadian prairie provinces*. Agriculture Canada.

Luer, C.A. 1975. *The native orchids of the United States and Canada*. The New York Botanical Garden.

Mackenzie, K.K. 1949. *North American* Cariceae. 2 Vols. New York Botanical Garden, Bronx, New York.

Marie-Victorin, Frere. 1964. *Flore Laurentienne*. University of Montreal Press, Montreal.

Masters, C.O. 1974. *Encyclopedia of the water-lily*. T.F.H. Publications Ltd., Neptune City, New Jersey.

Mohlenbrock, R.H. 1976. Sedges. *Cyperus to Scleria. The illustrated flora of Illinois*. Southern Illinois University Press. Carbondale, Illinois.

Moss, E.H. 1983. *Flora of Alberta*. 2nd edition, revised by J.G. Packer, University of Toronto Press, Toronto.

Newmaster, S.G., A.G. Harris, and L.J. Kershaw. 1997. *Wetland plants of Ontario*. Lone Pine Publishing, Edmonton.

Packer, J.G., and C.E. Bradley. 1984. *A checklist of the rare vascular plants of Alberta with maps*. Provincial Museum of Alberta, Edmonton.

Padgett, D.J. 1996. Pondering the pond-lilies: relationships within the genus *Nuphar*. *Aquatics* 18: 11, 14–16.

Padgett, D.J. 1997. Molecular study of yellow pond-lilies: the study of *Nuphar* DNA confirms and contradicts relationship theories of *Nuphar. The Water Garden Journal*, XIII(1): 34–37.

Porsild, A.E. 1974. *Rocky Mountain wild flowers*. National Museums of Canada, Ottawa.

Porsild, A.E. 1980. *Vascular plants of continental Northwest Territories, Canada*. National Museums of Canada, Ottawa.

Prescott, G.W. 1980. *How to know the aquatic plants*. Wm. C. Brown Company Publishers. Dubuque, Iowa.

Reimer, D.N. 1984. *Introduction to freshwater vegetation*. The AVI Publishing Comp., Inc.

Rydberg, P.A. 1965. *Flora of the prairies and plains of central North America*. Hafner Publishing, New York and London.

Sainty, G.R., and S.W.L. Jacobs. 1994. *Waterplants in Australia*. Sainty and Associates, Darlinghurst, Australia.

Schmidt, J.C. and J.R. Kannenberg. 1998. *How to identify and control water weeds and algae*. Applied Biochemistry, Milwaukee, Wisconsin.

Scoggan, H.J. 1957. *Flora of Manitoba*. Bulletin 140. National Museum of Canada, Ottawa.

Scoggan, H.J. 1978-1979. *The flora of Canada*. 4 parts. National Museum of Canada, Ottawa.

Slocum, P.D., and P. Robinson. 1996. *Water gardening—water lilies and lotuses*. Timber Press, Portland, Oregon.

Stearn, W.T. 1983. *Botanical Latin*. Fitzhenry and Whiteside Ltd., Ontario.

Steward, A.N., L.J. Dennis, and H.M. Gilkey. 1963. *Aquatic plants of the Pacific Northwest*. Oregon State University Press, Corvallis.

Stockerl, E.C., and R.L. Kent. 1984. *The distribution, identification, biology and management of Eurasian water milfoil: an Alberta perspective*. Alberta Environment, Pollution Control Division, Pesticide Chemicals Branch.

Stodola, J. 1967. *Encyclopedia of water plants*. T.F.H. Publications, Neptune City, New Jersey.

Stubbendieck, J., S.L. Hatch, C.H. Butterfield. 1997. *North American range plants*. University of Nebraska Press, Lincoln, Nebraska.

Vance, F.R., J.R. Jowsey, and J.S. McLean. 1999. *Wildflowers across the prairies*. Greystone Books, Douglas and McIntyre, Vancouver.

Wiersema, J.H. 1997. *Nymphaea tetragona* and *Nymphaea leibergii (Nymphaeaceae)*: two species of diminutive water-lilies in North America. *Brittonia* 48: 520–31.

Wilkinson, K. 1999. *Wildflowers of Alberta*. Lone Pine Publishing, Edmonton.

EDIBLE, MEDICINAL, AND HISTORICAL REFERENCES

Berglund, B., and C.E. Bolsby. 1974. *The edible wild*. Modern Canadian Library, Toronto.

Bleything, D., and R. Dawson. 1972. *Edible plants in the wilderness*. Life Support Technology, Oregon.

Coffey, T. 1993. *The history and folklore of North American wildflowers*. Facts on File, New York.

Coon, N. 1974. *The dictionary of useful plants*. Rodale Press, Pennsylvania.

Couplan, F. 1998. *The encyclopedia of edible plants of North America*. Keats Publishing, New Canaan, Connecticut.

Dawson, R., R. Landsburg, and J. Riggs. 1975. *Edible plant identification cards*. Life Support Technology, Oregon.

Duke, J.A. 1992. *Handbook of edible weeds*. CRC Press, Florida.

East, N.E.,and R.J. Higgins. 1988. Canary grass (*Phalaris* sp) toxicosis in sheep in California. *Journal of the American Veterinary Medical Association* 192: 667–69

Hutchens, A.R. 1973. *Indian herbology of North America*. Merco, Windsor, Ontario.

Lacki, M.J., W.T. Peneston, and K.B. Adams. 1990. Summer foraging patterns and diet selection of muskrats inhabiting a fen wetland. *Canadian Journal of Zoology* 68: 1163–67.

Lodge, R.W., A. McLean, and A. Johnston. 1975. *Stock-poisoning plants of western Canada*. Canada Department of Agriculture, Ottawa.

Martin, A.C., and F.M. Uhler. 1951. *Food of game ducks in the United States and Canada*. United States Department of Agriculture Technical Bulletin 634.

Maurice, D.V., J.E. Jones, amd C.R. Dillon. 1984. Chemical composition and nutritional value of Brazilian *elodea (Egeria densa)* for the chick. *Poultry Science* 63: 317–23.

McAtee, W.L. 1917. *Propagation of wild-duck foods*. United States Department of Agriculture Bulletin 465.

McDowell, L.R., L.C. Lizama, and J.E. Marion. 1990. Utilization of aquatic plants *Elodea canadensis* and *Hydrilla verticillata* in diets of laying hens. 1. Perfomance and egg-yolk pigmentation. *Poultry Science* 69: 673–78.

Moore, M. 1979. *Medicinal plants of the mountian west*. The Museum of New Mexico Press, New Mexico.

Neumann, A., R. Holloway, and C. Busby. 1989. Determination of prehistoric use of arrowhead (*Sagittaria, Alismataceae*) in the Great Basin of North America by scanning electron microscopy. *Economic Botany* 43: 287–96

Nicholson, S.S., B.M. Olcott, and E.A. Usenik. 1989. Delayed Phalaris grass toxicosis in sheep and cattle. *Journal of the American Veterinary Medical Association* 195: 345–46.

Peden, D.G. 1977. Waterfowl use of exotic wild rice habitat in northern Saskatchewan. *Canadian Field-Naturalist* 91: 286–87.

Smirnov, N. 1961. Consumption of emergent plants by insects. Verh. int. Verein theor. angew. Limnol. 14: 232–36.

Stark, R. 1981. *Guide to Indian herbs*. Hancock House Publishers, Vancouver.

Turner, N.J. 1997. *Food plants of interior first peoples*. University of British Columbia Press and Royal British Columbia Museum, Vancouver.

Turner, N.J., A.F. Szczawinski. 1988. *Edible wild fruits and nuts of Canada*. Fitzhenry and Whiteside in trust for the National Museum of Natural Sciences, Markham, Ontario.

Vaquer, A. 1973. Absorption and accumulation of pesticides and accumulation of pesticides residues and chlorinated biphenyls in both wild aquatic vegetation and rice in the Camargue Region. *Oecol. Plant* 4: 353–65.

von Reis, S., and F.J. Lipp Jr. 1982. *New plant sources for drugs and foods from the New York Botanical Garden Herbarium*. Harvard University Press.

Walker, M. 1984. *Harvesting the northern wild*. The Northern Publishers, Northwest Territories.

Ye, Z.H., A.J.M. Baker, M.H. Wong. 1997. Zinc, lead and cadmium tolerance, uptake and accumulation by the common reed,

Phragmites australis (Cav.) Trin. ex Steudel. *Annals of Botany* 80: 363–70.

Ye, Z.H., M.H. Wong, and A.J.M. Baker. 1998. Comparison of biomass and metal uptake between two populations of *Phragmites australis* grown in flooded and dry conditions. *Annals of Botany* 82(1): 83–87.

ECOLOGY, PHYSIOLOGY, AND WETLAND REFERENCES

Aiken, S.G., and R.R. Picard. 1980. The influence of substrate on the growth and morphology of *Myriophyllum exalbescens* and *Myriophyllum spicatum*. *Canadian Journal of Botany* 58(9): 1111–18.

Alberta Environment. 1989. *A preliminary investigation into the use of spike rush (*Eleocharis spp.*) for aquatic plant management in Edmonton, Alberta*. Research Management Division, Alberta Environment.

Alberta Water Resources Commission. 1990. *Wetland management in the settled area of Alberta—background for policy development*. Alberta Water Resources Commission, Edmonton.

Alexander, S.A., K.A. Hobson, and C.L. Gratto-Trevor. 1996. Conventional and isotopic determinations of shorebird diets at and inland stopover: the importance of invertebrates and *Potamogeton pectinatus* tubers (with appendix). *Canadian Journal of Zoology* 74: 1057–68.

Allan, J.R., T.G. Sommerfeldt, and J.A. Braglinmarsh. 1989. *Aquatic vegetation on the Canadian prairies: physiology, ecology, and management*. Technical Bulletin 1989-6E, Lethbridge Research Station Contribution No. 14, Research Branch, Agriculture Canada.

Anderson, M.K. 1996. The ethnobotany of deergrass, *Muhlenbergia rigens* (Poaceae): its uses and fire management by California Indian Tribes. *Economic Botany* 50: 409–22.

Archibald, J.H., G.D. Klappstein, and I.G.W. Corns. 1996. *Field guide to ecosites of southwestern Alberta*. Univerity of British Columbia Press, Vancouver.

Armour, G., D. Brown, and K. Marsden. 1979. *Studies on aquatic macrophytes. Part IV. Bottom barriers for aquatic weed control*. Water Investigations Branch, Report No. 2801, British Columbia Ministry of Environment.

Bayley, S.E.M. 1970. *The ecology and disease of Eurasian water milfoil (*Myriophyllum spicatum L.*) in the Chesapeake Bay*. Ph.D. Thesis, Johns Hopkins University, Baltimore, Maryland.

Bayley, S.R.H., and Southwick, C.H. 1968. Recent decline in the distribution and abundance of Eurasian milfoil in Chesapeake Bay. *Chesapeake Sci.* 9: 177–81.

Beckingham, J.D. and J.H. Archibald. 1996. *Field guide to ecosites of northern Alberta*. University of British Columbia Press, Vancouver.

Beckingham, J.D., I.W.G. Corns, and J.H. Archibald. 1996. *Field guide to ecosites of west-central Alberta*. University of British Columbia Press, Vancouver.

Bell, K.L. 1974. Autecology of *Kobresia bellardii*: why winter snow accumulation patterns affect local distribution. Department of Botany, University of Alberta, Edmonton.

Best, E.P.H., H. Woltman, and F.H.H. Jacobs. 1996. Sediment related growth limitation of *Elodea nuttallii* as indicated by a fertilization experiment. *Freshwater Biology* 36: 33–44.

Best, M.D., and K.E. Mantai. 1978. Growth of *Myriophyllum*: sediment or lake water as the source of nitrogen and phosphorous. *Ecology* 59(5): 1075–80.

Biesboer, D.D. 1984. Nitrogen fixation associated with natural and cultivated stands of *Typha latifolia* L. *(Typhaceae). American Journal of Botany* 71: 505–11.

Biesboer, D.D. 1984. Seasonal variation in nitrogen fixation, associated microbial populations, and carbohydrates in roots and rhizomes of *Typha latifolia (Typhaceae)*. *Canadian Journal of Botany* 62: 1965–67.

Boe, A., and R. Wynia. 1985. Germination, forage yield, and seed production of American sloughgrass (*Beckmannia syzigachne*). *Journal of Range Management* 38: 114–16.

Bonnewell, V., W.L. Koukkari, and D.C. Pratt. 1983. Light, oxygen, and temperature requirements for *Typha latifolia* seed germination. *Canadian Journal of Botany* 61: 1330–36

Boyd, C.E. 1970. Vascular aquatic plants for mineral nutrient removal from polluted waters. *Econ. Bot.* 24: 95–103.

Bristow, J.M., and M. Witcombe. 1971. The role of roots in the nutrition of aquatic vascular plants. *American Journal of Botany* 58(1): 8–13.

Brooker, M.P., and R.W. Edwards. 1974. Effects of the herbicide paraquat on the ecology of a reservoir. *Freshwater Biology* 4: 331–35.

Buttery, B. and J. Lambert. 1965. Competition between *Glyceria maxima* and *Phragmites communis* in the region of Surlingham Broad. I: the competition mechanism. *Journal of Ecology* 53: 163–81.

Canadian Oxford Atlas of the World. 1967. Cartographic Press. London, England.

Clay, S.A., and E.A. Oelke, E.A. 1987. Effects of giant burreed *(Sparganium eurycarpum)* and shade on wild rice *(Zizania palustris).* *Weed Science* 35: 640–46.

Conchov, O., and E. Fuster. 1988. Influence of hydrological fluctuations on the growth and nutrient dynamics of *Phalaris arundinaceae* L. in a riparian environment.

Cussans, G.W., S. Raudonius, and P. Brain. 1996. Effects of depth of seed burial and soil aggregate size on seedling emergence of *Alopecurus myosuroides, Galium aparine, Stellaria medea,* and wheat. *Weed Research* 36: 133–41.

Dale, H.M. 1981. Hydrostatic pressure as the controlling factor in the depth distribution of Eurasian water milfoil; *Myriophyllum spicatum* L. *Hydrobiologia* 79: 239–44.

Delesalle, B. 1998. *Understanding wetlands: a wetland handbook for British Columbia's interior.* Ducks Unlimited Canada, Kamloops, British Columbia.

Delesalle, V.A., and S. Blum. 1994. Variation in germination and survival among families of *Sagittaria latifolia* in response to salinity and temperature. *International Journal of Plant Sciences* 155: 187–95

Fisher, C. and J. Acorn. 1998. *Birds of Alberta.* Lone Pine Publishing, Edmonton.

Forsyth, A. 1985. *Mammals of the Canadian wild.* Camden House Publishing Ltd., Camden East, Ontario.

Gangstad, E.O. 1980. *Weed control methods for public health applications.* CRC Press, Raton, Florida.

Giesy, J.P., and L.E. Tessier. 1979. Distribution potential of *Myriophyllum spicatum* in softwater systems. *Arch. Hydrobiologia* 85(4): 437–47.

Grace, J.B. 1989. Effects of water depth on *Typha latifolia* and *Typha domingensis.* *American Journal of Botany* 76: 762–68.

Gryseels, M. 1989. Nature management experiments in a derelict reedgrass. Effects of

summer mowing. *Biological Conservation* 48(2) 85–99.

Habeck, D.H. 1983. The potential of *Parapoynx stratiotata* L. as a biological control agent for Eurasian water milfoil. *Journal of Aquatic Plant Management* 21: 26–29.

Hammer, D.A. 1997. *Creating freshwater wetlands.* Lewis Publishers, CRC Press, Raton, Florida.

Hartman, W.A., and D.B. Martin 1985. Effects of four agricultural pesticides on *Daphnia pulex, Lemna minor,* and *Potamogeton pectinatus. Bulletin of Environmental Contamination and Toxicology* 35: 646–51.

Haslam, S.M. 1970. The performance of *Phragmites communis* Trin. in relation to water-supply. *Annals of Botany* 34: 867–77

Hauser, W.J., E.F. Legner, R.A. Medved, and S. Platt. 1976. *Tilapia*—a management tool for biological control of aquatic weeds and insects. *Fisheries* 1(6): 24.

Hutchinson, G.E. 1978. Eutrophication. *Scientific American* 269–79.

Hyuonen, T., A. Ojala, and P. Kankaala. 1998. Methane release from stands of water horsetail *(Equisetum fluviatile)* in a boreal lake. *Freshwater Biology* 40(2): 275–84.

Kemball, W. G. 1985. *The new Canadian Oxford atlas.* Oxford University Press, Canada.

Knowles, R.P. 1986. Feasibility of production of commercial hybrids in reed canary grass, *Phalaris arundinaceae* L., using a yellow-seeded mutant. *Canadian Journal of Plant Science* 66: 111–16.

Lahring, H.M. 1979. Bog floral succession in the Red Deer River—James River delta (Alberta, Canada): resource management. unpublished paper, Unversity of Calgary.

Lahring, H.M. 1979. Introducing aquatic macrophytes into fish-ponds of the Rocky Mountain foothills (Alberta, Canada). unpublished paper, University of Calgary.

Landhousser, S.M., K.J. Stadt, and V.J. Lieffers. 1996. Rhizome growth of *Calamagrostis canadensis* in response to soil nutrient and bulk density. *Canadian Journal of Plant Science* 76: 545–50.

Lewis, D.H., I. Wile., and D.S. Painter. 1983. Evaluation of Terratrack and Aquascreen for control of aquatic macrophytes. *Journal of Aquatic Plant Management* 21: 103–04.

Madsen, J.D., and M.S. Adams. 1988. The germination of *Potamogeton pectinatus* tubers: environmental control by temperature and light. *Canadian Journal of Botany* 66: 2523–26.

Madsen, T.V., and H. Brix. 1997. Growth, photosynthesis and acclimation by two submerged macrophytes in relation to temperature. *Oecologia* 110: 320–27.

Marquis, L.Y., R.D. Comes, C-P. Yang. 1984. Relative tolerance of desert saltgrass (*Distichlis stricta*) and reed canary grass (*Phlaris arundinaceae*) to boron. *Weed Science* 32: 534–38.

Maxnuk, M.D. 1979. *Studies on aquatic macrophytes. Part XXII. Evaluation of rotavating and diver dredging for aquatic weed control in the Okanagan Valley.* Water investigations Branch Report No. 2823, British Columbia Ministry of Environment.

McCrimmon, H.R. 1968. *Carp in Canada.* Bulletin of the Fisheries Research Board of Canada 165.

McGahee, C.F., and G.J. Davis. 1971. Photosynthesis and respiration in *Myriophyllum spicatum* L. as related to salinity. *Limn. Ocean.* 16: 826–29.

Meyer, J.R. 1978. Aquatic weed management by benthic semi-barriers. *Journal of Aquatic Plant Management* 16: 31–33.

Mitchell, D.S. 1974. *Aquatic vegetation and its use and control.* United Nations Educational, Scientific, and Cultural Organization, Paris.

Moron-Rios, A., R. Dirzo, and V.J. Jaramillo. 1997. Defoliation and below-ground herbivory in the grass *Muhlenbergia quadidentata*: effects on plant performance and on the root-feeder *Phyllophaga* sp. (*Coleoptera, Melolonthidae*). *Oecologia* 110: 237–42.

Moyle, J.B. 1945. Some chemical factors influencing the distribution of aquatic plants in Minnesota. *The American Midland Naturalist* 34(2): 402–20.

Muenchow, G. and V. Delesalle. 1994. Pollinator response to male floral display size in two Sagittaria (*Alismataceae*) species. *American Journal of Botany* 81: 568–73.

Nichols, S., and G. Cottam. 1972. Harvesting as a control of aquatic plants. *Water Res. Bull.* 8(6): 1205–10.

Niering, W.A. 1985. *The Audubon Society nature guides. Wetlands.* Chanticleer Press, New York.

Ng, W.J., T.S. Sim, and S.L. Ong. 1990. The effect of *Elodea densa* on aquaculture water quality. *Aquaculture* 84: 267–76.

Oertli, B. and J. Lochavanne. 1995. The effects of shoot age on colonization of an emergent macrophyte (*Typha latifolia*) by macroinvertebrates. *Freshwater Biology* 34: 421–31.

Opuszynski, K. 1972. Use of phytophagous fish to control aquatic plants. *Aquaculture, Netherlands* (online journal) 1(1): 61–74.

Osborne, J.A. 1982. The potential of the hybrid grass carp as a weed control agent. *Journal of Freshwater Ecology* 1: 353–60.

Perkins, M.A., H.L. Boston, and E.F. Curren. 1980. The use of fiberglass screens for control of Eurasian water milfoil. *Journal of Aquatic Plant Management* 18: 13–19.

Philip, G. 1989. *Complete atlas of Canada and the world.* George Philip Ltd., London.

Powelson, R.A., and V.J. Lieffers. 1991. Growth of dormant buds on severed rhizomes of *Calamagrostis canadensis. Canadian Journal of Plant Science* 71: 1093–99.

Ransom, J.K., and E.A. Oelke. 1983. Cultural control of common waterplantain (*Alisma triviale*) in wild rice (*Zizania palustris*). *Weed Science* 31: 562–66

Ranwell, D.S. 1964. Spartina salt marshes in southern England. II: rate and seasonal pattern of sediment accretion. *Journal of Ecology* 52: 79–94.

Reed, C.F. 1977. History and distribution of Eurasian watermilfoil in United States and Canada. *Phytologia* 36(5): 417–36.

Rivard, P.G., and P.M. 1989. Light, ash, and pH effects on the germination and seedling growth of *Typha latifolia* (Cattail). *Canadian Journal of Botany* 67: 2783–87.

Rottman, R.V. 1977. Management of weed lakes and ponds with grass carp. *Fisheries* 2(5): 8–13.

Sain, P. 1983. Decomposition of wild rice (*Zizania aquatica* L.) straw and its effect on the depletion of oxygen during winter in natural lakes of northwestern Ontario. Ontario Fisheries Technical Report Series 8.

Schiller, D. 1994. *The little Zen companion.* Workman Publishing, New York.

Schoonbee, H.J. 1991. Biological control of fennel-leaves pondweed, *Potamogeton pectinatus* (*Potamogetonaceae*), in South Africa. *Agriculture, Ecosystems and Environment* 37: 231–37.

Scott, G. A. J. 1995. *Canada's vegetation—a world perspective.* McGill–Queen's University Press, Montreal & Kingston, Ontario.

Sculthorpe, C.D. 1967. *The biology of aquatic vascular plants.* Edward Arnold Publishers, London.

Seaman, D.E., and W.A. Porterfield. 1964. Control of aquatic weeds by the snail, *Marisa cornvarietis. Weeds* 12: 87–92.

Singh, S.B. 1962. Preliminary experiments on the relative manurial values of some aquatic weeds as composts. *Handbook of Utilization of Aquatic Plants,* E.C.S. Little, ed. Rome Food and Agriculture Organization of the United Nations.

Spence, D.H.N. 1967. Factors controlling the distribution of freshwater macrophytes with particular reference to the Lochs of Scotland. *J. of Ecol.* 55: 147–70.

Spencer, D.F. 1987. Tuber size and planting depth influence growth of *Potamogeton pectinatus* L. *The American Midland Naturalist,* 118: 77–84.

Spicer, K.W., and P.M. Catling. 1988. The biology of Canadian weeds. *Elodea canadensis* Michx. *Canadian Journal of Plant Science* 68: 1035–51.

Stanley, R.A. 1976. Response of Eurasian watermilfoil to subfreezing temperature. *Journal of Aquatic Plant Management* 14: 36–39.

Stanley, R.A., E. Shackelford, D. Wade, and C. Warren. 1976. Effects of season and water depth on Eurasian water milfoil. *Journal of Aquatic Plant Management* 14: 32–36.

Steeves, T.A., and G.P. Dewolf 1950. A note on the varieites of *Zizania aquatica* L. *Rhodora* 52: 34.

Strong, W.L., E.T. Oswald, and D.J. Downing. 1990. *The Canadian vegetation classification system: first approximation.* Minister of Supply and Services Canada.

Summers, J.E., and M.B. Jackson. 1994. Anaerobic conditions strongly promote extension by stems of overwintering tubers of *Potamogeton pectinatus* L. *Journal of Experimental Botany* 45: 1309–18.

Taylor, G.J., and A.A. Crowder. 1983. Uptake and accumulation of heavy metals by *Typha latifolia* in wetlands of the Sudbury, Ontario, region. *Canadian Journal of Botany* 61: 63–73.

Taylor, G.J., and A.A. Crowder. 1984. Copper and nickel tolerance in *Typha latifolia* clones from contaminated and uncontaminated environments. *Canadian Journal of Botany* 62: 1304–08.

Thieret, J.W. 1971. Observations on some aquatic plants in northwestern Minnesota. *Mich. Bot.* 10: 117–18.

Thomas, A.G., and J.M. Stewart. 1969. The effect of different water depths on the growth of wild rice. *Canadian Journal of Botany* 47: 1525–31.

Thompson, G., J. Coldrey, and G. Bernard. 1985. *The pond.* Williams Collins and Co., London, England.

Thursby, G.B., and M.M. Harlin. 1984. Interaction of leaves and roots of *Ruppia maritima* in the uptake of phosphate, ammonia and nitrate. *Marine Biology* 83: 61–67.

van der Bijl, L., K. Sand-Jenson and A.L. Hjermind. 1987. Photosynthesis and canopy structure of a submerged plant, *Potamogeton pectinatus,* in a Danish lowland stream. *The Journal of Ecology* 77: 947–62.

Warwick, S.E., and S.G. Aiken. 1986. Electrophoretic evidence for the recognition of two species in annual wild rice *(Zizania, Poaceae). Systematic Botany* 11: 464–73.

Weisner, S.E., W. Graneli, W., and B. Ekstram. Influence of submergence on growth of seedlings of *Scirpus lacustris* and *Phragmites australis. Freshwater Biology* 29: 371–75.

Wetzel, R.G., and G.E. Likens. 1979. *Limnological analyses.* W.B. Saunders Co., Toronto.

Wijte, A.H., and Gallagher, J.L. 1996. Effect of oxygen availability and salinity on early life history stages of salt marsh plants. I. Different germination strategies of *Spartina alterniflora* and *Phragmites australis (Poaceae). American Journal of Botany* 83: 1337–42.

Wijte, A.H., and Gallagher, J.L. 1996. Effect of oxygen availability and salinity on early life history stages of salt marsh plants. II. Early seedling development advantage of *Spartina alterniflora* over *Phragmites australis (Poaceae). American Journal of Botany* 83: 1343–50.

Wile, I. 1978. Environmental effects of mechanical harvesting. *Journal of Aquatic Plant Management* 16. 14–20.

Index to Family Names

(Common and Scientific)

COMMON NAME	SCIENTIFIC NAME	PAGES
MUSTARD FAMILY	*BRASSICACEAE*	23, 25, 199–202
NAIAD FAMILY	*NAJADACEAE*	20, 40–41
NETTLE FAMILY	*URTICACEAE*	23, 170–171
OLEASTER FAMILY	*ELAEAGNACEAE*	22, 152–153
ORCHID FAMILY	*ORCHIDACEAE*	21, 78–84
PEA FAMILY	*FABACEAE*	24, 25, 218–219
PHLOX FAMILY	*POLEMONIACEAE*	26, 256
PINK FAMILY	*CARYOPHYLLACEAE*	23, 24, 184–185
PITCHER-PLANT FAMILY	*SARRACENIACEAE*	23, 204–205
PLANTAIN FAMILY	*PLANTAGINACEAE*	25, 278–279
PONDWEED FAMILY	*POTAMOGETONACEAE*	20, 42–51
PRIMROSE FAMILY	*PRIMULACEAE*	25, 246–251
QUILLWORT FAMILY	*ISOETACEAE*	20, 29
ROSE FAMILY	*ROSACEAE*	23, 24, 25, 212–217
RUSH FAMILY	*JUNCACEAE*	21, 85, 132–134
SANDALWOOD FAMILY	*SANTALACEAE*	22, 173
SAXIFRAGE FAMILY	*SAXIFRAGACEAE*	22, 24, 25, 208–211
SEDGE FAMILY	*CYPERACEAE*	21, 85, 108–131
ST. JOHN'S-WORT FAMILY	*CLUSIACEAE*	23, 224
SUNDEW FAMILY	*DROSERACEAE*	24, 206–207
SWEET FLAG FAMILY	*ACORACEAE*	21, 64–65
TOUCH-ME-NOT FAMILY	*BALSAMINACEAE*	24, 25, 222–223
VALERIAN FAMILY	*VALERIANACEAE*	26, 282
VIOLET FAMILY	*VIOLACEAE*	24, 226–227
WATER-CLOVER FAMILY	*MARSILEACEAE*	20, 34
WATERLILY FAMILY	*NYMPHAEACEAE*	23, 186–191
WATER-MILFOIL FAMILY	*HALORAGACEAE*	22, 24, 232–234
WATER-PLANTAIN FAMILY	*ALISMATACEAE*	21, 58–61
WATER-STARWORT FAMILY	*CALLITRICHACEAE*	22, 23, 220–221
WATERWEED FAMILY	*HYDROCHARITACEAE*	20, 62–63
WATERWORT FAMILY	*ELATINACEAE*	24, 225
WILLOW FAMILY	*SALICACEAE*	22, 136–143

INDEX TO SCIENTIFIC NAMES BEGINS ON PAGE 312 • INDEX TO COMMON NAMES BEGINS ON PAGE 318

Index to Scientific Names

major entries in **bold face italics**, synonyms and minor entries in *regular italics*

Index to Common Names

major entries in **bold face**; synonyms and minor entries in regular type

Bulrush, *(continued)*
  Slender, 124, 127
  Small-fruited, 125, 128–129
  Softstem, 97, 124, 127
  Three-Square, 130
  Tufted, 124, 127
  Viscid Great, 126
Bur-marigold,
  Nodding, 288
  Smaller, 288
Bur-reed,
  Broad-fruited, 38
  Floating, 39
  Giant, 38–39, 57
  Narrow-leaved, 39
  Slender, 39
  Stemless, 39
Butter-root, 254
Buttercup,
  Boreal, 198
  White Water, 196
Butterwort,
  Common, 274–275
  Small, 275
  Western, 275

Calamus, 64
Calico Bush, 160
Calico-flower, 283
Calla
  Water, 66
  Wild, 66
Cane, 100
Capillaire, 158
Carrizo, 100
Cassandra, 156
Catchstraw, 280
Cattail,
  Common, 36–37
  Narrow-leaved, 37
  Pencil, 37
Chicken's-claws, 182
Chickweed, 184, 185
Children's Bane, 238
Chives, Wild, 70
Chocolate-root, 212

Cinquefoil,
  Brook, 215
  Bushy, 215
  Drummond's, 215
  Marsh, 209, 214–215
  Mountain, 215
  Rough, 215
  Smooth-leaved, 215
Cloudberry, 217
Clover, Marsh, 254
Coast-blite, 180
Colt's-foot,
  Arrow-leaved, 297, 298–299
  Palmate-leaved, 299
  Snowleaf, 299
  Sweet, 298
  Vine-leaved, 299
Comandra, Northern, 173
Coon's-tail, 192
Coontail, 192
Cotton-grass, 120
  Alpine, 125, 131
  Beautiful, 118, 121
  Close-sheathed, 118, 121
  Filiform, 118, 121
  Narrow-leaved, 118, 121
  One-spike, 118, 121
  Russett, 118, 121
  Sheathed, 118, 121
  Slender, 118, 120, 121
  Thin-leaved, 118, 120–121
  Virginia, 118, 121
Cowberry, 166
Cow Cabbage, 242
Cow-lily, 186
Cow-parsnip, 239, 242–243, 299
Cowslip, 194
Cranberry,
  Alpine, 166
  Bog, 166–167
    Dwarf, 164
      Small, 164–165, 166
  Dry-ground, 166
  Mountain, 166
  Small, 164
  Swamp, 164

Cress
  Bitter, 199, 201
    Meadow, 199
    Pennsylvania, 199
  Slender, 202
  Yellow,
    Marsh, 202
Crimson-berry, 216
Crowfoot,
  Gmelin's, 198
  Seaside, 197
  see also Water-crowfoot
Cudweed
  Low, 294
  Western Marsh, 294

Death Camas, 75
Devil's Pitchfork, 288
Devil-spoons, 58
Dewberry, 217
Ditch-grass, 52
Dock,
  Curly, 171, 177
  Field, 177
  Golden, 177
  Narrow-leaved, 177
  Western, 176–177
Downingia, 283
  Bright, 283
Dragonhead,
  False, 262–263
  Western False, 262
Duck-potato, 61
Duckweed
  Common, 68–69
  Ivy-leaved, 69
  Larger, 69
  Lesser, 69
Dutch-rush, 32

Elephant's-head, 270–271
Elk's Lip, 195
Everlasting, 294
  Obtuse-leaved, 294

Felwort, Marsh, 253

INDEX TO FAMILY NAMES ON PAGES 310–11 • INDEX TO SCIENTIFIC NAMES BEGINS ON PAGE 312   319

Kobresia, Bellard's, 122

Labrador Tea, 151, 162–163
  Common, 162
  Glandular, 163
  Marsh, 163
  Northern, 163
Ladies'-tresses,
  Hooded, 84
  Northern, 84
Lady's-slipper,
  Large, 78
  Northern, 79
  Sparrow's-egg, 79
  Yellow, 71, 78–79
Lady's-thumb, 175
Lamb-kill, 160
Laurel,
  American, 160
  Mountain, 160, 161
  Northern, 160
  Pale, 160
  Sheep, 160
  Swamp, 160
Lavender Musk, 229
Leatherleaf, 156–157
Licorice,
  American, 218
  Wild, 203, 218–219
Lily,
  Bullhead, 186
  Calla, 66
  Snake, 76
Lingonberry, 166
Little Red Elephant, 270
Lobelia,
  Brook, 284
  Kalm's, 284–285
  Water, 284, 285
Loosestrife,
  Fringed, 249
  Lance-leaved, 249
  Purple, 228–229, 249
  Spike, 228
  Swamp, 248
  Tufted, 248–249
Lousewort, 270
  Labrador, 271
  Swamp, 271

Mad-dog Weed, 58, 265
Maidenhair-berry, 158
Manomin, 106
Mare's-tail, 236–237
  Common, 236
  Four-leaved, 237
  Mountain, 237
Marsh Five-finger, 214
Marsh-marigold, 194–195
  Floating, 179, 195
  Mountain, 195
Marsh-collard, 186
Marsh-elder,
  Big, 295
  Burweed, 295
Marsh-trefoil, 254
Masterwort, American, 242
Masungu, 117
May-blob, 194
Meadow-bouts, 194
Meadow-bright, 194
Meadow-fern, 144
Milfoil, see Water-milfoil
Milkwort, Sea, 246
Millet, Hot-springs, 93
Mint,
  Canada, 260
  Corn, 260
  Field, 260
  Wild, 258, 260–261
  see also Spearmint
Moccasin-flower, 78
Monkey-flower,
  Blue, 229, 269
  Lewis, 268
  Red, 235, 268–269
  Small Yellow, 269
  Smooth, 269
  Yellow, 268, 269
Mother Die, 240
Mouthwort, 242
Moxie-plum, 158
Mud-purslane, 225
Mudweed, 267
Mudwort, 267
Muhly, 96
  Bog, 96

Muskrat-weed, 238
Musquash-root, 238
Myrtle,
  Bog, 254
  Dutch, 144

Nagoonberry, 216
Naiad,
  Slender, 40–41, 53
  Gaudalupe, 41
Nerve-root, 78
Nettle,
  Annual English, 171
  Common, 170–171
  European, 170
  Slender, 170
  Small, 171
  Stinging, 170
  Tall, 170
Noah's-ark, 78

Oats, Water, 106
Onion, Geyer's Wild, 70
Orache, 178
Orchid,
  Bracted Bog, 81
  Northern Green Bog,
    80–81
  Slender Bog, 81
  Tall White, 81

Palsywort, 194
Parsley,
  False, 238
  Poison, 240
Parsnip,
  Poison, 238
  Woolly, 242
  see also Cow-parsnip
  see also Water-parsnip
Partridgeberry, 166
Pepper-root, 64
Pepperwort, Hairy, 34
Persicaria, Swamp, 174
Pigeon's-foot, 182
Pipewort, Seven-angled, 284

Snake-weed, 240
Snowberry, Creeping,
158–159
Solomon's-seal,
False, 73
Star-flowered, 73
Three Leaf False, 72
Three-leaved, 72–73
Sourgrass, 54
Spangletop, 104
Spanish Needles, 288
Spatter-dock, 186
Spearmint, 261
Spearwort, Creeping, 198
Speedwell,
American, 272
Common, 272
Hairy, 273
Marsh, 273
Water, 273
Spike-rush,
Creeping, 116–117
Engelmann's, 117
Needle, 117
Spotted Cowbane, 238
Spotted Joe-pye Weed,
292–293
St. John's-wort,
Canada, 224
Large Canada, 224
Marsh, 224
Western, 224
Starwort, 184, 286
see also Water-starwort
Stick-tights, 288
Stickweed, 240
Stitchwort, Northern,
184–185
Strawberry Blite, 181
Sundew,
English, 207
Oblong-leaved, 207
Round-leaved, 206–207
Slender-leaved, 207
Swamp Candles, 249
Sweet Cinnamon, 64

Sweet Flag, 64–65
European, 64–65
Sweet Potato, Indian, 215
Sweet-root, 218

Teaberry, 158
Timothy, 86
Marsh, 96
Tobaccoroot, 282
Touch-me-not, 222
Spotted, 223
Trapper's Tea, 163
Trumpet-weed, 292
Tule, 126
Tules, 126
Twayblade,
Broad-lipped, 82
Heart-leaved, 82
Northern, 82
Western, 82
Twinberry, Red, 168

Valerian,
Greek, 256
Northern, 282
Venus's-shoe, 78
Violet,
Blue Marsh, 227
Kidney-leaved, 226–227
Kidney-shaped, 226
Macloskey's, 227
Marsh, 227
Northern Bog, 227
Northern White, 226

Wade-whistle, 240
Wapato, 61
Water Arum, 66
Water-berry, 168
Water Buttercup, White, 196
Water-carpet, 208
Water-clover, Hairy, 34
Water-collard, 186
Watercress, 200–201, 202, 273

Water-crowfoot,
Curly White, 197
Firm White, 197
Large-leaved, 196
White, 196–197
Yellow, 198
Waterdragon, 194
Water Dragon, 66
Water-hairbrush, 92
Water-hemlock, 195, 241, 243,
245, 293
Bulb-bearing, 239
Poisonous, 239
Spotted, 238–239
Water-horehound,
American, 258
Northern, 258
Western, 258
Waterlily,
Fragrant White, 188–189
Leiberg's, 190–191
Magnolia, 189
Pygmy White, 190
Small White, 191
Tuberous White, 189
Water-marigold, 296
Water-mat, 208
Water-meal,
Columbia, 69
Globose, 69
Northern, 69
Water-milfoil,
Alternate-flowered, 233,
234
Bracted, 233, 234
Eurasian, 233, 234
Little, 234
Northern, 232–234
Whorled, 234
Water-nymph, Northern, 40
Water-parsnip, 239, 241,
244–245
Hemlock, 244
Water-plantain,
Broad-leaved, 58–59
Common, 58
Large-flowered, 58
Narrow-leaved, 59
Western, 58

Water-starwort,
  Common, 220
  Northern, 221
  Vernal, 220–221, 225
Waterweed, Canada, 62–63
Waterwort, 225
  American, 225
  Long-stemmed, 225
Whip-poor-will-shoe, 78
Whitetop, 104, 291
Whortleberry, Red, 166
Widgeon-grass, 52
Wild Rice, *see* Rice, Wild
Willow,
  Autumn, 137
  Balsam, 137
  Basket, 137
  Bog, 137
  Beaked, 138–139
  Bebb's, 138
  Blueberry, 142

Willow, *(continued)*
  Changeable, 136
  Coyote, 140
  Ditchbank, 140
  Drummond's, 136
  Flat-leaved, 137
  Gray, 138
  Hoary, 136
  Long-beaked, 138
  Mackenzie, 137
  Mountain, 137
  Myrtle-leaved, 142–143
  Narrow-leaf, 140
  Pacific, 136
  Peach-leaved, 136
  Pussy, 136, 139
  Sandbar, 140–141
  Shrubby, 136
  Short-capsuled, 136
  Sweet, 144
  Velvet-fruited, 137
  Wolf, 152

Willowherb
  Marsh, 230–231
  Narrow-leaved, 231
  Northern, 231
Wintergreen, 159
  Alpine, 159
  Bog, 160
Wokas, 186
Wool-grass, 124, 129
  Black-scaled, 124, 129

Yerba del Oso, 242